Technologies, Social Media, and Society 12/13

Eighteenth Edition

EDITOR

Paul De Palma, PhD
Gonzaga University

Paul De Palma is Chair and Professor of Computer Science at Gonzaga University. When he discovered computers, he was working on a doctorate in English (at Berkeley). He retrained and worked for a decade in the computer industry. After further training (at Temple), he joined the computer science faculty at Gonzaga. He recently spent a sabbatical year studying computational linguistics (at the University of New Mexico). His interests include the social impact of computing and speech processing.

ANNUAL EDITIONS: TECHNOLOGIES, SOCIAL MEDIA, AND SOCIETY,
EIGHTEENTH EDITION

Published by McGraw-Hill, a business unit of The McGraw-Hill Companies, Inc., 1221 Avenue
of the Americas, New York, NY 10020. Copyright © 2013 by The McGraw-Hill Companies, Inc.
All rights reserved. Printed in the United States of America. Previous editions © 2012, 2011,
2008, and 2007. No part of this publication may be reproduced or distributed in any form or by
any means, or stored in a database or retrieval system, without the prior written consent of The
McGraw-Hill Companies, Inc., including, but not limited to, in any network or other electronic
storage or transmission, or broadcast for distance learning.

Some ancillaries, including electronic and print components, may not be available to customers
outside the United States.

This book is printed on acid-free paper.

Annual Editions® is a registered trademark of The McGraw-Hill Companies, Inc.

Annual Editions is published by the **Contemporary Learning Series** group within the
McGraw-Hill Higher Education division.

1 2 3 4 5 6 7 8 9 0 QDB/QDB 1 0 9 8 7 6 5 4 3 2

ISBN 978-0-07-352873-1
MHID 0-07-352873-0
ISSN 1094-2629 (print)
ISSN 2159-1024 (online)

Managing Editor: *Larry Loeppke*
Developmental Editor: *Dave Welsh*
Permissions Coordinator: *Lenny J. Behnke*
Marketing Specialist: *Alice Link*
Senior Project Manager: *Joyce Watters*
Design Coordinator: *Margarite Reynolds*
Cover Designer: *Studio Montage, St. Louis, Missouri*
Buyer: *Susan K. Culbertson*
Media Project Manager: *Sridevi Palani*

Compositor: Laserwords Private Limited
Cover Image Credits: Colin Anderson/Blend Images LLC (inset); © ERproductions Ltd/Blend
Images LLC (background)

Editors/Academic Advisory Board

Members of the Academic Advisory Board are instrumental in the final selection of articles for each edition of ANNUAL EDITIONS. Their review of articles for content, level, and appropriateness provides critical direction to the editors and staff. We think that you will find their careful consideration well reflected in this volume.

ANNUAL EDITIONS: Technologies, Social Media, and Society 12/13
18th Edition

EDITOR

Paul De Palma
Gonzaga University

ACADEMIC ADVISORY BOARD MEMBERS

Preface

In these the waning days of summer 2011, we might be forgiven for being a bit glum. Standard and Poor's downgraded U.S. debt, official unemployment is at least 9 percent, and if anyone in Washington knows how to jump-start the economy, either he or she isn't telling us or can't shout above the din. But the sun is shining over one part of the economy. The Nasdaq, an index weighted to tech stocks, is up almost 14 percent over a year ago. Facebook, with a half-billion-dollar boost from Goldman Sachs last winter, is valued at $50 billion or $80 billion or $100 billion, depending on the source. Google, the most successful company in history, seems poised to insert itself into every aspect of commerce and our lives: it just agreed to pay $12.5 for Motorola Mobility and Motorola's portfolio of patents. Apple is now the most valuable publicly traded company in the world, pushing past Exon with its billions of gallons of oil reserves. Average salaries for 2011 computer science graduates rose to $63,000 according to one survey, easily among the highest for all fields. The social media along with Google and Apple seem ready to eclipse even President Obama in visibility. *The New York Times* included Google, Facebook, Twitter, and Apple in headlines 1,017 times in the past year, exactly the number of headlines mentioning the President. Even enrollment in computer science programs across the country is bouncing back after a decade-long decline. All signs point to a tech boom. And no wonder. Digital devices continue to transform the way we live.

Our task as students of technology is to ask questions *before* we permit the transformations. Computer technology, for all its marvels, is deeply disruptive. As Neil Postman tells us in the opening chapter to this volume, "Technology giveth and technology taketh away." Put more simply, technology bites back.[1] Consider two very simple examples. The fifty most visited websites install an average of sixty-four files (see "The Web's New Gold Mine," Unit 6) on our computers to relay information on our habits back to websites who sell it to advertisers. For many reasons, including a growing reluctance of citizens of the United States and Western Europe to die on the battlefield, governments everywhere are investing in precision-guided munitions[2] and semi-autonomous robotic warriors. See "Don't Fear the Reaper" and "Autonomous Robots" to join the debate. Though this latest revolution in military affairs may be a lifesaver in the short run, and though the wealth of information on the Internet may seem a fair trade for our privacy, the wise student of technology will look at the promises critically.

In a well-remembered scene from the 1968 movie, *The Graduate,* the hapless Ben is pulled aside at his graduation party by his father's business partner. He asks Ben about his plans, now that the young man has graduated. As Ben fumbles, the older man whispers the single word "plastics" in his ear. Today, Ben—much to his dismay, I am sure—could well be collecting Social Security and showing his ID for the senior discount at movie theatres. What advice would he offer a new graduate? Surely not *plastics,* even though petrochemicals have transformed the way we have lived over the past four decades. Odds are that computers have replaced plastics in the imaginations of today's graduates. To test this hypothesis, I did a Google search on the words "plastics," and "plastic." This produced about 53,800,000 hits, an indication that Ben was given good advice. I followed this with a search on "computers," and "computer," to which Google replied with an astonishing 891,000,000 hits. The point is that computers are a phenomenon to be reckoned with.

In netting articles for *Technologies, Social Media, and Society* from the sea of contenders, I have tried to continue in the tradition of the previous editors. The writers are journalists, computer scientists, lawyers, economists, policy analysts, and academics, the kinds of professions you would expect to find represented in a collection on the social implications of computing. They write for newspapers, business and general circulation magazines, academic journals, professional publications, and, this year for the first time, books. Their writing is mostly free from both the unintelligible jargon and the breathless enthusiasm that prevents people from forming clear ideas about computing. This is by design, of course. I have long contended that it is possible to write clearly about any subject, even one as technically complex and clouded by marketing as information technology. I hope that after reading the selections, you will agree.

Annual Editions: Computers in Society is organized around important dimensions of society rather than of computing. The introduction begins the conversation with an article by the late Neil Postman who says "that every technology has a philosophy which is given expression in how the technology makes people use their minds." Sherry Turkle, one of the earliest and most eloquent commentators on the psychological changes wrought by computing, offers a speculative example in the final unit: "The question is not whether children will grow up to love their robots more than their toys, or indeed, their parents, but what will loving come to mean." Not only does technology come embedded with a philosophy that transforms how we use our minds as well as our bodies, it can alter, Turkle asserts, the very emotion that binds us to our families, our community, maybe even to our country and planet.

This is a large claim, but not so different from claims made about other technologies. We have been living with one of those technologies for so long that its place in the list of transformative inventions is easy to forget. I am speaking of writing here, first realized as cuneiform script in Mesopotamia about 3500 B.C.E. Its development utterly transformed human culture, a transformation only intensified by the subsequent inventions of the phonetic alphabet and moveable type. Once writing had been invented, people could for the first time in human history store words permanently (relatively speaking, of course). This simple act produced shifts, to use Postman's phrase, in the way "people use their minds": writing led to logical argumentation, to the decline of epic poetry, to the invention of the novel, and even to that collection of inner states we call the self. Thus Augustus in his fourth century *Confessions* reports surprise at seeing Bishop Ambrose of Milan reading silently, a practice we take for granted. Yet until recently (in cultural time, of course) reading was a communal act. A step beyond reading alone is writing in a diary, a practice unknown before the 17th century and now undergoing further change through social networking technologies. It is not surprising that a technology as transformative as writing had its critics. Readers might be surprised to learn that Plato, in the *Phaedrus,* sets Socrates arguing against writing on the grounds that it destroys memory and weakens minds, charges leveled against computers not so long ago. Writing in some societies was restricted to a priestly caste, thought able to mediate between the untutored and sacred texts. European intellectuals who used Latin as a *lingua franca* well into the 16th century were just such a priestly caste. Things only got worst with that new device, moveable type, and the mass availability of printed books. Thus we have Hieronimo Squarciafico arguing in 1477 that the "abundance of books makes men less studious," having the effect of replacing the man of wisdom with a portable compendium of knowledge. See Walter J. Ong's *Orality and Literacy* (Routledge, 2002) for the complete and fascinating story of this early, disruptive technology. The point here is that technologies are never only tools. They are transformative in sometimes subtle, sometimes not so subtle, ways.

In between the first and last units, with the help of many other writers, a crucial question recurs like a leitmotif in a complex piece of music: to what extent is technology of any kind without a bias of its own and to what extent does it embody the world view, intentionally or not, of its creators? If the answer were simply that the good and the ill of computing depend upon how computers are used, those of us interested in the interaction of computers and society would be hard-pressed to claim your attention. We could simply exhort you to do no evil, as Google tells its employees. Good advice, certainly. But information technology demands a more nuanced stance.

Sometimes, computing systems have consequences not intended by their developers. The threat to privacy in an era of social networking is one. A growing inability to concentrate is another. And at all times, "embedded in every technology there is a powerful idea" ("Five Things We Need to Know Technological Change," Unit 1). An essential task for students of technology is to learn to tease out these ideas, so that the consequences might be understood *before* the technology is adopted.

This book's major themes are the economy, community, politics considered broadly, and the balance of risk and reward. In a field as fluid as computing, the intersection of computers with each of these dimensions changes from year to year. Many articles in the 10th edition examined the growing importance of e-commerce. By the time of the 13th edition, e-commerce had nearly disappeared. This is not because e-commerce had become unimportant. Rather, in just a few years, it had moved into the mainstream. The 14th edition replaced over half of the articles from the 13th. The 15th edition eliminated a third from the 14th. The 16th edition removed 40 percent of the articles from the 15th edition, replacing them with eighteen new ones. The 17th edition eliminated 37 percent of the articles from the 16th edition. The current edition contains seventeen new articles. Computing is a rapidly moving target. We race to keep up.

In the current edition, for the first time, we have included an article from a scientific symposium. The speed with which computing changes makes writing on the topic sometimes seem frenetic, reflective of the industry itself. Much of current writing takes the form of blogs. Even nicely written blogs have a topical, to-be-skimmed-with-morning-coffee kind of feel to them. This is not to disparage the form. Blogs may well play a role in resurrecting the personal essay, an important literary form, now derided in some circles as mere opinion. Still, I think it is important in a field as fluid as computing to step back and take a more considered look. The long scientific piece, an article presented at the IEEE (Institute of Electrical and Electronics Engineers) Symposium on Security and Privacy, investigates the links in the chain of spam from the vendors through your e-mail box to the banks that process payments. Systems administrators have been wringing their hands for so long over the plague of spam that it might come as a bit of a surprise to learn that just three banks handle payments for 95 percent of advertised goods. Break this link and we've broken the back of spam—unless, like *The Terminator,* it regenerates itself. Though this article was ably summarized by John Markoff in *The New York Times* ("Study Sees Way to Win Spam Fight," 5/19/2011), we have included the full study here to show how much ingenuity and pure effort went into the discovery—in fact, goes into to the most technical discoveries.

The long piece forms a counterweight to the blogs and shorter articles we have included. Both kinds of writing tell the story of computing. One might even argue that shorter pieces tell the story not just by their content but by their form as well. This is a fast-moving, hard-driving field, directed in important ways by the very young. The average age of Google and Facebook employees is 30 and 31, respectively. "All that is solid melts into air," wrote those two 19th century students of another transformative technology, industrial capitalism. Marx and Engels could have been writing about computer technology. So, why a long scientific article? The scientific article gives the full picture of an investigation. It is in tone, content, and joint authorship the very opposite of a blog. The inclusion of this longer piece in this edition is an experiment. We are very interested in your thoughts on the matter.

In 1965, Gordon Moore, who would go on to found Intel, published a paper in which he observed that the number of transistors that could be squeezed onto a silicon chip had doubled each year since the invention of integrated circuits. In a slightly modified form this has come to be called Moore's Law. Scholars have been predicting its demise ever since, usually pointing out that integrated circuits, like everything else in the universe, must conform to the laws of physics, and nothing, not even the ingenuity of Silicon Valley engineers, is without limits. Nevertheless, despite the inevitable day of reckoning, Paul Ceruzzi ("Moore's Law and Technological Determinism," Unit 1) points out that Moore's Law has been operating for almost a half century.

To see why the articles in this volume describe a world not conceivable even a decade ago, perform this thought experiment. Imagine you have a chessboard and a supply of pennies. Put one penny on the upper left-most square. Put two pennies on the next square and so on, doubling each stack of pennies for each subsequent square. At the end of the first row, you will have a stack 256 pennies. Lots, but still manageable. By the end of the second row, the stack will have grown to 65,536 pennies, a big stack and worth a lot of money, but still within the budget of a college student. By the end of the third row—twenty-four years of the nearly fifty that Moore's Law has been operating—you will have a stack of 17 million pennies, over sixteen miles high, and worth in the neighborhood of $200,000. This pile of pennies tells you everything you need to know about how it is that bloggers and assorted online sources are putting newspapers out of business, threatening book publishers, and worrying libraries; how Twitterers inside and outside of Iran held the world's attention in 2009; and, above all, why the term "computer," refers to so much more than the device on your desk (or even in your backpack). Computing has expanded beyond the constraints of the machine—to the publishing industry, to our cognitive processes, to education, warfare, and law, to romance, to our self-presentation on Facebook and Twitter, and now even to how we choose to die ("Geek Life," Unit 8)—for the same reason that the stack of pennies grew incomprehensibly large. Any good thing that doubles in size with regularity is going to change its world in unimaginable ways.

More than other technologies, computers force us to think about limits. What does it mean to be human? Are there kinds of knowledge that should not be pursued? One of our contributors, Sherry Turkle, recounts an interview in which she was accused of species chauvinism because she expressed reluctance to sanction robot-human marriage ("In Good Company," Unit 8). To suggest that "our culture had clearly come to a new place" has to rank as one of the ironic understatements of the decade. Meanwhile, back in the world of real or existing computing, we find Google building an operating system into a browser and offering its cloud as the place where we'll be invited to store our increasingly digitized cultural heritage. This is a lot of responsibility to hand over to a private corporation, especially one that didn't exist much more than a decade ago and whose employees, with all due respect, have an average age of 30.

A word of caution. Each article has been selected because it is topical, interesting, and (insofar as the form permits) nicely written. To say that an article is interesting or well-written, however, does not mean that it is right. This is as true of the facts presented in each article as it is of the point of view. When reading startling claims, whether in this volume or anywhere else, it is wise to remember that writers gather facts from other sources who gathered them from still other sources, who may, ultimately, rely upon a selective method of fact-gathering. There may be no good solution to the problem of unsupported assertions, beyond rigorous peer review. But, then, most of us don't curl up each night with scientific journals (see "Click Trajectories," Unit 3 for a sample), and even these can be flawed. The real antidote to poorly supported arguments is to become critical readers, no less of experts than of day-time TV and talk-show hosts. With the demise of newspapers and at least the semblance of professional accountability, blogs and opinion pieces have stepped into the breach. We have to be more vigilant then ever. Cautions notwithstanding, I hope you will approach these articles as you might a good discussion among friends. You may not agree with all opinions, but you will come away nudged in one direction or another by reasoned arguments, holding a richer, more informed view of important issues.

This book includes several features that I hope will be helpful to students and professionals. Each article listed in the table of contents is preceded by a short abstract with key issues in bold italic type. The social implications of computing, of course, are not limited to the eight broad areas represented by the unit titles. A topic guide lists each key issue and the articles that explore that issue. I have included study questions after each article. Though some of the questions can be answered from within the article, many more invite further investigation, in essence, your own contributions. The articles I've gathered for this volume along with the questions that follow are intended to get the discussion moving.

We want *Annual Editions: Technologies, Social Media, and Society* to help you participate more fully in some of the most important discussions of the time, those about the promises and risks of computing. Your suggestions and comments are very important to us. If you complete and to incorporate them into the next edition.

Notes

1. See Edward Tenner, *Why Things Bite Back,* Vintage, 1996.
2. See Unit 5, but also, Thomas G. Mahnken, Weapons: The Growth & Spread of the Precision-Strike Regime, *Daedalus,* Summer 2011.

Paul De Palma
Editor

The Annual Editions Series

VOLUMES AVAILABLE

Adolescent Psychology

Aging

American Foreign Policy

American Government

Anthropology

Archaeology

Assessment and Evaluation

Business Ethics

Child Growth and Development

Comparative Politics

Criminal Justice

Developing World

Drugs, Society, and Behavior

Dying, Death, and Bereavement

Early Childhood Education

Economics

Educating Children with Exceptionalities

Education

Educational Psychology

Entrepreneurship

Environment

The Family

Gender

Geography

Global Issues

Health

Homeland Security

Human Development

Human Resources

Human Sexualities

International Business

Management

Marketing

Mass Media

Microbiology

Multicultural Education

Nursing

Nutrition

Physical Anthropology

Psychology

Race and Ethnic Relations

Social Problems

Sociology

State and Local Government

Sustainability

Technologies, Social Media, and Society

United States History, Volume 1

United States History, Volume 2

Urban Society

Violence and Terrorism

Western Civilization, Volume 1

World History, Volume 1

World History, Volume 2

World Politics

Contents

UNIT 1
Introduction

UNIT 2
The Economy

The concepts in bold italics are developed in the article. For further expansion, please refer to the Topic Guide.

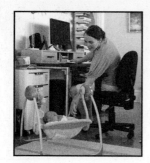

UNIT 3
Work and the Workplace

UNIT 4
Computers, People, and Social Participation

The concepts in bold italics are developed in the article. For further expansion, please refer to the Topic Guide.

UNIT 5
Societal Institutions: Law, Politics, Education, and the Military

UNIT 6
Risk and Avoiding Risk

The concepts in bold italics are developed in the article. For further expansion, please refer to the Topic Guide.

UNIT 7
International Perspectives and Issues

The concepts in bold italics are developed in the article. For further expansion, please refer to the Topic Guide.

UNIT 8
The Frontier of Computing

The concepts in bold italics are developed in the article. For further expansion, please refer to the Topic Guide.

Correlation Guide

The *Annual Editions* series provides students with convenient, inexpensive access to current, carefully selected articles from the public press. **Annual Editions: Technologies, Social Media, and Society 12/13** is an easy-to-use reader that presents articles on important topics such as *the economy, the workplace, social participation,* and many more. For more information on *Annual Editions* and other *McGraw-Hill Contemporary Learning Series* titles, visit www.mhhe.com/cls.

This convenient guide matches the units in **Annual Editions: Technologies, Social Media, and Society 12/13** with the corresponding chapters in three of our best-selling McGraw-Hill Computer Science textbooks by Haag/Cummings and Baltzan.

Annual Editions: Technologies, Social Media, and Society 12/13	Management Information Systems for the Information Age, 9/e by Haag/Cummings	Business-Driven Technology, 5/e by Baltzan	M: Information Systems, 2/e by Baltzan
Unit 1: Introduction	**Chapter 1:** The Information Age in Which You Live: Changing the Face of Business	**Chapter 1:** Business-Driven Technology	**Chapter 1:** Information Systems in Business
Unit 2: The Economy	**Chapter 1:** The Information Age in Which You Live: Changing the Face of Business **Chapter 2:** Major Business Initiatives: Gaining Competitive Advantage with IT **Chapter 5:** Electronic Commerce: Strategies for the New Economy	**Chapter 1:** Business-Driven Technology **Chapter 2:** Identifying Competitive Advantages **Chapter 14:** E-Business	**Chapter 2:** Decision and Processes: Value-Driven Business **Chapter 3:** Ebusiness: Electronic Business Value **Chapter 8:** Enterprise Applications: Business Communications
Unit 3: Work and the Workplace	**Chapter 2:** Major Business Initiatives: Gaining Competitive Advantage with IT **Chapter 4:** Analytics, Decision Support, and Artificial Intelligence: Brainpower for Your Business	**Chapter 9:** Enabling the Organization—Decision Making **Chapter 10:** Extending the Organization—Supply Chain Management **Chapter 11:** Building a Customer-Centric Organization—Customer Relationship Management **Chapter 12:** Integrating the Organization from End-to-End—Enterprise Resource Planning	**Chapter 6:** Data: Business Intelligence **Chapter 9:** Systems Development and Project Management: Corporate Responsibility
Unit 4: Computers, People, and Social Participation	**Chapter 9:** Emerging Trends and Technologies: Business, People, and Technology Tomorrow	**Chapter 14:** E-Business	**Chapter 4:** Ethics and Information Security: MIS Business Concerns
Unit 5: Societal Institutions: Law, Politics, Education, and the Military			**Chapter 4:** Ethics and Information Security: MIS Business Concerns
Unit 6: Risk	**Chapter 8:** Protecting People and Information: Threats and Safeguards	**Chapter 7:** Storing Organizational Information--Databases	**Chapter 4:** Ethics and Information Security: MIS Business Concerns
Unit 7: International Perspectives and Issues			
Unit 8: The Frontier of Computing	**Chapter 9:** Emerging Trends and Technologies: Business, People, and Technology Tomorrow		

Topic Guide

This topic guide suggests how the selections in this book relate to the subjects covered in your course. You may want to use the topics listed on these pages to search the Web more easily.

On the following pages a number of websites have been gathered specifically for this book. They are arranged to reflect the units of this Annual Editions reader. You can link to these sites by going to www.mhhe.com/cls

All the articles that relate to each topic are listed below the bold-faced term.

Publishing

Social Media and Google

Internet References

The following Internet sites have been selected to support the articles found in this reader. These sites were available at the time of publication. However, because websites often change their structure and content, the information listed may no longer be available. We invite you to visit www.mhhe.com/cls for easy access to these sites.

Annual Editions: Technologies, Social Media, and Society 12/13

General Sources

Livelink Intranet Guided Tour
www.opentext.com

Livelink Intranet helps companies to manage and control documents, business processes, and projects more effectively. Take this tour to see how.

www.youtube.com/results?search_query=medieval+helpdesk&aq=f

This clever YouTube video, called *Medieval Help Desk*, makes the point that writing and books are technologies.

UNIT 1: Introduction

Beyond the Information Revolution
www.theatlantic.com/magazine/archive/1999/10/beyond-the-information-revolution/4658

Peter Drucker has written a three-part article, available at this site, that uses history to gauge the significance of e-commerce—"a totally unexpected development"—to throw light on the future of, in his words, "the knowledge worker."

Short History of the Internet
http://ei.cs.vt.edu/~wwwbtb/book/chap1/index.html

Shahrooz Feizabadi presents the history of the World Wide Web as well as the history of several ideas and underlying technologies from which the World Wide Web emerged.

UNIT 2: The Economy

CAUCE: Coalition against Unsolicited Commercial Email
www.cauce.org

This all-volunteer organization was created to advocate for a legislative solution to the problem of UCE, better known as spam. Read about the fight and how you can help at this Web page.

E-Commerce Times
www.ecommercetimes.com

E-Commerce Times is a gateway to a wealth of current information and resources concerning e-commerce.

Fight Spam on the Internet
http://spam.abuse.net

This is an anti-spam site that has been in operation since 1996. Its purpose is to promote responsible net commerce, in part, by fighting spam. Up-to-date news about spam can be found on the home page.

AllAdvantage—The Rise of the Informediary
http://en.wikipedia.org/wiki/AllAdvantage

This Wikipedia article describes AllAdvantage's pathfinding role as, arguably, the first Internet infomediary.

Smart Cards: A Primer
www.smartcardbasics.com/overview.html

This site describes the smart card, its applications, and its value in e-commerce.

Smart Card Group
www.smartcard.co.uk

This website bills itself as "the definitive website for Smart Card Technology." At this site you can download Dr. David B. Everett's definitive "Introduction to Smart Cards."

UNIT 3: Work and the Workplace

American Telecommuting Association
www.yourata.com/telecommuting

What is good about telecommuting is examined at this site that also offers information regarding concepts, experiences, and the future of telecommuting.

Computers in the Workplace
www.cpsr.org/issues/industry

"Computers in the Workplace (initiated by the CPSR/Palo Alto chapter) became a national level project in 1988. The Participatory Design conferences have explored workplace issues since the conference's inception in 1992."

STEP ON IT! Pedals: Repetitive Strain Injury
www.bilbo.com/rsi2.html

Data on carpal tunnel syndrome are presented here with links to alternative approaches to the computer keyboard and links to related information.

What About Computers in the Workplace?
http://law.freeadvice.com/intellectual_ property/computer_law/computers_workplace.htm

This site, which is the leading legal site for consumers and small businesses, provides general legal information to help people understand their legal rights in 100 legal topics—including the answer to the question, "Can my boss watch what I'm doing?"

UNIT 4: Computers, People, and Social Participation

Alliance for Childhood: Computers and Children
http://drupal6.allianceforchildhood.org/computer_ position_statement

How are computers affecting the intellectual growth of children? Here is one opinion provided by the Alliance for Childhood.

Internet and American Life
www.pewinternet.org

Provides "reports exploring the impact of the Internet on families, communities, work and home, daily life, education, health care, and civic and political life."

American Scholar
www.theamericanscholar.org

Website for the American Scholar that includes William Zinsser's blog.

Internet References

Freakonomics
www.freakonomicsradio.com/hour-long-special-the-folly-of-prediction.html

A market-based explanation for why so many people, despite so many mistakes, continue to try to predict the future.

University of Phoenix
www.phoenix.edu

Home page for the University of Phoenix, the pioneer in online education.

The Core Rules of Netiquette
www.albion.com/netiquette/corerules.html

Excerpted from Virginia Shea's book *Netiquette,* this is a classic work in the field of online communication.

SocioSite: Networks, Groups, and Social Interaction
www.sociosite.net

This site provides sociological and psychological resources and research regarding the effect of computers on social interaction.

Wikipedia on Social Networking
http://en.wikipedia.org/wiki/List_of_social_networking_websites

Contains links to information about dozens of social networking sites.

UNIT 5: Societal Institutions: Law, Politics, Education, and the Military

Predator Drones Usage
www.youtube.com/watch?v=nMh8Cjnzen8

YouTube documentary on predator drones.

U.S. Department of Defense
www.defense.gov/home/features/2011/0411_cyberstrategy

Home page for the U.S. Department of Defense Cyber Strategy.

Berkman Center for Internet and Society at Harvard University
http://cyber.law.harvard.edu/about

A research center with many interesting links relating to the study of Internet "development, dynamics, norms, and standards."

ACLU: American Civil Liberties Union
www.aclu.org

Click on the Supreme Court's Internet decision, plus details of the case *Reno v. ACLU,* and the ACLU's campaign to restore information privacy, "Take Back Your Data"; and cyber-liberties and free speech for opinions on First Amendment rights as they apply to cyberspace.

United States Patent and Trademark Office
www.uspto.gov

This is the official home page of the U.S. Patent and Trademark Office. Use this site to search patents and trademarks, apply for patents, and more.

World Intellectual Property Organization
www.wipo.org

Visit the World Intellectual Property Organization website to find information and issues pertaining to virtual and intellectual property.

UNIT 6: Risk and Avoiding Risk

AntiOnline: Hacking and Hackers
www.antionline.com/index.php

This site is designed to help people learn how to protect against hackers.

Copyright & Trademark Information for the IEEE Computer Society
http://computer.org/copyright.htm

Here is an example of how a publication on the Web is legally protected. The section on Intellectual Property Rights Information contains further information about reuse permission and copyright policies.

Electronic Privacy Information Center (EPIC)
http://epic.org

EPIC is a private research organization that was established to focus public attention on emerging civil liberties issues and to protect privacy, the First Amendment, and constitutional values. This site contains news, resources, policy archives, and a search mechanism.

Internet Privacy Coalition
www.epic.org/crypto

The mission of the Internet Privacy Coalition is to promote privacy and security on the Internet through widespread public availability of strong encryption and the relaxation of export controls on cryptography.

Center for Democracy and Technology
www.cdt.org

These pages are maintained for discussion and information about data privacy and security, encryption, and the need for policy reform. The site discusses pending legislation, Department of Commerce Export Regulations, and other initiatives.

Survive Spyware
http://reviews.cnet.com/4520-3688_7-6456087-1.html

Internet spying is a huge problem. Advertisers, Web designers, and even the government are using the Net to spy on you. CNET .com provides information about spyware and detecting spying eyes that will help you eliminate the threat.

Cyber Warfare
http://en.wikipedia.org/wiki/Cyberwarfare

Wikipedia's up-to-the-minute account or the risks of cyber warfare. The site includes many interesting links in the short history of cyber warfare, 1982 to the present.

UNIT 7: International Perspectives and Issues

Oxford Internet Institute
www.oii.ox.ac.uk

Oxford University in England offers an international perspective on the social implications of the Internet, complete with interesting links and webcasts.

UNIT 8: The Frontier of Computing

Google Chrome Explanation
www.youtube.com/watch?v=0QRO3gKj3qw

A breezy YouTube video that explains Chrome.

Google Translation Software
http://translate.google.com

Google's free translation software is explained and provided here.

Google Reader Gadget
fttp://desktop.google.com/plugins/i/texttospeech_bijoy.html?hl=en

A Google gadget that reads out what you type in.

Internet References

Association for Computational Linguistics
www.aclweb.org

Some of the research in this article is in a field called "computational linguistics." This is the home page of the Association for Computational Linguistics.

IBM's Watson
www.ibm.com/watson

IBM website that contains links to a video series about the new *Jeopardy!* champ.

Alcor Life Extension Foundation
www.alcor.org

Home page of the Alcor Life Extension Foundation.

Introduction to Artificial Intelligence (AI)
www.formal.stanford.edu/jmc/aiintro/aiintro.html

This statement describes A.I. Click on John McCarthy's home page for a list of additional papers.

Kasparov vs. Deep Blue: The Rematch
www.research.ibm.com/deepblue/home/html/b.html

Video clips and a discussion of the historic chess rematch between Garry Kasparov and Deep Blue are available on this site.

PHP-Nuke Powered Site: International Society for Artificial Life
www.alife.org

Start here to find links to many a-life (artificial life) websites, including demonstrations, research centers and groups, and other resources.

UNIT 1

Introduction

Unit Selections

1. **Five Things We Need to Know about Technological Change,** Neil Postman
2. **Moore's Law and Technological Determinism: Reflections on the History of Technology,** Paul E. Ceruzzi
3. **A Passion for Objects,** Sherry Turkle

Learning Outcomes

After reading this Unit, you will be able to:

- Understand what is meant by the term technological determinism.
- Understand what is meant by the term social constructivism.
- Be able to argue for and against either a technological determinist or technological constructivist point of view.
- Be able to argue that things and the language used to describe things have a history.
- Be able to argue that technology comes embedded in a worldview.
- Be able to explain the oft-cited Moore's Law.
- Understand the role of objects in the education of young scientists.

Student Website

www.mhhe.com/cls

Internet Reference

Beyond the Information Revolution
www.theatlantic.com/issues/99oct/9910drucker.htm

Until not long ago, most people interested in the philosophy and sociology of science and technology considered them value-neutral. A given technology, it was supposed, carries no values of its own. The ethics of this or that technology depends on what is done with it. A vestige of this thinking is still with us. When people say, "Guns don't kill people. People kill people," they are asserting that technology somehow stands outside of society, waiting to be put to use for good or ill. The concern about intoxicated drivers is similar. All of us would live happier, safer lives if campaigns to remove drunk drivers from their cars were successful. But this still would not get to the heart of highway carnage that has to do with federal encouragement for far-flung suburbs, local patterns of land use, and a neglect of public transportation. Drunk driving would not be the issue it is, if driving were not so vital to American life, and driving would not be so vital to American life if a cascade of social and political decisions had not come together in the middle of the twentieth century to favor the automobile.

© Comstock/PunchStock

The first article, "Five Things We Need to Know about Technological Change," makes this point eloquently: "Embedded in every technology there is a powerful idea. . . ." The observation is an important one and is shared by most of the more reflective contemporary commentators on technology. The idea that technology can be studied apart from its social consequences owes some of its strength to the way many people imagine that scientific discoveries are made—since technology is just science applied. It is commonly imagined that scientists are disinterested observers of the natural world. In this view, science unfolds, and technology unfolds shortly after, according to the laws of nature and the passion of scientists. But, of course, scientists study those things that are socially valued. One expression of social value in the United States is National Science Foundation and National Institute of Health funding. We should not be surprised that the medical and computing sciences are funded generously, or, indeed, that our research physicians and computer scientists are paid better than English professors.

One eminent historian of science, Steven Shapin of Harvard, calls what I have just asserted—that science (and technology) is a human activity like any other—"tone-lowering." "Tone-lowering" is the removal of science and scientists from the quasi-religious status they held in the late nineteenth and early twentieth centuries to the world where mere mortals live their lives. This is the world where we act out of self-interest, make frequent errors in judgment and decorum, hold incompletely worked out and inconsistent opinions, jockey for position, and, generally, behave as human beings. If science and scientists (and by extension technology and engineers) have the moral authority of religion, then heresy is possible. Shapin offers many ways in which we might be heretical. Here are two:

- You could say that science happens within, not outside of, historical time, that it has a deep historicity, and that whatever transcendence it possesses is itself a historical accomplishment.

- You could say that science similarly belongs to place, that it bears the marks of the places where it is produced and

through which it is transmitted, and that whatever appearance of placelessness it possesses is itself a spatially grounded phenomenon.[1]

The relationship between technology and society is dialectical: social values affect technical discovery which, in turn, affect social values. It is this intricate dance between computers and society—now one leading, now the other—that the writers in this volume struggle to understand, though most of them do it implicitly.

This a good time to clarify what we mean by the title of this volume, *Technologies, Social Media, and Society*. As argued in the Preface, writing itself is a technology, probably one even more transformative than the digital computer. So also is the automobile, the network of highways built to accommodate it, as well as the desk at which I am sitting, the house that encloses us both, indeed, so is the pencil with which I made notes for this essay. Pencils are a modest technology, to be sure, but Henry Petroski, a professor of civil engineering at Duke, once wrote a long and highly praised book tracing its history.[2] Yet despite the word "technologies" in its title, this book includes no articles on the pencil, though a good one is deeply underrated. Even though technology is a big house, some artifacts are more typical residents than others. Though it would take some doing to convince most Americans that writing is a technology, no contemporary American would deny membership to the digital computer. In fact, the computer in all its many manifestations is the paradigmatic technological artifact of the early twenty-first century. So, really, when we say "technologies" in the title, we mean all of those technologies, every one of them, that owe their existence to the remarkable miniaturization of digital devices that began in the late forties and early fifties.

And "Social Media"? In a handful of years Facebook has morphed from a fairly unoriginal way for students in elite universities to communicate with others just like them[3] to a global phenomenon with a projected market value of $50–$100 billion. Facebook, Twitter, even Google with Gmail, are the giants of social media. But just as "technologies" is a metonym for all of digital technology, so also is "social media" metonymic for the many wonderful, transformative, and socially disruptive ways in which we can now communicate with one another.

Before the explosion of cell phones and social media in the past decade, a computer was a device that sat on your desk, perhaps networked to other devices just like it. Not long before that it was just a device on your desk, equipped with a word processor, a spreadsheet, and some primitive games. As recently as 1996, less than 1 in 5 Americans had used the Internet.[4] A decade before that, the word would have referred to a large, probably IBM, machine kept in an air-conditioned room and tended by an army of technicians. Prior to 1950, a "computer" meant someone particularly adept at arithmetic calculations. The point here is that as the meaning of a single word has shifted; our understanding of the dance has to shift with it.

That this shift in meaning has occurred in just a few decades helps us understand why so many commentators use the word "revolution" to describe what computing has wrought. Though political revolutions are usually thought to be chaotic and so undesirable—think French, Russian, Chinese, Cuban— "undesirable" drops a notch to "worrisome," at worst, when the chaos results from digitization (e.g., "those crazy kids and their Facebook pages"). Computing is thought to change quickly, but more, it is thought to bring many benefits. A survey conducted not long ago by the Brookings Institution indicated that 90 percent of Americans believe that science and technology will make their lives easier and more comfortable.[5] The real question to ask is more basic: not whether Americans believe it, but is it true? First, does the spread of computing constitute a revolution, or just, in Thoreau's words, "an improved means to an unimproved end." Second, revolutionary (worrisome or not), have we grown smarter, healthier, happier with the coming of the computer? This is still an open question—but, as the Internet morphs from a novelty to an appliance, to a shrinking number of commentators.

Nevertheless, as I warned in the Preface to this volume, read each of the articles critically, including this one. Paul Ceruzzi, a distinguished historian of computing, disagrees with me on how to understand the history of technology (see "Moore's Law and Technological Determinism"). He tells us that "computing power must increase because it can." This is raw technological determinism, a belief that technology has its "own internal logic and trajectory that human beings must follow." This is quite the opposite of the position that I've been arguing. Read the essay and see if you're convinced.

We end this section with a meditation by the person who, as much as anyone, first alerted us to some of the strange doings associated with the digital computer, Sherry Turkle. One can hardly pick up a newspaper—if, indeed, we pick up newspapers at all these days—without reading some cry from the heart about the decline in American schools. Front and center is the worry that American kids don't seem to want to study mathematics, science, and engineering. Everyone has his or her favorite cure: rigorous testing topped President Bush's list; charter schools and holding teachers accountable for their students' performance rank high with President Obama. Sherry Turkle has a much simpler solution that, ironically, lays part of the blame at the feet of that object without which modern science is inconceivable, the computer. Does she persuade you?

Notes

1. Steven Shapin, *Never Pure: Historical Studies of Science as if It Was Produced by People with Bodies, Situated in Time, Space, Culture, and Society, and Struggling for Credibility and Authority,* Johns Hopkins U. Press, 2010, p. 5.

2. Henry Petroski, *The Pencil: A History of Design and Circumstance,* Knopf, 1990.

3. See Charles Peterson, "In the World of Facebook," *The New York Review of Books,* 2/25/2010.

4. See R. Blendon, et al. "Whom to Protect and How?," *Brookings Review,* 2001.

5. Ibid.

Five Things We Need to Know about Technological Change

Neil Postman

Good morning your Eminences and Excellencies, ladies, and gentlemen.

The theme of this conference, "The New Technologies and the Human Person: Communicating the Faith in the New Millennium," suggests, of course, that you are concerned about what might happen to faith in the new millennium, as well you should be. In addition to our computers, which are close to having a nervous breakdown in anticipation of the year 2000, there is a great deal of frantic talk about the 21st century and how it will pose for us unique problems of which we know very little but for which, nonetheless, we are supposed to carefully prepare. Everyone seems to worry about this—business people, politicians, educators, as well as theologians.

The human dilemma is as it has always been, and it is a delusion to believe that the technological changes of our era have rendered irrelevant the wisdom of the ages and the sages.

At the risk of sounding patronizing, may I try to put everyone's mind at ease? I doubt that the 21st century will pose for us problems that are more stunning, disorienting or complex than those we faced in this century, or the 19th, 18th, 17th, or for that matter, many of the centuries before that. But for those who are excessively nervous about the new millennium, I can provide, right at the start, some good advice about how to confront it. The advice comes from people whom we can trust, and whose thoughtfulness, it's safe to say, exceeds that of President Clinton, Newt Gingrich, or even Bill Gates. Here is what Henry David Thoreau told us: "All our inventions are but improved means to an unimproved end." Here is what Goethe told us: "One should, each day, try to hear a little song, read a good poem, see a fine picture, and, if possible, speak a few reasonable words." Socrates told us: "The unexamined life is not worth living." Rabbi Hillel told us: "What is hateful to thee, do not do to another." And here is the prophet Micah: "What does the Lord require of thee but to do justly, to love mercy and to walk humbly with thy God." And

I could say, if we had the time, (although you know it well enough) what Jesus, Isaiah, Mohammad, Spinoza, and Shakespeare told us. It is all the same: There is no escaping from ourselves. The human dilemma is as it has always been, and it is a delusion to believe that the technological changes of our era have rendered irrelevant the wisdom of the ages and the sages.

. . . all technological change is a trade-off. . . . a Faustian bargain.

Nonetheless, having said this, I know perfectly well that because we do live in a technological age, we have some special problems that Jesus, Hillel, Socrates, and Micah did not and could not speak of. I do not have the wisdom to say what we ought to do about such problems, and so my contribution must confine itself to some things we need to know in order to address the problems. I call my talk *Five Things We Need to Know About Technological Change*. I base these ideas on my thirty years of studying the history of technological change but I do not think these are academic or esoteric ideas. They are the sort of things everyone who is concerned with cultural stability and balance should know and I offer them to you in the hope that you will find them useful in thinking about the effects of technology on religious faith.

First Idea

The first idea is that all technological change is a trade-off. I like to call it a Faustian bargain. Technology giveth and technology taketh away. This means that for every advantage a new technology offers, there is always a corresponding disadvantage. The disadvantage may exceed in importance the advantage, or the advantage may well be worth the cost. Now, this may seem to be a rather obvious idea, but you would be surprised at how many people believe that new technologies are unmixed blessings. You need only think of the enthusiasms with which most people approach their understanding of computers. Ask anyone who knows something about computers to talk about them, and you will find that they will, unabashedly and relentlessly, extol the wonders of computers. You will also find that in most cases they will completely neglect to mention any of the liabilities of computers. This is a dangerous imbalance, since the greater the wonders of a technology, the greater will be its negative consequences.

Think of the automobile, which for all of its obvious advantages, has poisoned our air, choked our cities, and degraded the beauty of our natural landscape. Or you might reflect on the paradox of medical technology which brings wondrous cures but is, at the same time, a demonstrable cause of certain diseases and disabilities, and has played a significant role in reducing the diagnostic skills of physicians. It is also well to recall that for all of the intellectual and social benefits provided by the printing press, its costs were equally monumental. The printing press gave the Western world prose, but it made poetry into an exotic and elitist form of communication. It gave us inductive science, but it reduced religious sensibility to a form of fanciful superstition. Printing gave us the modern conception of nationwide, but in so doing turned patriotism into a sordid if not lethal emotion. We might even say that the printing of the Bible in vernacular languages introduced the impression that God was an Englishman or a German or a Frenchman—that is to say, printing reduced God to the dimensions of a local potentate.

Perhaps the best way I can express this idea is to say that the question, "What will a new technology do?" is no more important than the question, "What will a new technology undo?" Indeed, the latter question is more important, precisely because it is asked so infrequently. One might say, then, that a sophisticated perspective on technological change includes one's being skeptical of Utopian and Messianic visions drawn by those who have no sense of history or of the precarious balances on which culture depends. In fact, if it were up to me, I would forbid anyone from talking about the new information technologies unless the person can demonstrate that he or she knows something about the social and psychic effects of the alphabet, the mechanical clock, the printing press, and telegraphy. In other words, knows something about the costs of great technologies.

Idea Number One, then, is that culture always pays a price for technology.

Second Idea

This leads to the second idea, which is that the advantages and disadvantages of new technologies are never distributed evenly among the population. This means that every new technology benefits some and harms others. There are even some who are not affected at all. Consider again the case of the printing press in the 16th century, of which Martin Luther said it was "God's highest and extremest act of grace, whereby the business of the gospel is driven forward." By placing the word of God on every Christian's kitchen table, the mass-produced book undermined the authority of the church hierarchy, and hastened the breakup of the Holy Roman See. The Protestants of that time cheered this development. The Catholics were enraged and distraught. Since I am a Jew, had I lived at that time, I probably wouldn't have given a damn one way or another, since it would make no difference whether a pogrom was inspired by Martin Luther or Pope Leo X. Some gain, some lose, a few remain as they were.

Let us take as another example, television, although here I should add at once that in the case of television there are

very few indeed who are not affected in one way or another. In America, where television has taken hold more deeply than anywhere else, there are many people who find it a blessing, not least those who have achieved high-paying, gratifying careers in television as executives, technicians, directors, newscasters and entertainers. On the other hand, and in the long run, television may bring an end to the careers of school teachers since school was an invention of the printing press and must stand or fall on the issue of how much importance the printed word will have in the future. There is no chance, of course, that television will go away but school teachers who are enthusiastic about its presence always call to my mind an image of some turn-of-the-century blacksmith who not only is singing the praises of the automobile but who also believes that his business will be enhanced by it. We know now that his business was not enhanced by it; it was rendered obsolete by it, as perhaps an intelligent blacksmith would have known.

The questions, then, that are never far from the mind of a person who is knowledgeable about technological change are these: Who specifically benefits from the development of a new technology? Which groups, what type of person, what kind of industry will be favored? And, of course, which groups of people will thereby be harmed?

. . . there are always winners and losers in technological change.

These questions should certainly be on our minds when we think about computer technology. There is no doubt that the computer has been and will continue to be advantageous to large-scale organizations like the military or airline companies or banks or tax collecting institutions. And it is equally clear that the computer is now indispensable to high-level researchers in physics and other natural sciences. But to what extent has computer technology been an advantage to the masses of people? To steel workers, vegetable store owners, automobile mechanics, musicians, bakers, bricklayers, dentists, yes, theologians, and most of the rest into whose lives the computer now intrudes? These people have had their private matters made more accessible to powerful institutions. They are more easily tracked and controlled; they are subjected to more examinations, and are increasingly mystified by the decisions made about them. They are more than ever reduced to mere numerical objects. They are being buried by junk mail. They are easy targets for advertising agencies and political institutions.

In a word, these people are losers in the great computer revolution. The winners, which include among others computer companies, multi-national corporations and the nation state, will, of course, encourage the losers to be enthusiastic about computer technology. That is the way of winners, and so in the beginning they told the losers that with personal computers the average person can balance a checkbook more neatly, keep better track of recipes, and make more logical shopping lists. Then they told them that computers will make it possible to vote at home, shop at home, get all the entertainment they wish at home, and thus make community life unnecessary. And now, of course, the winners speak constantly of the Age of Information, always implying that the more information we have, the better we will be in solving significant problems—not only personal ones but large-scale social problems, as well. But how true is this? If there are children starving in the world—and there are—it is not because of insufficient information. We have known for a long time how to produce enough food to feed every child on the planet. How is it that we let so many of them starve? If there is violence on our streets, it is not because we have insufficient information. If women are abused, if divorce and pornography and mental illness are increasing, none of it has anything to do with insufficient information. I dare say it is because something else is missing, and I don't think I have to tell this audience what it is. Who knows? This age of information may turn out to be a curse if we are blinded by it so that we cannot see truly where our problems lie. That is why it is always necessary for us to ask of those who speak enthusiastically of computer technology, why do you do this? What interests do you represent? To whom are you hoping to give power? From whom will you be withholding power?

I do not mean to attribute unsavory, let alone sinister motives to anyone. I say only that since technology favors some people and harms others, these are questions that must always be asked. And so, that there are always winners and losers in technological change is the second idea.

Third Idea

Here is the third. Embedded in every technology there is a powerful idea, sometimes two or three powerful ideas. These ideas are often hidden from our view because they are of a somewhat abstract nature. But this should not be taken to mean that they do not have practical consequences.

The third idea is the sum and substance of what Marshall McLuhan meant when he coined the famous sentence, "The medium is the message."

Perhaps you are familiar with the old adage that says: To a man with a hammer, everything looks like a nail. We may extend that truism: To a person with a pencil, everything looks like a sentence. To a person with a TV camera, everything looks like an image. To a person with a computer, everything looks like data. I do not think we need to take these aphorisms literally. But what they call to our attention is that every technology has a prejudice. Like language itself, it predisposes us to favor and value certain perspectives and accomplishments. In a culture without writing, human memory is of the greatest importance, as are the proverbs, sayings and songs which contain the accumulated oral wisdom of centuries. That is why Solomon was thought to be the wisest of men. In Kings I we are told he knew 3,000 proverbs. But in a culture with writing, such feats of memory are considered a waste of time, and proverbs are merely irrelevant fancies. The writing person favors logical organization and systematic analysis, not proverbs. The telegraphic person values speed, not introspection. The television person values

immediacy, not history. And computer people, what shall we say of them? Perhaps we can say that the computer person values information, not knowledge, certainly not wisdom. Indeed, in the computer age, the concept of wisdom may vanish altogether.

The consequences of technological change are always vast, often unpredictable and largely irreversible.

The third idea, then, is that every technology has a philosophy which is given expression in how the technology makes people use their minds, in what it makes us do with our bodies, in how it codifies the world, in which of our senses it amplifies, in which of our emotional and intellectual tendencies it disregards. This idea is the sum and substance of what the great Catholic prophet, Marshall McLuhan meant when he coined the famous sentence, "The medium is the message."

Fourth Idea

Here is the fourth idea: Technological change is not additive; it is ecological. I can explain this best by an analogy. What happens if we place a drop of red dye into a beaker of clear water? Do we have clear water plus a spot of red dye? Obviously not. We have a new coloration to every molecule of water. That is what I mean by ecological change. A new medium does not add something; it changes everything. In the year 1500, after the printing press was invented, you did not have old Europe plus the printing press. You had a different Europe. After television, America was not America plus television. Television gave a new coloration to every political campaign, to every home, to every school, to every church, to every industry, and so on.

That is why we must be cautious about technological innovation. The consequences of technological change are always vast, often unpredictable and largely irreversible. That is also why we must be suspicious of capitalists. Capitalists are by definition not only personal risk takers but, more to the point, cultural risk takers. The most creative and daring of them hope to exploit new technologies to the fullest, and do not much care what traditions are overthrown in the process or whether or not a culture is prepared to function without such traditions. Capitalists are, in a word, radicals. In America, our most significant radicals have always been capitalists—men like Bell, Edison, Ford, Carnegie, Sarnoff, Goldwyn. These men obliterated the 19th century, and created the 20th, which is why it is a mystery to me that capitalists are thought to be conservative. Perhaps it is because they are inclined to wear dark suits and grey ties.

I trust you understand that in saying all this, I am making no argument for socialism. I say only that capitalists need to be carefully watched and disciplined. To be sure, they talk of family, marriage, piety, and honor but if allowed to exploit new technology to its fullest economic potential, they may undo the institutions that make such ideas possible. And here I might just give two examples of this point, taken from the American encounter with technology. The first concerns education. Who, we may ask, has had the greatest impact on American education in this century? If you are thinking of John Dewey or any other education philosopher, I must say you are quite wrong. The greatest impact has been made by quiet men in grey suits in a suburb of New York City called Princeton, New Jersey. There, they developed and promoted the technology known as the standardized test, such as IQ tests, the SATs and the GREs. Their tests redefined what we mean by learning, and have resulted in our reorganizing the curriculum to accommodate the tests.

A second example concerns our politics. It is clear by now that the people who have had the most radical effect on American politics in our time are not political ideologues or student protesters with long hair and copies of Karl Marx under their arms. The radicals who have changed the nature of politics in America are entrepreneurs in dark suits and grey ties who manage the large television industry in America. They did not mean to turn political discourse into a form of entertainment. They did not mean to make it impossible for an overweight person to run for high political office. They did not mean to reduce political campaigning to a 30-second TV commercial. All they were trying to do is to make television into a vast and unsleeping money machine. That they destroyed substantive political discourse in the process does not concern them.

Fifth Idea

I come now to the fifth and final idea, which is that media tend to become mythic. I use this word in the sense in which it was used by the French literary critic, Roland Barthes. He used the word "myth" to refer to a common tendency to think of our technological creations as if they were God-given, as if they were a part of the natural order of things. I have on occasion asked my students if they know when the alphabet was invented. The question astonishes them. It is as if I asked them when clouds and trees were invented. The alphabet, they believe, was not something that was invented. It just is. It is this way with many products of human culture but with none more consistently than technology. Cars, planes, TV, movies, newspapers—they have achieved mythic status because they are perceived as gifts of nature, not as artifacts produced in a specific political and historical context.

When a technology become mythic, it is always dangerous because it is then accepted as it is, and is therefore not easily susceptible to modification or control. If you should propose to the average American that television broadcasting should not begin until 5 P.M. and should cease at 11 P.M., or propose that there should be no television commercials, he will think the idea ridiculous. But not because he disagrees with your cultural agenda. He will think it ridiculous because he assumes you are proposing that something in nature be changed; as if you are suggesting that the sun should rise at 10 A.M. instead of at 6.

**The best way to view technology
is as a strange intruder.**

Whenever I think about the capacity of technology to become mythic, I call to mind the remark made by Pope John Paul II. He said, "Science can purify religion from error and superstition. Religion can purify science from idolatry and false absolutes."

What I am saying is that our enthusiasm for technology can turn into a form of idolatry and our belief in its beneficence can be a false absolute. The best way to view technology is as a strange intruder, to remember that technology is not part of God's plan but a product of human creativity and hubris, and that its capacity for good or evil rests entirely on human awareness of what it does for us and to us.

Conclusion

And so, these are my five ideas about technological change. First, that we always pay a price for technology; the greater the technology, the greater the price. Second, that there are always winners and losers, and that the winners always try to persuade the losers that they are really winners. Third, that there is embedded in every great technology an epistemological, political or social prejudice. Sometimes that bias is greatly to our advantage. Sometimes it is not. The printing press annihilated the oral tradition; telegraphy annihilated space; television has humiliated the word; the computer, perhaps, will degrade community life. And so on. Fourth, technological change is not additive; it is ecological, which means, it changes everything and is, therefore too important to be left entirely in the hands of Bill Gates. And fifth, technology tends to become mythic; that is, perceived as part of the natural order of things, and therefore tends to control more of our lives than is good for us.

If we had more time, I could supply some additional important things about technological change but I will stand by these for the moment, and will close with this thought. In the past, we experienced technological change in the manner of sleepwalkers. Our unspoken slogan has been "technology über alles," and we have been willing to shape our lives to fit the requirements of technology, not the requirements of culture. This is a form of stupidity, especially in an age of vast technological change. We need to proceed with our eyes wide open so that we may use technology rather than be used by it.

Critical Thinking

1. All U.S. schoolchildren learn that the first message Samuel F. B. Morse transmitted over his newly invented telegraph were the words, "What hath God wrought." What they probably do not learn is that Morse was quoting from the poem of Balaam in the Book of Numbers, chapter 23. Read the text of this poem.
2. The overview to this unit presents two ways to understand technical and scientific discoveries. In which camp is Morse? Richard Lewontin, a Harvard geneticist, says ("The Politics of Science," *The New York Review of Books,* May 9, 2002) that "The state of American science and its relation to the American state are the product of war." What does he mean?

"Five Things We Need to Know About Technological Change," *Address to New Tech 98 Conference,* Denver, Colorado, March 27, 1998. Copyright © 1998 by Neil Postman. Reprinted by permission of the author.

Moore's Law and Technological Determinism

Reflections on the History of Technology

PAUL E. CERUZZI

Just over a year ago, the arrival in my mailbox of a book I had agreed to review triggered some thoughts about technology I had been meaning to articulate. The book was Ross Bassett's *To the Digital Age: Research Labs, Start-up Companies, and the Rise of MOS Technology* (Baltimore, 2002).[1] In it, Bassett describes the development of metal-oxide semiconductor (MOS) technology, which enabled semiconductor firms to place more and more transistors on a single silicon chip.[2] This became the basis for what is now known as Moore's law, after Gordon E. Moore. In April 1965, Moore, then the director of research and development at the semiconductor division of Fairchild Camera and Instrument Corporation, published a paper in which he observed that the number of transistors that could be placed on an integrated circuit had doubled every year since integrated circuits had been invented and predicted that that trend would continue.[3] Shortly afterward, Moore left Fairchild to cofound Intel—a company, Bassett notes, that staked its future on MOS technology.

It is important to note at the outset that Moore's law was an empirical observation; it is not analogous to, say, Ohm's law, which relates resistance to current. Moore simply looked at the circuits being produced, plotted their density on a piece of semi-log graph paper, and found a straight line. Furthermore, he made this observation in 1965, when the integrated circuit was only six years old and had barely found its way out of the laboratory. The name "Silicon Valley" did not even exist; it would be coined at the end of that decade. Nonetheless, Moore's prediction that the number of transistors that could be placed on an integrated circuit would continue to double at short, regular intervals has held true ever since, although the interval soon stretched from twelve to eighteen months.[4]

Moore's law has been intensively studied, mainly by those wondering when, if ever, fundamental physical constraints (such as the diameter of a hydrogen atom) will interrupt the straight line that Moore observed. These studies note the lengthening of the interval mentioned already: chip densities now double about every eighteen to twenty months, although no one is sure why.[5] Analysts have been predicting the failure of Moore's law for years. Interestingly, the moment of its demise seems always to be about ten years from whenever the prediction is made; that is, those writing in 1994 anticipated that it would fail in 2004, while some today put the likely date at about 2015. Obviously one of these predictions will pan out someday, but for now Moore's law is very much in force, as it has been for over forty-five years—a fact from which the lengthening of the doubling interval should not distract us. Over the same period, computer-disk memory capacity and fiber-optic cable bandwidth have also increased at exponential rates. Thus, in 2005 we see memory chips approaching a billion (10^9) bits of storage, Apple iPods with forty-gigabyte (3×10^{11} bits) disks, and local networks capable of transmitting a full-length Hollywood feature film in seconds.

But while industry analysts, engineers, and marketing people have studied Moore's law intensively, historians of science and technology have shown less interest. That is surprising, since it cuts to the heart of an issue that they have debated over the years: technological determinism.

Mel Kranzberg and his colleagues organized the Society for the History of Technology in part to foster a view of technology running counter to the notion that technology is an impersonal force with its own internal logic and a trajectory that human beings must follow. The society's founders spoke of a "contextual" approach to technology, in which the linear narrative of events from invention to application was accompanied by an understanding of the context in which those events occurred.[6] They named the society's journal *Technology and Culture* to emphasize the importance of all three words. Of course, the founding of SHOT and the establishment of *T&C* did not settle the framework for studying technology once and for all, and periodically the concept of determinism is revisited.[7] Nor did the contextual approach remain static. Led by a second generation of scholars including Thomas Parke Hughes, Wiebe Bijker, and Donald MacKenzie, it evolved into the notion (borrowed from elsewhere) of the "social construction" of technology.[8] At the risk of telescoping a complex and rich story, recall that part of the context of the founding of the Society for the History of Technology in 1957 was the Soviets' launch of *Sputnik* and its effect on the perception of U.S. and British technology.[9] The idea of free peoples choosing their destiny freely was very much on the minds of Americans and Britons, then engaged in a cold war with a nation whose citizens lacked such freedom.

I agree with and support this approach to the history of technology. But it must confront a serious challenge: the steady and unstoppable march of semiconductor density, which has led to the rapid introduction of an enormous number of new products, services, and ways of working and living. Think of all the cultural, political, and social events that have occurred in the West since 1965. Think of our understanding of the history of science and technology today compared to then. Now consider that throughout all of these years, the exponential growth of chip density has hardly deviated from its slope. Can anything other than the limit implied by Planck's constant have an effect on Moore's law?

That Moore's law plays a significant role in determining the current place of technology in society is not in dispute. Is it a determinant of our society? The public and our political leaders believe so. In the popular press, the term "technology" itself is today synonymous with "computers." Historians of technology find that conflation exasperating, as it excludes a vast array of technology-driven processes, such as textiles or food production.

The public acceptance of technological determinism is evident among the many visitors where I work, at the National Air and Space Museum, and a recent essay in this journal indicates that determinism is again very much on the minds of historians of technology as well. In "All that Is Solid Melts into Air: Historians of Technology in the Information Revolution," Rosalind Williams recounts her experiences as dean of students at the Massachusetts Institute of Technology during that institution's transition from a set of internally generated, ad hoc administrative computing systems to one supplied by a commercial vendor, SAP.[10] Williams noted that MIT faculty and administrators felt powerless to shape, much less resist, the administrative model embodied in the new software. Such feelings of powerlessness might be understandable elsewhere, but MIT faculty are supposed to be the masters of new technology—they are the ones who create the science and engineering that underpin SAP's products. How could *they* be powerless?

A close reading of Williams's essay reveals that MIT faculty and staff were not exactly passive consumers of SAP R/3. They may have conformed to the software's rigid structure, but not without a fight. The final implementation of this "reengineering," as it was called, was much more than a simple top-down process. Is that not a refutation of the notion that increases in semiconductor density drive society? If one looked instead at a liberal arts college, less technologically savvy than MIT, would the deterministic nature of computing assert itself more strongly?

Williams used her own institution and her own role as a dean as data points (although she did exclaim "There must be an easier way to do research").[11] I propose that we do the same: look not at other people and institutions but rather at ourselves, historians of

technology who live and work in a digital environment and who assert the right to criticize the blind acceptance of the products of the information age. How do we, as individuals, handle the consequences of Moore's law?

I begin with the ground on which we stand—or, more accurately, the chairs in which we sit. We spend our days in offices, staring into computer screens, using software provided by corporations such as Microsoft, Adobe, AOL, Novell, Lotus. We do not design or build the hardware or write the software, nor do we have more than a rudimentary notion of how to repair either when something breaks. "Wizards" install new applications for us; we insert a disk and press "Enter." The computer recognizes when a new device is attached, a process called "plug and play." How far removed this is from the days when many of us used jacks, wrenches, screwdrivers, and other tools to replace broken or worn parts on our cars, reinstalled everything, tested it, and then drove off![12]

We are trying to have it both ways. We pass critical and moral judgment on Harry Truman for his decision to use atomic bombs against Japan, we criticize a museum for showing, out of context, the aircraft that carried the first bomb, yet we ignore our inability to exert more than a smidgen of control over technologies that affect—determine—our daily lives.[13] In her recent book *User Error*, Ellen Rose, a professor of education and multimedia at the University of New Brunswick, writes that when it comes to software people uncritically accept technology without regard to its context or social dimension.[14] This time the villains are not Harry Truman, the Air Force Association, or senior management at the Smithsonian. We are responsible. Historians of technology find determinism distasteful. Yet we validate it every day.

Consider the tools that I and my colleagues used when I began my career as a historian of technology and a teacher:

16 mm movies
Triplicate 3″ × 5″ library cards (author, title, subject)
5″ × 8″ note cards, some with edge notches sorted by a
    knitting needle
35 mm film camera, producing color slides or 8″ × 10″
    black-and-white prints
Blackboard and chalk
Cassette tape recorder
Drafting table, for producing hand-drawn maps and charts
Hewlett-Packard pocket calculator
Microfilm
Mimeograph machine
Overhead transparencies, hand drawn on the fly during
    a lecture
Photocopier
Preprints or offprints of published papers
Telephone, rotary dial, leased from AT&T
Typed letters, sent through U.S. mail
Typewriter, manual

Now consider the tool set we use today in our daily work of teaching, researching, and writing. This list is based on an informal look around my own office and at nearby universities

Hardware	Software
Blackberry or PDA	JPEG image files
Compact disks	PDF files (plus Adobe Reader)
Cell phone	Electronic mail
Digital camera	Instant messaging or chat
DSL or cable modem	Groupware (Lotus Notes or
DVD player	Microsoft Outlook)
GPS receiver	Adobe Photoshop
MP3 player	Microsoft Excel
Laptop computer	Microsoft PowerPoint
Desktop personal computer	Microsoft Word
Scanner with digitizing software	Worldwide Web browser
Sony MiniDisc recorder	Amazon.com
VoIP telephone	Blackboard.com
Wireless ethernet (Wi-Fi)	Blogs
networking device	Google
	HTML documents
	JSTOR
	Listservs, Usenet or similar
	discussion groups
	ProQuest on-line newspaper
	retrieval
	QuickTime Virtual Reality
	Turnitin.com

in Maryland and Virginia where I have taught or lectured. For convenience I divide it into software and hardware. Strictly speaking only hardware obeys Moore's law, but in practice the advances in semiconductor technology allow for more and more complex software products, so both lists are appropriate.

I have probably left some out. Few readers will be enthusiastic users of every device or program or service listed above (though some will be). But I have made my point: Moore's law is at work.

Every three years, as chip capacity quadruples, a new generation of electronic products appears, along with new versions of existing software or new software products. Six years from now probably half the devices in my list of current hardware will be superseded. We see Moore's law at work in the progression of personal computer system software from CP/M to MS-DOS to Windows in its numerous versions, each integrating more and more functions (and triggering antitrust actions, to little avail). We see it, too, in the progression of personal computers, laptops, cell phones, digital cameras, MP3 players, and other devices far more powerful than the computer that accompanied Neil Armstrong, Michael Collins, and Buzz Aldrin to the Moon in 1969.[15]

It is this progression that drives the current relationship between culture and technology. Right now, many of us are abandoning film for digital photography. For those of us who took pleasure in working in a darkroom, this transition is painful. Do we have a choice? I vividly remember getting a pocket calculator and putting away my beloved slide rule.[16] It was a conscious decision that I made with an appreciation of its cultural

implications. But who thinks about the wholesale transition to digital technology? Ellen Rose argues that we adopt these things en masse, without questioning them. And if we do not question them, we are at the mercy of those who produce and sell them to us. How can we espouse theories of the social shaping of technology when our daily interaction with technology is driven to such a great extent by the push of engineering?

This phenomenon seems, furthermore, without regard for the themes of gender, race, and class to which historians of technology have devoted so much attention. This journal, for example, has published an excellent study of women's involvement with programming early computers.[17] The popular press carries almost daily reports on, for example, how technologies such as the cell phone are used in less-developed countries lacking extensive wired phone infrastructure, how such technologies are differently adopted in various developed countries, how such devices are manufactured in Asia, or the outsourcing of software production to countries like India.

These are second-order examples of social construction. Silicon Valley firms frequently introduce products that fail in the marketplace, and the consumer plays a role in that process. Race, class, and gender factor into consumers' decisions. But transistor density and memory capacity never stop growing. The MIT faculty may balk at implementing a particular database product, but not at the doubling of chip capacity every eighteen months. It is a prerequisite for employment at MIT, Microsoft, or in Silicon Valley that one buy into the perpetuation of Moore's law. People who do not believe it must find work elsewhere.

Is this belief, then, an indication of the social construction of computing? I think not. Rather, it is an indication of the reality of technological determinism. Computing power must increase because it can.

PowerPoint

In an earlier version of this essay I examined the debate over Microsoft PowerPoint as a possible refutation of the thesis of determinism. Many scholars have criticized this program. Edward Tufte, the well-known author of books on the visual presentation of information, is especially harsh, arguing that PowerPoint "elevates format over content, betraying an attitude of commercialism that turns everything into a sales pitch."[18] Vint Cerf, coinventor of the Internet protocols, prefers old-fashioned overhead transparencies and typically begins his public talks with the admonition, "Power corrupts; PowerPoint corrupts absolutely." For Cerf it is more of an apology; at most conferences he is the only speaker who does not use the program.[19] Originally I intended to add my own critique, but in the interval between early draft and later revision the debate was flattened by the steamroller of Moore's law. Neither Tufte nor Cerf has made the slightest dent in the adoption of PowerPoint. And if they could not, who can? Two years ago it was still possible to warn scholars not to use PowerPoint. Now that sounds like a crusty old newspaper reporter waxing nostalgic about his old Underwood (and the bottle of bourbon in the top desk drawer).

Comparing PowerPoint to Stalin, as Tufte does, does not advance the debate over technological determinism. Nor will it do to deny determinism because one uses only a fraction of the electronic devices listed above—or even none of them. In a famous and now fairly old essay titled "Why I Am Not Going to Buy a Computer," Wendell Berry raised many of the objections found in more recent critiques, albeit with a succinct eloquence that few can match.[20] One objection not found in many later commentaries that Berry nonetheless advanced was that his wife did the typing for him. That brought him a lot of criticism, of course, but no argument he could have raised would have made a difference. As Ellen Rose points out, even if one writes an essay in longhand, someone else will have to scan or key it into a computer before it can be published.[21] Who is kidding whom? All of these critiques wither before Moore's law. When I was preparing these remarks I found Berry's famous essay not by going to the library and looking for a print copy but by typing the title into Google. The full text came up in seconds. Whether Berry knows or cares that his writings can be found that way, I cannot say. Nor do I know if whoever put the essay onto the Worldwide Web did so with a sense of irony. It does not matter. That is how one retrieves information nowadays.

A common method by which scholars communicate today is via Microsoft Word files attached to e-mail messages. Most publishers and publications (including this journal) ask that manuscripts be submitted as e-mail attachments. Microsoft Word has its flaws; most of us who use it, for example, have encountered instances where the font suddenly changes, randomly, for no apparent reason.[22] Word is also a voracious consumer of memory, but thanks to Moore's law that does not matter. Attaching Word files to e-mail is simple and it works, and so the practice is ubiquitous. I compare it to the 4′8½″ railroad gauge, which experts say is slightly narrower than the optimum, in terms of engineering efficiency. That drawback is overshadowed by the virtue of being a standard.[23] But remember that the encoding of text in Word is controlled by Microsoft, and Microsoft has the right to change the code according to its needs—not ours. Indeed, Microsoft has done so in the past, and we may assume that it will do so again.[24] The same holds true of another "standard" now taking hold, Adobe's Portable Document Format (PDF). PDF files also take up a lot of memory, but that is not the problem. The coding of these files is owned by Adobe, not by the person who wrote the words or created the document. Before reading such a file, we have to look at a page of dense legalese that states that we "accept" whatever terms of use Adobe wants us to accept (I have never read it).

One response to these concerns is to adopt "open source" programs that do what Word and Acrobat do but run under some other operating system, such as Linux, and adhere to the GNU general public license. Such programs are available and their numbers are increasing. By definition, their source code is available publicly, without charge, and cannot ever come under the control of a private entity.[25] Users are encouraged to modify the software to fit their needs. The historian who learns how to write open-source code would be the present-day counterpart to one who could repair and modify his own automobile in the dim past.

But can open-source software refute the thesis that historians have no ability to control the pace of digital technology?

Thus far, the number of historians of technology who use these programs is miniscule. Perhaps open source will prevail, but the movement is mature and yet has not had much effect on us.

An Internal Logic at Work

Historians need to be cautious when predicting the future—or, for that matter, assessing the present. Using ourselves as data points, as I (like Rosalind Williams) have done, is also dangerous. Yet the data are there, and it would be foolish to ignore our own actions. Readers interested in critiques of the pace of digital technology besides the ones cited here can find a range of studies.[26] I have not dwelled more on them because, like everything else, they have had no effect on Moore's law. For the same reason, I do not offer this essay as yet another critique of digitization. My goal is more modest: to ask that we step back from a social constructionist view of technology and consider that, in at least one instance, raw technological determinism is at work. Only then can we begin to make intelligent observations about the details of this process. Ross Bassett's *To the Digital Age* is one such study. There ought to be many more, and they ought to address the question of why the exponential advance of computer power is so impervious to social, economic, or political contexts.

I do not deny that the digital world we inhabit is socially constructed. I am reminded of it every time I observe the celebrity status afforded to Steve Jobs—who, by the way, is not an engineer. Biographies of individuals like Jobs tell how they willed the future into being through the strength of their personalities. One must read these biographies with care, but their arguments are valid. Studying the history of computing in the context of social, political, and economic forces makes sense. It identifies us as like-minded thinkers who do not embrace every new gadget. But if we assert the right to look at technology that way, we must also recognize that in at least one case, Moore's law, an internal logic is at work, and that it is based on old-fashioned hardware engineering that an earlier generation of historians once celebrated.

Notes

1. My review appeared in the October 2004 issue of this journal, *Technology and Culture* 45 (2004): 892–93.

2. A variant, in which PNP-type transistors alternate with NPN types, is called "complementary MOS," or CMOS, and has the advantage of requiring very little power.

3. Gordon E. Moore, "Cramming More Components onto Integrated Circuits," *Electronics*, 19 April 1965, 114–17.

4. The mathematical relationship described by Moore is $n = 2^{((y - 1959) \div d)}$, where n is the number of circuits on a chip, y is the current year, and d is the doubling time, in years. For a doubling time of eighteen months, or $d = 1.5$, this equation predicts chip densities of about one billion in 2005. Chips with that density are not yet available commercially as far as I know, but are being developed in laboratories.

5. For early discussions on this topic among the principals, see Gordon E. Moore, "Progress in Digital Integrated Electronics" (paper presented at the International Electronic Devices Meeting, Washington, D.C., 1–3 December 1975, technical

digest 11–13); Robert N. Noyce, "Microelectronics," *Scientific American* 237 (September 1977): 65.

6. See, for example, Stephen H. Cutcliffe and Robert C. Post, eds., *In Context: History and the History of Technology—Essays in Honor of Melvin Kranzberg* (Bethlehem, Pa., 1989).

7. See, for example, Merritt Roe Smith and Leo Marx, eds., *Does Technology Drive History? The Dilemma of Technological Determinism* (Cambridge, Mass., 1994).

8. For example, Donald MacKenzie and Judy Wajcman, eds., *The Social Shaping of Technology,* 2nd ed. (Buckingham, 1999); Wiebe Bijker, Thomas P. Hughes, and Trevor Pinch, eds., *The Social Construction of Technological Systems* (Cambridge, Mass., 1987).

9. Mel Kranzberg, "The Newest History: Science and Technology," *Science,* 11 May 1962, 463–68.

10. Rosalind Williams, "All that Is Solid Melts into Air: Historians of Technology in the Information Revolution," *Technology and Culture* 41 (2000): 641–68. See also her more recent book, *Retooling: A Historian Confronts Technological Change* (Cambridge, Mass., 2002).

11. Williams, "All that Is Solid," 641.

12. I can no longer make such repairs, as the engine and basic components of the car I now drive are inaccessible. Its ignition, fuel, brake, and other systems are all heavily computerized.

13. Robert C. Post, "A Narrative for Our Time: The *Enola Gay* 'and after that, period,'" *Technology and Culture* 45 (2004): 373–95. But see also his "No Mere Technicalities: How Things Work and Why It Matters," *Technology and Culture* 40 (1999): 607–22, which expresses Post's concerns about the way historians of technology react to claims that "life without technology isn't an option."

14. Ellen Rose, *User Error: Resisting Computer Culture* (Toronto, 2003).

15. The Apollo Guidance Computer had a read-write memory capacity of two thousand sixteen-bit words, or four thousand bytes. See the History of Recent Science and Technology project web pages for the Apollo Guidance Computer, http:// hrst.mit.edu/ hrs/apollo/public/, accessed July 2005.

16. The calculator was a Hewlett-Packard HP-25C. The letter "C" meant that it used CMOS chips, novel at that time.

17. Jennifer S. Light, "When Computers Were Women," *Technology and Culture* 40 (1999): 455–83.

18. Edward Tufte, "Power Corrupts: PowerPoint Corrupts Absolutely," *Wired,* September 2003, 118–19; also Ian Parker, "Absolute PowerPoint," *New Yorker,* 28 May 2001, 86–87.

19. This is the title of Tufte's article cited above, of course, but I heard Cerf use the phrase on the two occasions when we were on the same program as speakers; we were the only two who did not use PowerPoint.

20. The essay was published in print in various places, but I found it on the Worldwide Web at www.tipiglen.dircon.co.uk/ berrynot.html (accessed July 2005).

21. Rose (n. 14 above), 175. She is referring to Neil Postman, who proudly claimed that he wrote all his work by hand.

22. This happened to me as I was preparing this essay.

23. George W. Hilton, *American Narrow Gauge Railroads* (Stanford, Calif., 1990).

24. And this does not address the question whether one can still read the disk on which a document was stored.

25. Paul Ceruzzi, "A War on Two Fronts: The U.S. Justice Department, Open Source, and Microsoft, 1995–2000," *Iterations,* an on-line journal, www.cbi.umn.edu/iterations/ ceruzzi.html (accessed July 2005). Among colleagues in SHOT, I note that Bryan Pffafenberger, of the University of Virginia, uses open source software. At home I use several open-source programs, but my employer in general does not allow them at work. GNU, a recursive acronym for "GNU's Not UNIX," is, among other things, an open-source operating system.

26. The best are written by computer-industry insiders. See, for example, Clifford Stoll, *Silicon Snake Oil: Second Thoughts on the Information Superhighway* (New York, 1996); Ben Shneiderman, *Leonardo's Laptop: Human Needs and the New Computing Technologies* (Cambridge, Mass., 2003); Steve Talbott, *The Future Does Not Compute* (Sebastopol, Calif., 1995); Thomas K. Landauer, *The Trouble with Computers: Usefulness, Usability, and Productivity* (Cambridge, Mass., 1995); Donald A. Norman, *The Invisible Computer: Why Good Products Fail, the Personal Computer Is So Complex, and Information Appliances Are the Solution* (Cambridge, Mass., 1998).

Critical Thinking

1. Early on in *Walden,* Thoreau famously remarks that "Our inventions are wont to be pretty toys, which distract our attention from serious things. They are but an improved means to an unimproved end, an end that it was already but too easy to arrive at. . . . We are in great haste to construct a magnetic telegraph from Maine to Texas; but Maine and Texas, it may be, have nothing important to communicate." Substitute "Internet" for "magnetic telegraph." Do you agree or disagree with Thoreau? How do you think Paul Ceruzzi might respond?

2. The two poles of thought that Paul Ceruzzi discusses are usually referred to as social constructivism and technological determinism. Use the Internet to explore both. Ceruzzi says that "public acceptance of technological determinism is evident among the many visitors where I work, at the National Air and Space Museum." Why?

3. Who is Moore of Moore's Law?

4. Ceruzzi says that "Moore's law was an empirical observation; it is not analogous to, say, Ohm's law, which relates resistance to current." This implies that Ohm's law is not an empirical observation. Is this true?

5. State clearly what is meant by *technological determinism* and *social constructivism.*

Paul Ceruzzi is curator of aerospace electronics and computing at the Smithsonian's National Air and Space Museum. A second edition of his book *A History of Modern Computing* appeared in 2004.

A Passion for Objects

How science is fueled by an attachment to things.

SHERRY TURKLE

In the ongoing national conversation about science education in America, there is a new consensus that we have entered a time of crisis in our relationship to the international scientific and engineering community. For generations we have led; now Americans wonder why our students are turning away from science and mathematics—at best content to be the world's brokers, broadcasters, and lawyers, and at worst simply dropping out—while foreign students press forward on a playing field newly leveled by the resources of the World Wide Web. Leaders in science and technology express dismay.

On this theme, Bill Gates stated flatly, "In the international competition to have the biggest and best supply of knowledge workers, America is falling behind." He went on: "In math and science, our fourth graders are among the top students in the world. By eighth grade, they're in the middle of the pack. By 12th grade, U.S. students are scoring near the bottom of all industrialized nations."

When the science committee of the House of Representatives asked the National Academies, the nation's leading scientific advisory group, for 10 recommendations to strengthen America's scientific competitiveness, the academies offered twice that number. There were recommendations to support early-career scientists and those who plan to become science teachers. There were recommendations to create a new government agency to sponsor energy research and to use tax policy to encourage research and development in corporate settings.

As sensible as these recommendations may be, they deal largely with financial incentives and big institutions. I would like to suggest a different tack.

From my very first days at the Massachusetts Institute of Technology in 1976, I found passion for objects everywhere. I had students and colleagues who spoke about how they were drawn into science by the mesmerizing power of a crystal radio, by the physics of sand castles, by playing with marbles, by childhood explorations of air-conditioning units.

They also spoke of new objects. I came to MIT in the early days of the computer culture. My students were beginning to talk about how they identified with their computers, how they experienced these machines as extensions of themselves. For some, computers were "objects to think with" for thinking about larger questions, questions about determinism and free will, mind and mechanism.

Trained as a humanist and social scientist, I began to ask, What is the role of objects in the creative life of the scientist? What makes certain objects good to think with? What part do objects take in the development of a young scientific mind?

Thinking about scientists and their objects raises the question of how to best exploit the power of things to improve science education.

Neither physical nor digital objects can be taken out of the equation; nor should either be fetishized. Over the past decades, we have seen an ongoing temptation to turn to computers to try to solve our educational crisis. It is natural, in a time of crisis, to avidly pursue the next new thing, but we need to not lose sight of the things that have already worked. Awash as we are in new teaching materials (from smart boards to simulated science laboratories), object-play is not something to which today's teachers are particularly attuned, although as early as third grade, young people interested in science can identify the objects that preoccupy them. Theirs are the minds we want to cultivate, but these students are often isolated, strangely alone with their thoughts.

One reason we don't pay enough attention to things and thinking is that we are distracted by our digital dreams; another is that traditionally, scientists have been reticent to talk about their object passions or, one might say, about passions of any kind. There was a canonical story about the objectivity and dispassion of scientific work, and scientists stuck to it. In 1856 the essayist Walter Bagehot described the young scientist as an aficionado of the object world, yet Bagehot was ready to declare that scientists' involvement with "minerals, vegetables, and animals" spoke to an absence within their constitutions of an "intense and vivid nature." Scientists, he wrote, "are by nature dull and rigid and calm. An aloofness, an abstractedness cleave to their greatness." In their autobiographical writings, scientists reinforced the idea that theirs was a discipline that faced nature with cool composure; lives in science were recounted in ways that separated reason and passion and usually left objects out altogether. But there has always been another story in which scientists' attachments to objects are red-hot. In recent years, this story is starting to be told.

The Nobel laureate Richard Feynman begins his autobiography, *Surely You're Joking, Mr. Feynman,* with a loving description of the "lamp bank" that he built when he was 10, a collection of sockets, bell wire, and serial and parallel switches, screwed down to a wooden base. Feynman plays with the lamp bank to get different voltages by setting switches up in different combinations, serial or parallel. He joyfully recounts his electronic universe: the radios he bought at rummage sales, his homemade burglar alarms and fuses. The fuses, made from tinfoil, offer spectacle as well as intellectual excitement. Feynman sets them up with light bulbs across them so that he can see when a fuse has been blown. And he puts brown candy wrappers in front of the light bulbs so that a blown fuse translates into a beautiful red spot on his switchboard. "They would gloooooooooow, very pretty—it was great."

Over time, there have been dramatic changes in the kinds of objects children have had presented to them. Yet in reviewing 25 years of science students' writing on their favored childhood objects, certain trends are apparent. One is an interest in transparency. Through the mid-1980s, MIT students who grew up in the 1960s wrote about radios, vacuum cleaners, wooden blocks, and broken air-conditioners. These are things to take apart and put back together again. Students describe childhoods in which they fix what is broken or at least try to. They write about the frustration of not getting things to work but learning from their furious efforts.

By the end of the 1980s, my students begin to write about growing up with electronic games, lasers, video games, and "home computers," objects that are investigated through the manipulation of program and code. Yet even with the passage from mechanical to electronic, and from analog to digital, students express a desire to get close to the inner workings of their machines. The early personal computers made it relatively easy to do so. Machines such as the TRS-80, the Atari 2600, and the Apple II came bundled with programming languages and, beyond this, gave users access to assembly languages that spoke directly to their hardware. Students write fondly about programming in assembler, of the pleasures of debugging complex programs. Metaphorically speaking, an early personal computer was like an old car in your garage. You could still "open up the hood and look inside."

However, by the 1990s, the industry trend was clear: Digital technology was to become increasingly opaque, reshaped as consumer products for a mass market. The new opacity was cast as transparency, redefined as the ability to make something work without knowing how it works. By the 1990s, personal-computer users were not given access to underlying machine processes; computers no longer arrived with programming languages as a standard feature. Beyond this, programming itself was no longer taught in most schools. Even so, young people with a scientific bent continued to approach technology looking for at least a metaphorical understanding of the mechanism behind the magic.

Beyond seeking a way to make any object transparent, young people across generations extol the pleasure of materials, of texture, of what one might call the resistance of the "real." In the early 1990s, the computer scientist Timothy Bickmore's experiments with lasers, "passing the laser through every substance I could think of (Vaseline on slowly rotating glass was one of the best)," recall the physical exuberance of Richard Feynman's candy-wrapped light bulbs of a half-century before. For Selby Cull in 2006, geology becomes real through her childhood experience of baking a chocolate meringue: "Basic ingredients heated, separated, and cooled equals planet. To add an atmospheric glaze, add gases from volcanoes and volatile liquids from comets and wait until they react. Then shock them all with bolts of lightning and stand back. Voilà. Organic compounds. How to bake a planet." Cull's joyful comments describe the moment of scientific exultation, the famed "Eureka" moment of raw delight.

Science is fueled by passion, a passion that often attaches to the world of objects much as the artist attaches to his paints, the poet to his or her words. Putting children in a rich object world is essential to giving science a chance. Children will make intimate connections, connections they need to construct on their own. At a time when science education is in crisis, giving science its best chance means guiding children to objects they can love.

At present, there is some evidence that we discourage object passions. Parents and teachers are implicitly putting down both science and scientists when they use phrases such as "boys and their toys," a devaluing commonplace. It discourages both young men and women from expressing their object enthusiasms until they can shape them into polite forms. One of the things that discourages adults from valuing children's object passions is fear that children will become trapped in objects, that they will come to prefer the company of objects to the company of other children. Indeed, when the world of people is too frightening, children may retreat into the safety of what can be predicted and controlled. This clear vocation should not give objects a bad name. We should ally ourselves with what objects offer: They can make children feel safe, valuable, and part of something larger than themselves.

The pleasures of the scientist are not so different from those of historians who inhabit other times and ways. What scientist and historian have in common is an experience that respects immersion rather than curricular pace. Their shared experience has little in common with lesson plans, accelerated drill and practice, or rapid-fire multiple simulations.

Digital media can be used to invite painstaking exploration, but here, velocity tempts because it is so easily achieved. More recent digital media rarely seem to "want" to be used slowly. Their great and unique virtue is that they are able to present an endless stream of what-ifs—thought experiments that try out possible branching structures of an argument or substitutions in an experimental procedure. At its heart, digital culture is about precision and an infinity of possibility. It is about creating a "second nature" under our control.

Object passions bring us to the same enthusiasm for what-is that computation inspires for the what-ifs. We now live the tension between these two impulses; we need to cultivate a balance between them. When we fall for science through objects, they ground us. We focus on what kind of sand is best for building castles, on the stubborn complexity of soap bubbles, on the details of light bent by a prism. I believe these moments open us, heart and mind, to fall for the what-is of our planet. In doing so, we may come home to wonder at it, not only as a frontier of science, but as where we live.

Critical Thinking

1. Sherry Turkle thinks that the temptation to turn to computers to try to solve our educational crisis is wrong-headed. Why?

2. Specifically, what does Turkle mean she says we have "entered a time of crisis in our relationship to the international scientific and engineering community"?

3. Turkle's says that the engineering students she studied in the 1980s expressed "a desire to get close to the inner workings of their machines." What does she say is frustrating that desire with the current generation of computers?

4. Turkle quotes 19th century essayist Walter Bagehot on the supposed personality of scientists. How close is Bagehot's portrayal to your own view?

5. Both Paul Ceruzzi ("Moore's Law and Technological Determinism") and Sherry Turkle evoke a time in when it was possible to work on your car. What is the significance of this story for each writer?

SHERRY TURKLE is a professor of the social studies of science and technology at the Massachusetts Institute of Technology, where she directs the Initiative on Technology and Self. This essay is excerpted from *Falling for Science: Objects in Mind,* which she edited and which is being published this month by MIT Press.

UNIT 2
The Economy

Unit Selections

Learning Outcomes

After reading this Unit, you will be able to:

- Understand the difficulties of picking tech winners and losers.

- Be able to explain the assertion in Gleick's article that "Google's business is not search but advertising," and how it came to be that way.

- Know something of booms and busts in the computer industry and how Facebook fits into the mix.

- Understand how Apple's approach to e-books appears to differ from Amazon's.

- Have experienced the precision and rhetorical difficulty of a peer-reviewed scientific article.

- Understand one clear—and counterintuitive—proposal for eliminating the plague of spam.

- Have a clearer idea of how computing fits into the larger American economy.

Student Website
www.mhhe.com/cls

Internet References

CAUCE: Coalition Against Unsolicited Commercial Email
    www.cauce.org
E-Commerce Times
    www.ecommercetimes.com
Fight Spam on the Internet
    http://spam.abuse.net
The Linux Home Page
    www.linux.org
AllAdvantage—The Rise of the Informediary
    http://en.wikipedia.org/wiki/AllAdvantage
Smart Cards: A Primer
    www.smartcardbasics.com/overview.html
Smart Card Group
    www.smartcard.co.uk

Living in the United States in the beginning of the twenty-first century, it is hard to imagine that the accumulation of wealth once bordered on the disreputable, at least among a certain class. Listen to William Wordsworth, writing 200 years ago:

> The world is too much with us; late and soon,
> Getting and spending, we lay waste our powers:
> Little we see in nature that is ours;
> We have given our hearts away, a sordid boon!

These are words that would quicken the pulse of any young protester of globalization. And no wonder. Wordsworth was writing a generation after James Watt perfected the steam engine. England was in the grips of the Industrial Revolution. Just as the developed world now appears to be heading away from an industrial and towards a service economy, so Wordsworth's world was moving from an agrarian to an industrial economy (see "Automation on the Job," Unit 3). And just as the steam engine has become the emblem of that transformation, the computer has become the symbol of this one.

It is a rare week when the papers do not include coverage of a plant closure, the weakness of trade unions, or the decline in living wage manufacturing jobs. A large part of this is due to plant relocations to countries with lower labor costs. To be convinced, take a look at where almost anything you purchase is made. Lay the blame on computing. It is impossible to imagine how a global manufacturing network, the "global supply-chain," in the argot of the industry, could be coordinated without computers. Products manufactured abroad—with or without the productivity benefits of computers—pass through a bewildering array of shippers and distributors until they arrive on the shelves of a big box retailer in a Phoenix suburb, or just-in-time to be bolted to the frame of an automobile being assembled outside St. Louis. Or, imagine how Federal Express, without computers, could track a parcel as it makes its way from an office in a San Jose suburb to one in Bangalore. "Technology giveth and technology taketh away."

People, of course, did not stop farming after the Industrial Revolution, nor have they stopped producing steel and automobiles after the information revolution, though many commentators write as if this is exactly what has happened. It is true that we in the United States have largely given up factory work. In the last three decades, the number of Americans employed has increased by over 50 million. During this same period, the number of manufacturing jobs declined by several hundred thousand. A large handful of these new workers are software and computer engineers, manipulators of digital images—the glamour jobs of the information age. A much larger portion provide janitorial, health, food, and child care services, leading to the charge that the American economy works because we take in one another's laundry.

© Simon Fell / Getty Images

No discussion of the economic impact of computing would be complete without a nod to Google and Facebook. This is not because they are employers of massive numbers of highly paid software engineers. As Bob Garfield points out ("The Revolution Will Not Be Monetized"), Facebook has about 2,000 employees. Although Google employees 30,000 around the world, neither company is a General Motors. In its glory days, *circa* 1955, GM employed a half million people in the United States alone. Even in its currently diminished state, GM employs over 250,000 people around the world. Neither Facebook nor Google is a mass employer. Instead, they fascinate us because of their almost effortless ability to make money. The Internet has been hopping with news about Facebook's planned initial public offering, thought to be worth $100 billion by some analysts according to *The Los Angeles Times* (June 13, 2011). But what about Google? Its IPO is not a promise. Google is a publicly traded company with 2010 revenues of $29 billion. According to James Gleick ("How Google Dominates Us"), "it has created more wealth faster than any company in history."

We close this unit with a consideration of spam, surely a downside of digital communication. Tens of billions of unwanted e-mail messages flood our in boxes each day. An international team of computer scientists recently reported on its efforts to untangle spam's business ecology, much as entomologists might study the ecology of a crop-destroying insect ("Click Trajectories"). They discovered that its most vulnerable point is the banking system, the mechanism by which consumer payments are transferred to advertisers. As it happens, "just three banks provide the payment servicing for over 95% of the spam-advertised goods." Is an organic pesticide on the way?

The Revolution Will Not Be Monetized

Stratospheric valuations for social media titans assume vast advertising revenue that will never arrive.

BOB GARFIELD

First thing you do, tear this article out of the magazine and carefully set it on fire. It's about the jockeying for position and revenue among the big players in social media: Facebook, Twitter, and Google's YouTube. And the analysis isn't bad for—whaddyacallit—history. But it wasn't written in the past 12 minutes. So more likely than not it's already hilariously out of date. ("*Google?*" you may be asking, perplexed. In case the brand has in the interim disappeared from the scene, like Webvan and John Tesh, listen up: "Google" was a *search engine.*)

Probably there's a new serial-killer app in town—CatRattle .com, or some such—that lets users know what everybody else really thinks of them, in real time. Probably sweeping the nation is the phrase "Dude, you've been totally rattled." But just in case events haven't made a mockery out of this exercise, let's try to address three basic questions:

1. If you build it and they come, does that guarantee that there's money to be made? (Hint: No.)
2. Which of Facebook, YouTube, and Twitter will amass the millennium's first megafortune and a borderless virtual state, with a vast population, political influence, economic clout, and a lair in a hollowed-out volcano from which to control the world's weather? (Well, you can probably eliminate Twitter.)
3. The Wall Street valuations of companies like Facebook, which is worth US $85 billion on the secondary market, are stratospheric. Should we stockpile ammo and canned goods for when the bubble bursts? (Not a bad idea; remember Pets.com.)

Once again, addressing such questions is a process both complicated and highly speculative. But let's give it a shot anyway, beginning with a glance at the status quo, and a little arithmetic.

US $29.3 billion
Google

$2 billion
Facebook

2010 Revenues. In its sixth year, 2010, Facebook's estimated revenues equaled Google's at the same age.

According to the Interactive Advertising Bureau, U.S. advertisers spent $25 billion online in 2010—representing about 15 percent of the $164 billion U.S. ad market and, for the first time, a bit more than their spending on print newspapers. That was no small milestone. But here's the thing: According to eMarketer, 31 percent of Americans' media-consuming *time* in 2010 was spent online. Which means, speaking broadly, marketers valued new-media time *only half as much* as old-media time. And that's the rose-colored view. Chris Anderson, curator of the TED Conferences, recently crunched numbers from Nielsen, Forrester Research, the Yankee Group, and other modelers to synthesize the value, medium by medium, of an individual's time. Globally, print publications fetched $1 per hour of reader attention. TV got a quarter for a viewer hour. Online fetched "less than a dime."

Why is online advertising such a poor stepchild? Well, extremely delightful and informative books with pale-blue and white covers have been written on this subject, but let's reduce the problem to its essence: The endless supply of online content means an endless supply of places where ads could go, which by definition depresses demand and, with it, price. Period.

The second problem is more basic still. Ever click on a banner ad? Have you? Ever? Of course not, because why would you leave what you're doing—especially socializing—to go listen to a sales pitch? The click-through rate, industry-wide, is less than 1 percent—and chalk some of that up to mouse error and click fraud. Some advertisers deal with this problem by popping ads into your face, blaring audio, or subjecting you to "preroll" video messages before the video you actually wish to see. As Anderson sagely observed to a Madison Avenue audience, that was an acceptable quid pro quo in the days of passive TV viewing. Online, though, users are active and in control. "If you take control away from them," he said, "they will hate you." Or, put another way: Online, *all advertising is spam.* These two structural problems leave two possibilities: Either advertising will never be the force in new media that it was in the five predigital centuries (a theory to which I personally subscribe), or someone will crack the code.

The holy grail, if it exists, resides in online advertising's central advantage: the ability to mine data and target individuals with an offer relevant to their lives and interests. In

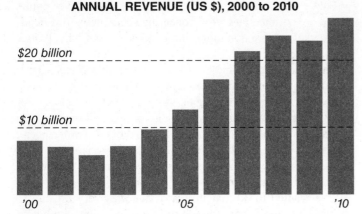

ANNUAL REVENUE (US $), 2000 to 2010

Online Ad Revenue Soars. Web revenues rose last year following a brief, recessionary fall.

Source: Interactive Advertising Bureau.

the case of social networks, there is also the ability to target *friends of existing customers*—what venture capitalist David Pakman calls "the most powerful form of advertising ever created, not counting search." Not only is such targeted advertising on average twice as lucrative as conventional ads, it can fetch 100 times as much revenue as mere spam, the sort that pushes random teeth-whitening miracles and predatory-loan-shilling dancing silhouettes. That's why Pakman believes Facebook's valuation will rise even higher.

"Social networking is a winner-take-all market," Pakman says. "They run the table." His firm recently bankrolled a start-up heavily dependent on Facebook in the social-advertising arena.

On the other hand, that very lucrative targeted messaging has another undesirable effect: It gives us, the target, a condition that experts call the heebie-jeebies. A word about data mining: It is automated and essentially anonymous, but it engenders a creepy sense of privacy invasion and personal violation. Which is why the Federal Trade Commission (FTC) and the U.S. Congress are warning the industry to fix the privacy problem or permit the government to fix it for them. As Anderson sums up the situation: "We're in danger of becoming stalkers. That strategy is going to end badly."

Nor is it beginning all that magnificently.

Facebook and Google's YouTube themselves achieved milestones in 2010. Both are said to have eclipsed $1 billion in ad revenues, and both have reportedly become cash-flow positive. Twitter has only just started attempting to monetize its microblogging utility, but it has similarly altered human behavior on a large scale. Absolutely nobody questions the transformative qualities of these services, nor their extraordinary reach. At this writing, Facebook boasts approximately 600 million users. At current rates of growth, by 2020 its membership will exceed the population of Earth, plus the International Space Station and the planet Krypton. Yet, as Pakman recently estimated, it generates no more than $3 per user per year in revenue (compared to Google, which brings in about $25 per user)—and a huge chunk of the revenue comes from the social-gaming firm Zynga to sell player credits for titles like *FarmVille,* itself a Facebook app.

Furthermore, Facebook's priceless asset is not its incomparable reach but its incomparable data set. Should legislators or

regulators intervene in the name of privacy—maybe by mandating a simple way for anyone to opt out of tracking—the value and sustainability of Facebook's data trove would be vastly degraded.

And that's not the only dark cloud. Facebook's ad strategy hinges not on ads that appear on Facebook pages but rather those served to third-party sites seeking to benefit from Facebook's data and reach. This strategy employs Facebook Connect, a bag of tricks that let developers build Web applications that invite visitors to share information with their friends. For instance, such an application allows subscribers to Netflix, the movie-rental service, to tell their friends which movies they've seen and how well they liked them.

It is precisely such third-party transactions that the FTC is at the moment proposing to regulate. Furthermore, not everyone on Madison Avenue is persuaded that social affinities are such a magical predictor of purchasing behavior. "This is old math," says Rob Norman, CEO of the media-buying colossus Group M North America. "It's the Bell Labs' 'network neighborhood' theory of selling long-distance calling plans. 'Birds of a feather flock together' blah, blah, blah." That's a decent theory but so far, he says, worthy of only "the Scottish Verdict: unproven."

So hold those thoughts for a moment.

If social targeting indeed represents the second most powerful ad engine in history, the first is surely Google search, which allows advertisers to pursue not those it suspects of being prospects but those raising their hands with search terms hollering "Yoo-hoo! I'm over here! And I'm looking for a deal on a new television." Google's 2010 revenues were $29 billion—equivalent to the monthly U.S.–China trade deficit, the Harvard endowment, or the GDP of Latvia plus the market value of the Philadelphia Eagles when Michael Vick is staying in the pocket

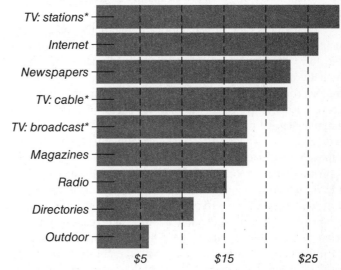

U.S. ADVERTISING MARKET, by MEDIA REVENUE, 2010 (US $, billions)

Online Advertising Surpasses Newspapers. Internet advertising revenue rose at the expense of other media, and last year it surpassed newspapers.

* "TV: stations" includes national and local TV station ads., as well as multichannel system ads. Cable and broadcast refer to TV networks.

Source: IAB Internet Advertising Revenue Report; PwC.

and refraining from killing dogs. In short, that's a chunk of change. It is so big, in fact, that nobody much sweats about when or whether YouTube will be significantly profitable, much less about how Google will amortize the $1.65 billion it paid YouTube's Chad Hurley, Steve Chen, and other owners.

By the same token, as the default platform for video distribution in the Milky Way galaxy, YouTube probably doesn't care how quickly Anderson fills with blind rage upon being presented a 20-second preroll ad before a 2-minute video of kittens on a sliding board. For those who want free content, says Norman, putting up with commercials "is an occupational hazard," and necessary, at least up to a point. The balance of ad time versus content time, he believes, must and will find its level. Meanwhile, the display ads on YouTube's home page have TV-like reach and "are of enormous value to advertisers. I don't think there is any question about that."

What YouTube mainly has going for it is its enormous value to users. In addition to being a bottomless bowl of video snacks, it provides convenient and free distribution for the genius and stupidity of countless video civilians. If Google executive chairman Eric Schmidt's vision is realized, it will also be the central purveyor of all video content, amateur and Hollywood alike, worldwide. For ever and ever. To this end, he has spoken of a 15-year monetization plan including not just advertising but also subscriptions and micropayments. On that journey, he might want to get started right quick.

If YouTube is profitable at $1 billion in revenues, it ain't by much. Acquisition of Hollywood content means fat licensing fees, and streaming all the world's video requires vast network capability beginning—but only beginning—with bandwidth. Alas, even in developed countries, the amount of available fiber and wireless bandwidth is insufficient to convey today's peak loads, much less tomorrow's. "I was sent on a jaunt for one client to buy as much bandwidth and distributed architecture as I could," says Tony Greenberg, chief executive of RampRate, the IT infrastructure consultancy. "I had an unlimited budget, but the Internet didn't have enough capacity."

Google chews up 10 percent of the Internet's capacity, and it has recently been speculated that much of that share is in the form of as-yet-unused optical cable, or dark fiber, that's actually owned by Google. Rather than paying a $500 million annual YouTube bandwidth bill, the company is known to conserve cash by "peering"—trading its excess bandwidth with Internet service providers, like Verizon, for access to their networks. But so what? To Google's accountants, the barter still represents a gigantic overhead expense.

And it's not the only one, as Greenberg notes, his voice rising in gathering annoyance. "In the cost of streaming media, I'm sick and tired of everyone talking about x pennies to move a movie on Netflix and then quoting only bandwidth cost. That's like computing the cost of a bathroom based on the price of toilet paper. You have to deal with the ability to scale, the servers, where the servers live, how it's routed, what the fault tolerances are in terms of milliseconds. And then there's 100 engineering and application issues that can go awry."

That's why, he says, so many massively multiplayer online games are defunct, and why pioneering social network Friendster, outside of Asia, is more like Dumpster. And why Twitter crashes frequently.

Ah, Twitter. Permit me to dispense with this perfunctorily: It is hard to imagine Twitter prospering long-term as a stand-alone company. Oh, the microblogging utility is surely utilitarian. For those who tweet among themselves, it's a means to make all life experiences interactive. For those who monitor the Twittersphere, it is a near-perfect, real-time zeitgeist engine. These are revolutionary benefits, but will the revolution be monetized? That entirely depends on the rather dubious value of "promoted tweets."

"We wanted to do that in a way that was very organic to Twitter and didn't seem foreign or in any way clash with how people were using the product," says Twitter cofounder Evan Williams. "Basically, we give companies the ability to give visibility to a topic that they want to give visibility to, and then when people see that and they click on it, they see a tweet from that advertiser. We have a few dozen advertisers who have gotten phenomenal results, and we're ramping that up now."

Maybe, but here again, a huge obstacle is defeating online inertia.

"If I'm going to be interrupted during a tweet, I want a deal," says Peter Hirshberg, CEO of the agency Reimagine Group and former chairman of Technorati. But such promotional offers are more or less the antithesis of brand building and therefore not necessarily attractive to leading national advertisers. "The point of a brand is to create brand equity and brand loyalty," Hirshberg says. The point is definitely *not* to attract bargain hunters, who are by definition the least loyal, least profitable customers. Many observers therefore assume Twitter will be gobbled up by Google or somebody else—perhaps as a competitive hedge against Groupon, the daily-bargain site, or Foursquare, the location-based social network.

So there. We've reduced the battle of social-media titans to Google/YouTube and Facebook. But who prevails? One of them? Both of them? Neither? That answer probably hinges on who dominates in three areas: mobile search (it's basically the same as search, but on wireless devices, with a few more branches but not really the Foursquare thing), e-mail, and e-currency.

In mobile search, Google doesn't just dominate—it enjoys a virtual monopoly. It also obviously has a huge advantage in e-mail, with its Gmail service, but Facebook, with its new combined e-mail/text/Facebook-message application, is trying to move into that territory—and thereby start siphoning a huge contextual-advertising revenue stream.

For my money, though, the segment to keep your eye on is "Facebook credits," the virtual currency now used primarily in places like *FarmVille*, to buy that game's own in-house money—say, to purchase a virtual cow. I say it will evolve into the long-sought-after mechanism for online micropayments. And you're reading it here first—or maybe the second or 18th time, because the thought isn't unique to me. But the other 17 folks are onto something. As smartphones evolve into transactional tools, Facebook credits could someday function as scrip in the brick-and-mortar world as well. Right now Facebook takes a 30 percent commission; if it can make the system work at 0.3 percent, it will not only overtake the rest of the social media, it will overtake Switzerland.

So, all of the above having been chewed over, the question remains: Who wins? Well, before we get there, I should probably own up to misleading you, because the three queries this essay used as points of departure leave out a possibility, namely that . . .

Those three questions are irrelevant! What if we evolve from an Internet-cloud environment to an app environment—in which case Steve Jobs, who defined his business in 1984 by portraying the competition as Big Brother, could wind up as Big Brother himself? As app-centric mobiles and tablets increasingly dominate our online lives, perhaps the CatRattle app or something else will materialize to make us all forget that Mark Zuckerberg, Chad Hurley, and Evan Williams ever existed.

Maybe yes, maybe no; my forecast is cloudy with a strong chance of iPads. But I must delay no longer. The assignment here was to make a prediction, and with all the above-mentioned caveats, and the further disclaimer that this is but one man's opinion, I will boldly do just that. The dominant online force with a significant social-media component over the next 20 years will be Amazon.com. This is part of *IEEE Spectrum*'s special report on the battle for the future of the social Web.

Critical Thinking

1. This article is about predicting the future of markets, specifically the winner in the race among the big social media companies. *Market Place,* American Public Radio's program on the economy, did a show on predictions August 9, 2011. Use the Internet to find out why people in the United States make so much money making predictions even though they are wrong so frequently.

2. What does the term "click-through rate" measure?

3. What does the low click-through rate in online advertising have to do with Facebook's high valuation?

4. What is the average age of a Facebook employee? Google?

BOB GARFIELD, cohost of WNYC's "On the Media," distributed by NPR, and longtime *Advertising Age* columnist, is author of *The Chaos Scenario,* which describes the collapse of mass media and mass marketing as a by-product of the digital revolution. He says that when he first floated his theories in 2005, he was wisely dismissed as a hysterical crackpot, whereas now, a mere six years later, he is widely dismissed for belaboring the obvious. He gives a précis of those theories in "The Revolution Will Not Be Monetized."

How Google Dominates Us

JAMES GLEICK

Tweets Alain de Botton, philosopher, author, and now online aphorist:

The logical conclusion of our relationship to computers: expectantly to type "what is the meaning of my life" into Google.

You can do this, of course. Type "what is th" and faster than you can find the *e* Google is sending choices back at you: what is the *cloud?* what is the *mean?* what is the *american dream?* what is the *illuminati?* Google is trying to read your mind. Only it's not your mind. It's the World Brain. And whatever that is, we know that a twelve-year-old company based in Mountain View, California, is wired into it like no one else.

Google is where we go for answers. People used to go elsewhere or, more likely, stagger along not knowing. Nowadays you can't have a long dinner-table argument about who won the Oscar for that Neil Simon movie where she plays an actress who doesn't win an Oscar; at any moment someone will pull out a pocket device and Google it. If you need the art-history meaning of "picturesque," you could find it in *The Book of Answers,* compiled two decades ago by the New York Public Library's reference desk, but you won't. Part of Google's mission is to make the books of answers redundant (and the reference librarians, too). "A hamadryad is a wood-nymph, also a poisonous snake in India, and an Abyssinian baboon," says the narrator of John Banville's 2009 novel, *The Infinities.* "It takes a god to know a thing like that." Not anymore.

The business of finding facts has been an important gear in the workings of human knowledge, and the technology has just been upgraded from rubber band to nuclear reactor. No wonder there's some confusion about Google's exact role in that— along with increasing fear about its power and its intentions.

Most of the time Google does not actually *have* the answers. When people say, "I looked it up on Google," they are committing a solecism. When they try to erase their embarrassing personal histories "on Google," they are barking up the wrong tree. It is seldom right to say that anything is true "according to Google." Google is the oracle of redirection. Go there for "hamadryad," and it points you to Wikipedia. Or the Free Online Dictionary. Or the Official Hamadryad Web Site (it's a rock band, too, wouldn't you know). Google defines its mission as "to organize the world's information," not to possess it or accumulate it. Then again, a substantial portion of the world's printed books have now been copied onto the company's servers, where they share space with millions of hours of video and detailed multilevel imagery of the entire globe, from satellites and from its squadrons of roving street-level cameras. Not to mention the great and growing trove of information Google possesses regarding the interests and behavior of, approximately, everyone.

When I say Google "possesses" all this information, that's not the same as owning it. What it means to own information is very much in flux.

In barely a decade Google has made itself a global brand bigger than Coca-Cola or GE; it has created more wealth faster than any company in history; it dominates the information economy. How did that happen? It happened more or less in plain sight. Google has many secrets but the main ingredients of its success have not been secret at all, and the business story has already provided grist for dozens of books. Steven Levy's new account, *In the Plex,* is the most authoritative to date and in many ways the most entertaining. Levy has covered personal computing for almost thirty years, for *Newsweek* and *Wired* and in six previous books, and has visited Google's headquarters periodically since 1999, talking with its founders, Larry Page and Sergey Brin, and, as much as has been possible for a journalist, observing the company from the inside. He has been able to record some provocative, if slightly self-conscious, conversations like this one in 2004 about their hopes for Google:

"It will be included in people's brains," said Page. "When you think about something and don't really know much about it, you will automatically get information."

"That's true," said Brin. "Ultimately I view Google as a way to augment your brain with the knowledge of the world. Right now you go into your computer and type a phrase, but you can imagine that it could be easier in the future, that you can have just devices you talk into, or you can have computers that pay attention to what's going on around them. . . ."

. . . Page said, "Eventually you'll have the implant, where if you think about a fact, it will just tell you the answer."

In 2004, Google was still a private company, five years old, already worth $25 billion, and handling about 85 percent of Internet searches. Its single greatest innovation was the algorithm called PageRank, developed by Page and Brin when they were Stanford graduate students running their research project from a computer in a dorm room. The problem was that most Internet searches produced useless lists of low-quality results.

The solution was a simple idea: to harvest the implicit knowledge already embodied in the architecture of the World Wide Web, organically evolving.

The essence of the Web is the linking of individual "pages" on websites, one to another. Every link represents a recommendation—a vote of interest, if not quality. So the algorithm assigns every page a rank, depending on how many other pages link to it. Furthermore, all links are not valued equally. A recommendation is worth more when it comes from a page that has a high rank itself. The math isn't trivial—PageRank is a probability distribution, and the calculation is recursive, each page's rank depending on the ranks of pages that depend . . . and so on. Page and Brin patented PageRank and published the details even before starting the company they called Google.

Most people have already forgotten how dark and unsignposted the Internet once was. A user in 1996, when the Web comprised hundreds of thousands of "sites" with millions of "pages," did not expect to be able to search for "Olympics" and automatically find the official site of the Atlanta games. That was too hard a problem. And what was a search supposed to produce for a word like "university"? AltaVista, then the leading search engine, offered up a seemingly unordered list of academic institutions, topped by the Oregon Center for Optics.

Levy recounts a conversation between Page and an AltaVista engineer, who explained that the scoring system would rank a page higher if "university" appeared multiple times in the headline. Alta Vista seemed untroubled that the Oregon center did not qualify as a major university. A conventional way to rank universities would be to consult experts and assess measures of quality: graduate rates, retention rates, test scores. The Google approach was to trust the Web and its numerous links, for better and for worse.

PageRank is one of those ideas that seem obvious after the fact. But the business of Internet search, young as it was, had fallen into some rigid orthodoxies. The main task of a search engine seemed to be the compiling of an index. People naturally thought of existing technologies for organizing the world's information, and these were found in encyclopedias and dictionaries. They could see that alphabetical order was about to become less important, but they were slow to appreciate how dynamic and ungraspable their target, the Internet, really was. Even after Page and Brin flipped on the light switch, most companies continued to wear blindfolds.

The Internet had entered its first explosive phase, boom and then bust for many ambitious startups, and one thing everyone knew was that the way to make money was to attract and retain users. The buzzword was "portal"—the user's point of entry, like Excite, Go.com, and Yahoo—and portals could not make money by rushing customers into the rest of the Internet. "Stickiness," as Levy says, "was the most desired metric in websites at the time." Portals did not want their search functions to be *too good*. That sounds stupid, but then again how did Google intend to make money when it charged users nothing? Its user interface at first was plain, minimalist, and emphatically free of advertising—nothing but a box for the user to type a query, followed by two buttons, one to produce a list of results and one with the famously brash tag "I'm feeling lucky."

The Google founders, Larry and Sergey, did everything their own way. Even in the unbuttoned culture of Silicon Valley they stood out from the start as originals, "Montessori kids" (per Levy), unconcerned with standards and proprieties, favoring big red gym balls over office chairs, deprecating organization charts and formal titles, showing up for business meetings in roller-blade gear. It is clear from all these books that they believed their own hype; they believed with moral fervor in the primacy and power of information. (Sergey and Larry did not invent the company's famous motto—"Don't be evil"—but they embraced it, and now they may as well own it.)

As they saw it from the first, their mission encompassed not just the Internet but all the world's books and images, too. When Google created a free e-mail service—Gmail—its competitors were Microsoft, which offered users two megabytes of storage of their past and current e-mail, and Yahoo, which offered four megabytes. Google could have trumped that with six or eight; instead it provided 1,000—a *giga*byte. It doubled that a year later and promised "to keep giving people more space forever."

They have been relentless in driving computer science forward. Google Translate has achieved more in machine translation than the rest of the world's artificial intelligence experts combined. Google's new mind-reading type-ahead feature, Google Instant, has "to date" (boasts the 2010 annual report) "saved our users over 100 billion keystrokes and counting." (If you are seeking information about the Gobi Desert, for example, you receive results well before you type the word "desert.")

Somewhere along the line they gave people the impression that they didn't care for advertising—that they scarcely had a business plan at all. In fact it's clear that advertising was fundamental to their plan all along. They did scorn conventional marketing, however; their attitude seemed to be that Google would market itself. As, indeed, it did. Google was a verb and a meme. "The media seized on Google as a marker of a new form of behavior," writes Levy.

Endless articles rhapsodized about how people would Google their blind dates to get an advance dossier or how they would type in ingredients on hand to Google a recipe or use a telephone number to Google a reverse lookup. Columnists shared their self-deprecating tales of Googling themselves. . . . A contestant on the TV show *Who Wants to Be a Millionaire?* arranged with his brother to tap Google during the Phone-a-Friend lifeline. . . . And a fifty-two-year-old man suffering chest pains Googled "heart attack symptoms" and confirmed that he was suffering a coronary thrombosis.

Google's first marketing hire lasted a matter of months in 1999; his experience included Miller Beer and Tropicana and his proposal involved focus groups and television commercials. When Doug Edwards interviewed for a job as marketing manager later that year, he understood that the key word was "viral." Edwards lasted quite a bit longer, and now he's the first Google insider to have published his memoir of the experience. He was, as he says proudly in his subtitle to *I'm Feeling Lucky,* Google employee number 59. He provides two other indicators of how early that was: so early that he nabbed the e-mail address doug@google.com; and so early that Google's entire server hardware lived in a rented "cage."

Less than six hundred square feet, it felt like a shotgun shack blighting a neighborhood of gated mansions. Every square inch was crammed with racks bristling with stripped-down CPUs [central processing units]. There were twenty-one racks and more than fifteen hundred machines, each sprouting cables like Play-Doh pushed through a spaghetti press. Where other cages were right-angled and inorganic, Google's swarmed with life, a giant termite mound dense with frenetic activity and intersecting curves.

Levy got a glimpse of Google's data storage a bit later and remarked, "If you could imagine a male college freshman made of gigabytes, this would be his dorm."

Not anymore. Google owns and operates a constellation of giant server farms spread around the globe—huge windowless structures, resembling aircraft hangars or power plants, some with cooling towers. The server farms stockpile the exabytes of information and operate an array of staggeringly clever technology. This is Google's share of the cloud (that notional place where our data live) and it is the lion's share.

How thoroughly and how radically Google has already transformed the information economy has not been well understood. The merchandise of the information economy is not information; it is attention. These commodities have an inverse relationship. When information is cheap, attention becomes expensive. Attention is what we, the users, give to Google, and our attention is what Google sells—concentrated, focused, and crystallized.

Google's business is not search but advertising. More than 96 percent of its $29 billion in revenue last year came directly from advertising, and most of the rest came from advertising-related services. Google makes more from advertising than all the nation's newspapers combined. It's worth understanding precisely how this works. Levy chronicles the development of the advertising engine: a "fantastic achievement in building a money machine from the virtual smoke and mirrors of the Internet." In *The Googlization of Everything (and Why We Should Worry),* a book that can be read as a sober and admonitory companion, Siva Vaidhyanathan, a media scholar at the University of Virginia, puts it this way: "We are not Google's customers: we are its product. We—our fancies, fetishes, predilections, and preferences—are what Google sells to advertisers."

The evolution of this unparalleled money machine piled one brilliant innovation atop another, in fast sequence:

1. Early in 2000, Google sold "premium sponsored links": simple text ads assigned to particular search terms. A purveyor of golf balls could have its ad shown to everyone who searched for "golf" or, even better, "golf balls." Other search engines were already doing this. Following tradition, they charged according to how many people saw each ad. Salespeople sold the ads to big accounts, one by one.

2. Late that year, engineers devised an automated self-service system, dubbed AdWords. The opening pitch went, "Have a credit card and 5 minutes? Get your ad on Google today," and suddenly thousands of small businesses were buying their first Internet ads.

3. From a short-lived startup called Go To (by 2003 Google owned it) came two new ideas. One was to charge per click rather than per view. People who click on an ad for golf balls are more likely to buy them than those who simply see an ad on Google's website. The other idea was to let advertisers bid for keywords—such as "golf ball"—against one another in fast online auctions. Pay-per-click auctions opened a cash spigot. A click meant a *successful* ad, and some advertisers were willing to pay more for that than a human salesperson could have known. Plaintiffs' lawyers seeking clients would bid as much as fifty dollars for a single click on the keyword "mesothelioma"—the rare form of cancer caused by asbestos.

4. Google—monitoring its users' behavior so systematically—had instant knowledge of which ads were succeeding and which were not. It could view "click-through rates" as a measure of ad quality. And in determining the winners of auctions, it began to consider not just the money offered but the appeal of the ad: an effective ad, getting lots of clicks, would get better placement.

   Now Google had a system of profitable cycles in place, positive feedback pushing advertisers to make more effective ads and giving them data to help them do it and giving users more satisfaction in clicking on ads, while punishing noise and spam. "The system enforced Google's insistence that advertising shouldn't be a transaction between publisher and advertiser but a three-way relationship that also included the user," writes Levy. Hardly an equal relationship, however. Vaidhyanathan sees it as exploitative: "The Googlization of everything entails the harvesting, copying, aggregating, and ranking of information about and contributions made by each of us."

   By 2003, AdWords Select was serving hundreds of thousands of advertisers and making so much money that Google was deliberating hiding its success from the press and from competitors. But it was only a launching pad for the next brilliancy.

5. So far, ads were appearing on Google's search pages, discreet in size, clearly marked, at the top or down the right side. Now the company expanded its platform outward. The aim was to develop a form of artificial intelligence that could analyze chunks of text—websites, blogs, e-mail, books—and match them with keywords. With two billion Web pages already in its index and with its close tracking of user behavior, Google had exactly the information needed to tackle this problem. Given a website (or a blog or an e-mail), it could predict which advertisements would be effective.

This was, in the jargon, "content-targeted advertising." Google called its program AdSense. For anyone hoping to—in the jargon—"monetize" their content, it was the Holy Grail. The biggest digital publishers, such as *The New York Times,* quickly signed up for AdSense, letting Google handle growing portions of their advertising business. And so did the smallest publishers, by the millions—so grew the "long tail" of possible advertisers, down to individual bloggers. They signed up because the ads were so powerfully, measurably productive. "Google conquered the advertising world with nothing more than applied mathematics," wrote Chris Anderson, the editor of *Wired.* "It didn't pretend to know anything about the culture and conventions of advertising—it just assumed that better data, with better analytical tools, would win the day. And Google was right." Newspapers and other traditional media have complained from time to time about the arrogation of their content, but it is by absorbing the world's advertising that Google has become their most destructive competitor.

Like all forms of artificial intelligence, targeted advertising has hits and misses. Levy cites a classic miss: a gory *New York Post* story about a body dismembered and stuffed in a garbage bag, accompanied on the *Post* website by a Google ad for plastic bags. Nonetheless, anyone could now add a few lines of code to their website, automatically display Google ads, and start cashing monthly checks, however small. Vast tracts of the Web that had been free of advertising now became Google partners. Today Google's ad canvas is not just the search page but the entire Web, and beyond that, great volumes of e-mail and, potentially, all the world's books.

Search and advertising thus become the matched edges of a sharp sword. The perfect search engine, as Sergey and Larry imagine it, reads your mind and produces the answer you want. The perfect advertising engine does the same: it shows you the ads you want. Anything else wastes your attention, the advertiser's money, and the world's bandwidth. The dream is virtuous advertising, matching up buyers and sellers to the benefit of all. But virtuous advertising in this sense is a contradiction in terms. The advertiser is paying for a slice of our limited attention; our minds would otherwise be elsewhere. If our interests and the advertisers' were perfectly aligned, they would not need to pay. There is no information utopia. Google users are parties to a complex transaction, and if there is one lesson to be drawn from all these books it is that we are not always witting parties.

Seeing ads next to your e-mail (if you use Google's free e-mail service) can provide reminders, sometimes startling, of how much the company knows about your inner self. Even without your e-mail, your search history reveals plenty—as Levy says, "your health problems, your commercial interests, your hobbies, and your dreams." Your response to advertising reveals even more, and with its advertising programs Google began tracking the behavior of individual users from one Internet site to the next. They observe our every click (where they can) and they measure in milliseconds how long it takes us to decide. If they didn't, their results wouldn't be so uncannily effective. They have no rival in the depth and breadth of their data mining. They make statistical models for everything they know, connecting the small scales with the large, from queries and clicks to trends in fashion and season, climate and disease.

It's for your own good—that is Google's cherished belief. If we want the best possible search results, and if we want advertisements suited to our needs and desires, we must let them into our souls.

The Google corporate motto is "Don't be evil." Simple as that is, it requires parsing.

It was first put forward in 2001 by an engineer, Paul Buchheit, at a jawboning session about corporate values. "People laughed," he recalled. "But I said, 'No, *really.*'" (At that time the booming tech world had its elephant-in-the-room, and many Googlers understood "Don't be evil" explicitly to mean "Don't be like Microsoft"; i.e., don't be a ruthless, take-no-prisoners monopolist.)

Often it is misquoted in stronger form: "Do no evil." That would be a harder standard to meet.

Now they're mocked for it, but the Googlers were surely sincere. They believed a corporation should behave ethically, like a person. They brainstormed about their values. Taken at face value, "Don't be evil" has a finer ring than some of the other contenders: "Google will strive to honor all its commitments" or "Play hard but keep the puck down."

"Don't be evil" does not have to mean transparency. None of these books can tell you how many search queries Google fields, how much electricity it consumes, how much storage capacity it owns, how many streets it has photographed, how much e-mail it stores; nor can you Google the answers, because Google values its privacy.

It does not have to mean "Obey all the laws." When Google embarked on its program to digitize copyrighted books and copy them onto its servers, it did so in stealth, deceiving publishers with whom it was developing business relationships. Google knew that the copying bordered on illegal. It considered its intentions honorable and the law outmoded. "I think we knew that there would be a lot of interesting issues," Levy quotes Page as saying, "and the way the laws are structured isn't really sensible."

Who, then, judges what is evil? "Evil is what Sergey says is evil," explained Eric Schmidt, the chief executive officer, in 2002.

As for Sergey: "I feel like I shouldn't impose my beliefs on the world. It's a bad technology practice." But the founders seem sure enough of their own righteousness. ("'Bastards!' Larry would exclaim when a blogger raised concerns about user privacy," recalls Edwards. "'Bastards!' they would say about the press, the politicians, or the befuddled users who couldn't grasp the obvious superiority of the technology behind Google's products.")

Google did some evil in China. It collaborated in censorship. Beginning in 2004, it arranged to tweak and twist its algorithms and filter its results so that the native-language Google.cn would omit results unwelcome to the government. In the most notorious example, "Tiananmen Square" would produce sightseeing guides but not history lessons. Google figured out what to censor by checking China's approved search engine, Baidu, and by accepting the government's supplementary guidance.

Yet it is also true that Google pushed back against the government as much as any other American company. When results were blocked, Google insisted on alerting users with a notice at the bottom of the search page. On balance Google clearly believed (and I think it was right, despite the obvious self-interest) that its presence benefited the people of China by increasing information flow and making clear the violation of transparency. The adventure took a sharp turn in January 2010, after organized hackers, perhaps with government involvement, breached Google's servers and got access to the e-mail accounts of human rights activists. The company shut down Google.cn and now serves China only from Hong Kong—with results censored not by Google but by the government's own ongoing filters.

So is Google evil? The question is out there now; it nags, even as we blithely rely on the company for answers—which now also means maps, translations, street views, calendars, video, financial data, and pointers to goods and services. The strong version of the case against Google is laid out starkly in *Search & Destroy,* by a self-described "Google critic" named Scott Cleland. He wields a blunt club; the book might as well been have been titled *Google: Threat or Menace?!* "There is evidence that Google is not all puppy dogs and rainbows," he writes.

Google's corporate mascot is a replica of a Tyrannosaurus Rex skeleton on display outside the corporate headquarters. With its powerful jaws and teeth, T-Rex was a terrifying predator. And check out the B-52 bomber chair in Google Chairman Eric Schmidt's office. The B-52 was a long range bomber designed to deliver nuclear weapons.

Levy is more measured: "Google professed a sense of moral purity . . . but it seemed to have a blind spot regarding the consequences of its own technology on privacy and property rights." On all the evidence Google's founders began with an unusually ethical vision for their unusual company. They believe in information—"universally accessible"—as a force for good in and of itself. They have created and led teams of technologists responsible for a golden decade of genuine innovation. They are visionaries in a time when that word is too cheaply used. Now they are perhaps disinclined to submit to other people's ethical standards, but that may be just a matter of personality. It is well to remember that the modern corporation is an amoral creature by definition, obliged to its shareholder financiers, not to the public interest.

The Federal Trade Commission issued subpoenas in June in an antitrust investigation into Google's search and advertising practices; the European Commission began a similar investigation last year. Governments are responding in part to organized complaints by Google's business competitors, including Microsoft, who charge, among other things, that the company manipulates its search results to favor its friends and punish its enemies. The company has always denied that. Certainly regulators are worried about its general "dominance"—Google seems to be everywhere and seems to know everything and offends against cherished notions of privacy.

The rise of social networking upends the equation again. Users of Facebook choose to reveal—even to flaunt—aspects of their private lives, to at least some part of the public world. Which aspects, and which part? On Facebook the user options are notoriously obscure and subject to change, but most users share with "friends" (the word having been captured and drained

bloodless). On Twitter, every remark can be seen by the whole world, except for the so-called "direct message," which former Representative Anthony Weiner tried and failed to employ. Also, the Library of Congress is archiving all tweets, presumably for eternity, a fact that should enter the awareness of teenagers, if not members of Congress.

Now Google is rolling out its second attempt at a social-networking platform, called Google+. The first attempt, eighteen months ago, was Google Buzz; it was an unusual stumble for the company. By default, it revealed lists of contacts with whom users had been chatting and e-mailing. Privacy advocates raised an alarm and the FTC began an investigation, quickly reaching a settlement in which Google agreed to regular privacy audits for the next twenty years. Google+ gives users finer control over what gets shared with whom. Still, one way or another, everything is shared with the company. All the social networks have access to our information and mean to use it. Are they our friends?

This much is clear: We need to decide what we want from Google. If only we can make up our collective minds. Then we still might not get it.

The company always says users can "opt out" of many of its forms of data collection, which is true, up to a point, for savvy computer users; and the company speaks of privacy in terms of "trade-offs," to which Vaidhyanathan objects:

Privacy is not something that can be counted, divided, or "traded." It is not a substance or collection of data points. It's just a word that we clumsily use to stand in for a wide array of values and practices that influence how we manage our reputations in various contexts. There is no formula for assessing it: I can't give Google three of my privacy points in exchange for 10 percent better service.

This seems right to me, if we add that privacy involves not just managing our reputation but protecting the inner life we may not want to share. In any case, we continue to make precisely the kinds of trades that Vaidhyanathan says are impossible. Do we want to be addressed as individuals or as neurons in the world brain? We get better search results and we see more appropriate advertising when we let Google know who we are. And we save a few keystrokes.

Critical Thinking

1. The author of this article is a well-known science writer. What is his most recent book about?

2. Much is made of Google's PageRank algorithm? What is it?

3. What is the overwhelming source of Google's revenue?

4. Google's model is "Don't be evil." Gleick tells a story about Google.cn. Do you think Google behaved ethically in its encounter with the Chinese government?

5. Type your address into Google Street View. Are you comfortable with what comes up? What if the federal government provided the same service? Would that affect your opinion?

Click Trajectories: End-to-End Analysis of the Spam Value Chain

Kirill Levchenko et al.

I. Introduction

We may think of email spam as a scourge—jamming our collective inboxes with tens of billions of unwanted messages each day—but to its perpetrators it is a potent marketing channel that taps latent demand for a variety of products and services. While most attention focuses on the problem of spam delivery, the email vector itself comprises only the visible portion of a large, multi-faceted business enterprise. Each click on a spam-advertised link is in fact just the start of a long and complex trajectory, spanning a range of both technical and business components that together provide the necessary infrastructure needed to monetize a customer's visit. Botnet services must be secured, domains registered, name servers provisioned, and hosting or proxy services acquired. All of these, in addition to payment processing, merchant bank accounts, customer service, and fulfillment, reflect necessary elements in the spam value chain.

While elements of this chain have received study in isolation (e.g., dynamics of botnets [20], DNS fast-flux networks [17], [42], Web site hosting [1], [22]), the relationship between them is far less well understood. Yet it is these very relationships that capture the structural dependencies—and hence the potential weaknesses—within the spam ecosystem's business processes. Indeed, each distinct path through this chain—registrar, name server, hosting, affiliate program, payment processing, fulfillment—directly reflects an "entrepreneurial activity" by which the perpetrators muster capital investments and business relationships to create value. Today we lack insight into even the most basic characteristics of this activity. How many organizations are complicit in the spam ecosystem? Which points in their value chains do they share and which operate independently? How "wide" is the bottleneck at each stage of the value chain—do miscreants find alternatives plentiful and cheap, or scarce, requiring careful husbanding?

The desire to address these kinds of questions empirically—and thus guide decisions about the most effective mechanisms for addressing the spam problem—forms the core motivation of our work. In this paper we develop a methodology for characterizing the end-to-end resource dependencies ("trajectories") behind individual spam campaigns and then analyze the relationships among them. We use three months of real-time source data, including captive botnets, raw spam feeds, and feeds of spam-advertised URLs to drive active probing of spam infrastructure elements (name servers, redirectors, hosting proxies). From these, we in turn identify those sites advertising three popular classes of goods—pharmaceuticals, replica luxury goods and counterfeit software—as well as their membership in specific affiliate programs around which the overall business is structured. Finally, for a subset of these sites we perform on-line purchases, providing additional data about merchant bank affiliation, customer service, and fulfillment. Using this data we characterize the resource footprint at each step in the spam value chain, the extent of sharing between spam organizations and, most importantly, the relative prospects for interrupting spam monetization at different stages of the process. The remainder of this paper is organized as follows. Section II provides a qualitative overview of the spam ecosystem coupled with a review of related research. Section III describes the data sources, measurement techniques and post-processing methodology used in our study. Section IV describes our analysis of spam activities between August and October of 2010, and the implications of these findings on the likely efficacy of different anti-spam interventions, followed by our conclusions in Section V.

II. Background and Related Work

As an advertising medium, spam ultimately shares the underlying business model of all advertising. So long as the revenue driven by spam campaigns exceeds their cost, spam remains a profitable enterprise. This glib description belives the complexity of the modern spam business. While a decade ago spammers might have handled virtually all aspects of the business including email distribution, site design, hosting, payment processing, fulfillment, and customer service [33], today's spam business involves a range of players and service providers. In this section, we review the broad elements in the spam value chain, the ways in which these components have adapted to adversarial pressure from the anti-spam community, and the prior research on applied e-crime economics that informs our study.

A. How Modern Spam Works

While the user experience of spam revolves principally around the email received, these constitute just one part of a larger value chain that we classify into three distinct stages: advertising, click support, and realization. Our discussion here reflects the modern understanding of the degree to which specialization and affiliate programs dominate the use of spam to sell products. To this end, we draw upon and expand the narrative of the "Behind Online Pharma" project [4], which documents the experience of a group of investigative journalists in exploring the market structure for online illegal pharmaceuticals; and Samosseiko's recent overview [46] of affiliate programs, including many that we discuss in this paper.

Advertising

Advertising constitutes all activities focused on reaching potential customers and enticing them into clicking on a particular URL. In this paper we focus on the email spam vector, but the same business model occurs for a range of advertising vectors, including blog spam [39], Twitter spam [12], search engine optimization [53], and sponsored advertising [26], [27]. The delivery of email spam has evolved considerably over the years, largely in response to increasingly complex defensive countermeasures. In particular, large-scale efforts to shut down open SMTP proxies and the introduction of well-distributed IP blacklisting of spam senders have pushed spammers to using more sophisticated delivery vehicles. These include botnets [13], [20], [56], Webmail spam [9], and IP prefix hijacking [45]. Moreover, the market for spam services has stratified over time; for example, today it is common for botnet operators to rent their services to spammers on a contract basis [40].

The advertising side of the spam ecosystem has by far seen the most study, no doubt because it reflects the part of spam that users directly experience. Thus, a broad and ongoing literature examines filtering spam email based on a variety of content features (e.g., [2], [19], [43], [57]). Similarly, the network characteristics of spam senders

have seen extensive study for characterizing botnet membership [58], identifying prefix hijacking [45], classifying domains and URLs [14], [32], [44], [55], [56], and evaluating blacklists [47], [48]. Finally, we note that most commercial anti-spam offerings focus exclusively on the delivery aspect of spam. In spite of this attention, spam continues to be delivered and thus our paper focuses strictly on the remaining two stages of the spam monetization pipeline.

Click Support

Having delivered their advertisement, a spammer depends on some fraction of the recipients to respond, usually by clicking on an embedded URL and thus directing their browser to a Web site of interest. While this process seems simple, in practice a spammer must orchestrate a great many moving parts and maintain them against pressure from defenders.

Redirection sites. Some spammers directly advertise a URL such that, once the recipient's browser resolves the domain and fetches the content from it, these steps constitute the fullness of the promoted Web site. However, a variety of defensive measures—including URL and domain blacklisting, as well as site takedowns by ISPs and domain takedowns by registrars—have spurred more elaborate steps. Thus, many spammers advertise URLs that, when visited, redirect to additional URLs [1], [22]. Redirection strategies primarily fall into two categories: those for which a legitimate third party inadvertently controls the DNS name resource for the redirection site (e.g., free hosting, URL shorteners, or compromised Web sites), and those for which the spammers themselves, or perhaps parties working on their behalf, manage the DNS name resources (e.g., a "throwaway" domain such as minesweet.ru redirecting to a more persistent domain such as greatjoywatches.com).

Domains. At some point, a click trajectory will usually require domain name resources managed by the spammer or their accomplices. These names necessarily come via the services of a domain registrar, who arranges for the root-level registry of the associated top-level domain (TLD) to hold NS records for the associated registered domain. A spammer may purchase domains directly from a registrar, but will frequently purchase instead from a domain reseller, from a "domaineer" who purchases domains in bulk via multiple sources and sells to the underground trade, or directly from a spam "affiliate program" that makes domains available to their affiliates as part of their "startup package."

Interventions at this layer of the spam value chain depend significantly on the responsiveness of individual registrars and the pressure brought to bear [29]. For example, a recent industry study by LegitScript and KnujOn documents heavy concentration of spam-advertised pharmacies with domains registered through a particular set of registrars who appear indifferent to complaints [28].

Name servers. Any registered domain must in turn have supporting name server infrastructure. Thus spammers must provision this infrastructure either by hosting DNS name servers themselves, or by contracting with a third party. Since such resources are vulnerable to takedown requests, a thriving market has arisen in so-called "bulletproof" hosting services that resist such requests in exchange for a payment premium [23].

Web servers. The address records provided by the spammer's name servers must in turn specify servers that host (or more commonly proxy) Web site content. As with name servers, spam-advertised Web servers can make use of bulletproof hosting to resist takedown pressure [3], [51]. Some recent interventions have focused on effectively shutting down such sites by pressuring their upstream Internet service providers to deny them transit connectivity [6].

To further complicate such takedowns and to stymie blacklisting approaches, many spammers further obfuscate the hosting relationship (both for name servers and Web servers) using fast-flux DNS [17], [41], [42]. In this approach, domain records have short-lived associations with IP addresses, and the mapping infrastructure can spread the domain's presence over a large number of machines (frequently many thousands of compromised hosts that in turn proxy requests back to the actual content server [5]). Furthermore, recently innovators have begun packaging this capability to offer it to third parties on a contract basis as a highly resilient content-hosting service [7].

Stores and affiliate programs. Today, spammers operate primarily as advertisers, rarely handling the back end of the value chain. Such spammers often work as affiliates of an online store, earning a commission (typically 30–50 percent) on the sales they bring in [46]. The affiliate program typically provides the storefront templates, shopping cart management, analytics support, and even advertising materials. In addition, the program provides a centralized Web service interface for affiliates to track visitor conversions and to register for payouts (via online financial instruments such as WebMoney). Finally, affiliate programs take responsibility for contracting for payment and fulfillment services with outside parties. Affiliate programs have proven difficult to combat directly—although, when armed with sufficient legal jurisdiction, law enforcement has successfully shut down some programs [8].

Realization

Finally, having brought the customer to an advertised site and convinced them to purchase some product, the seller realizes the latent value by acquiring the customer's payment through conventional payment networks, and in turn fulfilling their product request.

Payment services. To extract value from the broadest possible customer base, stores try to support standard credit card payments. A credit card transaction involves several parties in addition to the customer and merchant: money is transferred from the *issuing bank* (the customer's bank) to the *acquiring bank* (the bank of the merchant) via a *card association network* (i.e., Visa or MasterCard). In addition to the acquiring bank, issuing bank, and card association, the merchant frequently employs the services of a *payment processor* to facilitate this process and act as the technical interface between the merchant and the payment system.

Card associations impose contractual restrictions on their member banks and processors, including the threat of fines and de-association; but to our knowledge little public documentation exists about the extent to which the associations apply this pressure in practice nor the extent to which it plays an important role in moderating the spam business. Evidence from this study suggests that any such pressure is currently insufficient to stop this activity.

Fulfillment. Finally, a store arranges to fulfill an order[1] in return for the customer's payment. For physical goods such as pharmaceuticals and replica products, this involves acquiring the items and shipping them to the customer. Global business-to-business Web sites such as Alibaba, ECPlaza, and ECTrade offer connections with a broad variety of vendors selling a range of such goods, including prepackaged drugs—both brand (e.g., Viagra) and off-brand (e.g., sildenafil citrate capsules)—and replica luxury goods (e.g., Rolex watches or Gucci handbags). Generally, suppliers will offer direct shipping service ("drop shipping"), so affiliate programs can structure themselves around "just in time" fulfillment and avoid the overhead and risk of warehousing and shipping the product themselves.[2] Fulfillment for virtual goods such as software, music, and videos can proceed directly via Internet download.

B. Pharmacy Express: An Example

On October 27th, the Grum botnet delivered an email titled VIAGRAR ® *Official site*. The body of the message includes an image of male enhancement pharmaceutical tablets and their associated prices. The image provides a URL tag and thus when clicked directs the user's browser to resolve the associated domain name, medicshopnerx.ru.

This domain was registered by REGRU-REG-RIPN (a.k.a. reg.ru) on October 18th—it is still active as of this writing. The machine providing name service resides in China, while hosting resolves to a machine in Brazil. The user's browser initiates an HTTP request to the machine, and receives content that renders the storefront for "Pharmacy Express," a brand associated with the Mailien pharmaceutical affiliate program based in Russia.

After selecting an item to purchase and clicking on "Checkout", the storefront redirects the user to a payment portal served from payquickonline.com (this time serving content via an IP address in Turkey), which accepts the user's shipping, email contact, and payment information, and provides an order confirmation number. Subsequent email confirms the order, provides an EMS tracking number, and includes a contact email for customer questions. The bank that issued the user's credit card transfers money to the acquiring bank, in this case the Azerigazbank Joint-Stock Investment Bank in Baku, Azerbaijan (BIN 404610). Ten days later the product arrives, blister-packaged, in a cushioned white envelope with postal markings indicating a supplier named PPW based in Chennai, India as its originator.

C. Cybercrime Economics

Alongside the myriad studies of the various components employed in spam (e.g., botnets, fast flux, etc.), a literature has recently emerged that focuses on using economic tools for understanding cybercrime (including spam) in a more systematic fashion, with an aim towards enabling better reasoning about effective interventions. Here we highlight elements of this work that have influenced our study. Some of the earliest such work has aimed to understand the scope of underground markets based on the value of found goods (typically stolen financial credentials), either as seen on IRC chatrooms [10], forums [59], malware "dropzones" [16], or directly by intercepting communications to botnet C&C servers [50]. Herley and Florêncio critique this line of work as not distinguishing between claimed and true losses, and speculate that such environments inherently reflect "lemon markets" in which few participants are likely to acquire significant profits (particularly spammers) [15]. While this hypothesis remains untested, its outcome is orthogonal to our focus of understanding the structure of the value chain itself.

Our own previous work on spam conversion also used empirical means to infer parts of the return-on-investment picture in the spam business model [21]. By contrast, this study aims to be considerably more comprehensive in breadth (covering what we believe reflect most large spam campaigns) and depth (covering the fullness of the value chain), but offering less precision regarding specific costs.

Finally, another line of work has examined interventions from an economic basis, considering the efficacy of site and domain takedown in creating an economic impediment for cybercrime enterprises (notably phishing) [6], [35], [36]. Molnar et al. further develop this approach via comparisons with research on the illicit drug ecosystem [34]. Our work builds on this, but focuses deeply on the spam problem in particular.

III. Data Collection Methodology

In this section we describe our datasets and the methodology by which we collected, processed, and validated them. We start with a variety of full-message spam feeds, URL feeds, and our own botnet-harvested spam. Feed parsers extract embedded URLs from the raw feed data for further processing. A DNS crawler enumerates various resource record sets of the URL's domain, while a farm of Web crawlers visits the URLs and records HTTP-level interactions and landing pages. A clustering tool clusters pages by content similarity. A content tagger labels the content clusters according to the category of goods sold, and the associated affiliate programs. We then make targeted purchases from each affiliate program, and store the feed data and distilled and derived metadata in a database for subsequent analysis in Section IV. (Steps 5 and 6 are partially manual operations, the others are fully automated.) The rest of this section describes these steps in detail.

A. Collecting Spam-Advertised URLs

Our study is driven by a broad range of data sources of varying types, some of which are provided by third parties, while others we collect ourselves. Since the goal of this study is to decompose the spam ecosystem, it is natural that our seed data arises from spam email itself. More specifically, we focus on the URLs embedded within such email, since these are the vectors used to drive recipient traffic to particular Web sites. To support this goal, we obtained seven distinct URL feeds from third-party partners (including multiple commercial anti-spam providers), and harvested URLs from our own botfarm environment.

For this study, we used the data from these feeds from August 1, 2010 through October 31, 2010, which together comprised nearly 1 billion URLs. Table 1 summarizes our feed sources along with the "type" of each feed, the number of URLs received in the feed during this time period, and the number of distinct registered domains in those URLs. Note that the "bot" feeds tend to be focused spam sources, while the other feeds are spam sinks comprised of a blend of spam from a variety of sources. Further, individual feeds, particularly those gathered directly

Table 1 Feeds of Spam-Advertised URLs Used in this Study. We Collected Feed Data from August 1, 2010 through October 31, 2010

Feed Name	Feed Description	Received URLs	District Domains
Feed A	MX honeypot	32,548,304	100,631
Feed B	Seeded honey accounts	73,614,895	35,506
Feed C	MX honeypot	451,603,575	1,315,292
Feed D	Seeded honey accounts	30,991,248	79,040
Feed X	MX honeypot	198,871,030	2,127,164
Feed Y	Human identified	10,733,231	1,051,211
Feed Z	MX honeypot	12,517,244	67,856
Cutwail	Bot	3,267,575	65
Grum	Bot	11,920,449	348
MegaD	Bot	1,221,253	4
Rustock	Bot	141,621,731	13,612,815
Other bots	Bot	7,768	4
Total		968,918,303	17,813,952

from botnets, can be heavily skewed in their makeup. For example, we received over 11M URLs from the Grum bot, but these only contained 348 distinct registered domains. Conversely, the 13M distinct domains produced by the Rustock bot are artifacts of a "blacklist-poisoning" campaign undertaken by the bot operators that comprised millions of "garbage" domains [54]. Thus, one must be mindful of these issues when analyzing such feed data in aggregate.

From these feeds we extract and normalize embedded URLs and insert them into a large multi-terabyte Postgres database. The resulting "feed tables" drive virtually all subsequent data gathering.

B. Crawler Data

The URL feed data subsequently drives active crawling measurements that collect information about both the DNS infrastructure used to name the site being advertised and the Web hosting infrastructure that serves site content to visitors. We use distinct crawlers for each set of measurements.

DNS crawler: We developed a DNS crawler to identify the name server infrastructure used to support spam-advertised domains, and the address records they specify for hosting those names. Under normal use of DNS this process would be straightforward, but in practice it is significantly complicated by fast flux techniques employed to minimize central points of weakness. Similar to the work of [18], we query servers repeatedly to enumerate the set of domains collectively used for click support (Section II-A).

From each URL, we extract both the fully qualified domain name and the registered domain suffix (for example,

if we see a domain foo.bar.co.uk we will extract both foo. bar.co.uk as well as bar.co.uk). We ignore URLs with IPv4 addresses (just 0.36 percent of URLs) or invalidly formatted domain names, as well as duplicate domains already queried within the last day.

The crawler then performs recursive queries on these domains. It identifies the domains that resolve successfully and their authoritative domains, and filters out unregistered domains and domains with unreachable name servers. To prevent fruitless domain enumeration, it also detects wildcard domains (abc.example.com, def.example. com, etc.) where all child domains resolve to the same IP address. In each case, the crawler exhaustively enumerates all A, NS, SOA, CNAME, MX, and TXT records linked to a particular domain.

The crawler periodically queries new records until it converges on a set of distinct results. It heuristically determines convergence using standard maximum likelihood methods to estimate when the probability of observing a new unique record has become small. For added assurance, after convergence the crawler continues to query domains daily looking for new records (ultimately timing out after a week if it discovers none).

Web crawler: The Web crawler replicates the experience of a user clicking on the URLs derived from the spam feeds. It captures any application-level redirects (HTML, JavaScript, Flash), the DNS names and HTTP headers of any intermediate servers and the final server, and the page that is ultimately displayed—represented both by its DOM tree and as a screenshot from a browser. Although straightforward in theory, crawling spam URLs presents a number of practical challenges in terms of scale, robustness, and adversarial conditions.

Table 2 Summary Results of URL Crawling. We Crawl the Registered Domains Used by Over 98% of the URLs Received

Stage	Count	
Received URLs	968,918,303	
Distinct URLs	93,185,779	(9.6%)
Distinct domains	17,813,952	
Distinct domains crawled	3,495,627	
URLs covered	950,716,776	(98.1%)

For this study we crawled nearly 15 million URLs, of which we successfully visited and downloaded correct Web content for over 6 million (unreachable domains, blacklisting, etc., prevent successful crawling of many pages).[3] To manage this load, we replicate the crawler across a cluster of machines. Each crawler replica consists of a controller managing over 100 instances of Firefox 3.6.10 running in parallel. The controller connects to a custom Firefox extension to manage each browser instance, which incorporates the Screengrab! extension [38] to capture screen shots (used for manual investigations). The controller retrieves batches of URLs from the database, and assigns URLs to Firefox instances in a round-robin fashion across a diverse set of IP address ranges.[4]

Table 2 summarizes our crawling efforts. Since there is substantial redundancy in the feeds (e.g., fewer than 10 percent of the URLs are even unique), crawling every URL is unnecessary and resource inefficient. Instead, we focus on crawling URLs that cover the set of registered domains used by all URLs in the feed. Except in rare instances, all URLs to a registered domain are for the same affiliate program. Thus, the crawler prioritizes URLs with previously unseen registered domains, ignores any URLs crawled previously, and rate limits crawling URLs containing the same registered domain—both to deal with feed skew as well as to prevent the crawler from being blacklisted. For timeliness, the crawler visits URLs within 30 minutes of appearing in the feeds.

We achieve nearly complete coverage: Over 98 percent of the URLs received in the raw feeds use registered domains that we crawl. Note that we obtain this coverage even though we crawled URLs that account for only 20 percent of the nearly 18 million distinct registered domains in the feeds. This outcome reflects the inherent skew in the feed makeup. The vast majority of the remaining 80 percent of domains we did not crawl, and the corresponding 2 percent URLs that use those domains, are from the domain-poisoning spam sent by the Rustock bot and do not reflect real sites (Section III-A).

C. Content Clustering and Tagging

The crawlers provide low-level information about URLs and domains. In the next stage of our methodology, we process the crawler output to associate this information with higher-level spam business activities.

Note that in this study we exclusively focus on businesses selling three categories of spam-advertised products: pharmaceuticals, replicas, and software. We chose these categories because they are reportedly among the most popular goods advertised in spam [31]—an observation borne out in our data as well.[5]

To classify each Web site, we use content clustering to match sites with lexically similar content structure, category tagging to label clustered sites with the category of goods they sell, and program tagging to label clusters with their specific affiliate program and/or storefront brand. We use a combination of automated and manual analysis techniques to make clustering and tagging feasible for our large datasets, while still being able to manageably validate our results.

Table 3 summarizes the results of this process. It lists the number of received URLs with registered domains used by the affiliate programs we study, the number of registered domains in those URLs, the number of clusters formed based on the contents of storefront Web pages, and the number of affiliate programs that we identify from the clusters. As expected, pharmaceutical affiliate programs dominate the data set, followed by replicas and then software. We identify a total of 45 affiliate programs for the three categories combined, that are advertised via 69,002 distinct registered domains (contained within 38 percent of all URLs received in our feeds). We next describe the clustering and tagging process in more detail.

Table 3 Breakdown of Clustering and Tagging Results

Stage	Pharmacy	Software	Replicas	Total
URLs	346,993,046	3,071,828	15,330,404	365,395,278
Domain	54,220	7,252	7,530	69,002
Web clusters	968	51	20	1,039
Programs	30	5	10	45

Content clustering. The first step in our process uses a clustering tool to group together Web pages that have very similar content. The tool uses the HTML text of the crawled Web pages as the basis for clustering. For each crawled Web page, it uses a q-gram similarity approach to generate a fingerprint consisting of a set of multiple independent hash values over all 4-byte tokens of the HTML text. After the crawler visits a page, the clustering tool computes the fingerprint of the page and compares it with the fingerprints representing existing clusters. If the page fingerprint exceeds a similarity threshold with a cluster fingerprint (equivalent to a Jaccard index of 0.75), it places the page in the cluster with the greatest similarity. Otherwise, it instantiates a new cluster with the page as its representative.

Category tagging. The clusters group together URLs and domains that map to the same page content. The next step of category tagging broadly separates these clusters into those selling goods that we are interested in, and those clusters that do not (e.g., domain parking, gambling, etc.). We are intentionally conservative in this step, potentially including clusters that turn out to be false positives to ensure that we include all clusters that fall into one of our categories (thereby avoiding false negatives).

We identify interesting clusters using generic keywords found in the page content, and we label those clusters with category tags—"pharma", "replica", "software"—that correspond to the goods they are selling. The keywords consist of large sets of major brand names (Viagra, Rolex, Microsoft, etc.) as well as domain-specific terms (herbal, pharmacy, watches, software, etc.) that appear in the storefront page. These terms are tied to the content being sold by the storefront site, and are also used for search engine optimization (SEO). Any page containing a threshold of these terms is tagged with the corresponding keyword. The remaining URLs do not advertise products that we study and they are left untagged.

Even with our conservative approach, a concern is that our keyword matching heuristics might have missed a site of interest. Thus, for the remaining untagged clusters, we manually checked for such false negatives, i.e., whether there were clusters of storefront pages selling one of the three goods that should have a category tag, but did not. We examined the pages in the largest 675 untagged clusters (in terms of number of pages) as well as 1,000 randomly selected untagged clusters, which together correspond to 39 percent of the URLs we crawled. We did not find any clusters with storefronts that we missed.[6]

Program tagging. At this point, we focus entirely on clusters tagged with one of our three categories, and identify sets of distinct clusters that belong to the same affiliate program. In particular, we label clusters with specific *program tags* to associate them either with a certain affiliate program (e.g., EvaPharmacy—which in turn has many distinct storefront brands) or, when we cannot mechanically categorize the underlying program structure, with an individual storefront "brand" (e.g., Prestige Replicas). From insight gained by browsing underground forum discussions, examining the raw HTML for common implementation artifacts, and making product purchases, we found that some sets of the these brands are actually operated by the same affiliate program.

In total, we assigned program tags to 30 pharmaceutical, 5 software, and 10 replica programs that dominated the URLs in our feeds. Table 4 enumerates these affiliate programs and brands, showing the number of distinct registered domains used by those programs, and the number of URLs that use those domains. We also show two aggregate programs, Mailien and ZedCash, whose storefront brands we associated manually based on evidence gathered on underground Web forums (later validated via the purchasing process).[7] The "feed volume" shows the distribution of the affiliate programs as observed in each of the spam "sink" feeds (the feeds not from bots), roughly approximating the distribution that might be observed by users receiving spam.[8]

To assign these affiliate program tags to clusters, we manually crafted sets of regular expressions that match the page contents of program storefronts. For some programs, we defined expressions that capture the structural nature of the software engine used by all storefronts for a program (e.g., almost all EvaPharmacy sites contained unique hosting conventions). For other programs, we defined expressions that capture the operational modes used by programs that used multiple storefront templates (e.g., GlavMed).[9] For others, we created expressions for individual storefront brands (e.g., one for Diamond Replicas, another for Prestige Replicas, etc.), focusing on the top remaining clusters in terms of number of pages. Altogether, we assigned program tags to clusters comprising 86 percent of the pages that had category tags.

We manually validated the results of assigning these specific program tags as well. For every cluster with a program tag, we inspected the ten most and least common page DOMs contained in that cluster, and validated that our expressions had assigned them their correct program tags. Although not exhaustive, examining the most and least common pages validates the pages comprising both the "mass" and "tail" of the page distribution in the cluster.

Not all clusters with a category tag ("pharma") had a specific program tag ("EvaPharmacy"). Some clusters with category tags were false positives (they happened to have category keywords in the page, but were not

Table 4 Breakdown of the Pharmaceutical, Software, and Replica Affiliate Programs Advertising in Our URL Feeds

Affiliate Program		District Domains	Received URLs	Feed Volume
Rx Prm	Rx–Promotion	10,585	160,521,810	24.92%
Mailn	Mailien	14,444	69,961,207	23.49%
PhEx	Pharmacy Express	14,381	69,959,629	23.48%
EDEx	ED Express	63	1,578	0.01%
ZCashPh	ZedCash (Pharma)	6,976	42,282,943	14.54%
DrMax	Dr. Maxman	5,641	32,184,860	10.95%
Grow	Viagrow	382	5,210,668	1.68%
USHC	US HealthCare	167	3,196,538	1.31%
Max Gm	MaxGentleman	672	1,144,703	0.41%
VgREX	VigREX	39	426,873	.14%
Stud	Stud Extreme	42	68,907	0.03%
ManXt	ManXtenz	33	50,394	0.02%
GlvMd	GlavMed	2,933	28,313,136	10.32%
OLPh	Online Pharmacy	2,894	17,226,271	5.16%
Eva	EvaPharmacy	11,281	12,795,646	8.7%
WldPh	World Pharmacy	691	10,412,850	3.55%
PHOL	PH online	101	2,971,368	0.96%
Aptke	Swiss Apotheke	117	1,586,456	0.55%
HrbGr	HerbalGrowth	17	265,131	0.09%
Rx Pnr	RX Partners	449	229,257	0.21%
Stmul	Stimul-cash	50	157,537	0.07%
Maxx	MAXX Extend	23	104,201	0.04%
DrgRev	DrugRevenue	122	51,637	0.04%
UltPh	Ultimate Pharmacy	12	41,126	0.02%
Green	Greenline	1,766	25,021	0.36%
Vrlty	Virility	9	23,528	0.01%
Rx Rev	RX Rev Share	299	9,696	0.04%
Medi	MediTrust	24	6,156	0.01%
ClFr	Club-first	1,270	3,310	0.07%
CanPh	Canadian Pharmacy	133	1,392	0.03%
Rx Csh	RX Cash	22	287	<0.01%
Staln	Stallion	2	80	<0.01%
	Total	**54,220**	**346,993,046**	**93.18%**
Royal	Royal Software	572	2,291,571	0.79%
EuSft	EuroSoft	1,161	694,810	0.48%
ASR	Auth. Soft Resellers	4,117	65,918	0.61%
OEM	OEM Soft Store	1,367	19,436	0.24%
SftSl	Soft Sales	35	93	<0.01%
	Total	**7,252**	**3,071,828**	**2.12%**
ZCashR	ZedCash (Replica)	6,984	13,243,513	4.56%
UltRp	Ultimate Replica	5,017	10,451,198	3.55%
Dstn	Distinction Replica	127	1,249,886	0.37%
Exqst	Exquisite Replicas	128	620,642	0.22%
DrndRp	Diamond Replicas	1,307	506,486	0.27%
Prge	Prestige Replicas	101	382,964	0.1%
OneRp	One Replica	77	20,313	0.02%
Luxry	Luxury Replica	25	8,279	0.01%
AffAc	Aff. Accessories	187	3,669	0.02%
SwsRp	Swiss Rep. & Co.	15	76	<0.01%
WchSh	WatchShop	546	2,086,891	0.17%
	Total	**7,530**	**15,330,404**	**4.73%**
	Grand Total	**69,002**	**365,395,278**	**100%**

storefronts selling category goods), or they were small clusters corresponding to storefronts with tiny spam footprints. We inspected the largest 675 of these clusters and verified that none of them contained pages that should have been tagged as a particular program in our study.

D. Purchasing

Finally, for a subset of the sites with program tags, we also purchased goods being offered for sale. We attempted to place multiple purchases from each major affiliate program or store "brand" in our study and, where possible, we ordered the same "types" of product from different sites to identify differences or similarities in suppliers based on contents (e.g., lot numbers) and packaging (nominal sender, packaging type, etc.). We attempted 120 purchases, of which 76 authorized and 56 settled.[10]

Of those that settled, all but seven products were delivered. We confirmed via tracking information that two undelivered packages were sent several weeks after our mailbox lease had ended, two additional transactions received no follow-up email, another two sent a follow-up email stating that the order was re-sent after the mailbox lease had ended, and one sent a follow-up email stating that our money had been refunded (this refund, however, had not been processed three months after the fact).

Operational protocol. We placed our purchases via VPN connections to IP addresses located in the geographic vicinity to the mailing addresses used. This constraint is necessary to avoid failing common fraud checks that evaluate consistency between IP-based geolocation, mailing address and the Address Verification Service (AVS) information provided through the payment card association. During each purchase, we logged the full contents of any checkout pages as well as their domain names and IP addresses (frequently different from the sites themselves). We provided contact email addresses hosted on domain names purchased expressly for this project, as several merchants did not allow popular Web-based email accounts during the purchase process. We recorded all email sent to these accounts, as well as the domain names and IP addresses of any customer service sites provided. We also periodically logged into such sites to record the current status of our purchases. For physical goods, we always selected the quickest form of delivery, while software was provided via the Internet (here too we recorded the full information about the sites used for software fulfillment).

All of our purchases were conducted using prepaid Visa payment cards contracted through a specialty issuer. As part of our relationship with the issuer, we maintained the ability to create new cards on demand and to obtain the authorization and settlement records for each transaction.

We used a unique card for each transaction. We had goods shipped to a combination of individual residences and a suite address provided by a local commercial mailbox provider. We regularly picked up, tagged, and photographed shipments and then stored them in a centralized secure facility on our premises. We stored software purchases on a secure hard drive, checked for viruses using Microsoft Security Essentials and Kaspersky Free Trial, and compared against other copies of the same software (including a reference version that we owned).

Legal and ethical concerns. This purchasing portion of our study involved the most careful consideration of legal and ethical concerns, particularly because this level of active involvement has not been common in the academic community to date. We worked with both our own project legal advisors and with general counsel to design a protocol for purchasing, handling, analyzing and disposing of these products within a legal framework that minimizes any risk of harm to others. While the full accounting of the legal considerations are outside the scope of this paper, most of our effort revolved around item selection and controls. For example, we restricted our pharmaceutical purchasing to non-prescription goods such as herbal and over-the-counter products, and we restricted our software purchases to items for which we already possessed a site license (also communicating our intent with the publisher). We did not use any received products (physical or electronic) and, aside from a few demonstration lots, they are scheduled to be destroyed upon the completion of our analyses.

Finally, while these controls are designed to prevent any explicit harm from resulting through the study, a remaining issue concerns the ethics of any implicit harm caused by supporting merchants (through our purchasing) who are themselves potentially criminal or unethical. Since our study does not deal with human subjects our institutional review board did not deem it appropriate for their review. Thus, our decision to move forward is based on our own subjective evaluation (along with the implicit oversight we received from university counsel and administration). In this, we believe that, since any such implicit support of these merchants is small (no individual affiliate program received more than $277 dollars from us), the potential value from better understanding their ecosystem vastly outweighs the potential harm.[11]

IV. Analysis

A major goal of our work is to identify any "bottlenecks" in the spam value chain: opportunities for disrupting monetization at a stage where the fewest alternatives are available to spammers (and ideally for which switching cost is high as well). Thus, in this section we focus directly on analyzing the degree to which affiliate programs share infrastructure, considering both the click support (i.e., domain registration, name service and Web hosting service) and realization (i.e., payment and fulfillment) phases of the spam value chain. We explore each of these in turn and then return to consider the potential effectiveness of interventions at each stage.

A. Click Support

As described in Section III we crawl a broad range of domains—covering the domains found in over 98 percent of our spam feed URLs—and use clustering and tagging to associate the resulting Web sites with particular affiliate programs. This data, in combination with our DNS crawler and domain WHOIS data, allows us to associate each such domain with an affiliate program and its various click support resources (registrar, set of name server IP addresses and set of Web hosting IP addresses). However, before we proceed with our analysis, we first highlight the subtleties that result from the use of Web site redirection.

Redirection. As we mentioned, some Web sites will redirect the visitor from the initial domain found in a spam message to one or more additional sites, ultimately resolving the final Web page (we call the domain for this page the "final domain"). Thus, for such cases one could choose to measure the infrastructure around the "initial domains" or the "final domains".

To explain further, 32 percent of crawled URLs in our data redirected at least once and of such URLs, roughly 6 percent did so through public URL shorteners (e.g., bit.ly), 9 percent through well-known "free hosting" services (e.g., angelfire.com), and 40 percent were to a URL ending in .html (typically indicating a redirect page installed on a compromised Web server).[12] Of the remainder, the other common pattern is the use of low-quality "throw away" domains, the idea being to advertise a new set of domains, typically registered using random letters or combinations of words, whenever the previous set's traffic-drawing potential is reduced due to blacklisting [24].

Given this, we choose to focus entirely on the final domains precisely because these represent the more valuable infrastructure most clearly operated by an affiliate.

Returning to our key question, we next examine the set of resources used by sites for each affiliate program. In particular, we consider this data in terms of the service organization who is responsible for the resource and how many affiliate programs make use of their service.

Network infrastructure sharing. A spam-advertised site typically has a domain name that must be resolved to access the site.[13] This name must in turn be allocated via a registrar, who has the authority to shutdown or even take back a domain in the event of abuse [30]. In addition, to resolve and access each site, spammers must also provision servers to provide DNS and Web services. These servers receive network access from individual ISPs who have the authority to disconnect clients who violate terms of service policies or in response to complaints.

. . . . Network infrastructure sharing among affiliate programs—when it occurs—is concentrated in a small number of registrars and Autonomous Systems (ASes).[14] Many registrars and ASes host infrastructure for just one or two affiliate programs, only a small number host infrastructure for many affiliate programs, and no single registrar or AS hosts infrastructure for a substantial fraction of the programs overall. (As we will see in Section IV-C however, this situation can change drastically when we weight by the volume of spam advertising each domain.). . .

Although most registrars and ASes host infrastructure for just one affiliate program, each program could still engage many such registrars to serve their domains and many such ASes to host their DNS and Web servers. . . . Programs do not in general distribute their infrastructure across a large set of registrars or ASes: for most programs, each of them uses only a small fraction of registrars and ASes found in our data set. . . . For 50 percent of the affiliate programs, their domains, name servers, and Web servers are distributed over just 8 percent or fewer of the registrars and ASes, respectively; and 80 percent of the affiliate programs have their infrastructure distributed over 20 percent or fewer of the registrars and ASes. Only a handful of programs, such as EvaPharmacy, Pharmacy Express, and RX Partners, have infrastructure distributed over a large percentage (50 percent or more) of registrars and ASes. To summarize, there are a broad range of registrars and ISPs who are used to support spam-advertised sites, but there is only limited amounts of organized sharing and different programs appear to use different subsets of available resource providers.[15]

B. Realization

Next, we consider several aspects of the realization pipeline, including post-order communication, authorization and settlement of credit card transactions, and order fulfillment.

We first examined the hypothesis that realization infrastructure is the province of affiliate programs and not individual affiliates. Thus, we expect to see consistency in payment processing and fulfillment between different instances of the same affiliate program or store brand. Indeed, we found only two exceptions to this pattern and purchases from different sites appearing to represent the same affiliate program indeed make use of the same merchant bank and same pharmaceutical drop shipper.[16] Moreover, key customer support features including the email templates and order number formats are consistent across brands belonging to the same program. This allowed us to further confirm our understanding that a range of otherwise distinct brands all belong to the same underlying affiliate program, including most of the replica brands: Ultimate Replica, Diamond Replicas, Distinction Replica, Luxury Replica, One Replica, Exquisite Replicas, Prestige Replicas, Aff. Accessories; most of the herbal brands: MaxGentleman, ManXtenz, Viagrow, Dr. Maxman, Stud Extreme, VigREX; and the pharmacy: US HealthCare.[17]

Having found strong evidence supporting the dominance of affiliate programs over free actors, we now turn to the question how much realization infrastructure is being shared across programs.

Payment. The sharing of payment infrastructure is substantial. Table 5 documents that, of the 76 purchases for which we received transaction information, there were only 13 distinct banks acting as Visa acquirers. Moreover, there is a significant concentration even among this small set of banks. In particular, most herbal and replica purchases cleared through the same bank in St. Kitts (a by-product of ZedCash's dominance of this market, as per the previous discussion), while most pharmaceutical affiliate programs used two banks (in Azerbaijan and Latvia), and software was handled entirely by two banks (in Latvia and Russia).

Each payment transaction also includes a standardized "Merchant Category Code" (MCC) indicating the type of goods or services being offered [52]. Interestingly, most affiliate program transactions appear to be coded correctly.

For example, all of our software purchases (across all programs) were coded as 5734 (Computer Software Stores) and 85 percent of all pharmacy purchases (again across programs) were coded as 5912 (Drug Stores and Pharmacies). ZedCash transactions (replica and herbal) are an exception, being somewhat deceptive, and each was coded as 5969 (Direct Marketing—Other). The few other exceptions are either minor transpositions (e.g., 5921 instead of 5912), singleton instances in which a minor program uses a generic code (e.g., 5999, 8999) with a bank that we only observed in one transaction, and finally Greenline which is the sole pharmaceutical affiliate program that cleared transactions through a US Bank during our study (completely miscoded as 5732, Electronic Sales, across multiple purchases). The latter two cases suggest that some minor programs with less reliable payment relationships do try to hide the nature of their transactions, but generally speaking, category coding is correct. A key reason for this may be the substantial fines imposed by Visa on acquirers when miscoded merchant accounts are discovered "laundering" high-risk goods.

Finally, for two of the largest pharmacy programs, GlavMed and RX–Promotion, we also purchased from "canonical" instances of their sites advertised on their online support forums. We verified that they use the same bank, order number format, and email template as the spam-advertised instances. This evidence undermines the claim, made by some programs, that spammers have stolen their templates and they do not allow spam-based advertising.

Table 5 Merchant Banks Authorizing or Settling Transactions for Spam-Advertised Purchases, Their Visa-Assigned Bank Identification Number (BIN), Their Location, and the Abbreviation Used in Table 4 for Affiliate Program and/or Store Brand

Bank Name	BIN	Country	Affiliate Programs
Azerigazbank	404610	Azerbaijan	GlvMd, Rx Prm, PhEx, Stmul, RxPnr, WldPh
B&N	425175	Russia	ASR
B&S Card Service	490763	Germany	MaxGn
Borgun Hf	423262	Iceland	Trust
Canadian Imperial Bank of Commerce	452551	Canada	WldPh
Cartu Bank	478765	Georgia	DrgRev
DnB Nord (Pirma)	492175	Latvia	Eva, OLPh, USHC
Latvia Savings	490849	Latvia	EuSft, OEM, WchSh, Royal, SftSl
Latvijas Pasta Banka	489431	Latvia	SftSl
St. Kitts & Nevis Anguilla National Bank	427852	St. Kitts & Nevis	DmdRp, VgREX, Dstn, Luxry, SwsRp, OneRp
State Bank of Mauritius	474140	Mauritius	DrgRev
Visa Iceland	450744	Iceland	Staln
Wells Fargo	449215	USA	Green
Wirecard AG	424500	Germany	C1Fr

Fulfillment. Fulfillment for physical goods was sourced from 13 different suppliers (as determined by declared shipper and packaging), of which eight were again seen more than once (see Table 6). All pharmaceutical tablets shipped from India, except for one shipped from within the United States (from a minor program), while replicas shipped universally from China. While we received herbal supplement products from China and New Zealand, most (by volume) shipped from within the United States. This result is consistent with our expectation since, unlike the other goods, herbal products have weaker regulatory oversight and are less likely to counterfeit existing brands and trademarks. For pharmaceuticals, the style of blister packs, pill shapes, and lot numbers were all exclusive to an individual nominal sender and all lot numbers from each nominal sender were identical. Overall, we find that only modest levels of supplier sharing between pharmaceutical programs (e.g., Pharmacy Express, Stimul-cash, and Club-first all sourced a particular product from PPW in Chennai, while RX–Promotion and DrugRevenue both sourced the same drug from Rhine Inc. in Thane). This analysis is limited since we only ordered a small number of distinct products and we know (anecdotally) that pharmaceutical programs use a network of suppliers to cover different portions of their formulary.

We did not receive enough replicas to make a convincing analysis, but all ZedCash-originated replicas were low-quality and appear to be of identical origin. Finally, purchased software instances were bit-for-bit identical between sites of the same store brand and distinct across different affiliate programs (we found no malware in any of these images). In general, we did not identify any particularly clear bottleneck in fulfillment and we surmise that suppliers are likely to be plentiful.

C. Intervention Analysis

Finally, we now reconsider these different resources in the spam monetization pipeline, but this time explicitly from the standpoint of the defender. In particular, for any given registered domain used in spam, the defender may choose to intervene by either blocking its advertising (e.g., filtering spam), disrupting its click support (e.g., takedowns for name servers of hosting sites), or interfering with the realization step (e.g., shutting down merchant accounts).[18] But which of these interventions will have the most impact?

Ideally, we believe that such anti-spam interventions need to be evaluated in terms of two factors: their overhead to implement and their business impact on the spam value chain. In turn, this business impact is the sum of both the replacement cost (to acquire new resources equivalent to the ones disrupted) and the opportunity cost (revenue forgone while the resource is being replaced). While, at this point in time, we are unable to precisely quantify all of these values, we believe our data illustrates gross differences in scale that are likely to dominate any remaining factors.

To reason about the effects of these interventions, we consider the registered domains for the affiliate programs and storefront brands in our study and calculate their relative volume in our spam feeds (we particularly subtract the botnet feeds when doing this calculation as their inherent bias would skew the calculation in favor of certain programs). We then calculate the fraction of these domain trajectories that could be completely blocked (if only temporarily) through a given level of intervention at several resource tiers:

Table 6   List of Product Suppliers and Associated Affiliate Programs and/or Store Brands

Supplier	Item	Origin	Affiliate Programs
Aracoma Drug	Orange bottle of tablets (pharma)	WV, USA	C1Fr
Combitic Global Caplet Pvt. Ltd.	Blister-packed tablets (pharma)	Delhi, India	GlvMd
M.K. Choudhary	Blister-packed tablets (pharma)	Thane, India	OLPh
PPW	Blister-packed tablets (pharma)	Chennai, India	PhEx, Stmul, Trust, C1Fr
K. Sekar	Blister-packed tablets (pharma)	Villumpuram, India	WldPh
Rhine Inc.	Blister-packed tablets (pharma)	Thane, India	RxRrm, DrgRev
Supreme Suppliers	Blister-packed tablets (pharma)	Mumbai, India	Eva
Chen Hua	Small white plastic bottles (herbal)	Jiangmen, China	Stud
Etech Media Ltd.	Novelty-sized supplement (herbal)	Christchurch, NZ	Staln
Herbal Health Fulfillment Warehouse	White plastic bottle (herbal)	MA, USA	Eva
MK Sales	White plastic bottle (herbal)	WA, USA	GlvMd
Riverton, Utah shipper	White plastic bottle (herbal)	UT, USA	DrMax, Grow
Guo Zhonglei	Foam-wrapped replica watch	Baoding, China	Dstn, UltRp

Registrar

Here we examine the effect if individual registrars were to suspend their domains which are known to be used in advertising or hosting the sites in our study.

Hosting

We use the same analysis, but instead look at the number of distinct ASs that would need to be contacted (who would then need to agree to shut down all associated hosts in their address space) in order to interrupt a given volume of spam domain trajectories. We consider both name server and Web hosting, but in each case there may be multiple IP addresses recorded providing service for the domain. We adopt a "worst case" model that all such resources must be eliminated (i.e., every IP seen hosting a particular domain) for that domain's trajectory to be disrupted.

Payments

Here we use the same approach but focused on the role played by the acquiring banks for each program. We have not placed purchases via each domain, so we make the simplifying assumption that bank use will be consistent across domains belonging to the same brand or affiliate program. Indeed this is strongly borne out in our measurements. For the two small exceptions identified earlier, we assign banks proportionally to our measurements.

. . . . For both registrars and hosters there are significant concentrations among the top few providers and thus takedowns would seem to be an effective strategy. For example, almost 40 percent of spam-advertised domains in our feeds were registered by NauNet, while a single Romanian provider, Evolva Telecom, hosts almost 9 percent of name servers for spam-advertised domains and over 10 percent of the Web servers hosting their content; in turn, over 60 percent of these had payments handled via a single acquirer, Azerigazbank.

However, these numbers do not tell the entire story. Another key issue is the availability of alternatives and their switching cost.

For example, while only a small number of individual IP addresses were used to support spam-advertised sites, the supply of hosting resources is vast, with thousands of hosting providers and millions of compromised hosts.[19] The switching cost is also low and new hosts can be provisioned on demand and for low cost.[20]

By contrast, the situation with registrars appears more promising. The supply of registrars is fewer (roughly 900 gTLD registrars are accredited by ICANN as of this writing) and there is evidence that not all registrars are equally permissive of spam-based advertising [28]. Moreover, there have also been individual successful efforts to address malicious use of domain names, both by registries (e.g., CNNIC) and when working with individual registrars (e.g., eNom [25]). Unfortunately, these efforts have been slow, ongoing, and fraught with politics since they require global cooperation to be effective (only individual registrars or registries can take these actions). Indeed, in recent work we have empirically evaluated the efficacy of past registrar-level interventions and found that spammers show great agility in working around such actions [29]. Ultimately, the low cost of a domain name (many can be had for under $1 in bulk) and ease of switching registrars makes such interventions difficult.

Finally, it is the banking component of the spam value chain that is both the least studied and, we believe, the most critical. Without an effective mechanism to transfer consumer payments, it would be difficult to finance the rest of the spam ecosystem. Moreover, there are only two networks—Visa and Mastercard—that have the consumer footprint in Western countries to reach spam's principal customers. While there are thousands of banks, the number who are willing to knowingly process what the industry calls "high-risk" transactions is far smaller. . . .

More importantly, the replacement cost for new banks is high, both in setup fees and more importantly in time and overhead. Acquiring a legitimate merchant account directly with a bank requires coordination with the bank, with the card association, with a payment processor and typically involves a great deal of due diligence and delay (several days or weeks). Even for so-called third-party accounts (whereby a payment processor acts as middleman and "fronts" for the merchant with both the bank and Visa/Mastercard) we have been unable to locate providers willing to provide operating accounts in less than five days, and such providers have significant account "holdbacks" that they reclaim when there are problems.[21] Thus, unlike the other resources in the spam value chain, we believe payment infrastructure has far fewer alternatives and far higher switching cost.

Indeed, our subsequent measurements bear this out. For four months after our study we continued to place orders through the major affiliate programs. Many continued to use the same banks four months later (e.g., all replica and herbal products sold through ZedCash, all pharmaceuticals from Online Pharmacy and all software from Auth. Soft. Resellers). Moreover, while many programs did change (typically in January or February 2011), they still stayed within same set of banks we identified earlier. For example, transactions with EvaPharmacy, Greenline, and OEM Soft Store have started clearing through B&N Bank in Russia, while Royal Software, EuroSoft and Soft Sales, have rotated through two different Latvian Banks and B & S Card Service of Germany. Indeed, the only new bank appearing in our follow-on purchases is Bank Standard (a private commercial bank in Azerbaijan, BIN 412939); RX–Promotion, GlavMed, and Mailien (a.k.a. Pharmacy Express) all appear to have moved to this bank (from Azerigazbank) on or around January 25th. Finally, one order placed with DrugRevenue failed due to insufficient funds, and was promptly retried through two different banks (but again, from the same set). This suggests that while cooperating third-party payment processors may be able to route transactions through merchant accounts at difference banks, the set of banks currently available for such activities is quite modest.

D. Policy Options

There are two potential approaches for intervening at the payment tier of the value chain. One is to directly engage the merchant banks and pressure them to stop doing business with such merchants (similar to Legitscript's role with registrars [25], [28]). However, this approach is likely to be slow—very likely slower than the time to acquire new banking facilities. Moreover, due to incongruities in intellectual property protection, it is not even clear that the sale of such goods is illegal in the countries in which such banks are located. Indeed, a sentiment often expressed in the spammer community, which resonates in many such countries, is that the goods they advertise address a real need in the West, and efforts to criminalize their actions are motivated primarily by Western market protectionism.

However, since spam is ultimately supported by Western money, it is perhaps more feasible to address this problem in the West as well. To wit, if U.S. issuing banks (i.e., banks that provide credit cards to U.S. consumers) were to refuse to settle certain transactions (e.g., card-not-present transactions for a subset of Merchant Category Codes) with the banks identified as supporting spam-advertised goods, then the underlying enterprise would be dramatically demonetized. Furthermore, it appears plausible that such a "financial blacklist" could be updated very quickly (driven by modest numbers of undercover buys, as in our study) and far more rapidly than the turn-around time to acquire new banking resources—a rare asymmetry favoring the anti-spam community. Furthermore, for a subset of spam-advertised goods (regulated pharmaceuticals, brand replica products, and pirated software) there is a legal basis for enforcing such a policy.[22] While we suspect that the political challenges for such an intervention would be significant—and indeed merit thoughtful consideration—we note that a quite similar action has already occurred in restricting U.S. issuers from settling certain kinds of online gambling transactions [11].

V. Conclusion

In this paper we have described a large-scale empirical study to measure the spam value chain in an end-to-end fashion. We have described a framework for conceptualizing resource requirements for spam monetization and, using this model, we have characterized the use of key infrastructure—registrars, hosting and payment—for a wide array of spam-advertised business interests. Finally, we have used this data to provide a normative analysis of spam intervention approaches and to offer evidence that the payment tier is by far the most concentrated and valuable asset in the spam ecosystem, and one for which there may be a truly effective intervention through public policy action in Western countries.

Notes

1. In principle, a store could fail to fulfill a customer's order upon receiving their payment, but this would both curtail any repeat orders and would lead to chargebacks through the payment card network, jeopardizing their relationship with payment service providers.

2. Individual suppliers can differ in product availability, product quality, the ability to manage the customs process, and deliver goods on a timely basis. Consequently, affiliate programs may use different suppliers for different products and destinations.

3. By comparison, the spam hosting studies of Anderson et al. and Konte et al. analyzed 150,000 messages per day and 115,000 messages per month respectively [1], [22].

4. Among the complexities, scammers are aware that security companies crawl them and blacklist IP addresses they suspect are crawlers. We mitigate this effect by tunneling requests through proxies running in multiple disparate IP address ranges.

5. We did not consider two other popular categories (pornography and gambling) for institutional and procedural reasons.

6. The lack of false negatives is not too surprising. Missing storefronts would have no textual terms in their page content that relate to what they are selling (incidentally also preventing the use of SEO); this situation could occur if the storefront page were composed entirely of images, but such sites are rare.

7. Note, ZedCash is unique among programs as it has storefront brands for each of the herbal, pharmaceutical and replica product categories.

8. We remove botnet feeds from such volume calculations because their skewed domain mix would bias the results unfairly towards the programs they advertise.

9. We obtained the full source code for all GlavMed and RX–Promotion sites, which aided creating and validating expressions to match their templates.

10. Almost 50 percent of these failed orders were from ZedCash, where we suspect that our large order volume raised fraud concerns. In general, any such biases in the order completion rate do not impact upon our analysis, since our goal in purchasing is simply to establish the binding between individual programs and realization infrastructure; we obtained data from multiple transactions for each major program under study.

11. This is similar to the analysis made in our previous study of the CAPTCHA-solving ecosystem [37].

12. In our data, we identified over 130 shortener services in use, over 160 free hosting services and over 8,000 likely-compromised Web servers.

13. Fewer than half a percent use raw IP addresses in our study.

14. We use the AS number as a proxy for ISP.

15. We did find some evidence of clear inter-program sharing in the form of several large groups of DNS servers willing to authoritatively resolve collections of EvaPharmacy, Mailien and OEM Soft Store domains for which they were outside the DNS hierarchy (i.e., the name servers were never referred by the TLD). This overlap could reflect a particular affiliate advertising for multiple distinct programs and sharing resources internally or it could represent a shared service provider used by distinct affiliates.

16. In each of the exceptions, at least one order cleared through a different bank—perhaps because the affiliate program is interleaving payments across different banks, or (less likely) because the store "brand" has been stolen, although we are aware of such instances.

17. This program, currently called ZedCash, is only open by invitation and we had little visibility into its internal workings for this paper.

18. In each case, it is typically possible to employ either a "takedown" approach (removing the resource comprehensively) or cheaper "blacklisting" approach at more limited scope (disallowing access to the resource for a subset of users), but for simplicity we model the interventions in the takedown style.

19. Note, spam hosting statistics can be heavily impacted by the differences in spam volume produced by different affiliates/spammers. For example, while we find that over 80 percent of all spam received in this study leads to sites hosted by just 100 distinct IP addresses, there are another 2336 addresses used to host the remaining 20 percent of spam-advertised sites, many belonging to the same affiliate programs but advertising with lower volumes of spam email.

20. The cost of compromised proxies is driven by the market price for compromised hosts via Pay-Per-Install enterprises, which today are roughly $200/1000 for Western hosts and $5–10/1000 for Asian hosts [49]. Dedicated bulletproof hosting is more expensive, but we have seen prices as low as $30/month for virtual hosting (up to several hundred dollars for dedicated hosting).

21. To get a sense of the kinds of institutions we examined, consider this advertisement of one typical provider: "We have ready-made shell companies already incorporated, immediately available."

22. Herbal products, being largely unregulated, are a more complex issue.

References

D. S. Anderson, C. Fleizach, S. Savage, and G. M. Voelker. Spamscatter: Characterizing Internet Scam Hosting Infrastructure. In Proc. of 16th USENIX Security, 2007.

I. Androutsopoulos, J. Koutsias, K. Chandrinos, G. Paliouras, and C. D. Spyropoulos. An Evaluation of Naive Bayesian Anti-Spam Filtering. In Proc. of 1st MLNIA, 2000.

J. Armin, J. McQuaid, and M. Jonkman. Atrivo—Cyber Crime USA. http://fserror.com/pdf/Atrivo.pdf, 2008.

Behind Online Pharma. From Mumbai to Riga to New York: Our Investigative Class Follows the Trail of Illegal Pharma. http://behindonlinepharma.com, 2009.

C. Castelluccia, M. A. Kaafar, P. Manils, and D. Perito. Geolocalization of Proxied Services and Its Application to Fast-Flux Hidden Servers. In Proc. of 9th IMC, 2009.

R. Clayton. How Much Did Shutting Down McColo Help? In Proc. of 6th CEAS, 2009.

Dancho Danchev's Blog—Mind Streams of Information Security Knowledge. The Avalanche Botnet and the TROYAK-AS Connection. http://ddanchev.blogspot.com/2010/05/avalanche-botnet-and-troyak-as.html, 2010.

Federal Trade Commission. FTC Shuts Down, Freezes Assets of Vast International Spam E-Mail Network. http://ftc.gov/opa/2008/10/herbalkings.shtm, 2008.

W. Feng and E. Kaiser. kaPoW Webmail: Effective Disincentives Against Spam. In Proc. of 7th CEAS, 2010.

J. Franklin, V. Paxson, A. Perrig, and S. Savage. An Inquiry into the Nature and Causes of the Wealth of Internet Miscreants. In Proc. of 14th ACM CCS, 2007.

Gamblingplanet.org. Visa blocks gaming transactions for US players. www.gamblingplanet.org/news/Visa-blocksgaming-transactions-for-US-players/022310, 2010.

C. Grier, K. Thomas, V. Paxson, and M. Zhang. @spam: The Underground on 140 Characters or Less. In Proc. of 17th ACM CCS, 2010.

G. Gu, J. Zhang, and W. Lee. BotSniffer: Detecting Botnet Command and Control Channels in Network Traffic. In Proc. of 15th NDSS, 2008.

S. Hao, N. Feamster, A. Gray, N. Syed, and S. Krasser. Detecting Spammers with SNARE: Spatio-Temporal Network-Level Automated Reputation Engine. In Proc. of 18th USENIX Security, 2009.

C. Herley and D. Florencio. Nobody Sells Gold for the Price of Silver: Dishonesty, Uncertainty and the Underground Economy. In Proc. of 8th WEIS, 2009.

T. Holz, M. Engelberth, and F. Freiling. Learning More About the Underground Economy: A Case-Study of Keyloggers and Dropzones. In Proc. of 15th ESORICS, 2009.

T. Holz, C. Gorecki, K. Rieck, and F. C. Freiling. Measuring and Detecting Fast-Flux Service Networks. In Proc. of 15th NDSS, 2008.

X. Hu, M. Knysz, and K. G. Shin. RB-Seeker: Auto-detection of Redirection Botnets. In Proc. of 16th NDSS, 2009.

D. Irani, S. Webb, J. Giffin, and C. Pu. Evolutionary Study of Phishing. In eCrime Researchers Summit, pages 1–10, 2008.

J. P. John, A. Moshchuk, S. D. Gribble, and A. Krishnamurthy. Studying Spamming Botnets Using Botlab. In Proc. of 6th NSDI, 2009.

C. Kanich, C. Kreibich, K. Levchenko, B. Enright, G. M. Voelker, V. Paxson, and S. Savage. Spamalytics: An Empirical Analysis of Spam Marketing Conversion. In Proc. of 15th ACM CCS, 2008.

M. Konte, N. Feamster, and J. Jung. Dynamics of Online Scam Hosting Infrastructure. In Proc. of 10th PAM, 2009.

Krebs on Security. Body Armor for Bad Web Sites. http://krebsonsecurity.com/2010/11/body-armor-forbad-web-sites/, 2010.

C. Kreibich, C. Kanich, K. Levchenko, B. Enright, G. M. Voelker, V. Paxson, and S. Savage. Spamcraft: An Inside Look at Spam Campaign Orchestration. In Proc. of 2nd USENIX LEET, 2009.

LegitScript and eNom. LegitScript Welcomes Agreement with eNom (DemandMedia). www.legitscript.com/blog/ 142, 2010.

LegitScript and KnujOn. No Prescription Required: Bing.com Prescription Drug Ads. www.legitscript.com/download/ BingRxReport.pdf, 2009.

LegitScript and KnujOn. Yahoo! Internet Pharmacy Advertisements. www.legitscript.com/download/YahooRxAnalysis.pdf, 2009.

LegitScript and KnujOn. Rogues and Registrars: Are some Domain Name Registrars safe havens for Internet drug rings? www .legitscript.com/download/Roguesand-Registrars-Report.pdf, 2010.

H. Liu, K. Levchenko, M. F′elegyh′azi, C. Kreibich, G. Maier, G. M. Voelker, and S. Savage. On the Effects of Registrarlevel Intervention. In Proc. of 4th USENIX LEET, 2011.

B. Livingston. Web registrars may take back your domain name. http://news.cnet.com/2010-1071-281311.html, 2000.

M86 Security Labs. Top Spam Affiliate Programs. www .m86security.com/labs/traceitem.asp?article=1070, 2009.

J. Ma, L. K. Saul, S. Savage, and G. M. Voelker. Identifying Suspicious URLs: An Application of Large-Scale Online Learning. In Proc. of 26th ICML, 2009.

B. S. McWilliams. Spam Kings: The Real Story Behind the High-Rolling Hucksters Pushing Porn, Pills and @*#?% Enlargements. O'Reilly Media, Sept. 2004.

D. Molnar, S. Egelman, and N. Christin. This Is Your Data on Drugs: Lessons Computer Security Can Learn from the Drug War. In Proc. of 13th NSPW, 2010.

T. Moore and R. Clayton. The Impact of Incentives on Notice and Take-down. In Proc. of 7th WEIS, 2008.

T. Moore, R. Clayton, and H. Stern. Temporal Correlations between Spam and Phishing Websites. In Proc. of 2nd USENIX LEET, 2009.

M. Motoyama, K. Levchenko, C. Kanich, D. McCoy, G. M. Voelker, and S. Savage. Re: CAPTCHAs—Understanding CAPTCHA Solving from an Economic Context. In Proc. of 19th USENIX Security, 2010.

A. Mutton. Screengrab! www.screengrab.org/, 2010.

Y. Niu, Y.-M. Wang, H. Chen, M. Ma, and F. Hsu. A Quantitative Study of Forum Spamming Using Context-based Analysis. In Proc. of 14th NDSS, 2007.

C. Nunnery, G. Sinclair, and B. B. Kang. Tumbling Down the Rabbit Hole: Exploring the Idiosyncrasies of Botmaster Systems in a Multi-Tier Botnet Infrastructure. In Proc. of 3rd USENIX LEET, 2010.

E. Passerini, R. Paleari, L. Martignoni, and D. Bruschi. FluXOR: Detecting and Monitoring Fast-Flux Service Networks. In Proc. of 5th DIMVA, 2008.

R. Perdisci, I. Corona, D. Dagon, and W. Lee. Detecting Malicious Flux Service Networks through Passive Analysis of Recursive DNS Traces. In Proc. of 25th ACSAC, 2009.

A. Pitsillidis, K. Levchenko, C. Kreibich, C. Kanich, G. Voelkera, V. Paxson, N. Weaver, and S. Savage. Botnet Judo: Fighting Spam with Itself. In Proc. of 17th NDSS, 2010.

Z. Qian, Z. M. Mao, Y. Xie, and F. Yu. On Network-level Clusters for Spam Detection. In Proc. of 17th NDSS, 2010.

A. Ramachandran and N. Feamster. Understanding the Network-Level Behavior of Spammers. In Proc. of ACM SIGCOMM, 2006.

D. Samosseiko. The Partnerka—What is it, and why should you care? In Proc. of Virus Bulletin Conference, 2009.

S. Sinha, M. Bailey, and F. Jahanian. Shades of Grey: On the effectiveness of reputation-based "blacklists". In Proc. of 3rd MALWARE, 2008.

S. Sinha, M. Bailey, and F. Jahanian. Improving SPAM Blacklisting through Dynamic Thresholding and Speculative Aggregation. In Proc. of 17th NDSS, 2010.

K. Stevens. The Underground Economy of the Pay-Per-Install (PPI) Business. www.secureworks.com/research/threats/ppi, 2009.

B. Stone-Gross, M. Cova, L. Cavallaro, B. Gilbert, M. Szydlowski, R. Kemmerer, C. Kruegel, and G. Vigna. Your Botnet Is My Botnet: Analysis of a Botnet Takeover. In Proc. of 16th ACM CCS, 2009.

B. Stone-Gross, C. Kruegel, K. Almeroth, A. Moser, and E. Kirda. FIRE: FInding Rogue nEtworks. In Proc. of 25th ACSAC, 2009.

Visa Commercial Solutions. Merchant Category Codes for IRS Form 1099-MISC Reporting. http://usa.visa.com/download/corporate/ resources/mcc booklet.pdf.

Y.-M. Wang, M. Ma, Y. Niu, and H. Chen. Spam Double-Funnel: Connecting Web Spammers with Advertisers. In Proc. of 16th WWW, 2007.

G. Warner. Random Pseudo-URLs Try to Confuse Anti-Spam Solutions. http://garwarner.blogspot.com/2010/09/ randompseudo-urls-try-to-confuse-anti.html, Sept. 2010.

C. Whittaker, B. Ryner, and M. Nazif. Large-Scale Automatic Classification of Phishing Pages. In Proc. of 17th NDSS, 2010.

Y. Xie, F. Yu, K. Achan, R. Panigrahy, G. Hulten, and I. Osipkov. Spamming Botnets: Signatures and Characteristics. In Proc. of ACM SIGCOMM, 2008.

L. Zhang, J. Zhu, and T. Yao. An Evaluation of Statistical Spam Filtering Techniques. ACM Trans. on ALIP, 3(4), 2004.

Y. Zhao, Y. Xie, F. Yu, Q. Ke, Y. Yu, Y. Chen, and E. Gillum. BotGraph: Large-Scale Spamming Botnet Detection. In Proc. of 6th NSDI, 2009.

J. Zhuge, T. Holz, C. Song, J. Guo, X. Han, and W. Zou. Studying Malicious Websites and the Underground Economy on the Chinese Web. In Proc. of 7th WEIS, 2008.

Critical Thinking

1. How many authors does this article have? Notice that the names are not in alphabetical order. What does the order of author's names in scientific articles signify?

2. The authors speak of spam as being part of an ecosystem. Does the metaphor work?

3. What are the three stages of spam and what is accomplished at each stage?

4. The author's ultimately discover that the "banking component of the spam value chain is both the least studied and, we believe, the most critical." Why do you suppose what turns out to be the most critical and vulnerable component of the spam value chain is the least-studied?

5. The authors say that efforts to address inappropriate use of domain names "have been slow, ongoing, and fraught with

politics." This along with the conclusion cited in Question 4 suggests that spam is a business/political problem rather than a technical one. Recall that Postman's (Unit 1) fifth idea is "that media tend to become mythic . . . as if they were part of the natural order of things." Is confronting spam by blocking offending servers and domains an example of spam becoming mythic?

6. Why do you suppose there were neither economists nor business researchers of any sort involved in the study?

7. This is a difficult article. It was summarized (by John Markoff) in *The New York Times* on May 19, 2011. Use the Internet to read the summary. What are some of the differences between the original scientific article and the science journalism that appeared in the *Times?* Which did you enjoy most? Which did you learn the most from? Why would the Markoff summary not have been accepted at the peer-reviewed IEEE Symposium on Security and Privacy?

KIRILL LEVCHENKO Department of Computer Science and Engineering, University of California, San Diego. **ANDREAS PITSILLIDIS** Department of Computer Science and Engineering, University of California, San Diego. **NEHA CHACHRA** Department of Computer Science and Engineering, University of California, San Diego. **BRANDON ENRIGHT** Department of Computer Science and Engineering, University of California, San Diego. **MARK FELEGYHAZIZ** Laboratory of Cryptography and System Security (CrySyS) Budapest University of Technology and Economics. **CHRIS GRIERY** Computer Science Division University of California, Berkeley. **TRISTAN HALVORSON** Department of Computer Science and Engineering, University of California, San Diego. **CHRIS KANICH** Department of Computer Science and Engineering, University of California, San Diego. **CHRISTIAN KREIBICHY** Computer Science Division University of California, Berkeley International Computer Science Institute Berkeley, CA. **HE LIU** Department of Computer Science and Engineering, University of California, San Diego. **DAMON MCCOY** Department of Computer Science and Engineering, University of California, San Diego. **NICHOLAS WEAVERY** Computer Science Division University of California, Berkeley International Computer Science Institute Berkeley, CA. **VERN PAXSONY** Computer Science Division University of California, Berkeley International Computer Science Institute Berkeley, CA. **GEOFFREY M. VOELKER** Department of Computer Science and Engineering, University of California, San Diego. **STEFAN SAVAGE** Department of Computer Science and Engineering, University of California, San Diego.

Acknowledgments—This is, again, the most ambitious measurement effort our team has attempted and even with 15 authors it would have been impossible without help from many other individuals and organizations. First and foremost, we are indebted to our spam data providers: Jose Nazario, Chris Morrow, Barracuda Networks, Abusix and a range of other partners who wish to remain anonymous. Similarly, we received operational help, wisdom and guidance from Joe Stewart, Kevin Fall, Steve Wernikoff, Doug McKenney, Jeff Williams, Eliot Gillum, Hersh Dangayach, Jef Pozkanzer, Gabe Lawrence, Neils Provos, Kevin Fu and Ben Ransford among a long list of others. On the technical side of the study, we thank Jon Whiteaker for an early implementation of the DNS crawler and Brian Kantor for supporting our ever expanding needs for cycles, storage and bandwidth. On the purchasing side of the study, we are deeply indebted to the strong support of our card issuer and their staff. On the oversight side, we are grateful to Erin Kenneally and Aaron Burstein for their legal guidance and ethical oversight, to our Chief Counsel at UCSD, Daniel Park, and UC's Systemwide Research Compliance Director, Patrick Schlesinger, for their open-mindedness and creativity, and finally to Marianne Generales and Art Ellis representing UCSD's Office of Research Affairs for helping to connect all the dots. This work was supported in part by National Science Foundation grants NSF-0433668, NSF-0433702, NSF- 0831138 and CNS-0905631, by the Office of Naval Research MURI grant N000140911081, and by generous research, operational and/or in-kind support from Google, Microsoft, Yahoo, Cisco, HP and the UCSD Center for Networked Systems (CNS). Felegyhazi contributed while working as a researcher at ICSI. McCoy was supported by a CCC-CRANSF Computing Innovation Fellowship.

UNIT 3

Work and the Workplace

Unit Selections

Learning Outcomes

After reading this Unit, you will be able to:

* Understand that the need for software engineers and computer scientists continues to grow.

* Be able to enumerate some of the explanations for why women avoid computer science.

* Understand many of the subtle relationships between productivity, labor, and consumption.

* Understand the intellectual background of the concept of privacy along with one's legal right to privacy in the United States and Europe.

Student Website

www.mhhe.com/cls

Internet References

American Telecommuting Association
www.yourata.com/telecommuting

Computers in the Workplace
www.cpsr.org/issues/industry

STEP ON IT! Pedals: Repetitive Strain Injury
www.bilbo.com/rsi2.html

What About Computers in the Workplace
www.law.freeadvice.com/intellectual_ property/computer_law/computers_workplace.htm

Work is at the center of our lives. The kind of work we do plays a part in our standard of living, our social status, and our sense of worth. This was not always the case. Read some of the great Victorian novels, and you will find a society where paid employment, at least among the upper classes, does not exist. Even those men from the nineteenth century and before, whose discoveries and writings we study and admire, approached their work as an avocation. It is hard to imagine William Wordsworth, kissing his wife goodbye each morning, and heading off to the English Department where he directs a seminar in creative writing before going to work on a sticky line in "Ode Composed at Tintern Abbey." Or, think of Charles Darwin, donning a lab coat, and supervising an army of graduate students and post-docs before he touches up his latest National Science Foundation proposal. In the nineteenth century, there were a handful of professionals—doctor, lawyer, professor, clergyman, military officer, a larger handful of craftsmen—joiner, miller, cooper, blacksmith, an army of agricultural workers and an increasing number of displaced peasants toiling in factories, what William Blake famously called England's "dark Satanic mills."

U.S. Census records tell us that there were only 323 different occupations in 1850, the butcher, the baker, and the candlestick maker that all children read about. The butcher is still with us, as well as the baker, but both of them work for national supermarket chains, using digitally-controlled tools and managing their 401(k)s online. The candlestick maker has morphed into a refinery worker, watching digital displays in petrochemical plants that light up the Louisiana sky. The Canadian National Occupational Classification lists more than 25,000 occupational titles. It was once feared in the early twentieth century that industrial machines, and then later computers, would render work obsolete, transforming us into country gentlemen, like Charles Darwin in the utopian view or nomadic mobs of starving proletarians in the dystopian.

"Automation on the Job," written by a talented science writer, Brian Hayes, examines these once credible predictions. First agricultural then manufacturing labor became fabulously productive. As Hayes points out, "It's not too much of an exaggeration to say that before 1800 everyone in North American was a farmer, and now no one is." Then, the same thing happened to factories. General Motors, which employed a half million American workers in the mid-fifties, now employs half that many worldwide. Yet instead of working fifteen hours a week, as John Maynard Keynes predicted in 1930, and enjoying our considerable leisure sailing and traveling the world—yet another prediction by another expert—we work as sales clerks, health care workers, state license examiners, light truck drivers, equal opportunity compliance officers, and, yes, also as software engineers, database analysts, website designers, and entrepreneurs, all occupations that did not exist in Darwin's time or, for that matter in Keynes's. And this is if we are lucky. As of this writing (August 2011), 16 percent of the American labor force is either unemployed, underemployed or has given up looking for work altogether. As always, technology exists in a social context. We can produce more cars with fewer workers, feed the country with a tiny fraction of the workforce, and make vastly more phone calls with 10 percent of the 250,000 telephone operators employed at one time—all because of technology in one form or another. Yet how the benefits of technology are distributed is politically contested terrain.

Employment related to information technology is one area that appears to be growing in the United States, despite worries a while back that the Internet would make it easy to ship highly paid software engineering work to relatively low-wage economies like India and China. The U.S. Department of Labor's *Occupational Outlook Handbook* tells us that computer software engineers and computer scientists are among the occupations that will grow most quickly over the 2008–18 decade. This makes it even more important for universities and the computer industry to find out how to attract and retain women. Even though women earn more degrees at every level, they continue to be underrepresented in the so-call STEM disciplines: science, technology, engineering, and mathematics. "Women, Mathematics, and Computing" is one proposal among many, many, many to shift the imbalance.

Computers are everywhere in contemporary American life. We use them for study, entertainment, communication, medicine, record-keeping, and to control industrial processes. They are so ever-present and so seemingly benign that it is sometimes hard to remember that computing is a deeply disruptive technology. The physical and commercial landscape of the United States would be almost unrecognizable to a modern-day Rip van Winkel, one who had gone to sleep, say in 1980. Entire industries have gone out of (and come into) existence since then, and the cities that housed them have been eclipsed in our mental landscape by Seattle, Portland, and San Francisco, the glamour towns of our increasingly virtual world. In the seven years between 1995 and 2002, 22 million factory jobs around the world were eliminated, while global industrial output rose 30 percent in the same period.[1] Those two numbers, 22 million and 30 percent, tell us that software engineers, while producing Facebook, produce something else that is perhaps even more valuable (and more disruptive): tools that let us produce more goods with fewer workers, tools that let us develop supply chains that span the globe, tools that even let us transform service industries like banking and travel. This is not to fall into the technological determinist trap (see Unit 1). Computers transformed American life in the past thirty years, because our legal and political arrangements permitted it. You would like to headquarter your company in the Cayman Islands and produce goods in China for export to the United States? Fine. We're sorry that a few hundred or a few thousand jobs are lost, but most Americans will benefit from less expensive goods. Which brings us back to Neil Postman from Unit 1: technology giveth and technology taketh away, giving to and taking away from sectors of the population quite unevenly.

A dramatic instance of giving and taking may be seen in the tendency for many employers to do online background searches for prospective employees. Americans get the capacity to construct an online persona through Facebook and broadcast it to as many friends as will have them. They pay for that capacity when prospective employers find some aspects of their digital self less than attractive in new hires.

Note

1. Collins, D., and Ryan, M. (2007). The Strategic Implications of Technology on Job Loss. *Academy of Strategic Management Journal*, 27–46.

Automation on the Job

**Computers were supposed to be labor-saving devices.
How come we're still working so hard?**

Brian Hayes

Automation was a hot topic in the 1950s and '60s—a subject for congressional hearings, blue-ribbon panels, newspaper editorials, think-tank studies, scholarly symposia, documentary films, World's Fair exhibits, even comic strips and protest songs. There was interest in the technology itself—everybody wanted to know about "the factory of the future"—but the editorials and white papers focused mainly on the social and economic consequences of automation. Nearly everyone agreed that people would be working less once computers and other kinds of automatic machinery became widespread. For optimists, this was a promise of liberation: At last humanity would be freed from constant toil, and we could all devote our days to more refined pursuits. But others saw a threat: Millions of people would be thrown out of work, and desperate masses would roam the streets.

Looking back from 50 years hence, the controversy over automation seems a quaint and curious episode. The dispute was never resolved; it just faded away. The factory of the future did indeed evolve; but at the same time the future evolved away from the factory, which is no longer such a central institution in the economic scheme of things, at least in the United States. As predicted, computers guide machine tools and run assembly lines, but that's a minor part of their role in society. The computer is far more pervasive in everyday life than even the boldest technophiles dared to dream back in the days of punch cards and mainframes.

As for economic consequences, worries about unemployment have certainly not gone away—not with job losses in the current recession approaching 2 million workers in the U.S. alone. But recent job losses are commonly attributed to causes other than automation, such as competition from overseas or a roller-coaster financial system. In any case, the vision of a world where machines do all the work and people stand idly by has simply not come to pass.

The Problem of Leisure

In 1930 the British economist John Maynard Keynes published a short essay titled "Economic Possibilities for Our Grandchildren." At the time, the economic possibilities looked pretty grim, but Keynes was implacably cheerful. By 2030, he predicted, average income would increase by a factor of between four and eight. This prosperity would be brought about by gains in productivity: Aided by new technology, workers would produce more with less effort.

Keynes did not mention *automation*—the word would not be introduced until some years later—but he did refer to *technological unemployment,* a term that goes back to Karl Marx. For Keynes, a drop in the demand for labor was a problem with an easy solution: Just work less. A 3-hour shift and a 15-hour workweek would become the norm for the grandchildren of the children of 1930, he said. This would be a momentous development in human history. After millennia of struggle, we would have finally solved "the economic problem": How to get enough to eat. The new challenge would be the problem of leisure: How to fill the idle hours.

Decades later, when automation became a contentious issue, there were other optimists. The conservative economist Yale Brozen wrote in 1963:

> Perhaps the gains of the automation revolution will carry us on from a mass democracy to a mass aristocracy. . . . The common man will become a university-educated world traveler with a summer place in the country, enjoying such leisure-time activities as sailing and concert going.

But others looked at the same prospect and saw a darker picture. Norbert Wiener had made important contributions to the theory of automatic control, but he was wary of its social implications. In *The Human Use of Human Beings* (1950) he wrote:

> Let us remember that the automatic machine . . . is the precise economic equivalent of slave labor. Any labor which competes with slave labor must accept the economic conditions of slave labor. It is perfectly clear that this will produce an unemployment situation, in comparison with which the present recession and even the depression of the thirties will seem a pleasant joke.

A. J. Hayes, a labor leader (and no relation to me), wrote in 1964:

> Automation is not just a new kind of mechanization but a revolutionary force capable of overturning our social order. Whereas mechanization made workers more efficient—and thus more valuable—automation threatens to make them superfluous—and thus without value.

Keynes's "problem of leisure" is also mentioned with much anxiety throughout the literature of the automation era. In a 1962 pamphlet Donald N. Michael wrote:

> These people will work short hours, with much time for the pursuit of leisure activities. . . . Even with a college education, what will they do all their long lives, day after day, four-day weekend after weekend, vacation after vacation . . . ?

The opinions I have cited here represent extreme positions, and there were also many milder views. But I think it's fair to say that most early students of automation, including both critics and enthusiasts, believed the new technology would lead us into a world where people worked much less.

Where's My 15-Hour Workweek?

Keynes's forecast of growth in productivity and personal income seemed wildly optimistic in 1930, but in fact he underestimated. The upper bound of his prediction—an eightfold increase over 100 years—works out to an annual growth rate of 2.1 percent. So far, the observed average rate comes to 2.9 percent per year. If that rate is extrapolated to 2030, worldwide income will have increased by a factor of 17 in a century. (These calculations are reported by Fabrizio Zilibotti of the University of Zurich in a recent book reassessing Keynes's 1930 essay.)

Keynes's promise of affluence has already been more than fulfilled—at least for citizens of wealthier nations. It's a remarkable achievement, even if we have not yet truly and permanently "solved the economic problem." If Keynes was right about the accumulation of wealth, however, he missed the mark in predicting time spent on the job. By most estimates, the average workweek was about 60 hours in 1900, and it had fallen to about 50 hours when Keynes wrote in 1930. There was a further decline to roughly 40 hours per week in the 1950s and '60s, but since then the workweek has changed little, at least in the U.S. Western Europeans work fewer hours, but even there the trend doesn't look like we're headed for a 15-hour week anytime soon.

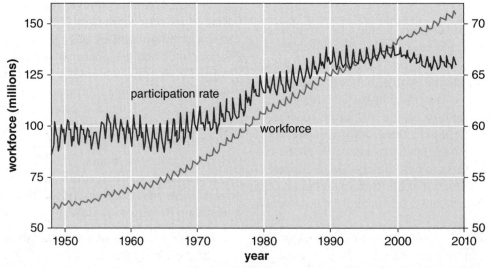

The size of the U.S. labor force has increased steadily throughout the period in which automation has taken hold. The increase is not merely an effect of population growth. The participation rate—the percentage of the adult population that is working or seeking work—has also risen, largely because of women entering the workforce. The data are from the Bureau of Labor Statistics of the U.S. Department of Labor. The saw-tooth fluctuations are seasonal.

Other measures of how hard people are working tell a similar story. The total labor force in the U.S. has increased by a factor of 2.5 since 1950, growing substantially faster than the working-age population. Thus labor-force participation (the percentage of people who hold jobs, among all those who could in principle be working) has risen from 59 percent to 66 percent.

These trends contradict almost all the expectations of early writers on automation, both optimists and pessimists. So far, automation has neither liberated us from the need to work nor deprived us of the opportunity to work. Instead, we're working more than ever.

Economists reflecting on Keynes's essay suggest he erred in supposing that people would willingly trade income for leisure. Instead, the commentators say, people work overtime to buy the new wide-screen TV even if they then have no time to enjoy it. Perhaps so. I would merely add that many who are working long hours (post-docs, say, or parents of young children) do not see their behavior as a product of conscious choice. And they do not think society has "solved the economic problem."

On the Factory Floor

Perhaps the most thoughtful and knowledgeable of the early writers on automation was John Diebold, a consultant and author. It was Diebold who introduced the word *automation* in its broad, modern sense. He clearly understood that there was more to it than reducing labor costs in factories. He foresaw applications to many other kinds of work, including clerical tasks, warehousing and even retailing. Nevertheless, when he chose examples for detailed description, they almost always came from manufacturing.

Automatic control first took hold in continuous-process industries such as oil refining. A closed-loop control mechanism could regulate the temperature of a distilling tower, eliminating the need for a worker to monitor a gauge and adjust valve settings. As such instruments proliferated, a refinery became a depopulated industrial landscape. An entire plant could be run by a few technicians, huddled together in a glass-walled control room. This hands-off mode of operation became the model that other industries strove to emulate.

In the automation literature of the 1950s and '60s, attention focuses mainly on manufacturing, and especially on the machining of metal. A celebrated example was the Ford Motor Company's Cleveland Engine Plant No. 1, built in 1951, where a series of interconnected machines took in raw castings at one end and disgorged finished engine blocks at the other. The various tools within this complex performed several hundred boring and milling operations on each engine, with little manual intervention.

A drawback of the Ford approach to automation was inflexibility. Any change to the product would require an extensive overhaul of the machinery. But this problem was overcome with the introduction of programmable metalworking tools, which eventually became computer-controlled devices.

Other kinds of manufacturing also shifted to automated methods, although the result was not always exactly what had been expected. In the early years, it was easy to imagine a straightforward substitution of machines for labor: Shove aside a worker and install a machine in his or her place. The task to be performed would not change, only the agent performing it. The ultimate expression of this idea was the robot—a one-for-one replacement for the factory worker. But automation has seldom gone this way.

Consider the manufacture of electronic devices. At the outset, this was a labor-intensive process of placing components on a chassis, stringing wires between them and soldering the connections one by one. Attempts to build automatic equipment to perform the same operations proved impractical. Instead, the underlying technology was changed by introducing printed circuit boards, with all the connections laid out in advance. Eventually, machines were developed for automatically placing the parts on the boards and for soldering the connections all at once.

The further evolution of this process takes us to the integrated circuit, a technology that was automated from birth. The manufacture of microprocessor chips could not possibly be carried out as a handicraft business; no sharp-eyed artisan could draw the minuscule circuit patterns on silicon wafers. For many other businesses as well, manual methods are simply unthinkable. Google could not operate by hiring thousands of clerks to read Web pages and type out the answers to queries.

The automation of factories has gone very much according to the script written by Diebold and other early advocates. Computer control is all but universal. Whole sections of automobile assembly plants are now walled off to exclude all workers. A computer screen and a keyboard are the main interface to most factory equipment.

Meanwhile, though, manufacturing as a whole has become a smaller part of the U.S. economy—12 percent of gross domestic product in 2005, down from more than double that in the 1950s. And because of the very success of industrial automation, employment on production lines has fallen even faster than the share of GDP. Thus, for most Americans, the factory automation that was so much the focus of early commentary is all but invisible. Few of us ever get a chance to see it at work.

But automation and computer technology have infiltrated other areas of the economy and daily life—office work, logistics, commerce, finance, household tasks. When you look for the impact of computers on society, barcodes are probably more important than machine tools.

The Do-It-Yourself Economy

In the 1950s, digital computers were exotic, expensive, unapproachable and mysterious. It was far easier to see such a machine becoming the nexus of control in a vast industrial enterprise than to imagine the computer transformed into a household object, comparable to a telephone or a typewriter—or even a toy for the children to play with. Donald Michael wrote:

> Most of our citizens will be unable to understand the cybernated world in which they live. . . . There will be a small, almost separate, society of people in rapport with the advanced computers. . . . Those with the talent for the work probably will have to develop it from childhood and will be trained as intensively as the classical ballerina.

If this attitude of awestruck reverence had persisted, most of the computer's productive potential would have been wasted. Computers became powerful when they became ubiquitous—not inscrutable oracles guarded by a priestly elite but familiar appliances found on every desk. These days, we are all expected to have rapport with computers.

The spread of automation outside of the factory has altered its social and economic impact in some curious ways. In many cases, the net effect of automation is not that machines are doing work that people used to do. Instead we've dispensed with the people who used to be paid to run the machines, and we've learned to run them ourselves. When you withdraw money from the bank via an ATM, buy an airline ticket online, ride an elevator or fill up the gas tank at a self-service pump, you are interacting directly with a machine to carry out a task that once required the intercession of an employee.

The dial telephone is the archetypal example. My grandmother's telephone had no dial; she placed calls by asking a switchboard operator to make the connection. The dial (and the various other mechanisms that have since replaced it) empowers you to set up the communications channel without human assistance. Thus it's not quite accurate to say that the operator has been replaced by a machine. A version of the circuit-switching machine was there all along; the dial merely provided a convenient interface to it.

The process of making travel arrangements has been transformed in a similar way. It was once the custom to telephone a travel agent, who would search an airline database for a suitable flight with seats available. Through the Web, most of us now access that database directly; we even print our own boarding passes. Again, what has happened here is not exactly the substitution of machines for people; it is a matter of putting the customer in control of the machines.

Other Internet technologies are taking this process one more dizzy step forward. Because many Web sites have published interface specifications, I now have the option of writing a program to access them. Having already removed the travel agent, I can now automate myself out of the loop as well.

The Full-Employment Paradox

Enabling people to place their own phone calls and make their own travel reservations has put whole categories of jobs on the brink of extinction. U.S. telephone companies once employed more than 250,000 telephone operators; the number remaining is a tenth of that, and falling fast. It's the same story for gas-station attendants, elevator operators and dozens of other occupations. And yet we have not seen the great contraction of the workforce that seemed inevitable 50 years ago.

One oft-heard explanation holds that automation brings a net increase in employment by creating jobs for people who design, build and maintain machines. A strong version of this thesis is scarcely plausible. It implies that the total labor requirement per unit of output is higher in the automated process than in the manual one; if that were the case, it would be hard to see the economic incentive for adopting automation. A weaker but likelier version concedes that labor per unit of output declines under automation, but total output increases enough to compensate. Even for this weaker prediction, however, there is no guarantee of such a rosy outcome. The relation may well be supported by historical evidence, but it has no theoretical underpinning in economic principles.

For a theoretical analysis we can turn to Herbert A. Simon, who was both an economist and a computer scientist and would thus seem to be the ideal analyst. In a 1965 essay, Simon noted that economies seek equilibrium, and so "both men and machines can be fully employed regardless of their relative productivity." It's just a matter of adjusting the worker's wage until it balances the cost of machinery. Of course there's no guarantee that the equilibrium wage will be above the subsistence level. But Simon then offered a more complex argument showing that any increase in productivity, whatever the underlying cause, should increase wages as well as the return on capital investment. Do these two results add up to perpetual full employment at a living wage in an automated world? I don't believe they offer any such guarantee, but perhaps the calculations are reassuring nonetheless.

Another kind of economic equilibrium also offers a measure of cheer. The premise is that whatever you earn, you eventually spend. (Or else your heirs spend it for you.) If technological progress makes some commodity cheaper, then the money that used to go that product will have to be spent on something else. The flow of funds toward the alternative sectors will drive up prices there and create new economic opportunities. This mode of reasoning offers an answer to questions such as, "Why has health care become so expensive in recent years?" The answer is: Because everything else has gotten so cheap.

I can't say that any of these formulations puts my mind at ease. On the other hand, I do have faith in the resilience of people and societies. The demographic history of agriculture offers a precedent that is both sobering and reassuring. It's not too much of an exaggeration to say that before 1800 everyone in North America was a farmer, and now no one is. In other words, productivity gains in agriculture put an entire population out of work. This was a wrenching experience for those forced to leave the farm, but the fact remains that they survived and found other ways of life. The occupational shifts caused by computers and automation cannot possibly match the magnitude of that great upheaval.

The Future of the Future

What comes next in the march of progress? Have we reached the end point in the evolution of computerized society?

Since I have poked fun at the predictions of an earlier generation, it's only fair that I put some of my own silly notions on the record, giving some future pundit a chance to mock me in turn. I think the main folly of my predecessors was not being reckless enough. I'll probably make the same mistake myself. So here are three insufficiently outrageous predictions.

1. We'll automate medicine. I don't mean robot surgeons, although they're in the works too. What I have in mind is Internet-enabled, do-it-yourself diagnostics. Google is already the primary-care physician for many of us; that role can be expanded in various directions. Furthermore, as mentioned above, medical care is where the money is going, and so that's where investment in cost-saving technologies has the most leverage.

2. We'll automate driving. The car that drives itself is a perennial on lists of future marvels, mentioned by a number of the automation prophets of the 50s and 60s. A fully autonomous vehicle, able to navigate ordinary streets and roads, is not much closer now than it was then, but a combination of smarter cars and smarter roads could be made to work. Building those roads would require a major infrastructure project, which might help make up for all the disemployed truckers and taxi drivers. I admit to a certain boyish fascination with the idea of a car that drops me at the office and then goes to fetch the dry cleaning and fill up its own gas tank.

3. We'll automate warfare. I take no pleasure in this one, but I see no escaping it either. The most horrific weapons of the 20th century had the redeeming quality that they are difficult and expensive to build, and this has limited their proliferation. When it comes to the most fashionable weapons of the present day—pilotless aircraft, cruise missiles, precision-guided munitions—the key technology is available on the shelf at Radio Shack.

What about trades closer to my own vital interests? Will science be automated? Technology already has a central role in many areas of research; for example, genome sequences could not be read by traditional lab-bench methods. Replacing the scientist will presumably be a little harder that replacing the lab technician, but when a machine exhibits enough curiosity and tenacity, I think we'll just have to welcome it as a companion in zealous research.

And if the scientist is elbowed aside by an automaton, then surely the science writer can't hold out either. I'm ready for my 15-hour workweek.

Bibliography

Buckingham, Walter S. 1961. *Automation: Its Impact on Business and People.* New York: Harper and Row.

Cortada, James W. 2004. *The Digital Hand: How Computers Changed the Work of American Manufacturing, Transportation, and Retail Industries.* Oxford: Oxford University Press.

Diebold, John. 1952. *Automation: The Advent of the Automatic Factory.* New York: D. Van Nostrand Company.

Einzig, Paul. 1956. *The Economic Consequences of Automation.* London: Secker and Warburg.

Hayes, A. J. 1964. Automation: A real "H" bomb. In *Jobs, Men, and Machines: Problems of Automation,* ed. Charles Markham, New York: Frederick A. Praeger, pp. 48–57.

Keynes, John Maynard. 1930. Economic possibilities for our grandchildren. Reprinted in *Revisiting Keynes: Economic Possibilities for Our Grandchildren,* ed. Lorenzo Pecchi and Gustavo Piga, Cambridge, Mass.: The MIT Press.

Leontief, Wassily. 1952. Machines and man. *Scientific American* 187(3):150–160.

Lilley, S. 1957. *Automation and Social Progress.* New York: International Publishers.

Michael, Donald N. 1962. *Cybernation: The Silent Conquest.* Santa Barbara, Calif.: Center for the Study of Democratic Institutions.

Pecchi, Lorenzo, and Gustavo Piga. 2008. *Revisiting Keynes: Economic Possibilities for Our Grandchildren.* Cambridge, Mass.: The MIT Press.

Philipson, Morris. 1962. *Automation: Implications for the Future.* New York: Vintage Books.

Pollock, Frederick. 1957. *Automation: A Study of Its Economic and Social Consequences.* Translated by W. O. Henderson and W. H. Chaloner. New York: Frederick A. Praeger.

Simon, Herbert A. 1965. *The Shape of Automation for Men and Management.* New York: Harper and Row.

Whaples, Robert. 2001. Hours of work in U.S. history. *EH.Net Encyclopedia,* Economic History Association. eh.net/encyclopedia/article/whaples.work.hours.us.

Wiener, Norbert. 1954. *The Human Use of Human Beings: Cybernetics and Society.* New York: Avon Books.

Critical Thinking

1. Who was John Maynard Keynes? His name is associated with a particular way of stimulating a sluggish economy. Use the Internet to find out more about it. Would he be more closely aligned with the modern democratic or republican parties?

2. Hayes says that labor force participation has risen from 59 percent to 66 percent since 1950. That is, more and more of us are working. What change in cultural mores allowed this shift to happen?

3. The decline in manufacturing employment parallels a decline in union membership since the 1950s. Are they related? Use the Internet (and a reference librarian) to try to untangle them.

4. What is the "full-employment paradox"? What are some of the explanations that Hayes offers?

5. Hayes has very little to say about a globalized labor force. Investigate labor productivity in Chinese factories. How has the cost of labor in China affected the incentive to automate?

6. Hayes sometimes writes of technological progress as if it were a force of nature (e.g., "If technological progress makes some commodity cheaper . . ."). Does he slip on Postman's fifth big idea, that is, the tendency to think of technology as a force of its own rather than a specific response to a specific set of circumstances?

Computer Software Engineers and Computer Programmers

Significant Points

- Computer software engineers are among the occupations projected to grow the fastest and add the most new jobs over the 2008–18 decade, resulting in excellent job prospects.
- Employment of computer programmers is expected to decline by 3 percent through 2018.
- Job prospects will be best for applicants with a bachelor's or higher degree and relevant experience.

Nature of the Work

Computer software engineers design and develop software. They apply the theories and principles of computer science and mathematical analysis to create, test, and evaluate the software applications and systems that make computers work. The tasks performed by these workers evolve quickly, reflecting changes in technology and new areas of specialization, as well as the changing practices of employers. (A separate section on computer hardware engineers appears in the engineers section of the *Handbook.*)

Software engineers design and develop many types of software, including computer games, business applications, operating systems, network control systems, and middleware. They must be experts in the theory of computing systems, the structure of software, and the nature and limitations of hardware to ensure that the underlying systems will work properly.

Computer software engineers begin by analyzing users' needs, and then design, test, and develop software to meet those needs. During this process they create flowcharts, diagrams, and other documentation, and may also create the detailed sets of instructions, called algorithms, that actually tell the computer what to do. They also may be responsible for converting these instructions into a computer language, a process called programming or coding, but this usually is the responsibility of *computer programmers.*

Computer software engineers can generally be divided into two categories: applications engineers and systems engineers. *Computer applications software engineers* analyze end users' needs and design, construct, deploy, and maintain general computer applications software or specialized utility programs. These workers use different programming languages, depending on the purpose of the program and the environment in which the program runs. The programming languages most often used are C, C++, Java, and Python. Some software engineers develop packaged computer applications, but most create or adapt customized applications for business and other organizations. Some of these workers also develop databases.

Computer systems software engineers coordinate the construction, maintenance, and expansion of an organization's computer systems. Working with the organization, they coordinate each department's computer needs—ordering, inventory, billing, and payroll recordkeeping, for example—and make suggestions about its technical direction. They also might set up the organization's intranets—networks that link computers within the organization and ease communication among various departments. Often, they are also responsible for the design and implementation of system security and data assurance.

Systems software engineers also work for companies that configure, implement, and install the computer systems of other organizations. These workers may be members of the marketing or sales staff, serving as the primary technical resource for sales workers, or providing logistical and technical support. Since the selling of complex computer systems often requires substantial customization to meet the needs of the purchaser, software engineers help to identify and explain needed changes. In addition, systems software engineers are responsible for ensuring security across the systems they are configuring.

Computer programmers write programs. After computer software engineers and systems analysts design software programs, the programmer converts that design into a logical series of instructions that the computer can follow. (A section on computer systems analysts appears elsewhere in the *Handbook.*) The programmer codes these instructions in any of a number of programming languages, depending on the need. The most common languages are C++ and Python.

Computer programmers also update, repair, modify, and expand existing programs. Some, especially those working on large projects that involve many programmers, use computer-assisted software engineering (CASE) tools to automate much of the coding process. These tools enable a programmer to concentrate on writing the unique parts of a program. Programmers working on smaller projects often use "programmer environments," applications that increase productivity by combining compiling, code walk-through, code generation, test data generation, and debugging functions. Programmers also use

Projections Data from the National Employment Matrix

Occupational Title	SOC Code	Employment, 2008	Projected Employment, 2018	Change, 2008–2018	
				Number	Percent
Computer software engineers and computer programmers	–	1,336,300	1,619,300	283,000	21
Computer programmers...	15–1021	426,700	414,400	–12,300	–3
Computer software engineers....................................	15–1030	909,600	1,204,800	295,200	32
Computer software engineers, applications.............................	15–1031	514,800	689,900	175,100	34
Computer software engineers, systems software	15–1032	394,800	515,000	120,200	30

Note: Data in this table are rounded. See the discussion of the employment projections table in the *Handbook* introductory chapter on *Occupational Information Included in the Handbook.*

libraries of basic code that can be modified or customized for a specific application. This approach yields more reliable and consistent programs and increases programmers' productivity by eliminating some routine steps.

As software design has continued to advance, and some programming functions have become automated, programmers have begun to assume some of the responsibilities that were once performed only by software engineers. As a result, some computer programmers now assist software engineers in identifying user needs and designing certain parts of computer programs, as well as other functions.

Work Environment

Computer software engineers and programmers normally work in clean, comfortable offices or in laboratories in which computer equipment is located. Software engineers who work for software vendors and consulting firms frequently travel to meet with customers. Telecommuting is becoming more common as technological advances allow more work to be done from remote locations.

Most software engineers and programmers work 40 hours a week, but about 15 percent of software engineers and 11 percent of programmers worked more than 50 hours a week in 2008. Injuries in these occupations are rare. However, like other workers who spend long periods in front of a computer terminal typing at a keyboard, engineers and programmers are susceptible to eyestrain, back discomfort, and hand and wrist problems such as carpal tunnel syndrome.

Training, Other Qualifications, and Advancement

A bachelor's degree commonly is required for software engineering jobs, although a master's degree is preferred for some positions. A bachelor's degree also is required for many computer programming jobs, although a 2-year degree or certificate may be adequate in some cases. Employers favor applicants who already have relevant skills and experience. Workers who keep up to date with the latest technology usually have good opportunities for advancement.

Education and Training

For software engineering positions, most employers prefer applicants who have at least a bachelor's degree and broad knowledge of, and experience with, a variety of computer systems and technologies. The usual college majors for applications software engineers are computer science, software engineering, or mathematics. Systems software engineers often study computer science or computer information systems. Graduate degrees are preferred for some of the more complex jobs.

Many programmers require a bachelor's degree, but a 2-year degree or certificate may be adequate for some positions. Some computer programmers hold a college degree in computer science, mathematics, or information systems, whereas others have taken special courses in computer programming to supplement their degree in a field such as accounting, finance, or another area of business.

Employers who use computers for scientific or engineering applications usually prefer college graduates who have a degree in computer or information science, mathematics, engineering, or the physical sciences. Employers who use computers for business applications prefer to hire people who have had college courses in management information systems and business, and who possess strong programming skills. A graduate degree in a related field is required for some jobs.

In addition to educational attainment, employers highly value relevant programming skills and experience. Students seeking software engineering or programming jobs can enhance their employment opportunities by participating in internships. Some employers, such as large computer and consulting firms, train new employees in intensive, company-based programs.

As technology advances, employers will need workers with the latest skills. To help keep up with changing technology, workers may take continuing education and professional development seminars offered by employers, software vendors, colleges and universities, private training institutions, and professional computing societies. Computer software engineers also need skills related to the industry in which they work. Engineers working for a bank, for example, should have some expertise in finance so that they understand banks' computing needs.

Certification and Other Qualifications

Certification is a way to demonstrate a level of competence and may provide a jobseeker with a competitive advantage. Certification programs are generally offered by product vendors or software firms, which may require professionals who work with their products to be certified. Voluntary certification also is available through various other organizations, such as professional computing societies.

Computer software engineers and programmers must have strong problem-solving and analytical skills. Ingenuity and creativity are particularly important in order to design new, functional software programs. The ability to work with abstract concepts and to do technical analysis is especially important for systems engineers because they work with the software that controls the computer's operation. Engineers and programmers also must be able to communicate effectively with team members, other staff, and end users. Because they often deal with a number of tasks simultaneously, they must be able to concentrate and pay close attention to detail. Business skills are also important, especially for those wishing to advance to managerial positions.

Advancement. For skilled workers who keep up to date with the latest technology, prospects for advancement are good. Advancement opportunities for computer software engineers increase with experience. Eventually, they may become a project manager, manager of information systems, or chief information officer, especially if they have business skills and training. Some computer software engineers with several years of experience or expertise can find lucrative opportunities working as systems designers or independent consultants, particularly in specialized fields such as business-to-business transactions or security and data assurance.

In large organizations, programmers may be promoted to lead programmer and be given supervisory responsibilities. Some applications programmers may move into systems programming after they gain experience and take courses in systems software. With general business experience, programmers may become programmer-analysts or systems analysts, or may be promoted to managerial positions. Programmers with specialized knowledge and experience with a language or operating system may become computer software engineers. As employers increasingly contract with outside firms to do programming jobs, more opportunities should arise for experienced programmers with expertise in a specific area to work as consultants.

Employment

Computer software engineers and computer programmers held about 1.3 million jobs in 2008. Approximately 514,800 were computer applications software engineers, about 394,800 were computer systems software engineers, and about 426,700 were computer programmers. Although computer software engineers and computer programmers can be found in a wide range of industries about 32 percent were employed in computer systems design and related services. Many also worked for software publishers, manufacturers of computers and related electronic equipment, financial institutions, and insurance providers.

About 48,200 computer software engineers and computer programmers were self-employed in 2008.

Job Outlook

Overall, employment of computer software engineers and computer programmers is projected to increase much faster than the average for all occupations. Job prospects should be best for those with a bachelor's degree and relevant experience.

Employment Change

Overall, employment of computer software engineers and computer programmers is projected to increase by 21 percent from 2008 to 2018, much faster than the average for all occupations. This will be the result of rapid growth among computer software engineers, as employment of computer programmers is expected to decline.

Employment of computer software engineers is expected to increase by 32 percent from 2008–2018, which is much faster than the average for all occupations. In addition, this occupation will see a large number of new jobs, with more than 295,000 created between 2008 and 2018. Demand for computer software engineers will increase as computer networking continues to grow. For example, expanding Internet technologies have spurred demand for computer software engineers who can develop Internet, intranet, and World Wide Web applications. Likewise, electronic data-processing systems in business, telecommunications, healthcare, government, and other settings continue to become more sophisticated and complex. Implementing, safeguarding, and updating computer systems and resolving problems will fuel the demand for growing numbers of systems software engineers.

New growth areas will also continue to arise from rapidly evolving technologies. The increasing uses of the Internet, the proliferation of Web sites, and mobile technology such as the wireless Internet have created a demand for a wide variety of new products. As more software is offered over the Internet, and as businesses demand customized software to meet their specific needs, applications and systems software engineers will be needed in greater numbers. In addition, the growing use of handheld computers will create demand for new mobile applications and software systems. As these devices become a larger part of the business environment, it will be necessary to integrate current computer systems with this new, more mobile technology.

In addition, information security concerns have given rise to new software needs. Concerns over "cyber security" should result in the continued investment in software that protects computer networks and electronic infrastructure. The expansion of this technology over the next 10 years will lead to an increased need for software engineers to design and develop secure applications and systems, and to integrate them into older systems.

As with other information technology jobs, offshore outsourcing may temper employment growth of computer software engineers. Firms may look to cut costs by shifting operations to foreign countries with lower prevailing wages and highly educated workers. Jobs in software engineering are less prone to being offshored than are jobs in computer programming, however, because software engineering requires innovation and intense research and development.

Employment of computer programmers is expected to decline slowly, decreasing by 3 percent from 2008 to 2018. Advances in programming languages and tools, the growing ability of users to write and implement their own programs, and the offshore outsourcing of programming jobs will contribute to this decline.

Because they can transmit their programs digitally, computer programmers can perform their job function from anywhere in the world, allowing companies to employ workers in countries that have lower prevailing wages. Computer programmers are at a much higher risk of having their jobs offshored than are workers involved in more complex and sophisticated information technology functions, such as software engineering. Much of the work of computer programmers requires little localized or specialized knowledge and can be made routine once knowledge of a particular programming language is mastered.

Nevertheless, employers will continue to need some local programmers, especially those who have strong technical skills and who understand an employer's business and its programming requirements. This means that programmers will have to keep abreast of changing programming languages and techniques. Furthermore, a recent trend of domestic sourcing may help to keep a number of programming jobs onshore. Instead of hiring workers in foreign locations, some organizations have begun to contract with programmers in low-cost areas of the United States. This allows them to reduce payroll expenses, while eliminating some of the logistical issues that arise with offshore outsourcing.

Job Prospects

As a result of rapid employment growth over the 2008 to 2018 decade, job prospects for computer software engineers should be excellent. Those with practical experience and at least a bachelor's degree in a computer-related field should have the best opportunities. Employers will continue to seek computer professionals with strong programming, systems analysis, interpersonal, and business skills. In addition to jobs created through employment growth, many job openings will result from the need to replace workers who move into managerial positions, transfer to other occupations, or leave the labor force. Consulting opportunities for computer software engineers also should continue to grow as businesses seek help to manage, upgrade, and customize their increasingly complicated computer systems.

Although employment of computer programmers is projected to decline, numerous job openings will result from the need to replace workers who leave the labor force or transfer to other occupations. Prospects for these openings should be best for applicants with a bachelor's degree and experience with a variety of programming languages and tools. As technology evolves, however, and newer, more sophisticated tools emerge, programmers will need to update their skills in order to remain competitive. Obtaining vendor-specific or language-specific certification also can provide a competitive edge.

Earnings

In May 2008, median annual wages of wage-and-salary computer applications software engineers were $85,430. The middle 50 percent earned between $67,790 and $104,870. The lowest 10 percent earned less than $53,720, and the highest 10 percent earned more than $128,870. Median annual wages in the industries employing the largest numbers of computer applications software engineers in May 2008 were as follows:

Professional and commercial equipment
   and supplies merchant wholesalers.........................93,740
Software publishers 87,710
Management of companies and enterprises...............85,990
Computer systems design and related services 84,610
Insurance carriers...80,370

In May 2008, median annual wages of wage-and-salary computer systems software engineers were $92,430. The middle 50 percent earned between $73,200 and $113,960. The lowest 10 percent earned less than $57,810, and the highest 10 percent earned more than $135,780. Median annual wages in the industries employing the largest numbers of computer systems software engineers in May 2008 were as follows:

Scientific research and development services $102,090
Computer and peripheral equipment
   manufacturing 101,270
Software publishers 93,590
Navigational measuring electromedical
   and control instruments manufacturing 91,720
Computer systems design and related services 91,610

Median annual wages of wage-and-salary computer programmers were $69,620 in May 2008. The middle 50 percent earned between $52,640 and $89,720 a year. The lowest 10 percent earned less than $40,080, and the highest 10 percent earned more than $111,450. Median annual wages in the industries employing the largest numbers of computer programmers in May 2008 are shown below:

Software publishers 81,780
Management of companies and enterprises................71,040
Computer systems design and related services 70,270
Employment services...70,070
Insurance carriers...69,790

According to the National Association of Colleges and Employers, starting salary offers for graduates with a bachelor's degree in computer science averaged $61,407 in July 2009.

Related Occupations

Other professional workers who deal extensively with computer technology or data include:

Actuaries

Computer network, systems, and database administrators

Computer scientists

Computer support specialists

Computer systems analysts

Engineers

Mathematicians

Operations research analysts

Statisticians

Sources of Additional Information

State employment service offices can provide information about job openings for computer programmers. Municipal chambers of commerce are an additional source of information on an area's largest employers.

Further information about computer careers is available from:

- Association for Computing Machinery, 2 Penn Plaza, Suite 701, New York, NY 10121–0701. Internet: http://computingcareers.acm.org
- Institute of Electrical and Electronics Engineers Computer Society, Headquarters Office, 2001 L St. NW., Suite 700 Washington, DC 20036–4910. Internet: www.computer.org
- National Workforce Center for Emerging Technologies, 3000 Landerholm Circle SE., Bellevue, WA 98007. Internet: www.nwcet.org

- University of Washington Computer Science and Engineering Department, AC101 Paul G. Allen Center, Box 352350, 185 Stevens Way, Seattle, WA 98195–2350. Internet: www.cs.washington.edu/WhyCSE
- National Center for Women and Information Technology, University of Colorado, Campus Box 322 UCB, Boulder, CO 80309-0322. Internet: www.ncwit.org

The Occupational Information Network (O*NET) provides information on a wide range of occupational characteristics. Links to O*NET appear at the end of the Internet version of this occupational statement, accessible at www.bls.gov/ooh/ocos303.htm

Critical Thinking

1. What is the distinction between computer programmers and computer software engineers?

2. Ask the human resources department of a company in your area that develops software if it distinguishes between computer programmers and computer software engineers.

3. Use the Internet to find out how many degrees in computer science were awarded in the United States in each of the years from 1997 to 2009. Be sure to keep in mind the total number of degrees offered each year.

From *Occupational Outlook Handbook*, 2010–2011.

Computer Scientists

Significant Points

- Most computer scientists are required to possess a PhD.
- Employment is projected to increase much faster than the average for all occupations.
- Job prospects are expected to be excellent.

Nature of the Work

The widespread and increasing use of computers and information technology has generated a need for highly trained, innovative workers with extensive theoretical expertise. These workers, called *computer scientists,* are the designers, creators, and inventors of new technology. By creating new technology, or finding alternative uses for existing resources, they solve complex business, scientific, and general computing problems. Some computer scientists work on multidisciplinary projects, collaborating with electrical engineers, mechanical engineers, and other specialists.

Computer scientists conduct research on a wide array of topics. Examples include computer hardware architecture, virtual reality, and robotics. Scientists who research hardware architecture discover new ways for computers to process and transmit information. They design computer chips and processors, using new materials and techniques to make them work faster and give them more computing power. When working with virtual reality, scientists use technology to create life-like situations. For example, scientists may invent video games that make users feel like they are actually in the game. Computer scientists working with robotics try to create machines that can perform tasks on their own—without people controlling them. Robots perform many tasks, such as sweeping floors in peoples' homes, assembling cars on factory production lines, and "auto-piloting" airplanes.

Computer science researchers employed by academic institutions . . . have job functions that are similar in many ways to those employed by other organizations. In general, researchers in academic settings have more flexibility to focus on pure theory, while those working in business or scientific organizations, covered here, usually focus on projects that have the possibility of producing patents and profits. Some researchers in non-academic settings, however, have considerable latitude in determining the direction of their research.

Work environment. Computer scientists normally work in offices or laboratories in comfortable surroundings. Like other workers who spend long periods in front of a computer terminal typing on a keyboard, computer scientists are susceptible to eyestrain, back discomfort, and hand and wrist problems such as carpal tunnel syndrome.

Training, Other Qualifications, and Advancement

A PhD is required for most jobs, and an aptitude for math is important.

Education and training. Most computer scientists are required to possess a PhD in computer science, computer engineering, or a closely related discipline. For some positions in the Federal Government, a bachelor's degree in a computer-related field may be adequate.

In order to be admitted to a PhD program, applicants generally are required to obtain a bachelor's degree with a strong computer science or computer engineering component. Popular undergraduate majors for PhD program applicants include computer science, computer engineering, software engineering, information systems, and information technology. A bachelor's degree generally takes 4 years to complete. A PhD generally requires at least 5 years of study beyond the bachelor's degree. PhD students usually spend the first two years taking classes on advanced topics, including computer and software systems, artificial intelligence, digital communication, and microprocessors. Students spend the remaining years conducting research on topics in computer science or computer engineering.

Other qualifications. Computer scientists must be able to think logically and creatively. They must possess a strong aptitude for math and other technical topics, as these are critical to the computing field. Because they often deal with a number of tasks simultaneously, the ability to concentrate and pay close attention to detail also is important.

Projections Data from the National Employment Matrix

Occupational Title	SOC Code	Employment, 2008	Projected Employment, 2018	Change, 2008–2018	
				Number	Percent
Computer and information scientists, research	15–1011	28,900	35,900	7,000	24

Note: Date in this table are rounded.

Although computer scientists sometimes work independently, they frequently work in teams on large projects. As a result, they must be able to communicate effectively with computer personnel, such as programmers and managers, as well as with users or other staff who may have no technical computer background.

Advancement. After they gain experience with an organization, computer scientists may advance into managerial or project leadership positions. Some choose to leave private industry for academic positions.

Employment

Computer scientists held about 28,900 jobs in 2008. Although they are increasingly employed in every sector of the economy, the greatest concentration of these workers, about 23 percent, was in the computer systems design and related services industry. Many computer scientists were also employed by software publishing firms, scientific research and development organizations, and in education.

Job Outlook

Employment growth is expected to be much faster than the average, and job prospects should be excellent.

Employment change. Employment of computer scientists is expected to grow by 24 percent from 2008 to 2018, which is much faster than the average for all occupations. Employment of these computer specialists is expected to grow as individuals and organizations continue to demand increasingly sophisticated technologies. Job increases will be driven, in part, by very rapid growth in computer systems design and related services industry, as well as the software publishing industry, which are projected to be among the fastest growing industries in the U.S. economy.

Computer scientists develop the theories that allow many new technologies to be developed. The demand for increasing efficiency in areas such as networking technology, computing speeds, software performance, and embedded systems will lead to employment growth. In addition, the growing emphasis on information security will lead to new jobs.

Job prospects. Computer scientists should enjoy excellent job prospects. Graduates from PhD programs in computer science and engineering are in high demand, and many companies report difficulties finding sufficient numbers of these highly skilled workers. In addition to openings resulting from rapid growth in the occupation, some additional job openings will arise from the need to replace workers who move into other occupations or who leave the labor force.

Earnings

Median annual wages of computer and information scientists were $97,970 in May 2008. The middle 50 percent earned between $75,340 and $124,370. The lowest 10 percent earned less than $57,480, and the highest 10 percent earned more than $151,250. Median annual wages of computer and information scientists employed in computer systems design and related services in May 2008 were $99,900.

Related Occupations

Others who work with information technology, or who engage in research and development include:

Computer and information systems managers
Computer network, systems, and database administrators
Computer software engineers
Computer support specialists
Engineers
Teachers—postsecondary

Sources of Additional Information

Further information about computer careers is available from:

- Association for Computing Machinery (ACM), 2 Penn Plaza, Suite 701, New York, NY 10121-0701. Internet: http://computingcareers.acm.org
- Institute of Electrical and Electronics Engineers Computer Society, Headquarters Office, 2001 L St. NW., Suite 700 Washington, DC 20036-4910. Internet: www.computer .org

- National Center for Women and Information Technology, University of Colorado, Campus Box 322 UCB, Boulder, CO 80309-0322. Internet: www.ncwit.org
- National Workforce Center for Emerging Technologies, 3000 Landerholm Circle SE., Bellevue, WA 98007. Internet: www .nwcet.org
- University of Washington Computer Science and Engineering Department, AC101 Paul G. Allen Center, Box 352350, 185 Stevens Way, Seattle, WA 98195-2350. Internet: www .cs.washington.edu/WhyCSE

Critical Thinking

1. What is the distinction between computer scientists and computer software engineers?

2. The article says that most computer scientists have doctorates. Use the Internet to find people described as computer scientists without PhDs, indeed, without any degree at all.

3. If your professor is a computer scientist, ask him/her to tell you about his/her dissertation.

4. The article says that there are 28,900 computer scientists is the United States. Use the Internet to find out how many doctors and lawyers there are.

The Occupational Information Network (O*NET) provides information on a wide range of occupational characteristics. Links to O*NET appear at the end of the Internet version of this occupational statement, accessible at www.bls.gov/ooh/ocos304.htm.

From *Occupational Outlook Handbook*, 2010/2011.

Women, Mathematics, and Computing[1]

PAUL DE PALMA

Introduction

In 1963, Betty Friedan wrote these gloomy words:

> The problem lay buried, unspoken, for many years in the minds of American women. . . . Each suburban wife struggled with it alone. As she made the beds, shopped for groceries, matched slipcover material, ate peanut butter sandwiches with her children, chauffeured Cub Scouts and Brownies, lay beside her husband at night—she was afraid to ask even of herself the silent question—"Is this all?"

The passage, of course, is from the *The Feminine Mystique* (Friedan, 1983: p. 15). Though, it took another decade for the discontent that Friedan described to solidify into a political movement, even in 1963 women were doing more than making peanut butter sandwiches. They also earned 41% of the bachelor's degrees. By 1995, the number of degrees conferred had nearly tripled. The fraction going to women more than kept pace at almost 55%. Put another way, women's share of bachelor's degrees increased by 25% since Betty Friedan first noticed the isolation of housewives. Consider two more sets of numbers. In 1965, 478 women graduated from medical school. These 478 women accounted for only 6.5% of the new physicians. Law was even less hospitable. Only 404 women, or just 3% of the total, received law degrees in 1965. By 1996, however, almost 39% of medical degrees and 43% of law degrees were going to women (Anderson, 1997).

If so many women are studying medicine and law, why are so few studying computer science? That's a good question, and one that has been getting a lot of attention. A search of an important index of computing literature, the *ACM Digital Portal* (ACM, 2005a), using the key words "women" and "computer," produced 2,223 hits. Of the first 200, most are about the underrepresentation of women in information technology. Judging by the volume of research, what we can do to increase the numbers of women studying computer science remains an open question.

While most investigators fall on one side or the other of the essentialist/social constructivist divide (Trauth, Quesenberry & Morgan, 2005), this article sidesteps the issue altogether in favor of offering a testable hypothesis: Girls and young women would be drawn to degree programs in computer science in greater numbers if the field were structured with the precision of mathematics. How we arrived at this hypothesis requires a look at the number of women earning degrees in computer science historically and in relation to other apparently similar fields.

Background

In 1997, *The Communications of the ACM* published an article entitled "The Incredible Shrinking Pipeline" (Camp, 1997). The article points out that the fraction of computer science degrees going to women decreased from 1986 to 1994. This bucks the trend of women entering male-dominated professions in increasing numbers. The graph below shows the percent of women earning degrees in various scientific disciplines between 1970–71 and 1994–95 (National Center for Educational Statistics, 1997).

If you did not look at the data over time, you would be justified in concluding that the 13% or so of engineering degrees going to women represents a terrible social injustice. Yet the most striking feature of the degrees conferred in engineering and the physical and life sciences is how closely their curves match that of all degrees conferred to women. Stated another way, the fraction of degrees in engineering

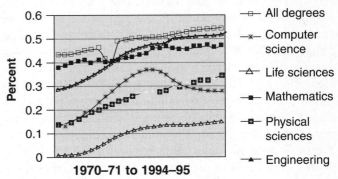

Percent of Women Earning Degrees by Year

Legend:
- —□— All degrees
- —✳— Computer science
- —△— Life sciences
- —■— Mathematics
- —⊞— Physical sciences
- —▲— Engineering

1970–71 to 1994–95

Figure 1

and the sciences going to women have increased enormously in a single generation. It has, in fact, outpaced the fraction of all degrees going to women. The curves for engineering and the life sciences both have that nice S shape that economists use to describe product acceptance. When a new kind of product comes to market, acceptance is initially slow. When the price comes down and the technology improves, it accelerates. Acceptance finally flattens out as the market becomes saturated. This appears to be exactly what has happened in engineering. Following the growth of the women's movement in the early 1970s, women slowly began to account for a larger share of degrees conferred. By the early 1980s, the fraction grew more rapidly, and then, by the 1990s, the rate of growth began to slow. A parallel situation has occurred in the life sciences, but at a much higher fraction. Women now earn more than 50% of undergraduate degrees in biology.

Computer science is the anomaly. Rapid growth in the mid-1980s was followed by a sharp decline. The fraction of women graduating in computer science flattens out in the 1990s. What is going on here? A study of German women noticed that the sharp increase in the number of degrees in computer science going to women followed the commercial introduction of the microcomputer in the early 1980s (Oechtering, 1993). This is a crucial observation. In a very few years, computers went from something most people were only vaguely aware of to a consumer product. What the graph does not tell you is that great numbers of men also followed the allure of computing in the early and mid-1980s—numbers that declined by the end of the decade.

Despite many earnest attempts to explain why women do not find computer science as appealing as young men (e.g., Bucciarelli, 1997; Wright, 1994), it is important to point out that computer science is not like the other areas we have been considering. Unlike physics, chemistry, mathematics, and electrical engineering, there is not an agreed-upon body of knowledge that defines the field. An important textbook in artificial intelligence, for instance, has grown three-fold in 10 years. A common programming language used to teach introductory computing barely existed a decade ago. Noam Chomsky has suggested that the maturity of a scientific discipline is inversely proportional to the amount of material that forms its core. By this measure, computer science is far less mature than other scientific and engineering disciplines.

Many studies have shown that girls are consistently less confident about their abilities in mathematics and science than are boys, even when their test scores show them to be more able (e.g., Mittelberg & Lev-Ari, 1999). Other studies attribute the shortage of women to lack of confidence along with the perception that computing is a male domain (Moorman & Johnson, 2003). Unfortunately, computer science, at least as presently constituted, requires a good bit of confidence. The kinds of problems presented to computer science majors tend to be open-ended. Unlike mathematics, the

answers are not in the back of the book—even for introductory courses. There is often not a single best way to come up with a solution and, indeed, the solutions themselves, even for trivial problems, have a stunning complexity to them. The tools that students use to solve these problems tend to be vastly more complex than the problems themselves. The reason for this is that the tools were designed for industrial-scale software development. The move over the last decade to object-oriented languages has only exacerbated an existing problem (Hsia, Simpson, Smith, & Cartwright, 2005). A typical lab assignment to write a program in the C++ or Java language will require that the student have a working knowledge of an operating system, a graphical user interface, text editor, debugger and the programming language itself.

One surrogate for complexity is the size of text-books. Kernighan and Ritchie's classic, *The C Programming Language* (1978) is 228 pages long. The first program in the book, the famous "Hello world," appears on page 6. Deitel, Deitel, Lipari, and Yaeger's (2004) *Visual C++ .NET: How to Program,* on the other hand, weighs in at a hefty four pounds and runs to 1,319 pages. Students have to wade through 52 pages before they reach the book's program equivalent to "Hello, world." The key to successful mastery in this environment is the willingness to tinker and the confidence to press forward with a set of tools that one only partially understands. Although we exhort our students to design a solution before they begin to enter it at the keyboard, in fact, the ready availability of computers has encouraged students to develop a trial-and-error attitude to their work. Those students willing to spend night after night at a computer screen acquire the kind of informal knowledge necessary to write successful programs. This is a world that will welcome only very self-assured young women.

Mathematics, Engineering, and Tinkering

Recall Chomsky's observation that the most mature disciplines are the most tightly defined. What discipline can boast the tightness and precision of mathematics? As it happens, many reasonable people have attributed at least some of the shortage of women in science and computing as well as the less-than-positive attitudes toward computers to so-called math anxiety among girls (e.g., Chang, 2002; Jennings & Onwuegbuzie, 2001; Mark, 1993). One study says that "The culture of engineering places particular stress on the importance of mathematical ability. Math is both the most complicated and the purest form of mental activity. It is also the most 'masculine' of subjects" (McIlwee & Robinson, 1992, p. 19, referring to Hacker, 1981). At first glance, the heavier reliance on mathematics might appear to explain why women avoid physics and electrical engineering while embracing biology and oceanography. But this explanation is insufficient for the simple reason that women receive nearly half of the undergraduate degrees in mathematics itself and were receiving almost 40% of them well before the women's movement became a mass phenomenon.

Here, then, is a hypothesis. What if the precision of mathematics is exactly what has appealed to women for so long? And what if the messiness of computing is what has put them off? So far, so good, but we still have to account for electrical engineering and physics. These have a smaller fraction of women than computer science, but are well defined and rely heavily on sophisticated mathematics. What is it about physics and electrical engineering that women find unattractive? The answer is really quite simple. Students drawn to engineering and physics like to tinker with gadgets (e.g., Crawford, Wood, Fowler, & Norell, 1994). That paper describes a grade school curriculum designed to encourage young engineers. It relieves heavily upon "levers, wheels, axles, cams, pulleys, forms of energy to create motion, etc." (p. 173). McIlwee and Robinson (1992) report that 57% of male engineers surveyed chose the field because they like to tinker. Only 16% of women surveyed chose engineering for this reason. It should come as no surprise that the men associated with the microcomputer—Bill Gates, the Paul Allen, Jobs and Wozniak—all got their start as tinkerers. And as all parents know but are hard-pressed to explain, their infant sons are drawn to trucks more readily than their infant daughters (Serbin, Poulin-Dubois, Colburne, Sen, & Eichstedt, 2001).

Microcomputers, a Problem with Computer Science Education

Here we find a convergence with computer science and, finally, an explanation for the steep rise in the number of women in the field following the introduction of the microcomputer and its drop a few years later. The development of the microcomputer changed computing enormously. In 1971, a small number of computer science departments awarded fewer than 2,400 degrees. Most people who worked in the thriving data processing industry had received their training in the military, for-profit vocational schools or on the job. By 1986, that number had jumped to nearly 42,000, including almost 15,000 women. Clearly, the microcomputer played a large part in the growth of the academic discipline of computing. Like the dot-com boom, the growth could not be maintained. If the production of computer science degrees had continued to climb at the rate it climbed between 1975 and 1985, by 2001 every American would have had a Bachelor of Science degree in the field. In fact, the number of degrees awarded began to drop sharply in 1987.

We know why both men and women entered IT in the 1980s. Why did the numbers drop by the late 1980s? We can

not really know the answer to this, of course, short of polling those who did not major in computer science during that period; but we can guess. Computer science is hard. What's more, it is not a real profession. There are no licensing barriers to entry, an issue that has been hotly debated in computing literature for at least two decades (ACM, 2005b). Until computing societies agree on licensing and convince state legislatures to go along, students need not earn a degree in computer science to work in the field.

These things are equally true for women, of course, but the tinker factor is an additional burden. Before the mid-1980s and the mass availability of microcomputers, programmers could almost ignore hardware. This article's author wrote programs for a large manufacturer of mainframe computers in the early 1980s without ever having seen the computer he was working on, nor, for that matter, the printer that produced the green bar paper delivered to his cubicle every two hours. There was tinkering going on in those days too, of course. But it was all software tinkering; only computer operators touched the machine. The micro changed all that. Suddenly, those young men who had spent their adolescence installing exotic operating systems and swapping memory chips were in great demand. By adding hardware tinkering to the supposed repertoire of skills necessary to program, the microcomputer reinforced the male-dominated culture of IT (for an account of this very male atmosphere, see De Palma, 2005).

Conclusion

Until the day when baby girls like gadgets as much as baby boys, let us look to mathematics itself to see what we can do about attracting young women to computer science. Well before other fields welcomed women, a significant fraction of degrees in mathematics were going to females. Let us assume that the mathematicians have been on the right track all along. A testable hypothesis presents itself. If we make computer science education more like mathematics education, we will make computer science more appealing to women. Computer science grew out of mathematics. How do we get back to basics?

First, teach girls who like to manipulate symbols how to program. Programming is weaving patterns with logic. If girls can do calculus, they can write programs. Second, try not to stray from logic. If we make computer science education less dependent on complex software tools, we remove some of the barriers between the student and logic. Third, minimize the use of microcomputers. Microcomputers, for all their cleverness, misrepresent computer science, the study of algorithms, as hardware tinkering. Fourth, ask students new to computer science to write many small functions, just as students of mathematics work countless short problems. Since there is something about the precision of mathematics that young women seem to like, let us try to make computing more precise. Later, as their confidence grows, they can take on larger projects. Fifth, regard programming languages as notation. It could well be that for complex systems, modern languages will produce a better product in a shorter time. But students do not produce complex systems. They produce relatively simple systems with extraordinarily complex tools. Choose a notation appropriate to the problem and do not introduce another until students become skilled programmers. Taken together, these suggestions outline a program to test the hypothesis.

Suppose we test the hypothesis and it turns out to have been correct. Suppose that, as a result, we give computing a makeover, and it comes out as clearly defined and as appropriate to the job as mathematics. Now imagine that able young women flock to the field. How might this change computing? To begin, students will no longer confuse half-formed ideas about proprietary products with computer science. Nor will they confuse the ability to plug in Ethernet cards with system design. It might mean that with a critical mass of women holding undergraduate degrees in computing, systems will be designed, not by tinkerers, but by women (and men) for whom the needs of computer users are front and center. Since stories of systems that failed through an over fondness for complexity are legion (De Palma, 2005), the makeover might even reduce the number of jerry-rigged systems. Thus, does social justice converge with the market place—a very happy outcome, indeed.

Note

1. This article grew out of a shorter opinion piece in the "Viewpoint" column of *Communications of the ACM* (De Palma, 2001).

References

ACM (2005a). Search using key words: "Women" and "computer." *The Digital Library*. Retrieved August 23, 2005 from www.acm.org.

ACM (2005b). Search using key words: "license" and "profession." *The Digital Library*. Retrieved August 27, 2005 from www.acm.org.

Anderson, C. (1998). *Fact Book on Higher Education: 1997 edition*. American Council on Education. Phoenix: Oryx Press.

Bucciarelli, L. & Kuhn, S. (1997). Engineering education and engineering practice: improving the fit. In S. R. Barley & J. Orr (Eds.), *Between Craft and Science: Technical Work in U.S. settings* (pp. 210–229). Ithaca, NY: Cornell University Press.

Camp, T. (1997). The incredible shrinking pipeline. *Communications of the ACM, 40*(10), 103–110.

Chang, J. (2002). Women and minorities in the sciences, mathematics, and engineering pipeline. *Eric Clearinghouse for Community Colleges*. Retrieved February 23, 2006, from Eric Digest (ED467855).

Crawford, R., Wood, K., Fowler, M., & Norell, J. (1994, April). An engineering design curriculum for the elementary grades. *Journal of Engineering Education, 83*(2), 172–181.

De Palma, P. (2001). Viewpoint: Why women avoid computer science. *The Communications of the ACM, 44*(6), 27–29.

De Palma, P. (2005). The Software Wars. *The American Scholar, 74*(1), 69–83.

Deitel, H., Deitel, P., Liperi, J., & Yaeger, C. (2003). *Visual C++ .NET: How to Program*. Upper Saddle River, NJ: Pearson Education, Inc.

Friedan, B. (1983). *The feminine mystique*. New York: W.W. Norton & Co.

Hacker, S. (1981). The culture of engineering: Women, workplace and machine. *Women's Studies International Journal Quarterly,* 4, 341–533.

Hsia, J., Simpson, E., Smith, D., & Cartwright, R. (2005). Taming Java for the classroom. Proceedings of the 36th SIGCSE technical symposium on Computer science education. *ACM SIGCSE Bulletin, 37*(1), 327–331.

Kernighan, B., & Ritchie, D. (1978). *The C Programming Language*. Englewood Cliffs: Prentice-Hall.

Mark, J. (1993). Beyond equal access: Gender equity in learning with computers. The Eisenhower National Clearinghouse for Mathematics and Science Education. Retrieved August 27, 2005, from www.enc.org/topics/equity/articles.

McIlwee, J. & Robinson, J. G. (1992). *Women in Engineering: Gender, Power and Workplace Culture*. Albany: State University of New York Press.

Mittelberg D. & Lev-Ari, L. (1999). Confidence in mathematics and its consequences: Gender differences among Israeli Jewish and Arab youth. *Gender and Education, 11*(1), 75–92.

Moorman, P., & Johnson, E. (2003). Still a stranger here: Attitudes among secondary school students towards computer science. *Proceedings of the 8th Annual Conference on Innovation and Technology in Computer Science Education*, 193–197.

National Center for Educational Statistics. (1997). *Digest of educational statistics NCES 98–015*. Washington, D.C. U.S. Government Printing Office.

Oechtering, V., & Behnke, R. (1995). Situations and advancement measures in Germany. *Communications of the ACM, 38*(1), 75–82.

Serbin, L., Poulin-Dubois, D., Colburne, K., Sen, M., & Eichstedt, J. (2001). Gender stereotyping in infancy: Visual preferences for and knowledge of gender-stereotyped *toys* in the second year. *International Journal of Behavioral Development, 25*(1), 7–15.

Trauth, E., Quesenberry, J., & Morgan, A. (2004). *Proceedings of the 2004 SIGMIS Conference on Computer Personnel Research, 114–119*. New York: ACM Press.

Wright, R., & Jacobs, J. (1994). Male flight from computer work. *American Sociological Review, 59*, 511–536.

Key Terms

Computer Science: An academic discipline that studies the design and implementation of algorithms. Algorithms are step-by-step procedures for solving well-defined problems. A precise description of a technique for putting words in alphabetical order is an algorithm.

Ethernet Card: Hardware that allows a computer to be attached to a network of computers.

Memory Chip: An informal term for RAM (random access memory) or just plain memory. It is internal to a computer and loses its contents when the power is shut off. Programs must be loaded into RAM to execute.

Microcomputer: Also called a personal computer. The machine on your desk is a microcomputer.

Operating System: The collection of programs that controls all of the computer's hardware and software. Important operating systems are Windows XP and Unix.

Program: A sequence of instructions that tells a computer how to accomplish a well-defined task.

Programming Language: The notational system that a programmer uses to construct a program. This program is transformed by another program, known as a compiler, into the instructions that a computer can execute. Important languages are Java and C++.

Critical Thinking

1. Are you persuaded that computer science would more appealing to women if computer science education were more like mathematics education?

2. There have been many hypotheses about why women find computer science relatively unattractive. Name two mentioned in the article.

3. Do you agree with Noam Chomsky's observation that the maturity of scientific discipline is inversely proportional to the amount of material that forms its core? Is this observation true outside of science? Use the Internet to find out how long it takes to earn a PhD., on average, in a selection of scientific disciplines compared to a selection of disciplines from the social sciences and humanities.

UNIT 4

Computers, People, and Social Participation

Unit Selections

Learning Outcomes

After reading this Unit, you will be able to:

- Be able to argue for and against the proposition that humans were more studious and attentive before the Internet.

- Not use the term "generation" quite so easily.

- Have a clear sense of role of solitude in Western history.

- Understand what one futurist thinks the world holds for us.

- Have seen examples of virtual worlds reproducing cultural behaviors found in the real world.

Student Website
www.mhhe.com/cls

Internet References

Alliance for Childhood: Computers and Children
www.drupal6.allianceforchildhood.org/computer_position_statement
The Core Rules of Netiquette
www.albion.com/netiquette/corerules.html
Internet and American Life
www.pewinternet.org
SocioSite: Networks, Groups, and Social Interaction
www.sociosite.net

The early and astute observer of American culture, Alexis de Tocqueville (1805–1859), had this to say about the proclivity of Americans to form civic associations:

> Americans of all ages, all conditions, and all-dispositions constantly form associations. . . . The Americans make associations to give entertainments, to found seminaries, to build inns, to construct churches, to diffuse books, to send missionaries to the Antipodes; in this manner they found hospitals, prisons, and schools. If it is proposed to inculcate some truth or to foster some feeling by the encouragement of a great example, they form a society. Wherever at the head of some new undertaking you see the government in France, or a man of rank in England, in the United States you will be sure to find an association. . . . The first time I heard in the United States that a hundred thousand men had bound themselves publicly to abstain from spiritous liquors, it appeared to me more like a joke than a serious engagement, and I did not at once perceive why these temperate citizens could not content themselves with drinking water by their own firesides. . . . Nothing, in my opinion, is more deserving of our attention than the intellectual and moral associations of America. . . . In democratic countries the science of association is the mother of science; the progress of all the rest depends upon the progress it has made.[1]

He laid this tendency squarely at the feet of democracy. If all men—we're talking about the first half of the ninteenth century here—are equal before the law, then, to do any civic good requires that these equal, but individually powerless, men band together.

A century and a half later, we have the technical means to communicate almost instantly and effortlessly across great distances. But we are banding together less. In 1995, Robert Putnam made the news with an article called "Bowling Alone," later expanded into a book of the same name (Simon and Schuster, 2000). He argued that the civil associations de Tocqueville had noticed so long ago were breaking down. Americans were not joining the PTA, the Boy Scouts, the local garden club, or bowling leagues in their former numbers. Putnam discovered that although more people are bowling than ever, participation in leagues was down by 40 percent since 1980. The consequences for a functioning democracy are severe.

Although the articles in this unit do not directly address the idea of civic participation, one question is the glue that holds them together. Do computers assist or detract from civic life? Another French social observer, Emile Durkheim (1858–1917), argued that a vital society must have members who feel a sense of community. Community is easily evident in pre-industrial societies where kinship ties, shared religious belief, and custom reinforce group identity and shared values. Not so in modern societies, particularly in the United States, where a mobile population commutes long distances and retreats each evening to the sanctity and seclusion of individual homes. Contemporary visitors to the United States are struck by the cultural cafeteria available to Americans. They find a dizzying array of religions, beliefs, moral and philosophical perspectives, modes of social

© Peter Scholey/Photographer's Choice/Getty Images

interaction, entertainment venues and, now, digital gadgets. One need only observe a teenager frantically updating his Facebook page from a darkened bedroom to know that while computer technology has surely given us great things, it has taken away something as well.

Or has it? One can argue that the new communications technologies permit relationships that were never before possible. To cite a large example, the organization, *moveon.org,* organized many thousands of people, in a matter of weeks, entirely over the Internet, to oppose the invasion of Iraq in the spring of 2003. Or a smaller one. Immigration, always a wrenching experience, is less wrenching now, since immigrants to the United States can be in daily touch with their families across the globe. Or consider how the virtual bazaar, eBay, surely one of the extraordinary aspects of the Internet, puts Americans in touch with Japanese, Latvians, Montenegrans, peoples whom we might never have known. Recall Postman: "Technology giveth and technology taketh away."

What technology seems to have taken away in the past few years is the ability either to concentrate or to be alone, at least according to the first two articles in this unit. The first, "Is Google Making Us Stupid?," was received so well that the author expanded it into an eminently readable book (*The Shallows,* W.W. Norton, 2011). The book takes the reader on a long, fascinating journey from our pre-literate forbears through the discovery of writing right up to our current cultural fascination with the social media. Media scholars have long argued that the invention of writing,[2] moveable type, and electronic media like radio and television changed the way we think. Carr begins that journey in the article reprinted here: "my concentration [when reading] often starts to drift after two or three pages." For a contrary view, see Steven Johnson's book, *Everything Bad is Good for You* (Riverhead, 2005).

It is difficult to be a full participant in the modern world without bumping up against the social media in some form or another. Even my own aunts and uncles, now in their seventies and eighties, keep track of far-flung children, grandchildren, nieces, and nephews using Facebook. It seems appropriate, then, to present counter voices. What if the social media do not contribute to a new kind of community but rather to the destruction of the sense of solitude made possible, some argue, by the invention of writing. But connectivity has a price. William Deresiewicz in "The End of Solitude" argues counterintuitively, "the Internet is as powerful a machine for the production of loneliness as television is for the manufacture of boredom."

Nevertheless, more and more our social lives appear to be spent online. One could lament this as does Deresiewicz or embrace it, teasing all of its implications, especially for commerce. This is the stance taken by Arnold Brown in "Relationships, Community, and Identity in the New Virtual Society." "Clearly," he writes, "the Internet has radically reshaped our social lives over the span of just a couple of decades, luring us into a virtual metaworld where traditional interactions—living, loving, belonging, and separating, as well as finding customers and keeping them—require new protocols." Among those new protocols is just how you are to behave with your digital devices when face-to-face with a real person.

Here's the rub. Those of us inhabiting the contemporary American social landscape stepped onto its soil at different times in our lives. Were we, to twist Shakespeare, born to fluent digital discourse, did we achieve it after much study, or have our devices thrust been upon us? "Pundits, professors, and pop critics" appear to assume that the current cohort of eighteen to twenty-two year olds form a "digital generation." But overuse of the word "generation" is an invitation to sloppy thinking, argues Siva Vaidhyanathan in "Generational Myth." Even the baby boomers, who once thought their numbers would transform the world, now share little more than sore knees and anxiety about Medicare.

The final piece in this section, "Expressing My Inner Gnome," indirectly addresses the idea of social transformation and digital technology. Turns out that when we play online role-playing games (MMORPGs to the initiated), we reproduce many of the social relationships found in the non-virtual world. Gender, attractiveness, interpersonal distance, and eye gaze are all mirrored in our avatars.

Where does this leave us? With a lot of questions, really. Do the social media promote or hinder the conviviality that de Tocqueville found so much a part of American culture a century and a half ago? And how exactly could we have been that convivial if we were spending all of our time in solitude pondering complex writing as Derseiewicz laments? And if digital technology is changing our mental makeup, why do we reproduce, for example, gender stereotypical behavior online? Interesting questions, though none likely to be answered. The greatest pleasure of all, and something that de Tocqueville *would* have understood, is to join that great cacophonous community of writers, talkers, and, now, bloggers, trying to persuade the rest of us that they're right.

Notes

1. Alexis de Tocqueville, *Democracy in American,* Vintage Books, 2000, vol. 2, 114–118.

2. Beginning about 3500 B.C.E. See the Preface to this volume for a discussion of writing as a technology.

Is Google Making Us Stupid?

What the Internet is doing to our brains.

NICHOLAS CARR

"Dave, stop. Stop, will you? Stop, Dave. Will you stop, Dave?" So the supercomputer HAL pleads with the implacable astronaut Dave Bowman in a famous and weirdly poignant scene toward the end of Stanley Kubrick's *2001: A Space Odyssey*. Bowman, having nearly been sent to a deep-space death by the malfunctioning machine, is calmly, coldly disconnecting the memory circuits that control its artificial brain. "Dave, my mind is going," HAL says, forlornly. "I can feel it. I can feel it. I'm afraid."

I can feel it, too. Over the past few years I've had an uncomfortable sense that someone, or something, has been tinkering with my brain, remapping the neural circuitry, reprogramming the memory. My mind isn't going—so far as I can tell—but it's changing. I'm not thinking the way I used to think. I can feel it most strongly when I'm reading. Immersing myself in a book or a lengthy article used to be easy. My mind would get caught up in the narrative or the turns of the argument, and I'd spend hours strolling through long stretches of prose. That's rarely the case anymore. Now my concentration often starts to drift after two or three pages. I get fidgety, lose the thread, begin looking for something else to do. I feel as if I'm always dragging my wayward brain back to the text. The deep reading that used to come naturally has become a struggle.

I think I know what's going on. For more than a decade now, I've been spending a lot of time online, searching and surfing and sometimes adding to the great databases of the Internet. The Web has been a godsend to me as a writer. Research that once required days in the stacks or periodical rooms of libraries can now be done in minutes. A few Google searches, some quick clicks on hyperlinks, and I've got the telltale fact or pithy quote I was after. Even when I'm not working, I'm as likely as not to be foraging in the Web's info-thickets, reading and writing e-mails, scanning headlines and blog posts, watching videos and listening to podcasts, or just tripping from link to link to link. (Unlike footnotes, to which they're sometimes likened, hyperlinks don't merely point to related works; they propel you toward them.)

For me, as for others, the Net is becoming a universal medium, the conduit for most of the information that flows through my eyes and ears and into my mind. The advantages of having immediate access to such an incredibly rich store of information are many, and they've been widely described and duly applauded. "The perfect recall of silicon memory," *Wired*'s Clive Thompson has written, "can be an enormous boon to thinking." But that boon comes at a price. As the media theorist Marshall McLuhan pointed out in the 1960s, media are not just passive channels of information. They supply the stuff of thought, but they also shape the process of thought. And what the Net seems to be doing is chipping away my capacity for concentration and contemplation. My mind now expects to take in information the way the Net distributes it: in a swiftly moving stream of particles. Once I was a scuba diver in the sea of words. Now I zip along the surface like a guy on a Jet Ski.

I'm not the only one. When I mention my troubles with reading to friends and acquaintances—literary types, most of them—many say they're having similar experiences. The more they use the Web, the more they have to fight to stay focused on long pieces of writing. Some of the bloggers I follow have also begun mentioning the phenomenon. Scott Karp, who writes a blog about online media, recently confessed that he has stopped reading books altogether. "I was a lit major in college, and used to be [a] voracious book reader," he wrote. "What happened?" He speculates on the answer: "What if I do all my reading on the Web not so much because the way I read has changed, i.e., I'm just seeking convenience, but because the way I THINK has changed?"

Bruce Friedman, who blogs regularly about the use of computers in medicine, also has described how the Internet has altered his mental habits. "I now have almost totally lost the ability to read and absorb a longish article on the web or in print," he wrote earlier this year. A pathologist who has long been on the faculty of the University of Michigan Medical School, Friedman elaborated on his comment in a telephone conversation with me. His thinking, he said, has taken on a "staccato" quality, reflecting the way he quickly scans short passages of text from many sources online. "I can't read *War and Peace* anymore," he admitted. "I've lost the ability to do that. Even a blog post of more than three or four paragraphs is too much to absorb. I skim it."

Anecdotes alone don't prove much. And we still await the long-term neurological and psychological experiments that will provide a definitive picture of how Internet use affects cognition. But a recently published study of online research habits, conducted by scholars from University College London, suggests that we may well be in the midst of a sea change in the way we read and think. As part of the five-year research program, the scholars examined computer logs documenting the behavior of visitors to two popular research sites, one operated by the British Library and one by a U.K. educational consortium, that provide access to journal articles, e-books, and other sources of written information. They found that people using the sites exhibited "a form of skimming activity," hopping from one source to another and rarely returning to any source they'd already visited. They typically read no more than one or two pages of an article or book before they would "bounce" out to another site. Sometimes they'd save a long article, but there's no evidence that they ever went back and actually read it. The authors of the study report:

> It is clear that users are not reading online in the traditional sense; indeed there are signs that new forms of "reading" are emerging as users "power browse" horizontally through titles, contents pages and abstracts going for quick wins. It almost seems that they go online to avoid reading in the traditional sense.

Thanks to the ubiquity of text on the Internet, not to mention the popularity of text-messaging on cell phones, we may well be reading more today than we did in the 1970s or 1980s, when television was our medium of choice. But it's a different kind of reading, and behind it lies a different kind of thinking—perhaps even a new sense of the self. "We are not only *what* we read," says Maryanne Wolf, a developmental psychologist at Tufts University and the author of *Proust and the Squid: The Story and Science of the Reading Brain.* "We are *how* we read." Wolf worries that the style of reading promoted by the Net, a style that puts "efficiency" and "immediacy" above all else, may be weakening our capacity for the kind of deep reading that emerged when an earlier technology, the printing press, made long and complex works of prose commonplace. When we read online, she says, we tend to become "mere decoders of information." Our ability to interpret text, to make the rich mental connections that form when we read deeply and without distraction, remains largely disengaged.

Reading, explains Wolf, is not an instinctive skill for human beings. It's not etched into our genes the way speech is. We have to teach our minds how to translate the symbolic characters we see into the language we understand. And the media or other technologies we use in learning and practicing the craft of reading play an important part in shaping the neural circuits inside our brains. Experiments demonstrate that readers of ideograms, such as the Chinese, develop a mental circuitry for reading that is very different from the circuitry found in those of us whose written language employs an alphabet. The variations extend across many regions of the brain, including those that govern such essential cognitive functions as memory and the interpretation of visual and auditory stimuli. We can expect as well that the circuits woven by our use of the Net will be different from those woven by our reading of books and other printed works.

Also See

Living with a Computer
(July 1982)

"The process works this way. When I sit down to write a letter or start the first draft of an article, I simply type on the keyboard and the words appear on the screen . . ."
—James Fallows

Sometime in 1882, Friedrich Nietzsche bought a typewriter—a Malling-Hansen Writing Ball, to be precise. His vision was failing, and keeping his eyes focused on a page had become exhausting and painful, often bringing on crushing headaches. He had been forced to curtail his writing, and he feared that he would soon have to give it up. The typewriter rescued him, at least for a time. Once he had mastered touch-typing, he was able to write with his eyes closed, using only the tips of his fingers. Words could once again flow from his mind to the page.

But the machine had a subtler effect on his work. One of Nietzsche's friends, a composer, noticed a change in the style of his writing. His already terse prose had become even tighter, more telegraphic. "Perhaps you will through this instrument even take to a new idiom," the friend wrote in a letter, noting that, in his own work, his " 'thoughts' in music and language often depend on the quality of pen and paper."

"You are right," Nietzsche replied, "our writing equipment takes part in the forming of our thoughts." Under the sway of the machine, writes the German media scholar Friedrich A. Kittler, Nietzsche's prose "changed from arguments to aphorisms, from thoughts to puns, from rhetoric to telegram style."

The human brain is almost infinitely malleable. People used to think that our mental meshwork, the dense connections formed among the 100 billion or so neurons inside our skulls, was largely fixed by the time we reached adulthood. But brain researchers have discovered that that's not the case. James Olds, a professor of neuroscience who directs the Krasnow Institute for Advanced Study at George Mason University, says that even the adult mind "is very plastic." Nerve cells routinely break old connections and form new ones. "The brain," according to Olds, "has the ability to reprogram itself on the fly, altering the way it functions."

As we use what the sociologist Daniel Bell has called our "intellectual technologies"—the tools that extend our mental rather than our physical capacities—we inevitably begin to take on the qualities of those technologies. The mechanical clock, which came into common use in the 14th century, provides a compelling example. In *Technics and Civilization,* the historian and cultural critic Lewis Mumford described how the clock "disassociated time from human events and helped create the belief in an independent world of mathematically measurable sequences." The "abstract framework of divided time" became "the point of reference for both action and thought."

The clock's methodical ticking helped bring into being the scientific mind and the scientific man. But it also took something away. As the late MIT computer scientist Joseph Weizenbaum observed in his 1976 book, *Computer Power and Human Reason: From Judgment to Calculation,* the conception of the world that emerged from the widespread use of timekeeping instruments "remains an impoverished version of the older one, for it rests on a rejection of those direct experiences that formed the basis for, and indeed constituted, the old reality." In deciding when to eat, to work, to sleep, to rise, we stopped listening to our senses and started obeying the clock.

The process of adapting to new intellectual technologies is reflected in the changing metaphors we use to explain ourselves to ourselves. When the mechanical clock arrived, people began thinking of their brains as operating "like clockwork." Today, in the age of software, we have come to think of them as operating "like computers." But the changes, neuroscience tells us, go much deeper than metaphor. Thanks to our brain's plasticity, the adaptation occurs also at a biological level.

The Internet promises to have particularly far-reaching effects on cognition. In a paper published in 1936, the British mathematician Alan Turing proved that a digital computer, which at the time existed only as a theoretical machine, could be programmed to perform the function of any other information-processing device. And that's what we're seeing today. The Internet, an immeasurably powerful computing system, is subsuming most of our other intellectual technologies. It's becoming our map and our clock, our printing press and our typewriter, our calculator and our telephone, and our radio and TV.

When the Net absorbs a medium, that medium is recreated in the Net's image. It injects the medium's content with hyperlinks, blinking ads, and other digital gewgaws, and it surrounds the content with the content of all the other media it has absorbed. A new e-mail message, for instance, may announce its arrival as we're glancing over the latest headlines at a newspaper's site. The result is to scatter our attention and diffuse our concentration.

The Net's influence doesn't end at the edges of a computer screen, either. As people's minds become attuned to the crazy quilt of Internet media, traditional media have to adapt to the audience's new expectations. Television programs add text crawls and pop-up ads, and magazines and newspapers shorten their articles, introduce capsule summaries, and crowd their pages with easy-to-browse info-snippets. When, in March of this year, *The New York Times* decided to devote the second and third pages of every edition to article abstracts, its design director, Tom Bodkin, explained that the "shortcuts" would give harried readers a quick "taste" of the day's news, sparing them the "less efficient" method of actually turning the pages and reading the articles. Old media have little choice but to play by the new-media rules.

Never has a communications system played so many roles in our lives—or exerted such broad influence over our thoughts—as the Internet does today. Yet, for all that's been written about the Net, there's been little consideration of how, exactly, it's reprogramming us. The Net's intellectual ethic remains obscure.

About the same time that Nietzsche started using his typewriter, an earnest young man named Frederick Winslow Taylor carried a stopwatch into the Midvale Steel plant in Philadelphia and began a historic series of experiments aimed at improving the efficiency of the plant's machinists. With the approval of Midvale's owners, he recruited a group of factory hands, set them to work on various metalworking machines, and recorded and timed their every movement as well as the operations of the machines. By breaking down every job into a sequence of small, discrete steps and then testing different ways of performing each one, Taylor created a set of precise instructions—an "algorithm," we might say today—for how each worker should work. Midvale's employees grumbled about the strict new regime, claiming that it turned them into little more than automatons, but the factory's productivity soared.

More than a hundred years after the invention of the steam engine, the Industrial Revolution had at last found its philosophy and its philosopher. Taylor's tight industrial choreography—his "system," as he liked to call it—was embraced by manufacturers throughout the country and, in time, around the world. Seeking maximum speed, maximum efficiency, and maximum output, factory owners used time-and-motion studies to organize their work and configure the jobs of their workers. The goal, as Taylor defined it in his celebrated 1911 treatise, *The Principles of Scientific Management,* was to identify and adopt, for every job, the "one best method" of work and thereby to effect "the gradual substitution of science for rule of thumb throughout the mechanic arts." Once his system was applied to all acts of manual labor, Taylor assured his followers, it would bring about a restructuring not only of industry but of society, creating a utopia of perfect efficiency. "In the past the man has been first," he declared; "in the future the system must be first."

Taylor's system is still very much with us; it remains the ethic of industrial manufacturing. And now, thanks to the growing power that computer engineers and software coders wield over our intellectual lives, Taylor's ethic is beginning to govern the realm of the mind as well. The Internet is a machine designed for the efficient and automated collection, transmission, and manipulation of information, and its legions of programmers are intent on finding the "one best method"—the perfect algorithm—to carry out every mental movement of what we've come to describe as "knowledge work."

Google's headquarters, in Mountain View, California—the Googleplex—is the Internet's high church, and the religion practiced inside its walls is Taylorism. Google, says its chief executive, Eric Schmidt, is "a company that's founded around the science of measurement," and it is striving to "systematize everything" it does. Drawing on the terabytes of behavioral data it collects through its search engine and other sites, it carries out thousands of experiments a day, according to the *Harvard Business Review,* and it uses the results to refine the algorithms that increasingly control how people find information and extract meaning from it. What Taylor did for the work of the hand, Google is doing for the work of the mind.

The company has declared that its mission is "to organize the world's information and make it universally accessible and useful." It seeks to develop "the perfect search engine," which it defines as something that "understands exactly what you mean and gives you back exactly what you want." In Google's view, information is a kind of commodity, a utilitarian resource that can be mined and processed with industrial efficiency. The more pieces of information we can "access" and the faster we can extract their gist, the more productive we become as thinkers.

Where does it end? Sergey Brin and Larry Page, the gifted young men who founded Google while pursuing doctoral degrees in computer science at Stanford, speak frequently of their desire to turn their search engine into an artificial intelligence, a HAL-like machine that might be connected directly to our brains. "The ultimate search engine is something as smart as people—or smarter," Page said in a speech a few years back. "For us, working on search is a way to work on artificial intelligence." In a 2004 interview with *Newsweek,* Brin said, "Certainly if you had all the world's information directly attached to your brain, or an artificial brain that was smarter than your brain, you'd be better off." Last year, Page told a convention of scientists that Google is "really trying to build artificial intelligence and to do it on a large scale."

Such an ambition is a natural one, even an admirable one, for a pair of math whizzes with vast quantities of cash at their disposal and a small army of computer scientists in their employ. A fundamentally scientific enterprise, Google is motivated by a desire to use technology, in Eric Schmidt's words, "to solve problems that have never been solved before," and artificial intelligence is the hardest problem out there. Why wouldn't Brin and Page want to be the ones to crack it?

Still, their easy assumption that we'd all "be better off" if our brains were supplemented, or even replaced, by an artificial intelligence is unsettling. It suggests a belief that intelligence is the output of a mechanical process, a series of discrete steps that can be isolated, measured, and optimized. In Google's world, the world we enter when we go online, there's little place for the fuzziness of contemplation. Ambiguity is not an opening for insight but a bug to be fixed. The human brain is just an outdated computer that needs a faster processor and a bigger hard drive.

The idea that our minds should operate as high-speed data-processing machines is not only built into the workings of the Internet, it is the network's reigning business model as well. The faster we surf across the Web—the more links we click and pages we view—the more opportunities Google and other companies gain to collect information about us and to feed us advertisements. Most of the proprietors of the commercial Internet have a financial stake in collecting the crumbs of data we leave behind as we flit from link to link—the more crumbs, the better. The last thing these companies want is to encourage leisurely reading or slow, concentrated thought. It's in their economic interest to drive us to distraction.

Maybe I'm just a worrywort. Just as there's a tendency to glorify technological progress, there's a countertendency to expect the worst of every new tool or machine. In Plato's *Phaedrus,* Socrates bemoaned the development of writing. He feared that, as people came to rely on the written word as a substitute for the knowledge they used to carry inside their heads, they would, in the words of one of the dialogue's characters, "cease to exercise their memory and become forgetful." And because they would be able to "receive a quantity of information without proper instruction," they would "be thought very knowledgeable when they are for the most part quite ignorant." They would be "filled with the conceit of wisdom instead of real wisdom." Socrates wasn't wrong—the new technology did often have the effects he feared—but he was shortsighted. He couldn't foresee the many ways that writing and reading would serve to spread information, spur fresh ideas, and expand human knowledge (if not wisdom).

The arrival of Gutenberg's printing press, in the 15th century, set off another round of teeth gnashing. The Italian humanist Hieronimo Squarciafico worried that the easy availability of books would lead to intellectual laziness, making men "less studious" and weakening their minds. Others argued that cheaply printed books and broadsheets would undermine religious authority, demean the work of scholars and scribes, and spread sedition and debauchery. As New York University professor Clay Shirky notes, "Most of the arguments made against the printing press were correct, even prescient." But, again, the doomsayers were unable to imagine the myriad blessings that the printed word would deliver.

So, yes, you should be skeptical of my skepticism. Perhaps those who dismiss critics of the Internet as Luddites or nostalgists will be proved correct, and from our hyperactive, data-stoked minds will spring a golden age of intellectual discovery and universal wisdom. Then again, the Net isn't the alphabet, and although it may replace the printing press, it produces something altogether different. The kind of deep reading that a sequence of printed pages promotes is valuable not just for the knowledge we acquire from the author's words but for the intellectual vibrations those words set off within our own minds. In the quiet spaces opened up by the sustained, undistracted reading of a book, or by any other act of contemplation, for that matter, we make our own associations, draw our own inferences and analogies, foster our own ideas. Deep reading, as Maryanne Wolf argues, is indistinguishable from deep thinking.

If we lose those quiet spaces, or fill them up with "content," we will sacrifice something important not only in our selves but in our culture. In a recent essay, the playwright Richard Foreman eloquently described what's at stake:

> I come from a tradition of Western culture, in which the ideal (my ideal) was the complex, dense and "cathedral-like" structure of the highly educated and articulate personality—a man or woman who carried inside themselves a personally constructed and unique version of the entire heritage of the West. [But now] I see within us all (myself included) the replacement of complex inner density with a new kind of self—evolving under the pressure of information overload and the technology of the "instantly available."

As we are drained of our "inner repertory of dense cultural inheritance," Foreman concluded, we risk turning into

" 'pancake people'—spread wide and thin as we connect with that vast network of information accessed by the mere touch of a button."

I'm haunted by that scene in *2001*. What makes it so poignant, and so weird, is the computer's emotional response to the disassembly of its mind: its despair as one circuit after another goes dark, its childlike pleading with the astronaut— "I can feel it. I can feel it. I'm afraid"—and its final reversion to what can only be called a state of innocence. HAL's outpouring of feeling contrasts with the emotionlessness that characterizes the human figures in the film, who go about their business with an almost robotic efficiency. Their thoughts and actions feel scripted, as if they're following the steps of an algorithm. In the world of *2001,* people have become so machinelike that the most human character turns out to be a machine. That's the essence of Kubrick's dark prophecy: as we come to rely on computers to mediate our understanding of the world, it is our own intelligence that flattens into artificial intelligence.

Critical Thinking

1. Carr ("Is Google Making Us Stupid?") quotes Friedrich Nietsche on the typewriter: "You are right, . . . , our writing equipment takes part in forming our thoughts." Use the Internet to find out who Walter J. Ong was. What does he have to say about writing and thought? How about Marshall McLuhan? How did these two early students of media studies know one another?

2. Is Google making us stupid?

3. For a completely different view on the relationship between computers and intelligence, see Steven Johnson's book, *Everything Bad Is Good for You* (Riverhead 2005). Who is most persuasive, Carr or Johnson?

The End of Solitude

WILLIAM DERESIEWICZ

As everyone seeks more and broader connectivity, the still, small voice speaks only in silence.

What does the contemporary self want? The camera has created a culture of celebrity; the computer is creating a culture of connectivity. As the two technologies converge—broadband tipping the Web from text to image, social-networking sites spreading the mesh of interconnection ever wider—the two cultures betray a common impulse. Celebrity and connectivity are both ways of becoming known. This is what the contemporary self wants. It wants to be recognized, wants to be connected: It wants to be visible. If not to the millions, on *Survivor* or *Oprah,* then to the hundreds, on Twitter or Facebook. This is the quality that validates us, this is how we become real to ourselves—by being seen by others. The great contemporary terror is anonymity. If Lionel Trilling was right, if the property that grounded the self, in Romanticism, was sincerity, and in modernism it was authenticity, then in postmodernism it is visibility.

So we live exclusively in relation to others, and what disappears from our lives is solitude. Technology is taking away our privacy and our concentration, but it is also taking away our ability to be alone. Though I shouldn't say taking away. We are doing this to ourselves; we are discarding these riches as fast as we can. I was told by one of her older relatives that a teenager I know had sent 3,000 text messages one recent month. That's 100 a day, or about one every 10 waking minutes, morning, noon, and night, weekdays and weekends, class time, lunch time, homework time, and toothbrushing time. So on average, she's never alone for more than 10 minutes at once. Which means, she's never alone.

I once asked my students about the place that solitude has in their lives. One of them admitted that she finds the prospect of being alone so unsettling that she'll sit with a friend even when she has a paper to write. Another said, why would anyone want to be alone?

To that remarkable question, history offers a number of answers. Man may be a social animal, but solitude has traditionally been a societal value. In particular, the act of being alone has been understood as an essential dimension of religious experience, albeit one restricted to a self-selected few. Through the solitude of rare spirits, the collective renews its relationship with divinity. The prophet and the hermit, the sadhu and the yogi, pursue their vision quests, invite their trances, in desert or forest or cave. For the still, small voice speaks only in silence. Social life is a bustle of petty concerns, a jostle of quotidian interests, and religious institutions are no exception. You cannot hear God when people are chattering at you, and the divine word, their pretensions notwithstanding, demurs at descending on the monarch and the priest. Communal experience is the human norm, but the solitary encounter with God is the egregious act that refreshes that norm. (Egregious, for no man is a prophet in his own land. Tiresias was reviled before he was vindicated, Teresa interrogated before she was canonized.) Religious solitude is a kind of self-correcting social mechanism, a way of burning out the underbrush of moral habit and spiritual custom. The seer returns with new tablets or new dances, his face bright with the old truth.

Like other religious values, solitude was democratized by the Reformation and secularized by Romanticism. In Marilynne Robinson's interpretation, Calvinism created the modern self by focusing the soul inward, leaving it to encounter God, like a prophet of old, in "profound isolation." To her enumeration of Calvin, Marguerite de Navarre, and Milton as pioneering early-modern selves we can add Montaigne, Hamlet, and even Don Quixote. The last figure alerts us to reading's essential role in this transformation, the printing press serving an analogous function in the 16th and subsequent centuries to that of television and the Internet in our own. Reading, as Robinson puts it, "is an act of great inwardness and subjectivity." "The soul encountered itself in response to a text, first Genesis or Matthew and then 'Paradise Lost' or 'Leaves of Grass.'" With Protestantism and printing, the quest for the divine voice became available to, even incumbent upon, everyone.

But it is with Romanticism that solitude achieved its greatest cultural salience, becoming both literal and literary. Protestant solitude is still only figurative. Rousseau and Wordsworth made it physical. The self was now encountered not in God but in Nature, and to encounter Nature one had to go to it. And go to it with a special sensibility: The poet displaced the saint as social seer and cultural model. But because Romanticism also inherited the 18th-century idea of social sympathy, Romantic solitude existed in a dialectical relationship with sociability— if less for Rousseau and still less for Thoreau, the most famous solitary of all, then certainly for Wordsworth, Melville, Whitman, and many others. For Emerson, "the soul environs itself with friends, that it may enter into a grander self-acquaintance or solitude; and it goes alone, for a season, that it may exalt its conversation or society." The Romantic practice of solitude is neatly captured by Trilling's "sincerity": the belief that the self is validated by a congruity of public appearance and private essence, one that stabilizes its relationship with both itself and others. Especially, as Emerson suggests, one beloved other. Hence the famous Romantic friendship pairs: Goethe and Schiller, Wordsworth and Coleridge, Hawthorne and Melville.

Modernism decoupled this dialectic. Its notion of solitude was harsher, more adversarial, more isolating. As a model of the self and its interactions, Hume's social sympathy gave way to Pater's thick wall of personality and Freud's narcissism—the sense that the soul, self-enclosed and inaccessible to others, can't choose but be alone. With exceptions, like Woolf, the modernists fought shy of friendship. Joyce and Proust disparaged it; D.H. Lawrence was wary of it; the modernist friendship pairs—Conrad and Ford, Eliot and Pound, Hemingway and Fitzgerald—were altogether cooler than their Romantic counterparts. The world was now understood as an assault on the self, and with good reason.

The Romantic ideal of solitude developed in part as a reaction to the emergence of the modern city. In modernism, the city is not only more menacing than ever, it has become inescapable, a labyrinth: Eliot's London, Joyce's Dublin. The mob, the human mass, presses in. Hell is other people. The soul is forced back into itself—hence the development of a more austere, more embattled form of self-validation, Trilling's "authenticity," where the essential relationship is only with oneself. (Just as there are few good friendships in modernism, so are there few good marriages.) Solitude becomes, more than ever, the arena of heroic self-discovery, a voyage through interior realms made vast and terrifying by Nietzschean and Freudian insights. To achieve authenticity is to look upon these visions without flinching; Trilling's exemplar here is Kurtz. Protestant self-examination becomes Freudian analysis, and the culture hero, once a prophet of God and then a poet of Nature, is now a novelist of self—a Dostoyevsky, a Joyce, a Proust.

But we no longer live in the modernist city, and our great fear is not submersion by the mass but isolation from the herd. Urbanization gave way to suburbanization, and with it the universal threat of loneliness. What technologies of transportation exacerbated—we could live farther and farther apart—technologies of communication redressed—we could bring ourselves closer and closer together. Or at least, so we have imagined. The first of these technologies, the first simulacrum of proximity, was the telephone. "Reach out and touch someone." But through the 70s and 80s, our isolation grew. Suburbs, sprawling ever farther, became exurbs. Families grew smaller or splintered apart, mothers left the home to work. The electronic hearth became the television in every room. Even in childhood, certainly in adolescence, we were each trapped inside our own cocoon. Soaring crime rates, and even more sharply escalating rates of moral panic, pulled children off the streets. The idea that you could go outside and run around the neighborhood with your friends, once unquestionable, has now become unthinkable. The child who grew up between the world wars as part of an extended family within a tight-knit urban community became the grandparent of a kid who sat alone in front of a big television, in a big house, on a big lot. We were lost in space.

Under those circumstances, the Internet arrived as an incalculable blessing. We should never forget that. It has allowed isolated people to communicate with one another and marginalized people to find one another. The busy parent can stay in touch with far-flung friends. The gay teenager no longer has to feel like a freak. But as the Internet's dimensionality has grown, it has quickly become too much of a good thing. Ten years ago we were writing e-mail messages on desktop computers and transmitting them over dial-up connections. Now we are sending text messages on our cellphones, posting pictures on our Facebook pages, and following complete strangers on Twitter. A constant stream of mediated contact, virtual, notional, or simulated, keeps us wired in to the electronic hive—though contact, or at least two-way contact, seems increasingly beside the point. The goal now, it seems, is simply to become known, to turn oneself into a sort of miniature celebrity. How many friends do I have on Facebook? How many people are reading my blog? How many Google hits does my name generate? Visibility secures our self-esteem, becoming a substitute, twice removed, for genuine connection. Not long ago, it was easy to feel lonely. Now, it is impossible to be alone.

As a result, we are losing both sides of the Romantic dialectic. What does friendship mean when you have 532 "friends"? How does it enhance my sense of closeness when my Facebook News Feed tells me that Sally Smith (whom I haven't seen since high school, and wasn't all that friendly with even then) "is making coffee and staring off into space"? My students told me they have little time for intimacy. And of course, they have no time at all for solitude.

But at least friendship, if not intimacy, is still something they want. As jarring as the new dispensation may be for people in their 30s and 40s, the real problem is that it has become completely natural for people in their teens and 20s. Young people today seem to have no desire for solitude, have never heard of it, can't imagine why it would be worth having. In fact, their use of technology—or to be fair, our use of technology—seems to involve a constant effort to stave off the possibility of solitude, a continuous attempt, as we sit alone at our computers, to maintain the imaginative presence of others. As long ago as 1952, Trilling wrote about "the modern fear of being cut off from the social group even for a moment." Now we have equipped ourselves with the means to prevent that fear from ever being realized. Which does not mean that we have put it to rest. Quite the contrary. Remember my student, who couldn't even write a paper by herself. The more we keep aloneness at bay, the less are we able to deal with it and the more terrifying it gets.

There is an analogy, it seems to me, with the previous generation's experience of boredom. The two emotions, loneliness and boredom, are closely allied. They are also both characteristically modern. The Oxford English Dictionary's earliest citations of either word, at least in the contemporary sense, date from the 19th century. Suburbanization, by eliminating the stimulation as well as the sociability of urban or traditional village life, exacerbated the tendency to both. But the great age of boredom, I believe, came in with television, precisely because television was designed to palliate that feeling. Boredom is not a necessary consequence of having nothing to do, it is only the negative experience of that state. Television, by obviating the need to learn how to make use of one's lack of occupation, precludes one from ever discovering how to enjoy it. In fact, it renders that condition fearsome, its prospect intolerable. You are terrified of being bored—so you turn on the television.

I speak from experience. I grew up in the 60s and 70s, the age of television. I was trained to be bored; boredom was cultivated within me like a precious crop. (It has been said that consumer society wants to condition us to feel bored, since boredom creates a market for stimulation.) It took me years to discover—and my nervous system will never fully adjust to this idea; I still have to fight against boredom, am permanently damaged in this respect—that having nothing to do doesn't have to be a bad thing. The alternative to boredom is what Whitman called idleness: a passive receptivity to the world.

So it is with the current generation's experience of being alone. That is precisely the recognition implicit in the idea of solitude, which is to loneliness what idleness is to boredom. Loneliness is not the absence of company, it is grief over that absence. The lost sheep is lonely; the shepherd is not lonely. But the Internet is as powerful a machine for the production of loneliness as television is for the manufacture of boredom. If six hours of television a day creates the aptitude for boredom, the inability to sit still, a hundred text messages a day creates the aptitude for loneliness, the inability to be by yourself. Some degree of boredom and loneliness is to be expected, especially among young people, given the way our human environment has been attenuated. But technology amplifies those tendencies. You could call your schoolmates when I was a teenager, but you couldn't call them 100 times a day. You could get together with your friends when I was in college, but you couldn't always get together with them when you wanted to, for the simple reason that you couldn't always find them. If boredom is the great emotion of the TV generation, loneliness is the great emotion of the Web generation. We lost the ability to be still, our capacity for idleness. They have lost the ability to be alone, their capacity for solitude.

And losing solitude, what have they lost? First, the propensity for introspection, that examination of the self that the Puritans, and the Romantics, and the modernists (and Socrates, for that matter) placed at the center of spiritual life—of wisdom, of conduct. Thoreau called it fishing "in the Walden Pond of [our] own natures," "bait[ing our] hooks with darkness." Lost, too, is the related propensity for sustained reading. The Internet brought text back into a televisual world, but it brought it back on terms dictated by that world—that is, by its remapping of our attention spans. Reading now means skipping and skimming; five minutes on the same Web page is considered an eternity. This is not reading as Marilynne Robinson described it: the encounter with a second self in the silence of mental solitude.

But we no longer believe in the solitary mind. If the Romantics had Hume and the modernists had Freud, the current psychological model—and this should come as no surprise—is that of the networked or social mind. Evolutionary psychology tells us that our brains developed to interpret complex social signals. According to David Brooks, that reliable index of the social-scientific zeitgeist, cognitive scientists tell us that "our decision-making is powerfully influenced by social context"; neuroscientists, that we have "permeable minds" that function in part through a process of "deep imitation"; psychologists, that "we are organized by our attachments"; sociologists, that our behavior is affected by "the power of social networks." The ultimate implication is that there is no mental space that is not social (contemporary social science dovetailing here with postmodern critical theory). One of the most striking things about the way young people relate to one another today is that they no longer seem to believe in the existence of Thoreau's "darkness."

The MySpace page, with its shrieking typography and clamorous imagery, has replaced the journal and the letter as a way of creating and communicating one's sense of self. The suggestion is not only that such communication is to be made to the world at large rather than to oneself or one's intimates, or graphically rather than verbally, or performatively rather than narratively or analytically, but also that it can be made completely. Today's young people seem to feel that they can make themselves fully known to one another. They seem to lack a sense of their own depths, and of the value of keeping them hidden.

If they didn't, they would understand that solitude enables us to secure the integrity of the self as well as to explore it. Few have shown this more beautifully than Woolf. In the middle of *Mrs. Dalloway,* between her navigation of the streets and her orchestration of the party, between the urban jostle and the social bustle, Clarissa goes up, "like a nun withdrawing," to her attic room. Like a nun: She returns to a state that she herself thinks of as a kind of virginity. This does not mean she's a prude. Virginity is classically the outward sign of spiritual inviolability, of a self untouched by the world, a soul that has preserved its integrity by refusing to descend into the chaos and self-division of sexual and social relations. It is the mark of the saint and the monk, of Hippolytus and Antigone and Joan of Arc. Solitude is both the social image of that state and the means by which we can approximate it. And the supreme image in *Mrs. Dalloway* of the dignity of solitude itself is the old woman whom Clarissa catches sight of through her window. "Here was one room," she thinks, "there another." We are not merely social beings. We are each also separate, each solitary, each alone in our own room, each miraculously our unique selves and mysteriously enclosed in that selfhood.

To remember this, to hold oneself apart from society, is to begin to think one's way beyond it. Solitude, Emerson said, "is to genius the stern friend." "He who should inspire and lead his race must be defended from traveling with the souls of other men, from living, breathing, reading, and writing in the daily, time-worn yoke of their opinions." One must protect oneself from the momentum of intellectual and moral consensus—especially, Emerson added, during youth. "God is alone," Thoreau said, "but the Devil, he is far from being alone; he sees a great deal of company; he is legion." The university was to be praised, Emerson believed, if only because it provided its charges with "a separate chamber and fire"—the physical space of solitude. Today, of course, universities do everything they can to keep their students from being alone, lest they perpetrate self-destructive acts, and also, perhaps, unfashionable thoughts. But no real excellence, personal or social, artistic, philosophical, scientific or moral, can arise without solitude. "The saint and poet seek privacy," Emerson said, "to ends the most public and universal." We are back to the seer, seeking signposts for the future in splendid isolation.

Solitude isn't easy, and isn't for everyone. It has undoubtedly never been the province of more than a few. "I believe," Thoreau said, "that men are generally still a little afraid of the dark." Teresa and Tiresias will always be the exceptions, or to speak in more relevant terms, the young people—and they still exist—who prefer to loaf and invite their soul, who step to the beat of a different drummer. But if solitude disappears as a social value and social idea, will even the exceptions remain possible? Still, one is powerless to reverse the drift of the culture. One can only save oneself—and whatever else happens, one can still always do that. But it takes a willingness to be unpopular.

The last thing to say about solitude is that it isn't very polite. Thoreau knew that the "doubleness" that solitude cultivates, the ability to stand back and observe life dispassionately, is apt to make us a little unpleasant to our fellows, to say nothing of the offense implicit in avoiding their company. But then, he didn't worry overmuch about being genial. He didn't even like having to talk to people three times a day, at meals; one can only imagine what he would have made of text-messaging. We, however, have made of geniality—the weak smile, the polite interest, the fake invitation—a cardinal virtue. Friendship may be slipping from our grasp, but our friendliness is universal. Not for nothing does "gregarious" mean "part of the herd." But Thoreau understood that securing one's self-possession was worth a few wounded feelings. He may have put his neighbors off, but at least he was sure of himself. Those who would find solitude must not be afraid to stand alone.

Critical Thinking

1. Deresiewicz's piece is a cry from the heart. Do you agree when he says that "If six hours of television a day creates the aptitude for boredom, the inability to sit still, a hundred text messages a day creates the aptitude for loneliness, the inability to be by yourself"?

2. Do you read books for pleasure? According to Steve Jobs (Article 5), 40% of Americans read one book or fewer last year. Do some research to find out if this represents a decline. Be sure to take into account income and educational status.

3. Walter J. Ong (use the Internet to learn more about him) says in *Orality and Literacy* (Routledge 2002) that the personal diary was unknown before the 17th century. What is the relationship between solitude and the personal diary?

4. Is there a difference between keeping a diary with pen and ink and maintaining a blog?

5. Are you alone when you are updating your Facebook page, even though you might be the only person in the room?

WILLIAM DERESIEWICZ writes essays and reviews for a variety of publications. He taught at Yale University from 1998 to 2008.

Relationships, Community, and Identity in the New Virtual Society

As we spend more of our social lives online, the definitions of relationships and families are shifting. A business futurist offers an overview of these trends and what they imply for organizations in the coming years.

ARNOLD BROWN

In India, where for centuries marriages have been arranged by families, online dating services such as BharatMatrimony.com are profoundly changing embedded traditions.

MyGamma, a Singapore-based mobile phone social networking site, has millions of users throughout Asia and Africa, giving social networking capability to people across continents—no personal computer necessary.

In China, individuals have been participating in *wang hun* (online role-play marriages). These gaming sites are causing actual married couples to get divorced on the grounds that this constitutes adultery—even though no face-to-face meetings ever took place.

And Web sites such as GeneTree.com and Ancestry.com, which offer inexpensive cheek-swab DNA tests, link up people throughout the world who have similar DNA, thus combining genealogy, medical technology, and social networking.

Clearly the Internet has radically reshaped our social lives over the span of just a couple of decades, luring us into a virtual metaworld where traditional interactions—living, loving, belonging, and separating, as well as finding customers and keeping them—require new protocols.

Relationships Take on a Digital Dimension

The future of falling in love may be online. Dating sites, once considered a gimmicky way to meet and connect with new people, have grown immensely in popularity, thanks in part to the convergence of information technologies and digital entertainment. Facilitating and managing relationships online is projected to become close to a billion-dollar industry in the United States in 2011.

In the new Virtual Society, we will see an increasing transition from basic matchmaking sites to sites that enable people to actually go out on online "dates" without ever leaving their desks. While face-to-face dating will never entirely disappear, the process—and even relationships themselves—will happen more and more in virtual space.

Especially for young people, relationships made in virtual space can be just as powerful and meaningful as those formed in the real world. Additionally, as more people gain access to broadband technologies, an increasing number are seeking social connectivity this way. There are already at least 500 million mobile broadband users globally. The speed and flexibility with which people communicate and socialize online will likely only continue to increase.

Technology doesn't just bring people together, though. As Douglas Rushkoff points out in *Program or Be Programmed* (OR Books, 2010), cyberspace creates a temporal and spatial separation from which it becomes seemingly easier to accomplish unpleasant interpersonal tasks. Hence, the *techno brush-off:* breaking up with a significant other via e-mail or text message.

This will increasingly be a dominant fixture of the global youth culture. Young people everywhere link up through IM, Twitter, blogs, smart-phones, and social networking sites that are proliferating at an accelerating rate. This is a critical point for businesses to understand. The emerging generation is part of what is, in essence, a vast new cross-border empire. It is marked by an instant awareness of what's new, what's hot, what's desirable—and what's not. This is the group that pollster John Zogby, in his book *The Way We'll Be* (Random House, 2008), calls the First Globals. His research shows that their expectations of products and services will be vastly different and that they will force businesses to redefine their offerings.

Young people will not, as their elders did, simply adapt to the technology. The new youth cyberculture will continue to find ways to adapt the technology to their needs and desires. For example, Ning, created in 2005 by Netscape co-founder Marc Andreessen, enables people to create their own individual social network—not join a preexisting world but actually build their own. A Web site called paper.li creates a personalized newspaper for you everyday based on whom you follow on Twitter and whether or not they said anything particularly important in the last 24 hours (as measured by retweets). Your friend's brilliant blog post about last night's St. Patrick's Day party could appear directly next to Tim O'Reilly or Bruce Sterling's most recent missive on China's Internet policy. It's hard to imagine a local newspaper providing that sort of personalized content.

But online relationships are not exclusively reserved for young people. As the elderly become more comfortable with the Internet, they will increasingly turn to alternative spaces, such as virtual worlds, to find company or meet people with similar interests. By 2008, more than 20 million social networkers in the United States were over the age of 50, according to a study by Deloitte. There have been a slew of media reports playing up the fact that many seniors are joining Facebook and Twitter, as well as becoming an increasingly significant part of the growing commercial activity in virtual worlds.

Commercializing Communities

More and more people regard the virtual world as a place where they can establish and maintain safer, less demanding relationships on their own time. Ease, flexibility, and relative anonymity will continue to be three key components of dating online. Monetization will happen quickly, as virtual restaurants, movie theaters, concerts, and even wedding chapels are established.

In addition to using virtual worlds as test markets for real-life products and services, as is done now, businesses will offer a much wider variety of virtual products and services. Having these options would give a substantive feel to online relationships. The more real and satisfying these relationships can be made to seem, the more they will attract and hold people, and the more money they will generate.

Commercialized virtual venues such as upscale bars and coffeehouses could even be looked to as testing grounds to develop the social skills necessary to form meaningful human relationships. Businesses could use game applications like Mall World or Café World on Facebook as platforms to advertise various specials that occur in virtual space, ranging from coupons for those aforementioned simulations of bars and coffeehouses to discounts for two to "live" streaming concert events. Advertising boards could promote online activities and events such as speed dating in a virtual nightclub setting. All this will dramatically change the nature of relationships.

As social researchers have pointed out, the Internet is programming us as well, starting at an early age. For example, there are combination social networking and gaming sites for children such as Disney's Club Penguin. Children are developing social skills within these virtual worlds. What this will mean in terms of how they will start, maintain, and end "real" friendships and relationships in the future is anyone's guess.

But the Internet can also strengthen family ties because it provides a continuously connected presence. In Norway, for example, one study showed that college students were in touch with their parents on average 10 times a week. Young people use mobile devices to Skype, text, upload photos and videos to Facebook, and more, with increasing frequency. Cyberspace enables families and friends to converse, in effect, as if they were in the same room. This is part of the reason that the Millennial generation reported feeling closer to their parents than did their older siblings during adolescence, according to the Pew Internet and American Life Survey.

So what does all this tell us? For one thing, the temporal and spatial "here-and-now" limitations that formerly characterized social interactions such as dating and family get-togethers have broken down. The composition of, and behavior in, relationships and households in the future will therefore change seriously. These trends are powerfully affecting how companies and organizations will design, sell, and market a wide range of products and services to consumers, with a growing emphasis on individualization and personalization. For instance, if relationships and families are more virtual, we should see an increase in the construction of new kinds of single-person housing units or dual sleeping quarters.

Family formation will need to be flexible and adaptive. The nuclear family was a response to the Industrial Age, in large measure replacing the extended family that characterized the Agricultural Era. It spurred vast economic shifts and led to new multibillion-dollar industries, from autos to washing machines to personal telephones. We are already seeing indications that the family is morphing into other forms as the Virtual Age approaches. Employers and governments will see their social, human resources, financial services, and benefits programs challenged, as the new economy takes great advantage of these multiple, newly unfolding personal relationships. For instance, should a "virtual spouse" be able to claim the Social Security benefits of a partner? The easy answer is, of course not. But what if it's the virtual spouse who is charged with monitoring the health of an aged parent remotely? What if he or she does the household bill-paying, or even contributes half of the household income? In other words, what if the virtual spouse performs many if not all of the tasks associated with a traditional spouse? And should the same polygamy laws applied to regular marriages also apply to virtual marriages? Should such marriages be subject to the same taxation laws?

With the advent of an electronic era, many social scientists and other "experts" decried what they saw as a loss of social capital—the so-called "Bowling Alone" theory—because people were supposedly decreasing their participation in such things as bowling leagues. The big mistake that the fearful always make is to equate change with destruction. The social turmoil of the 1970s was heralded by such observers as "the destruction of the family." But the family did not die; it just changed—and it is still changing.

Similarly, social capital is not going away; it is too intrinsic to human nature, although aspects of it may well be changing, and it is important that you view these changes objectively if you want to understand what they are and what they mean to you.

Social ties are being created, strengthened, and—yes—weakened in an almost unbelievable variety of ways. This has to entail, as well, the remaking and establishing of both a deeper and a shallower social capital. Someone with more than

The Reality of Virtual Feelings

Advances in brain research and multisensory perception could play an important role in the development of virtual relationships. Neural devices already allow people to control electronic equipment such as wheelchairs, televisions, and video games via brain–computer interfaces.

One day soon, avatars may also be controllable this way. Virtual reality may become so advanced that it could trick the brain into thinking the invented images it is responding to are real—and human emotions would follow accordingly. Avatars will cause people to feel love, hate, jealousy, etc. And as haptic technologies improve, our abilities to respond physically to our virtual partners will also improve.

Sexual pleasure may be routinely available without any inter-human stimulation at all.

If it becomes possible to connect virtual reality programs directly to the brain, thoughts and emotions may also be digitized, rendered binary and reduced to 0s and 1s. Feelings of satisfaction and pleasure (two key components in any relationship) could be created between avatars without any "real" stimulus at all. But would they be real or mimetic?

Once humans begin to perceive virtual social interactions as actually having occurred, it will greatly impact individuals, relationships, communities, and society as a whole.

—Arnold Brown

3,000 Facebook friends probably has more than 2,000 shallow friendships, but there's a tremendous amount of variety in that number; some of these friendships are viable clients, others may be service providers, others may be long-term friend prospects, or secret crushes, or members of a social circle to which the person with 3,000 friendships wants access; some of them will be annoying people encountered only once at a party, be grudgingly given the status of "friend" to avoid seeming rude. All of these friendships have their own unique value. But Facebook sees little difference among them outside of how they are designated in privacy settings (some people can see more private posts than others). Outside institutions don't recognize any distinction among these virtual friendships, if they recognize such friendships at all.

Sociologist Richard Ling has labeled the new communication phenomenon *micro-coordination*—as people are constantly planning, coordinating, and changing plans because their cyberconnections are always on. University of Southern California sociologist Manuel Castells says that adolescents today build and rebuild social networks via constant messaging. This is helped by the fact that they have what he calls "a safe autonomous pattern," in that their parents are only a speed dial away.

Sociologists describe two kinds of social ties: strong ties of family members and those with shared values, beliefs, and identities; and weak ties to acquaintances and other people with shallower connections. According to some researchers, the Internet and, in particular, mobile devices are enabling the strong community ties to be reinforced, often at the expense of the weak ties. At a time when technology is being lauded for encouraging diversity and facilitating cross-cultural communication, there is, consequently, a strong and growing counter-trend: digital tribalism. Aside from strengthening ties to family and close friends, people are using the technology to find others with whom they share important affinities, ranging from genomes to beliefs to lifestyle choices. This digital form of tribalism is an unexpectedly strong trend, as observed by social critics such as Christine Rosen.

Information—including product and service information—spreads electronically with speed and power. Effectively getting a positive message on a tribal network could well be tomorrow's best marketing strategy. Although the tribal identity can be deep and solid, brand connections may not necessarily be so. Maintaining the connection will require constant monitoring of the electronic tribal village and quickness to reposition or reinforce when required.

Bridal showers, for instance, can be attended by distant guests through Skype, and e-registries allow gift givers to view what others have bought. There is much room for innovation here, in terms of bringing people together who would not otherwise be in the same place for business meetings, financial planning, meal sharing, celebrations, and more. Associations might capitalize on online events for far-flung and numerous businesses, professionals, and friends and families of members. Employers might do the same for their employees' personal networks, perhaps offering discounts, education, job postings, and new products to all "friends of friends."

Expat workers and members of the armed forces might be more easily enabled to stay in touch with their families if their employers organized better around online communications and communities. This would ease the burden on relocated personnel, improve morale, attract more people, increase productivity, and spin the sale of products and service to these populations. This could also be true for alumni networks and other diaspora groups.

The Identity Industry

Social scientists make the distinction between a found identity and a made identity. The found identity is one created by your circumstances—who your parents were, your ethnic background, your religion, your sex, where you went to school, your profession, and all the other external factors that people use to categorize and describe you. The made identity, on the other hand, is the one you create for yourself. It is how you wish to see yourself and how you want others to see you.

In the past, people who wanted to escape what they saw as the trap of their found identity did such things as change their name or appearance. They moved somewhere else. Now, and increasingly in the future, technology will let you make and remake your identity at will—virtually. This extraordinary, even revolutionary, development will profoundly affect fundamental societal values such as trust and reliability.

In addition to engaging directly online with other individuals, you can also interact with them through avatars, the images that represent you (or an idealized version of yourself) in virtual worlds. Each virtual world requires a separate avatar, so in effect you can be as many different people as there are virtual worlds. In the future, you will be able to create avatars that will literally take on lives of their own. They will, once created, be able to "think" on their own, without further input from you. They may be able to perform intensive research tasks for you, start and even manage online companies, maintain your social relationships by reading your Facebook updates and blog posts and analyzing them for significant news so you don't have to.

Increasingly, over time, distinctions between real and virtual identity will become less sharply defined, particularly for people who spend substantial amounts of time in the virtual world—or some enhanced combination of the real and the virtual. A company called Total Immersion combines 3-D and augmented reality technology on the Internet, inserting people and physical objects into live video feeds. According to the company's Web site, "this digital processing mixes real and virtual worlds together, in real time."

All this could lead to growing confusion about identity. We will go from "Who am I?" to "Who, when, and where am I?" What in the twentieth century was seen as a problem that needed treatment—multiple personalities—will increasingly be seen in the twenty-first century as a coping mechanism, greatly affecting the evolving economy, as multiple personas split their expenditures in multiple ways. Companies that provide such services will be a great growth industry as we move further into the "Who are you, really?" era.

Critical Thinking

1. Count the number of times the future tense is used in this article. Now use the Internet to listen to: http://freakonomicsradio.com/hour-lonq-special-the-folly-of-prediction.html. What is Freakonomics?

2. Brown says that "Clearly the Internet has radically reshaped our social lives over the span of just a couple of decades. . . ." Who is "our"? Ask your parents if their social lives are different now than they were two decades ago.

3. Brown says "face-to-face dating will never entirely disappear." This suggests that it has been around for millennia. Do some research to find out when face-to-face dating, as you understand it, first appeared in the United States and Europe.

4. Arnold distinguishes between *found* and *made* identities. What are they?

5. Do you distinguish between your real and virtual identity? How is your online presentation different from your "real" identity? Why do you suppose *real* is enclosed within quotes?

ARNOLD BROWN is the chairman of Weiner, Edrich, Brown, Inc., and the coauthor (with Edie Weiner) of *FutureThink: How to Think Clearly in a Time of Change* (Pearson Prentice Hall, 2006). E-mail arnold@weineredrichbrown.com. Web site www.weineredrichbrown.com.

Generational Myth
Not All Young People Are Tech-Savvy

Siva Vaidhyanathan

Consider all the pundits, professors, and pop critics who have wrung their hands over the inadequacies of the so-called digital generation of young people filling our colleges and jobs. Then consider those commentators who celebrate the creative brilliance of digitally adept youth. To them all, I want to ask: Whom are you talking about? There is no such thing as a "digital generation."

In the introduction to his book *Print Is Dead: Books in Our Digital Age* (Macmillan) last year, Jeff Gomez posits that young Americans constitute a distinct generation that shares a sensibility: resistance to the charms of printed and bound books. Gomez, who has been a sales-and-marketing director for a number of global publishers, has written a trade book whose title and thesis demands that we ignore it. Alas, I could not.

"The needs of an entire generation of 'Digital Natives'—kids who have grown up with the Internet, and are accustomed to the entire world being only a mouse click away—are going unanswered by traditional print media like books, magazines, and newspapers," Gomez writes. "For this generation—which Googles rather than going to the library—print seems expensive, a bore, and a waste of time."

When I read that, I shuddered. I shook my head. I rolled my eyes. And I sighed. I have been hearing some version of the "kids today" or "this generation believes" argument for more than a dozen years of studying and teaching about digital culture and technology. As a professor, I am in the constant company of 18- to-23-year-olds. I have taught at both public and private universities, and I have to report that the levels of comfort with, understanding of, and dexterity with digital technology varies greatly within every class. Yet it has not changed in the aggregate in more than 10 years.

Every class has a handful of people with amazing skills and a large number who can't deal with computers at all. A few lack mobile phones. Many can't afford any gizmos and resent assignments that demand digital work. Many use Facebook and MySpace because they are easy and fun, not because they are powerful (which, of course, they are not). And almost none know how to program or even code text with Hypertext Markup Language (HTML). Only a handful come to college with a sense of how the Internet fundamentally differs from the other major media platforms in daily life.

College students in America are not as "digital" as we might wish to pretend. And even at elite universities, many are not rich enough. All this mystical talk about a generational shift and all the claims that kids won't read books are just not true. Our students read books when books work for them (and when I tell them to). And they all (I mean all) tell me that they prefer the technology of the bound book to the PDF or Web page. What kids, like the rest of us, don't like is the price of books.

Of course they use Google, but not very well—just like my 75-year-old father. And they fill the campus libraries at all hours, just as Americans of all ages are using libraries in record numbers. (According to the American Library Association, visits to public libraries in the United States increased 61 percent from 1994 to 2004.)

What do we miss when we pay attention only to the perceived digital prejudices of American college students? Most high-school graduates in the United States do not end up graduating from four-year universities with bachelor's degrees. According to the National Center for Education Statistics, in 2007 only some 28 percent of adults 25 and older had completed bachelor's degrees or higher. Is it just college-educated Americans who are eligible for generational status?

Talk of a "digital generation" or people who are "born digital" willfully ignores the vast range of skills, knowledge, and experience of many segments of society. It ignores the needs and perspectives of those young people who are not socially or financially privileged. It presumes a level playing field and equal access to time, knowledge, skills, and technologies. The ethnic, national, gender, and *class biases* of any sort of generation talk are troubling. And they could not be more obvious than when discussing assumptions about digital media.

As Henry Jenkins, a media-studies professor at the Massachusetts Institute of Technology, wrote on his blog last year, "Talking about youth as digital natives implies that there is a world which these young people all share and a body of knowledge they have all mastered, rather than seeing the online world as unfamiliar and uncertain for all of us." Such discussions, he said, also risk ignoring the different ways young people use digital tools, from listening to compact discs to blogging to posting clever videos on YouTube to buying stuff on eBay.

In reaction to Jenkins's post, Leslie Johnston, now at the Library of Congress, wrote on her blog, "I have worked with faculty in their 60s who saw something in being digital decades ago and have worked in that realm for years. I have worked with colleagues—librarians and faculty—in my own age group (I'm 44) who hate all technology with a passion and others who embrace it in all ways. I have worked with students at three different research universities who could not care less about being digital."

On my blog, Sivacracy, Elizabeth Losh, writing director of the humanities core course at the University of California at Irvine and author of the forthcoming *Virtualpolitik: An Electronic History of Government Media-Making in Time of War, Scandal, Disaster, Miscommunication, and Mistakes* (MIT Press, 2009), kept the online conversation going: "Unlike many in today's supposed 'digital generation,' we learned real programming skills—with punch cards in the beginning—from the time we were in elementary school. What passes for 'media literacy' now is often nothing more than teaching kids to make prepackaged PowerPoint presentations." Losh also pointed out that the supposed existence of a digital generation has had an impact on education, as distance-learning corporations with bells-and-whistles technology get public attention while traditional classroom teaching is ignored.

Once we assume that all young people love certain forms of interaction and hate others, we forge policies and design systems and devices that match those presumptions. By doing so, we either pander to some marketing cliché or force an otherwise diverse group of potential users into a one-size-fits-all system that might not meet their needs. Then, lo and behold, young people rush to adapt to those changes that we assumed all along that they wanted. More precisely, we take actions like rushing to digitize entire state-university library systems with an emphasis on speed and size rather than on quality and utility.

Ask any five people when Generation X started and ended. You will get five different answers. The borders of membership could not be more arbitrary. Talking as if all people born between 1964 and (pick a year after 1974) share some discernible, unifying traits or experiences is about as useful as saying that all Capricorns are the same. Such talk is not based on any sociological or demographic definition of a generation; it's based on whatever topic is in question.

Invoking "generations" demands an exclusive focus on people of wealth and means, because they get to express their preferences (for music, clothes, technology, etc.) in ways that are easy to count. It tends to exclude immigrants and non-English-speaking Americans, not to mention those who live beyond the borders of the United States. And it excludes anyone on the margins of mainstream consumer or cultural behavior.

The baby boom was a real demographic event. But what baby boomers share is Medicare—or at least they will soon. That's pretty much the end of the list. America, even in the 1950s and 1960s, was too diverse a place for uniform assumptions to hold true. It's even more diverse now.

Historical phenomena such as the Vietnam War matter to entire populations in complicated ways. Vietnam affected almost everyone in America who was 18 to 25 at the time. But it affected everyone differently. Let's not pretend that the war was not traumatic to those older than 25. Those who served did not share the zeitgeist with those who resisted. Women and men experienced it differently. The poor tended to serve. The rich did not. Remember how many people assumed in 1972 that there was some great generational mood or attitude that would pull voters to George McGovern in the first election in which 18- to 20-year-olds could vote? Why don't we ask President McGovern how that turned out?

By focusing on wealthy, white, educated people, as journalists and pop-trend analysts tend to do, we miss out on the whole truth. Generation X and the Greatest Generation are just the stuff of book titles. And they are not even good books.

The strongest argument against the idea of generations was raised first by the 18th-century philosopher David Hume. People are constantly being born and dying, Hume noted. So political sensibilities (to cite one phenomenon often assigned to generations) tend not to be cleanly associated with a single cohort. They change gradually. That's why human history has so few revolutions. And when there are revolutions, they tend not to separate generations.

I realize that by puncturing the myth of generations, I am pitting myself against one of the giants of 20th-century social theory, Karl Mannheim. In his 1927 essay, "The Problem of Generations," Mannheim answered Hume by positing that generations are not demographically determined, but historically. Big events forge common identities. And proximity to an experience matters more than birth year. In other words, a Mannheimian generation might exist among all people who breathed in the ash and dust of the Twin Towers in New York City in 2001. But it might exclude people of the same age who merely watched the event on television from a comfortable couch in Madison, Wis.

Nor, Mannheim wrote, is a generation like an association, in which one claims membership or allegiance. Generation is a fluid and messy social category, not unlike class, he argued. As with class, members don't always know they are members. Members of generations, like classes, share "a common location in the social and historical process," he wrote, that predisposes them to certain modes of thought and action. A generation is one element of a fuller theory of cultural cohesion, mutation, and transmission.

Mannheim was arguing for an eclectic model of social analysis, one that does not rely too heavily on positivist principles of precision and accountability. He also wanted to use the concept of generation to delineate a set of human traits that biology alone could not explain. Finally, he wanted to establish that one's intellectual position in society is influenced by much more than class position, as orthodox Marxism of the day insisted. Thus generations were important explanatory mechanisms in his "sociology of knowledge."

By trying to do all that work, Mannheim's generations quickly crumbled. Generations seemed only to exist within nations, not across them; continuity existed between and among age cohorts; diversity of thought existed among members of a generation. Even if Mannheim's generations might have existed as a stable social category, they no longer do. Germany, Hungary, and England in the 1920s were hardly as diverse and globalized as those countries are now.

None of this means that nothing changes. Nor that we should not study youth, even privileged subcultures of youth, and their particular needs and problems. History is not static. Demography matters. But today's young people—including college students—are just more complicated than an analysis of imaginary generations can ever reveal. There are far better ways to study and write about them and their interactions with digital technologies than our current punditry offers.

A short list of the best of those who are studying and writing about the effects of digital media on youth must include Eszter Hargittai, a sociologist and associate professor of communications studies at Northwestern University, who has received a major grant from the John D.

and Catherine T. MacArthur Foundation to study digital communication and youth. In a recent paper in *Information, Communication & Society,* "The Participation Divide: Content Creation and Sharing in the Digital Age," Hargittai and Gina Walejko conclude that the habit of creating digital content and sharing it across digital platforms correlates with a person's identity traits. When asked in an interview in the May 2 issue of *The Chronicle* which demographic groups are less Web-savvy than others, Hargittai responded that women, students of Hispanic origin, African-American students, and students whose parents have lower levels of education tend to have less mastery of the inner workings of digital technology than other groups do.

Hargittai explained why we tend to overestimate the digital skills of young people: "I think the assumption is that if [digital technology] was available from a young age for them, then they can use it better. Also, the people who tend to comment about technology use tend to be either academics or journalists or techies, and these three groups tend to understand some of these new developments better than the average person. Ask your average 18-year-old: Does he know what RSS means? And he won't."

A 2007–8 fellow at the Berkman Center for Internet and Society, at Harvard University, and a doctoral candidate at the University of California at Berkeley, danah boyd, has done a series of in-depth qualitative studies of young people's use of digital communication. In her paper "Why Youth (Heart) Social Network Sites: The Role of Networked Publics in Teenage Social Life," published in a volume edited by David Buckingham, *Youth, Identity, and Digital Media* (MIT Press, 2008), she has observed how digital spaces give young people a sense of autonomy and control that, for example, planned access and limited loitering spaces at shopping malls do not. She has also sparked an online conversation, however, by noting how the migration of some young people from MySpace to Facebook reflects a strong class component.

As Susan Herring urges in an insightful article, "Questioning the Generational Divide," also in the Buckingham volume, we should move our gaze from dazzling technologies and two-dimensional exotic beings—so-called "digital natives"—to young people themselves.

Even in her unfortunately titled yet sharp book, *Generation Digital: Politics, Commerce, and Childhood in the Age of the Internet* (MIT Press, 2007), the American University communications professor Kathryn C. Montgomery has criticized the news media for characterizing "all young people in monolithic and simplistic terms, defining them almost exclusively on the basis of technology."

But Montgomery is not alone in selling a book about a generation while undermining belief in its existence. The most prominent scholarly project aimed at making sense of the effects of digitization on young people remains invested in the notion that they "constitute a distinct tribe": Digital Natives, conducted at the Berkman center by its former executive director, John Palfrey. In August, Palfrey and Urs Gasser gave us *Born Digital: Understanding the First Generation of Digital Natives* (Basic Books), which argues that kids today are fundamentally different from the rest of us because their default modes of interaction involve mixing and mashing digital files and exposing (and rewriting) themselves through online profiles and avatars. That assumption bolsters the policy positions that the investigators already embraced: that the law should allow young people to remix and share bits of culture, while helping them respect and manage privacy. The policy goals are laudable. And the research is interesting. But Palfrey and Gasser did not need to render young people exotic to make their points. The concept of "born digital" flattens out the needs and experiences of young people into a uniform wish list of policies that conveniently matches the agenda of digital enthusiasts and entrepreneurs of all ages. Indeed, it is interesting that Palfrey and Gasser deny that their subjects constitute a "generation," conceding in their introduction that they are describing only the challenges of privileged young people.

Most alarming, Mark Bauerlein, a professor of English at Emory University, has recently written a jeremiad against young people and their digital habits, *The Dumbest Generation: How the Digital Age Stupefies Young Americans and Jeopardizes our Future* (Jeremy P. Tarcher/Penguin, 2008). Well, if there is one way to ensure that young people do not read more books than necessary, it is to call them dumb in the title of a book. The book is strongly argued, but the voices of those who concern the author are curiously absent.

There is much to admire in the book. Bauerlein assembles impressive evidence that American youth are terribly served by our current educational system. He deflates the grand folly of strategies like putting computers in the classroom and assuming that students will learn skills by sitting in front of them. But in blaming the digital moment for the problems of education, and government in general, he is off the mark.

Yes, young people may favor social-networking sites to the exclusion of political, news, or in-depth intellectual or cultural-commentary sites. But if the form is different, the malady is old. After all, Neil Postman, the late New York University professor who originated the anti-media jeremiad with *Amusing Ourselves to Death* (Viking, 1985), blamed television for restructuring our thought patterns and retarding our ability to think complex thoughts.

If the concept of a generation is unenlightening at best and harmful at worst, why do we persist in describing cultural, historical, and social change as generational? Sociologists have subsumed Mannheim's generational declarations within sophisticated theories of the "sociology of knowledge" and the "collective memory" of inherited culture. And professional historians rarely employ generations as historically determinative categories. Still, sociologist-sounding consultants like Neil Howe and the late William Strauss have built nice careers publishing shallow primers—like their books on millennials—on how to market goods and services to cartoon versions of various generations. They have pretty much owned the generations field to the point where real scholars will even cite their definitions of when baby boomers and Generation X begin and end. Howe and Strauss go to show you that you'll never go broke in America marketing to marketers. Or marketing to those who claim membership in particular generations. Journalists like Tom Brokaw invoke generations to forge rickety generalizations about people who were young in the 1940s and 1960s. Americans love thinking in generations because they keep us from examining uncomfortable ethnic, gender, and class distinctions too closely. Generations seem to explain everything.

But there is more to it. People fervently declare and defend generational identity. They clearly get something out it. Perhaps it's the same satisfaction that one gets out of other tribal identities, what Emile Durkheim called the "collective effervescence" of performed rituals. Feeling part of the "Woodstock generation" must generate some sort of warmth, comfort, or false nostalgia for those who caught the 1970 documentary film but missed the bus to the festival back in 1969.

We should drop our simplistic attachments to generations so we can generate an accurate and subtle account of the needs of young people—and all people, for that matter. A more responsible assessment would divorce itself from a pro-or anti-technology agenda and look at multiple causes for problems we note: state malfeasance or benign neglect of education, rampant consumerism in our culture, moral panics that lead us to scapegoat technology, and, yes, technology itself. Such work would reflect the fact that technologies do not emerge in a vacuum. They are subject to market forces, political ideologies, and policy incentives. More important, such work would not use young people as fodder for attacking wider social problems.

Too often we reach for easy, totalizing explanations for cultural phenomena, constructing cartoons of digital youth that have a tone of "gee whiz" or "shame, shame" to describe these new and odd creatures. The Who may have started this whole mess by recording an anthem steeped in the collective effervescence of "My Generation." But the Who also assured us that "The Kids Are Alright."

Critical Thinking

1. Who is the digital generation?

2. Take the author's suggestion: "Ask any five people when Generation X started and ended." Did you get, as he suggests, five different answers?

3. The author says that there is a strong class bias built-in to the assumption of digital natives. Do you agree?

4. The author says that "Germany, Hungary, and England in the 1920s were hardly as diverse and globalized as those countries are now." Wikipedia says that seven different languages were spoken in Hungary in 1910. How many are spoken there now?

5. Do you agree or disagree that the digital skills of young people are exaggerated? Use the Internet to find the names of five programming languages. How many have you used?

SIVA VAIDHYANATHAN is an associate professor of media studies and law at the University of Virginia. His next book, *The Googlization of Everything,* will be published in 2009 by the University of California Press.

Expressing My Inner Gnome: Appearance and Behavior in Virtual Worlds

Role-playing gamers take on the behavior they think appropriate for the "body" they inhabit in a virtual environment.

SHYONG (TONY) K. LAM AND JOHN RIEDL

Massively multiplayer online role-playing games, or MMORPGs, have captivated millions of videogame players worldwide. In games such as *World of Warcraft* (*WoW*) and *Second Life,* players can create unique avatars to represent them as they venture through virtual worlds with thousands of their peers. Although MMORPGs differ wildly in setting, ambiance, and game play, they all involve social interactions among players to accomplish tasks like defeating powerful monsters, exchanging goods and services, or simply getting to know one another.

In virtual worlds, avatars mediate social interactions. This raises the interesting question of how avatar appearance impacts those interactions. Does a three-foot-tall, pink-haired gnome behave and get treated differently than a giant, hulking orc, even if the same person controls both avatars? Nick Yee, a researcher at the Palo Alto Research Center (PARC), has conducted a series of studies exploring the relationship between avatar appearance and virtual behavior.

The 'Proteus Effect'

In one of the earliest studies, Yee and Jeremy Bailenson examined what they called the "Proteus Effect," named for the shape-changing Greek god ("The Proteus Effect: The Effect of Transformed Self-Representation on Behavior," *Human Communication Research,* July 2007, pp. 271–290). Their goal was to test the extent to which the "feeling" of having a character with a certain appearance shapes player behavior. In the real world, more attractive people tend to dominate social interactions in certain ways: they move closer to the people they are interacting with and are more open about sharing personal information about themselves. Yee and Bailenson wanted to know

whether that same behavior would occur with more attractive avatars in a virtual world.

. . . In a pilot study the researchers created an immersive 3-D environment that users could navigate with goggles and motion-sensitive headsets and ran a lab experiment in which participants interacted with a confederate in the virtual environment. Each participant was randomly assigned an avatar of high, medium, or low attractiveness, while the confederate's avatar was always of medium attractiveness. The researchers didn't tell the participants the purpose of the study and recorded everything that occurred during the interactions.

To prevent the experimental manipulation from impacting the confederate's behavior, the system was designed to reveal different views of the participant's avatar to the participant and to the confederate. Thus a participant might see himself or herself in a virtual mirror as very attractive, but the confederate saw every participant as having a generic human face. In this way, Yee and Bailenson ensured that any difference in how participants behaved was due only to self-perception and not to the confederate's reaction to how the participant's avatar looked.

The striking result of the pilot study was that participants assigned more attractive avatars did indeed behave more intimately when interacting. Compared to participants with less attractive avatars, they moved closer to the confederate's avatar when asked to do so and revealed more information when prompted to introduce themselves during a conversation.

In a second study with a similar setup, the researchers found that participants with tall avatars were much more confident in a negotiation task than those with shorter avatars. Participants with taller avatars tended to make offers more tilted in their own favor, while those with shorter avatars were twice as likely to capitulate and accept a patently unfair deal—even though the avatar's height was randomly assigned and independent of the participant's actual height.

Social Norms and Stereotypes

To examine the Proteus Effect in a more natural setting, Yee and his PARC colleagues explored the role of social norms and stereotypes in MMORPGs. In one study, Yee's team analyzed 8,418 dyads (pairs of people) interacting in *Second Life,* looking specifically at how each person's avatar was positioned and what it was looking at (N. Yee et al., "The Unbearable Likeness of Being Digital: The Persistence of Nonverbal Social Norms in Online Virtual Environments," *CyberPsychology & Behavior,* Feb. 2007, pp. 115–121). They found that real-world norms regarding gender, interpersonal distance, and eye gaze are also present in the virtual world.

In the real world, males tend to position themselves farther apart and are less likely to look at one another than females. Yee's group observed the same behavior in *Second Life:* male-male dyads positioned their avatars significantly farther apart than female-female or mixed-gender dyads, and male-male dyads maintained significantly less eye contact than female-female dyads. This result is intriguing because players in *Second Life* must use mice and keyboards to control their avatars' position and gaze, whereas in the real world people simply use their legs and eyes. Despite the difference in modalities, people apparently adhere to social norms in the virtual world.

Another study by Yee and his colleagues examined the relationship between player gender and avatar gender in *World of Warcraft* (Yee et al., "Do Men Heal More When in Drag? Conflicting Identity Cues between User and Avatar," *Proc. 2011 Ann. Conf. Human Factors in Computing Systems,* ACM Press, 2011, pp. 773–776).

Most players choose an avatar that matches their own gender, but a survey of 1,040 *WoW* players showed that a substantial proportion (about 25 percent) of players gender-bend for their primary character—that is, they intentionally choose to role-play as a character of the opposite gender. Gender-bending by players may cloud gender roles in a virtual world, as physical and virtual identity cues are in conflict with one another when players are gender-bending.

To study this phenomenon more closely, the researchers looked at two different activities in *WoW:* healing and player versus player (PvP) combat. Healing involves using an avatar's special abilities to help others by restoring health that they may have lost during combat. In PvP combat, players try to kill other players' avatars to complete various objectives such as capturing an opposing team's base. In many MMORPGs, PvP combat is a sanctioned competitive activity. The "Griefers in MMORPGs" sidebar provides examples of less consensual PvP activities.

A pretest survey confirmed gender stereotypes associated with these activities: healing is seen as preferred by females, while PvP combat is generally associated with males. Combining the survey data with information about players' in-game activities, Yee's team correlated both player and avatar gender to the amount of healing and PvP combat.

Griefers in MMORPGs

MMORPG players known as "griefers" are perhaps best described as the bullies and sociopaths of the virtual world. Griefers' motivations for attacking fellow players are largely intrinsic—they bask in schadenfreude as they watch their peers react, often angrily, to being killed.

In the science fiction MMORPG *EVE Online,* one group of griefers known as GoonFleet measures their success not by wealth or character advancement but by their ability to drive others away from the game. In an interview with technology journalist Julian Dibbell, GoonFleet's leader, Isaiah Houston, said "the ability to inflict that huge amount of actual, real-life damage on someone is amazingly satisfying. . . . The way that you win in *EVE* is you basically make life so miserable for someone else that they actually quit the game and don't come back" (www.wired.com/gaming/virtualworlds/magazine/16-02/mf_goons).

In one major space battle, GoonFleet was able to destroy one of the most powerful ships in the game, a Titan-class vessel with an estimated cost of about US$10,000 in virtual components. To accomplish this, they used hundreds of small, inexpensive ships to overwhelm not only the Titan, but also the *EVE Online* servers and players' network bandwidth. This tactic, considered by some to be an unsportsmanlike technical exploit, is intended to increase network latency and reduce game performance to the point where organizing an effective defense is difficult.

Griefers also take pleasure in causing general disruption.

Consider, for example, the Corrupted Blood incident in the MMORPG *World of Warcraft* that occurred in late 2005 (http://en.wikipedia.org/wiki/Corrupted_Blood_incident). Corrupted Blood was a contagious virtual disease that advanced players were exposed to when fighting Hakkar, a demon that had just been introduced to the game at the time. Corrupted Blood was intentionally designed to be a very short-term disease so that it would be confined to the immediate area around Hakkar. However, some players found loopholes in the game that enabled them to spread the disease to major cities and cause widespread outbreaks.

The effect of these virtual bioterrorists' actions was immediate and profound. Many players in the cities were not powerful enough to cope with the disease and quickly died. In the ensuing fallout, players abandoned the cities en masse as griefers continued to spread Corrupted Blood. In a *Wired* magazine interview, one griefer, Robert Allen, succinctly justified his actions: "It's just funny to watch people run away screaming" (www.wired.com/gaming/virtualworlds/news/2008/03/wow_terror).

The researchers found activity to be predominantly impacted by avatar gender, with player gender either marginally significant (PvP combat) or insignificant (healing), and they observed no interaction effects. In other words, male avatars participated in more PvP combat and performed less healing than female avatars, regardless of player gender. The results indicate that in virtual worlds, behaviors tend to conform to the expectations associated with the avatar's gender, not with the player's gender. Virtual identity apparently takes precedence over real-world identity.

Taken together, Yee's studies on avatar appearance and online behavior suggest that people take on the behavior they think appropriate for the "body" they are inhabiting, even if that body is only assumed for a short period of time in a virtual environment. What implications might these results have for interactions in virtual worlds?

Yee observes that there is no reason for social interactions in virtual worlds to be the same as interactions in the physical world (N. Yee, J. Ellis, and N. Ducheneaut, "The Tyranny of Embodiment," *Artifact,* vol. 2, 2008, pp. 88–93). In the attractiveness study, for example, different people saw different virtual faces for the same avatar. Some researchers have discovered that virtual brainstorming sessions are much more effective when the boss adopts an anonymous avatar, so all participants feel equal socially.

But these ideas have more profound implications. For instance, when people meet someone in a virtual world, they are more likely to agree with them if they look alike. In principle, a programmer could create an avatar that automatically adapts its appearance to look like the person it is facing. A candidate for political office might exploit this idea in a virtual town hall meeting by showing a different face to every participant. And you thought "twofaced" politicians were bad!

Our understanding of the effect of avatars on behavior is still in its early stages. How could the results of research on avatar appearance and behavior in virtual worlds be used to improve the way we work and play together? How could they be used to damage the structure of our social relationships?

Critical Thinking

1. What does MMORPG refer to?

2. Have you played World of Warcraft or similar games? What avatars have you chosen? Why?

3. Do you agree that gender and other stereotypical social relationships found in the real world reproduce themselves in the virtual world?

4. Have you ever taken on an avatar of another gender (or impersonated a person of another gender anywhere in cyberspace)? What did it feel like?

5. Is your online behavior different than your real behavior? Are you angrier, more aggressive, friendlier, more nurturing, etc.?

Shyong (Tony) K. Lam is a PhD student in the Department of Computer Science and Engineering at the University of Minnesota. Contact him at lam@cs.umn.edu. **John Riedl,** Social Computing column editor, is a professor in the Department of Computer Science and Engineering at the University of Minnesota. Contact him at riedl@cs.umn.edu.

UNIT 5

Societal Institutions: Law, Politics, Education, and the Military

Unit Selections

Learning Outcomes

After reading this Unit, you will be able to:

- Know the risks of maintaining an online presence.

- Understand Google's role in the effort to digitize books.

- Understand the implications of digital technology for cultural history.

- Understand some of the educational and economic dynamics underlying online education.

- Understand some of the issues surrounding citizen journalists and the new media.

- Understand that the role of social media in political change is more nuanced than is generally supposed.

- Be able to give an informed argument about the costs and benefits of robotic warfare.

Student Website

www.mhhe.com/cls

Internet References

Berkman Center for Internet and Society at Harvard University
www.cyber.law.harvard.edu/about

ACLU: American Civil Liberties Union
www.aclu.org

United States Patent and Trademark Office
www.uspto.gov

World Intellectual Property Organization
www.wipo.org

After the collapse of the Soviet Union, many Americans believed that democracy and a market economy would develop in short order. Commentators seemed to have taken a cue from Francis Fukuyama's imposingly entitled essay, "The End of History," that appeared in *The National Interest* in 1989. "What we may be witnessing," he wrote, is "not just the end of the Cold War, or the passing of a particular period of post-war history, but . . . the universalization of Western liberal democracy as the final form of human government." Fukuyama, deputy director of the State Department's planning staff in the elder Bush administration, hedged a bit. He was careful to argue that the victory of liberal capitalism "has occurred primarily in the realm of ideas or consciousness and is as yet incomplete in the real or material world."

We have grown wiser since those heady times. The events of September 11, 2001, showed Americans, in the most brutal fashion, that not everyone shares their values. More importantly, the political and economic chaos that has been so much a part of Russian life since the collapse of the Soviet Union has led many commentators to conclude that liberal democracy and a market economy require more than "the realm of ideas or consciousness." They need, above all else, institutions that govern political and economic relationships. They require mechanisms for business contracts and land use, courts to adjudicate disputes, government agencies to record titles and regulate resources, and, not just a mechanism but a tradition of representative government. In a phrase, democracy and a market economy require the institutions of civil society.

We in the United States and Western Europe have long traditions of civil society, in some cases reaching back hundreds of years. The French sociologist, Emile Durkheim (1858–1917), hoped that as traditional societies gave way to urban industrial societies, rule by contract and law would provide the glue for social cohesion. To a very large extent this has been the case in the United States. The room in which I am writing is part of a house that sits on a small piece of property that belongs to me. I am confident that my title to this property is part of the public record. Were someone to appear on my doorstep with a claim to my property, a procedure exists to adjudicate our dispute. If I do not personally understand the rule, I can hire a lawyer, a specialist in civil procedures, to make my case before an independent judiciary.

What the law seems not to have been prepared for, however, is a set of permanent unofficial records documenting not only my title to the house in which I live, but also what I had for lunch, whom I met for dinner last night, what I think about allowing the Bush-era tax cuts to expire, plus a thousand other things that, were I so inclined, I might post to my Facebook page. The problem here is that as a middle-aged adult, the temptation to post a picture of myself in a pirate hat, drinking from a plastic cup—assuming such a picture existed—is close to none at all. Not so for Stacy Snyder, once a student at Millersville University in Pennsylvania, who was denied a teaching degree for just such a youthful indiscretion. And no, suing didn't help. Ms. Snyder now works in human resources. Read Jeffrey Rosen's "The End of Forgetting" to see just how we might recreate a civil society from the chaotic digital world we've stumbled into.

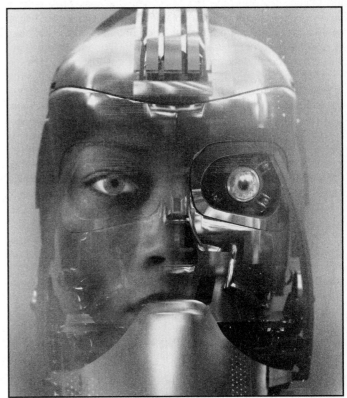

© Colin Anderson/Blend Images LLC

The ability to write, publish, and distribute books along with contractual mechanisms to enforce intellectual property seems essential to a civil society. The publishing industry is struggling to integrate e-books into a profitable publication and distribution model. While Amazon and Apple are shaking things up on that front, Google, as it digitizes books from several large research libraries, is pushing against the limits of intellectual property. Many books undergoing digitization are still protected by copyright. Therein lay the shoals on which the ship of Google has foundered. As it happens, many writers were not happy and sued Google in 2005. After yet more negotiations, Judge Denny Chin rejected the settlement between Google and its plaintiffs, mostly because the settlement gives "Google exclusive legal protection against potential competitors"; in essence Google would be a monopoly in potential violation of the Sherman Antitrust Act. Robert Darnton ("Google's Loss: The Public's Gain") has presented a balanced view of Google's efforts in *The New York Review of Books* over the past few years. His is an important voice, since he directs the Harvard library, one of the largest research libraries in the country, and a good example of the kind of civil institution that has undergone enormous change with the introduction of networked computers. One of those changes is the nature of the archive itself. At least until paper rots—rather sooner than we might like, given the number of books printed on paper made from wood pulp—the contents of traditional libraries is available to anyone with eyes to see. Not so with the digital library, as Steve

Kolowich points out ("Archiving Writers' Work in the Age of E-Mail"). John Updike's papers recently arrived at Harvard on floppy disk.

Education is yet another piece of civil society. American students in public schools study the mechanism of government, recite the Pledge of Allegiance, and learn to revere the sacred texts of American democracy, the Declaration of Independence, the Constitution, and the Bill of Rights. One task of American public education is to instill a common ideal of citizenship into a diverse and changing population. The contribution of computing to education—if not always uncontroversial—has been substantial. From educational software, to wired college campuses, to Internet-mediated distance education, computing has been a part of education since the introduction of personal computers in the early eighties. If you throw in mass, standardized testing, an enterprise nearly unthinkable without computers, computing has been a part of American education since the fifties. As state legislatures increasingly withdraw funds from public education, the demand to lower the cost of on-site education has prompted some unlikely universities to begin offering online courses. The nation's premier public university and one of the world's most prestigious research institutions, the University of California at Berkeley, receives only 15 percent of its funding from the state of California. As "Degrees, Distance, and Dollars" reports, Berkeley is considering some form of online instruction. Meanwhile, the University of Phoenix, a pioneer in online education, registers almost 456,000 students, 200,000 more than the ten campuses of the University of California system combined. There is clearly something going on here. One might easily argue that the collection of private and public research universities is a civil treasure found nowhere else on the planet. How this treasure will negotiate diminished civil funding and competition from online institutions remains to be seen.

No concerned citizen could be unaware of the problems facing newspapers. Advertising lost to online media, increasing costs, and declining readership has brought many of them to their knees in the past decade. This does not mean that Americans are willing to do without a fourth estate, a free press that informs them of the doings of governments around the world while keeping their own government in line. Into the breach created by the decline of newspapers has stepped the citizen journalist. Armed with a blogs and Twitter accounts, they increasingly provide content not provided by mainstream media outlets. Some professional journalists argue that there are risks associated with democratizing reporting. The author of the piece seems to stake his claim in the middle ground.

Perhaps the most surprising piece in this section is Malcolm Gladwell's "Small Change." A popular writer at *The New Yorker,* Gladwell has made a career of writing eloquent pieces that take counterintuitive positions. Ever since President Obama's masterful marshaling of the new media in the last presidential campaign, writers everywhere have been praising its power to mobilize people for one cause or another. Gladwell argues that real change requires real old-fashioned organizing. We end this unit with two pieces on modern warfare. The use of predator drones in Pakistan and Afghanistan has been very much in the news this past year, following at least a decade in which we have been hearing about a military that increasingly operates with high-tech weaponry. "Don't Fear the Reaper" unpacks a set of four "misconceptions" about robotic warfare. "Autonomous Robots" is different in that it is written not by a policy analyst but by an engineer who has built military robots for two decades. What she has to say about their abilities (and inabilities) is worth listening to.

The End of Forgetting

JEFFREY ROSEN

Four years ago, Stacy Snyder, then a 25-year-old teacher in training at Conestoga Valley High School in Lancaster, Pa., posted a photo on her MySpace page that showed her at a party wearing a pirate hat and drinking from a plastic cup, with the caption "Drunken Pirate." After discovering the page, her supervisor at the high school told her the photo was "unprofessional," and the dean of Millersville University School of Education, where Snyder was enrolled, said she was promoting drinking in virtual view of her under-age students. As a result, days before Snyder's scheduled graduation, the university denied her a teaching degree. Snyder sued, arguing that the university had violated her First Amendment rights by penalizing her for her (perfectly legal) after-hours behavior. But in 2008, a federal district judge rejected the claim, saying that because Snyder was a public employee whose photo didn't relate to matters of public concern, her "Drunken Pirate" post was not protected speech.

When historians of the future look back on the perils of the early digital age, Stacy Snyder may well be an icon. The problem she faced is only one example of a challenge that, in big and small ways, is confronting millions of people around the globe: how best to live our lives in a world where the Internet records everything and forgets nothing—where every online photo, status update, Twitter post and blog entry by and about us can be stored forever. With websites like LOL Facebook Moments, which collects and shares embarrassing personal revelations from Facebook users, ill-advised photos and online chatter are coming back to haunt people months or years after the fact. Examples are proliferating daily: there was the 16-year-old British girl who was fired from her office job for complaining on Facebook, "I'm so totally bored!!"; there was the 66-year-old Canadian psychotherapist who tried to enter the United States but was turned away at the border—and barred permanently from visiting the country—after a border guard's Internet search found that the therapist had written an article in a philosophy journal describing his experiments 30 years ago with L.S.D.

According to a recent survey by Microsoft, 75 percent of U.S. recruiters and human-resource professionals report that their companies require them to do online research about candidates, and many use a range of sites when scrutinizing applicants—including search engines, social-networking sites, photo- and video-sharing sites, personal websites and blogs, Twitter and online-gaming sites. Seventy percent of U.S. recruiters report

that they have rejected candidates because of information found online, like photos and discussion-board conversations and membership in controversial groups.

Technological advances, of course, have often presented new threats to privacy. In 1890, in perhaps the most famous article on privacy ever written, Samuel Warren and Louis Brandeis complained that because of new technology—like the Kodak camera and the tabloid press—"gossip is no longer the resource of the idle and of the vicious but has become a trade." But the mild society gossip of the Gilded Age pales before the volume of revelations contained in the photos, video and chatter on social-media sites and elsewhere across the Internet. Facebook, which surpassed MySpace in 2008 as the largest social-networking site, now has nearly 500 million members, or 22 percent of all Internet users, who spend more than 500 billion minutes a month on the site. Facebook users share more than 25 billion pieces of content each month (including news stories, blog posts and photos), and the average user creates 70 pieces of content a month. There are more than 100 million registered Twitter users, and the Library of Congress recently announced that it will be acquiring—and permanently storing—the entire archive of public Twitter posts since 2006.

In Brandeis's day—and until recently, in ours—you had to be a celebrity to be gossiped about in public: today all of us are learning to expect the scrutiny that used to be reserved for the famous and the infamous. A 26-year-old Manhattan woman told The New York Times that she was afraid of being tagged in online photos because it might reveal that she wears only two outfits when out on the town—a Lynyrd Skynyrd T-shirt or a basic black dress. "You have movie-star issues," she said, "and you're just a person."

We've known for years that the Web allows for unprecedented voyeurism, exhibitionism and inadvertent indiscretion, but we are only beginning to understand the costs of an age in which so much of what we say, and of what others say about us, goes into our permanent—and public—digital files. The fact that the Internet never seems to forget is threatening, at an almost existential level, our ability to control our identities; to preserve the option of reinventing ourselves and starting anew; to overcome our checkered pasts.

In a recent book, "Delete: The Virtue of Forgetting in the Digital Age," the cyberscholar Viktor Mayer-Schönberger cites

Stacy Snyder's case as a reminder of the importance of "societal forgetting." By "erasing external memories," he says in the book, "our society accepts that human beings evolve over time, that we have the capacity to learn from past experiences and adjust our behavior." In traditional societies, where missteps are observed but not necessarily recorded, the limits of human memory ensure that people's sins are eventually forgotten. By contrast, Mayer-Schönberger notes, a society in which everything is recorded "will forever tether us to all our past actions, making it impossible, in practice, to escape them." He concludes that "without some form of forgetting, forgiving becomes a difficult undertaking."

It's often said that we live in a permissive era, one with infinite second chances. But the truth is that for a great many people, the permanent memory bank of the Web increasingly means there are *no* second chances—no opportunities to escape a scarlet letter in your digital past. Now the worst thing you've done is often the first thing everyone knows about you.

The Crisis—and the Solution?

All this has created something of a collective identity crisis. For most of human history, the idea of reinventing yourself or freely shaping your identity—of presenting different selves in different contexts (at home, at work, at play)—was hard to fathom, because people's identities were fixed by their roles in a rigid social hierarchy. With little geographic or social mobility, you were defined not as an individual but by your village, your class, your job or your guild. But that started to change in the late Middle Ages and the Renaissance, with a growing individualism that came to redefine human identity. As people perceived themselves increasingly as individuals, their status became a function not of inherited categories but of their own efforts and achievements. This new conception of malleable and fluid identity found its fullest and purest expression in the American ideal of the self-made man, a term popularized by Henry Clay in 1832. From the late 18th to the early 20th century, millions of Europeans moved from the Old World to the New World and then continued to move westward across America, a development that led to what the historian Frederick Jackson Turner called "the significance of the frontier," in which the possibility of constant migration from civilization to the wilderness made Americans distrustful of hierarchy and committed to inventing and reinventing themselves.

In the 20th century, however, the ideal of the self-made man came under siege. The end of the Western frontier led to worries that Americans could no longer seek a fresh start and leave their past behind, a kind of reinvention associated with the phrase "G.T.T.," or "Gone to Texas." But the dawning of the Internet age promised to resurrect the ideal of what the psychiatrist Robert Jay Lifton has called the "protean self." If you couldn't flee to Texas, you could always seek out a new chat room and create a new screen name. For some technology enthusiasts, the Web was supposed to be the second flowering of the open frontier, and the ability to segment our identities with an endless supply of pseudonyms, avatars and categories of friendship was supposed to let people present different sides of their personalities in different contexts. What seemed within our grasp was a power that only Proteus possessed: namely, perfect control over our shifting identities.

But the hope that we could carefully control how others view us in different contexts has proved to be another myth. As social-networking sites expanded, it was no longer quite so easy to have segmented identities: now that so many people use a single platform to post constant status updates and photos about their private and public activities, the idea of a home self, a work self, a family self and a high-school-friends self has become increasingly untenable. In fact, the attempt to maintain different selves often arouses suspicion. Moreover, far from giving us a new sense of control over the face we present to the world, the Internet is shackling us to everything that we have ever said, or that anyone has said about us, making the possibility of digital self-reinvention seem like an ideal from a distant era.

Concern about these developments has intensified this year, as Facebook took steps to make the digital profiles of its users generally more public than private. Last December, the company announced that parts of user profiles that had previously been private—including every user's friends, relationship status and family relations—would become public and accessible to other users. Then in April, Facebook introduced an interactive system called Open Graph that can share your profile information and friends with the Facebook partner sites you visit.

What followed was an avalanche of criticism from users, privacy regulators and advocates around the world. Four Democratic senators—Charles Schumer of New York, Michael Bennet of Colorado, Mark Begich of Alaska and Al Franken of Minnesota—wrote to the chief executive of Facebook, Mark Zuckerberg, expressing concern about the "instant personalization" feature and the new privacy settings. The reaction to Facebook's changes was such that when four N.Y.U. students announced plans in April to build a free social-networking site called Diaspora, which wouldn't compel users to compromise their privacy, they raised more than $20,000 from more than 700 backers in a matter of weeks. In May, Facebook responded to all the criticism by introducing a new set of privacy controls that the company said would make it easier for users to understand what kind of information they were sharing in various contexts.

Facebook's partial retreat has not quieted the desire to do something about an urgent problem. All around the world, political leaders, scholars and citizens are searching for responses to the challenge of preserving control of our identities in a digital world that never forgets. Are the most promising solutions going to be technological? Legislative? Judicial? Ethical? A result of shifting social norms and cultural expectations? Or some mix of the above? Alex Türk, the French data-protection commissioner, has called for a "constitutional right to oblivion" that would allow citizens to maintain a greater degree of anonymity online and in public places. In Argentina, the writers Alejandro Tortolini and Enrique Quagliano have started a campaign to "reinvent forgetting on the Internet," exploring a range of political and technological ways of making data disappear.

In February, the European Union helped finance a campaign called "Think B4 U post!" that urges young people to consider the "potential consequences" of publishing photos of themselves or their friends without "thinking carefully" and asking permission. And in the United States, a group of technologists, legal scholars and cyberthinkers are exploring ways of recreating the possibility of digital forgetting. These approaches share the common goal of reconstructing a form of control over our identities: the ability to reinvent ourselves, to escape our pasts and to improve the selves that we present to the world.

Reputation Bankruptcy and Twittergation

A few years ago, at the giddy dawn of the Web 2.0 era—so called to mark the rise of user-generated online content—many technological theorists assumed that self-governing communities could ensure, through the self-correcting wisdom of the crowd, that all participants enjoyed the online identities they deserved. Wikipedia is one embodiment of the faith that the wisdom of the crowd can correct most mistakes—that a Wikipedia entry for a small-town mayor, for example, will reflect the reputation he deserves. And if the crowd fails—perhaps by turning into a digital mob—Wikipedia offers other forms of redress. Those who think their Wikipedia entries lack context, because they overemphasize a single personal or professional mistake, can petition a group of select editors that decides whether a particular event in someone's past has been given "undue weight." For example, if the small-town mayor had an exemplary career but then was arrested for drunken driving, which came to dominate his Wikipedia entry, he can petition to have the event put in context or made less prominent.

In practice, however, self-governing communities like Wikipedia—or algorithmically self-correcting systems like Google—often leave people feeling misrepresented and burned. Those who think that their online reputations have been unfairly tarnished by an isolated incident or two now have a practical option: consulting a firm like ReputationDefender, which promises to clean up your online image. ReputationDefender was founded by Michael Fertik, a Harvard Law School graduate who was troubled by the idea of young people being forever tainted online by their youthful indiscretions. "I was seeing articles about the 'Lord of the Flies' behavior that all of us engage in at that age," he told me, "and it felt un-American that when the conduct was online, it could have permanent effects on the speaker and the victim. The right to new beginnings and the right to self-definition have always been among the most beautiful American ideals."

ReputationDefender, which has customers in more than 100 countries, is the most successful of the handful of reputation-related start-ups that have been growing rapidly after the privacy concerns raised by Facebook and Google. (ReputationDefender recently raised $15 million in new venture capital.) For a fee, the company will monitor your online reputation, contacting websites individually and asking them to take down offending items. In addition, with the help of the kind of search-optimization technology that businesses use to raise their Google profiles, ReputationDefender can bombard the Web with positive or neutral information about its customers, either creating new Web pages or by multiplying links to existing ones to ensure they show up at the top of any Google search. (Services begin from $10 a month to $1,000 a year; for challenging cases, the price can rise into the tens of thousands.) By automatically raising the Google ranks of the positive links, ReputationDefender pushes the negative links to the back pages of a Google search, where they're harder to find. "We're hearing stories of employers increasingly asking candidates to open up Facebook pages in front of them during job interviews," Fertik told me. "Our customers include parents whose kids have talked about them on the Internet— 'Mom didn't get the raise'; 'Dad got fired'; 'Mom and Dad are fighting a lot, and I'm worried they'll get a divorce.'"

Companies like ReputationDefender offer a promising short-term solution for those who can afford it; but tweaking your Google profile may not be enough for reputation management in the near future, as Web 2.0 swiftly gives way to Web. 3.0—a world in which user-generated content is combined with a new layer of data aggregation and analysis and live video. For example, the Facebook application Photo Finder, by Face.com, uses facial-recognition and social-connections software to allow you to locate any photo of yourself or a friend on Facebook, regardless of whether the photo was "tagged"—that is, the individual in the photo was identified by name. At the moment, Photo Finder allows you to identify only people on your contact list, but as facial-recognition technology becomes more widespread and sophisticated, it will almost certainly challenge our expectation of anonymity in public. People will be able to snap a cellphone picture (or video) of a stranger, plug the images into Google and pull up all tagged and untagged photos of that person that exist on the Web.

In the nearer future, Internet searches for images are likely to be combined with social-network aggregator search engines, like today's Spokeo and Pipl, which combine data from online sources—including political contributions, blog posts, YouTube videos, Web comments, real estate listings and photo albums. Increasingly these aggregator sites will rank people's public and private reputations, like the new website Unvarnished, a reputation marketplace where people can write anonymous reviews about anyone. In the Web 3.0 world, Fertik predicts, people will be rated, assessed and scored based not on their creditworthiness but on their trustworthiness as good parents, good dates, good employees, good baby sitters or good insurance risks.

Anticipating these challenges, some legal scholars have begun imagining new laws that could allow people to correct, or escape from, the reputation scores that may govern our personal and professional interactions in the future. Jonathan Zittrain, who teaches cyberlaw at Harvard Law School, supports an idea he calls "reputation bankruptcy," which would give people a chance to wipe their reputation slates clean and start over. To illustrate the problem, Zittrain showed me an iPhone app called Date Check, by Intelius, that offers a "sleaze detector" to let you investigate people you're thinking about dating—it reports their criminal histories, address histories and summaries of their social-networking profiles. Services like Date Check, Zittrain said, could soon become even more sophisticated, rating a person's social desirability based on minute social measurements—like how often he or she was approached or avoided by others at parties (a ranking that would be easy to calibrate under existing technology using cellphones and Bluetooth). Zittrain also speculated that, over time, more and more reputation queries will be processed by a handful of de facto reputation brokers—like the existing consumer-reporting agencies Experian and Equifax, for example—which will provide ratings for people based on their sociability, trustworthiness and employability.

To allow people to escape from negative scores generated by these services, Zittrain says that people should be allowed to declare "reputation bankruptcy" every 10 years or so, wiping out certain categories of ratings or sensitive information. His model is the Fair Credit Reporting Act, which requires consumer-reporting agencies to provide you with one free credit report a year—so you can dispute negative or inaccurate information—and prohibits the agencies from retaining negative information about bankruptcies, late payments or tax liens for more than 10 years. "Like personal financial bankruptcy, or the way in which a state often seals a juvenile criminal record and gives a child a 'fresh start' as an adult," Zittrain writes in his book "The Future of the Internet and How to Stop It," "we ought to consider how to implement the idea of a second or third chance into our digital spaces."

The cyberlaw expert Jonathan Zittrain says that the law should permit people to declare 'reputation bankruptcy' every 10 years or so, wiping out certain categories of personal information online.

Another proposal, offered by Paul Ohm, a law professor at the University of Colorado, would make it illegal for employers to fire or refuse to hire anyone on the basis of legal off-duty conduct revealed in Facebook postings or Google profiles. "Is it really fair for employers to know what you've put in your Facebook status updates?" Ohm asks. "We could say that Facebook status updates have taken the place of water-cooler chat, which employers were never supposed to overhear, and we could pass a prohibition on the sorts of information employers can and can't consider when they hire someone."

Ohm became interested in this problem in the course of researching the ease with which we can learn the identities of people from supposedly anonymous personal data like movie preferences and health information. When Netflix, for example, released 100 million purportedly anonymous records revealing how almost 500,000 users had rated movies from 1999 to 2005, researchers were able to identify people in the database by name with a high degree of accuracy if they knew even only a little bit about their movie-watching preferences, obtained from public data posted on other ratings sites.

Ohm says he worries that employers would be able to use social-network-aggregator services to identify people's book and movie preferences and even Internet-search terms, and then fire or refuse to hire them on that basis. A handful of states—including New York, California, Colorado and North Dakota—broadly prohibit employers from discriminating against employees for legal off-duty conduct like smoking. Ohm suggests that these laws could be extended to prevent certain categories of employers from refusing to hire people based on Facebook pictures, status updates and other legal but embarrassing personal information. (In practice, these laws might be hard to enforce, since employers might not disclose the real reason for their hiring decisions, so employers, like credit-reporting agents, might also be required by law to disclose to job candidates the negative information in their digital files.)

Another legal option for responding to online setbacks to your reputation is to sue under current law. There's already a sharp rise in lawsuits known as Twittergation—that is, suits to force websites to remove slanderous or false posts. Last year, Courtney Love was sued for libel by the fashion designer Boudoir Queen for supposedly slanderous comments posted on Twitter, on Love's MySpace page and on the designer's online marketplace-feedback page. But even if you win a U.S. libel lawsuit, the website doesn't have to take the offending material down any more than a newspaper that has lost a libel suit has to remove the offending content from its archive.

Some scholars, therefore, have proposed creating new legal rights to force websites to remove false or slanderous statements. Cass Sunstein, the Obama administration's regulatory czar, suggests in his new book, "On Rumors," that there might be "a general right to demand retraction after a clear demonstration that a statement is both false and damaging." (If a newspaper or blogger refuses to post a retraction, they might be liable for damages.) Sunstein adds that websites might be required to take down false postings after receiving notice that they are false—an approach modeled on the Digital Millennium Copyright Act, which requires websites to remove content that supposedly infringes intellectual property rights after receiving a complaint.

As Stacy Snyder's "Drunken Pirate" photo suggests, however, many people aren't worried about false information posted by others—they're worried about true information they've posted about themselves when it is taken out of context or given undue weight. And defamation law doesn't apply to true information or statements of opinion. Some legal scholars want to expand the ability to sue over true but embarrassing violations of privacy—although it appears to be a quixotic goal.

Daniel Solove, a George Washington University law professor and author of the book "The Future of Reputation," says that laws forbidding people to breach confidences could be expanded to allow you to sue your Facebook friends if they share your embarrassing photos or posts in violation of your privacy settings. Expanding legal rights in this way, however, would run up against the

First Amendment rights of others. Invoking the right to free speech, the U.S. Supreme Court has already held that the media can't be prohibited from publishing the name of a rape victim that they obtained from public records. Generally, American judges hold that if you disclose something to a few people, you can't stop them from sharing the information with the rest of the world.

That's one reason that the most promising solutions to the problem of embarrassing but true information online may be not legal but technological ones. Instead of suing after the damage is done (or hiring a firm to clean up our messes), we need to explore ways of pre-emptively making the offending words or pictures disappear.

Expiration Dates

Jorge Luis Borges, in his short story "Funes, the Memorious," describes a young man who, as a result of a riding accident, has lost his ability to forget. Funes has a tremendous memory, but he is so lost in the details of everything he knows that he is unable to convert the information into knowledge and unable, as a result, to grow in wisdom. Viktor Mayer-Schönberger, in "Delete," uses the Borges story as an emblem for the personal and social costs of being so shackled by our digital past that we are unable to evolve and learn from our mistakes. After reviewing the various possible legal solutions to this problem, Mayer-Schönberger says he is more convinced by a technological fix: namely, mimicking human forgetting with built-in expiration dates for data. He imagines a world in which digital-storage devices could be programmed to delete photos or blog posts or other data that have reached their expiration dates, and he suggests that users could be prompted to select an expiration date before saving any data.

This is not an entirely fanciful vision. Google not long ago decided to render all search queries anonymous after nine months (by deleting part of each Internet protocol address), and the upstart search engine Cuil has announced that it won't keep any personally identifiable information at all, a privacy feature that distinguishes it from Google. And there are already small-scale privacy apps that offer disappearing data. An app called TigerText allows text-message senders to set a time limit from one minute to 30 days after which the text disappears from the company's servers on which it is stored and therefore from the senders' and recipients' phones. (The founder of TigerText, Jeffrey Evans, has said he chose the name before the scandal involving Tiger Woods's supposed texts to a mistress.)

Expiration dates could be implemented more broadly in various ways. Researchers at the University of Washington, for example, are developing a technology called Vanish that makes electronic data "self-destruct" after a specified period of time. Instead of relying on Google, Facebook or Hotmail to delete the data that is stored "in the cloud"—in other words, on their distributed servers—Vanish encrypts the data and then "shatters" the encryption key. To read the data, your computer has to put the pieces of the key back together, but they "erode" or "rust" as time passes, and after a certain point the document can no longer be read. Tadayoshi Kohno, a designer of Vanish, told

me that the system could provide expiration dates not only for e-mail but also for any data stored in the cloud, including photos or text or anything posted on Facebook, Google or blogs. The technology doesn't promise perfect control—you can't stop someone from copying your photos or Facebook chats during the period in which they are not encrypted. But as Vanish improves, it could bring us much closer to a world where our data didn't linger forever.

Researchers at the University of Washington are developing a technology called Vanish that makes electronic data— e-mail messages as well as photos and text posted on the Web—'self-destruct' after a specified period of time.

Kohno told me that Facebook, if it wanted to, could implement expiration dates on its own platform, making our data disappear after, say, three days or three months unless a user specified that he wanted it to linger forever. It might be a more welcome option for Facebook to encourage the development of Vanish-style apps that would allow individual users who are concerned about privacy to make their own data disappear without imposing the default on all Facebook users.

So far, however, Zuckerberg, Facebook's C.E.O., has been moving in the opposite direction—toward transparency rather than privacy. In defending Facebook's recent decision to make the default for profile information about friends and relationship status public rather than private, Zuckerberg said in January to the founder of the publication TechCrunch that Facebook had an obligation to reflect "current social norms" that favored exposure over privacy. "People have really gotten comfortable not only sharing more information and different kinds but more openly and with more people, and that social norm is just something that has evolved over time," he said.

Privacy's New Normal

But not all Facebook users agree with Zuckerberg. Plenty of anecdotal evidence suggests that young people, having been burned by Facebook (and frustrated by its privacy policy, which at more than 5,000 words is longer than the U.S. Constitution), are savvier than older users about cleaning up their tagged photos and being careful about what they post. And two recent studies challenge the conventional wisdom that young people have no qualms about having their entire lives shared and preserved online forever. A University of California, Berkeley, study released in April found that large majorities of people between 18 and 22 said there should be laws that require websites to delete all stored information about individuals (88 percent) and that give people the right to know all the information websites know about them (62 percent)—percentages that mirrored the privacy views of older adults. A recent Pew study found that 18-to-29-year-olds are actually more concerned about their online profiles than older people are, vigilantly deleting unwanted posts, removing their names from tagged photos and censoring themselves as they share personal information, because they are coming to understand the dangers of oversharing.

Still, Zuckerberg is on to something when he recognizes that the future of our online identities and reputations will ultimately be shaped not just by laws and technologies but also by changing social norms. And norms are already developing to recreate off-the-record spaces in public, with no photos, Twitter posts or blogging allowed. Milk and Honey, an exclusive bar on Manhattan's Lower East Side, requires potential members to sign an agreement promising not to blog about the bar's goings on or to post photos on social-networking sites, and other bars and nightclubs are adopting similar policies. I've been at dinners recently where someone has requested, in all seriousness, "Please don't tweet this"—a custom that is likely to spread.

But what happens when people transgress those norms, using Twitter or tagging photos in ways that cause us serious embarrassment? Can we imagine a world in which new norms develop that make it easier for people to forgive and forget one another's digital sins?

That kind of social norm may be harder to develop. Alessandro Acquisti, a scholar at Carnegie Mellon University, studies the behavioral economics of privacy—that is, the conscious and unconscious mental trade-offs we make in deciding whether to reveal or conceal information, balancing the benefits of sharing with the dangers of disclosure. He is conducting experiments about the "decay time" and the relative weight of good and bad information—in other words, whether people discount positive information about you more quickly and heavily than they discount negative information about you. His research group's preliminary results suggest that if rumors spread about something good you did 10 years ago, like winning a prize, they will be discounted; but if rumors spread about something bad that you did 10 years ago, like driving drunk, that information has staying power. Research in behavioral psychology confirms that people pay more attention to bad rather than good information, and Acquisti says he fears that "20 years from now, if all of us have a skeleton on Facebook, people may not discount it because it was an error in our youth."

On the assumption that strangers may not make it easy for us to escape our pasts, Acquisti is also studying technologies and strategies of "privacy nudges" that might prompt people to think twice before sharing sensitive photos or information in the first place. Gmail, for example, has introduced a feature that forces you to think twice before sending drunken e-mail messages. When you enable the feature, called Mail Goggles, it prompts you to solve simple math problems before sending e-mail messages at times you're likely to regret. (By default, Mail Goggles is active only late on weekend nights.) Acquisti is investigating similar strategies of "soft paternalism" that might nudge people to hesitate before posting, say, drunken photos from Cancún. "We could easily think about a system, when you are uploading certain photos, that immediately detects how sensitive the photo will be."

A silly but surprisingly effective alternative might be to have an anthropomorphic icon—a stern version of Microsoft's Clippy—that could give you a reproachful look before you hit the send button. According to M. Ryan Calo, who runs the consumer-privacy project at Stanford Law School, experimenters studying strategies of "visceral notice" have found that when people navigate a website in the presence of a human-looking online character who seems to be actively following the cursor, they disclose less personal information than people who browse with no character or one who appears not to be paying attention. As people continue to experience the drawbacks of living in a world that never forgets, they may well learn to hesitate before posting information, with or without humanoid Clippys.

Forgiveness

In addition to exposing less for the Web to forget, it might be helpful for us to explore new ways of living in a world that is slow to forgive. It's sobering, now that we live in a world misleadingly called a "global village," to think about privacy in actual, small villages long ago. In the villages described in the Babylonian Talmud, for example, any kind of gossip or tale-bearing about other people—oral or written, true or false, friendly or mean—was considered a terrible sin because small communities have long memories and every word spoken about other people was thought to ascend to the heavenly cloud. (The digital cloud has made this metaphor literal.) But the Talmudic villages were, in fact, far more humane and forgiving than our brutal global village, where much of the content on the Internet would meet the Talmudic definition of gossip: although the Talmudic sages believed that God reads our thoughts and records them in the book of life, they also believed that God erases the book for those who atone for their sins by asking forgiveness of those they have wronged. In the Talmud, people have an obligation not to remind others of their past misdeeds, on the assumption they may have atoned and grown spiritually from their mistakes. "If a man was a repentant [sinner]," the Talmud says, "one must not say to him, 'Remember your former deeds.' "

Unlike God, however, the digital cloud rarely wipes our slates clean, and the keepers of the cloud today are sometimes less forgiving than their all-powerful divine predecessor. In an interview with Charlie Rose on PBS, Eric Schmidt, the C.E.O. of Google, said that "the next generation is infinitely more social online"—and less private—"as evidenced by their Facebook pictures," which "will be around when they're running for president years from now." Schmidt added: "As long as the answer is that I chose to make a mess of myself with this picture, then it's fine. The issue is when somebody else does it." If people chose to expose themselves for 15 minutes of fame, Schmidt says, "that's their choice, and they have to live with it."

Schmidt added that the "notion of control is fundamental to the evolution of these privacy-based solutions," pointing to Google Latitude, which allows people to broadcast their locations in real time.

This idea of privacy as a form of control is echoed by many privacy scholars, but it seems too harsh to say that if people like Stacy Snyder don't use their privacy settings responsibly, they have to live forever with the consequences. Privacy protects us from being unfairly judged out of context on the basis of snippets of private information that have been exposed against our will; but we can be just as unfairly judged out of context on the basis of snippets of public information that we have unwisely chosen to reveal to the wrong audience.

Moreover, the narrow focus on privacy as a form of control misses what really worries people on the Internet today. What people seem to want is not simply control over their privacy settings; they want control over their online reputations. But the idea that any of us can control our reputations is, of course, an unrealistic fantasy. The truth is we can't possibly control what others say or know or think about us in a world of Facebook and Google, nor can we realistically demand that others give us the deference and respect to which we think we're entitled. On the Internet, it turns out, we're not entitled to demand any particular respect at all, and if others don't have the empathy necessary to forgive our missteps, or the attention spans necessary to judge us in context, there's nothing we can do about it.

But if we can't control what others think or say or view about us, we can control our own reaction to photos, videos, blogs and Twitter posts that we feel unfairly represent us. A recent study suggests that people on Facebook and other social-networking sites express their real personalities, despite the widely held assumption that people try online to express an enhanced or idealized impression of themselves. Samuel Gosling, the University of Texas, Austin, psychology professor who conducted the study, told the Facebook blog, "We found that judgments of people based on nothing but their Facebook profiles correlate pretty strongly with our measure of what that person is really like, and that measure consists of both how the profile owner sees him or herself and how that profile owner's friends see the profile owner."

By comparing the online profiles of college-aged people in the United States and Germany with their actual personalities and their idealized personalities, or how they wanted to see themselves, Gosling found that the online profiles conveyed "rather accurate images of the profile owners, either because people aren't trying to look good or because they are trying and failing to pull it off." (Personality impressions based on the online profiles were most accurate for extroverted people and least accurate for neurotic people, who cling tenaciously to an idealized self-image.)

Gosling is optimistic about the implications of his study for the possibility of digital forgiveness. He acknowledged that social technologies are forcing us to merge identities that used to be separate—we can no longer have segmented selves like "a home or family self, a friend self, a leisure self, a work self." But although he told Facebook, "I have to find a way to reconcile my professor self with my having-a-few-drinks self," he also suggested that as all of us have to merge our public and private identities, photos showing us having a few drinks on Facebook will no longer seem so scandalous. "You see your accountant going out on weekends and attending clown conventions, that no

longer makes you think that he's not a good accountant. We're coming to terms and reconciling with that merging of identities."

Perhaps society will become more forgiving of drunken Facebook pictures in the way Gosling says he expects it might. And some may welcome the end of the segmented self, on the grounds that it will discourage bad behavior and hypocrisy: it's harder to have clandestine affairs when you're broadcasting your every move on Facebook, Twitter and Foursquare. But a humane society values privacy, because it allows people to cultivate different aspects of their personalities in different contexts; and at the moment, the enforced merging of identities that used to be separate is leaving many casualties in its wake. Stacy Snyder couldn't reconcile her "aspiring-teacher self" with her "having-a-few-drinks self": even the impression, correct or not, that she had a drink in a pirate hat at an off-campus party was enough to derail her teaching career.

That doesn't mean, however, that it had to derail her life. After taking down her MySpace profile, Snyder is understandably trying to maintain her privacy: her lawyer told me in a recent interview that she is now working in human resources; she did not respond to a request for comment. But her success as a human being who can change and evolve, learning from her mistakes and growing in wisdom, has nothing to do with the digital file she can never entirely escape. Our character, ultimately, can't be judged by strangers on the basis of our Facebook or Google profiles; it can be judged by only those who know us and have time to evaluate our strengths and weaknesses, face to face and in context, with insight and understanding. In the meantime, as all of us stumble over the challenges of living in a world without forgetting, we need to learn new forms of empathy, new ways of defining ourselves without reference to what others say about us and new ways of forgiving one another for the digital trails that will follow us forever.

Critical Thinking

1. Rosen refers to Frederick Jackson Turner early in his article. He is best known for what's been called the Frontier Hypothesis. What is the Frontier Hypothesis? Rosen cites it approvingly as the state of affairs before the 20th century. What do contemporary historians think about Frederick Jackson Turner?

2. Rosen says that the "Internet never seems to forget." Is this true? Read Article 18 ("Archiving Writers' Work in the Age of E-Mail"), then investigate how libraries are handling the transition from one digital format to another.

3. Do you agree with Paul Ohm that it should be illegal for employers to fire or refuse to hire anyone on the basis of legal off-duty conduct revealed in Facebook postings or Google profiles?

JEFFREY ROSEN, a law professor at George Washington University, is a frequent contributor to the magazine. He is writing a book about Louis Brandeis.

Google's Loss: The Public's Gain

ROBERT DARNTON

It is too early to do a postmortem on Google's attempt to digitize and sell millions of books, despite the decision by Judge Denny Chin on March 23 to reject the agreement that seemed to make Google's project possible. Google Book Search may rise from the ashes, reincarnated in some new settlement with the authors and publishers who had taken Google to court for alleged infringement of their copyrights. But this is a good time to take a backward look at the ground covered by Google since it first set out to provide access to all the books in the world. What went wrong?

In the forty-eight-page opinion that accompanied his decision, Judge Chin indicated some of the wrong turns and paths not taken. His reasoning ran through each stage in the evolution of the enterprise:

- 2004: Google started digitizing books from research libraries and displaying snippets of them for online searches. You could find short excerpts from a book online but not the 2005: The Authors Guild and the Association of American Publishers sued Google for violation of their copyrights.
- October 28, 2008: After arduous negotiations, Google and the plaintiffs filed a proposed settlement with the Southern Federal District Court of New York.
- November 13, 2009: In response to hundreds of objections filed with the court, Google and the plaintiffs submitted an Amended Settlement Agreement (ASA).
- February 18, 2010: Judge Chin conducted a fairness hearing at which more objections were raised.
- March 23, 2011: Judge Chin rejected the ASA.

What began as a project for online searching metamorphosed during those seven years into an attempt to create the largest library and book business ever imagined. Had Google kept to its original plan, it might have won its case by invoking the doctrine of fair use. To display a few sentences in the form of snippets could hardly be equated with reproducing so much text that Google was effectively appropriating the bulk of a book. The early version of Google Book Search did not amount to commercial competition with publishers, because Google provided its search service free of charge, although it linked its displays to advertisements.

Then the lawyers took over. For more than two years, the legal teams of Google and the plaintiffs wrangled over details of how their differences could be resolved by a partnership in a common commercial enterprise. (The lawyers' fees for the various parties eventually came to $45 million.) The result, Google Book Search,

had many positive aspects. Above all, it promised to provide millions of readers with access to millions of books. It also gave authors an opportunity to have their out-of-print works revived and circulated widely, instead of lying unread on the shelves of research libraries. The authors would collect fees from the retail sales of the digital copies, and the libraries would gain access to the entire data bank, consisting of millions of books, by paying an annual subscription fee. If the prices were moderate, everyone would benefit.

The settlement had many other advantages: free service on at least one terminal at public libraries, special measures to help the visually impaired, and access to Google's database for large-scale quantitative research. Its main disadvantage, according to many critics, was its commercial aspect. Google asked libraries to supply it with their books free of charge—not quite free, actually: Google paid for the digitizing but the libraries shouldered heavy transactional costs. (Harvard paid $1.9 million to process the 850,000 public domain books that it furnished to Google.) In return, the libraries were required to buy back access to those books in digital form for a subscription price that might escalate to a ruinous level. The subscription rate would be set by a Book Rights Registry composed of representatives of the authors and publishers who had an interest in maximizing their income. Therefore, the settlement could look like a way to conquer and divide a lucrative market: 37 percent of the income would go to Google, 63 percent to the plaintiffs, the authors and publishers who had become its partners. No one represented the public interest, and no public authority was empowered to monitor an operation that seemed likely to determine the fate of books far into the digital future.

In his opinion, Judge Chin did not dwell on the commercial aspects of Google Book Search, except insofar as they posed a threat to restrain competition. Two memoranda from the Department of Justice had alerted him to the danger of a violation of the Sherman Antitrust Act, and he especially objected to the way that threat applied to the digitization and marketing of "orphan" books—books whose copyright owners have not been identified. Orphan books—and unclaimed copyrights in general—are crucial to the entire enterprise, because there are so many of them, perhaps five million, according to a recent estimate. Most of them date from the period between 1923 and 1964, when copyright law is particularly ambiguous. Any database that excluded them would be disastrously deficient, but any enterprise that included them would expose the digitizer to ruinously expensive lawsuits. Damages would probably run to at least $100,000 per title. The settlement solved this problem by giving Google exclusive exemption from litigation. If any owners of unclaimed copyrights identified themselves, they would be compensated, but they could not collect damages.

In its original version, the settlement went further. It made Google and the plaintiffs effective proprietors of the orphan books and permitted them to pocket the income from their sale, even though hardly anyone involved in Google's enterprise had ever had anything to do with the creation of those works. The amended version of the settlement eliminated that provision, but it continued to give Google exclusive legal protection in a manner that would discriminate against potential competitors. It amounted to changing copyright law by litigation instead of legislation.

In objecting to this aspect of the settlement, Judge Chin insisted that issues of such importance should be decided by Congress, all the more so since the settlement would determine future activities instead of merely remedying damages that took place in the past. Class action suits that affect the future look dubious in court, and the Google Book Search case also included a doubtful opt-out provision. It provided that any author of a book that was covered by copyright but no longer commercially available (that is, essentially, in print) would be deemed to have accepted the terms of the settlement unless he or she explicitly notified Google to the contrary. Judge Chin noted that 6,800 authors had opted out, an indication that the settlement may not have looked acceptable to a considerable proportion of the class that the Authors Guild claimed to represent.

How large is that class? The Guild has 8,000 members, but there must be far more than 100,000 living writers who have published a book during the last fifty years. Many of them are academic authors who do not depend on the sale of books to make a living. Some of them sent memoranda to the court saying that they preferred to have their out-of-print books made available free of charge, because they cared more about the diffusion of their ideas than what little income they might derive from sales. Of course, professional writers have a vital interest in sales, and they understandably pressed hard to make the most from the deal with Google. Judge Chin did not disparage anyone's motives, but he showed concern for the representativeness of the class composed of authors that was involved in the class action suit and the antagonistic interests of different groups of its members.

Judge Chin also mentioned other problems that had been stressed in the five hundred amicus briefs and memoranda that had been submitted to the court. Two stand out.

Foreign authors and publishers objected that the settlement violated international copyright law. Google digitized many of their works without their permission, even though they held copyrights in their home countries. The settlement treated them as if they belonged to the same class as the American rightsholders, despite the fact that they had little possibility of studying the terms of the settlement and opting out of it. The ASA met most of those objections by eliminating copyrighted books that were published abroad, except in the United Kingdom, Canada, and Australia. But foreigners continued to protest about the potential violation of their rights and noted that they, too, had an orphan book problem.

To many who sent their objections to the court, as well as others, Google Book Search threatened to violate their privacy. In the course of administering its sales, both of individual books and of access to its database by means of institutional subscriptions, it would accumulate information about the private activity of reading. It would know who read what, including in many cases the precise passages that were read and the exact time when the readers consulted them. The ASA provided some assurances about this danger, but Judge Chin recommended more, should the ASA be revised and resubmitted to the court.

He also urged the possibility that a further revision of the settlement might be acceptable to the court if its key provisions were switched from opt-out to opt-in requirements. In that case, presumably, the authors of copyrighted, out-of-print books would not be considered to have accepted the settlement unless they gave notice of their intention to do so. If enough of those authors could be located, or volunteered to consent to the settlement, Google Book Search might build up a large database of books published since 1923. But the logistics and the transaction costs might make that task unfeasible, and the problem of orphan books would remain unsolvable without congressional legislation.

The cumulative effect of these various objections, many of them endorsed by Judge Chin's decision, could give the impression that the settlement, even in its amended version, is so flawed that it deserves to be pronounced dead and buried. But that would mean the loss of its many positive features. How could its advantages be preserved without the accompanying drawbacks? The answer that I and others have proposed is to create a Digital Public Library of America (DPLA)—that is, a collection of works in all formats that would make our cultural heritage available online and free of charge to everyone everywhere.

Having argued so often for this alternative to Google Book Search, I may fall victim to the syndrome known in France as preaching for one's own saint. Instead of repeating the arguments previously made in these pages and elsewhere,[1] I would like to show how the case for the Digital Public Library would look if seen from the perspective of similar projects in other countries.

The most impressive attempts to create national digital libraries are taking shape in Norway and the Netherlands. They have state support, and they involve plans to digitize books covered by copyright, even those that are currently in print, by means of collective agreements—not legalistic devices like the class action suit employed by Google and its partners, but voluntary arrangements that reconcile the interests of the authors and publishers who own the rights with those of readers who want access to everything in their national languages. Of course, the number of books in Norwegian and Dutch is small compared with those in English. To form an idea of what could be done in the United States, it is better to study another venture, the pan-European digital library known as Europeana.

Europeana—which already has offices in The Hague—is still in a formative phase, but its basic structure is well developed. Instead of accumulating collections of its own, it will function as an aggregator of aggregators. Information will be accumulated and coordinated at three levels: particular libraries will digitize their collections; national or regional centers will integrate them into central databases; and Europeana will transform those databases, from twenty-seven constituent countries, into a single, seamless network. To the users, all these currents of information will remain invisible. They will simply search for an item—a book, an image, a recording, or a video—and the system will direct them to a digitized version of it, wherever it may be, making it available for downloading on a personal computer or a handheld device.

To deliver such service, the system will require not only an effective technological architecture but also a way of coordinating the information required to locate the digitized items—"metadata," as librarians call it. The staff of Europeana at The Hague has perfected a code to harmonize the metadata that will flow into it from every corner of Europe. Unlike Google, it will not store digital files in a single database or server farm. It will operate as a nerve center for what is known as a "distributed network," leaving libraries, archives, and museums to digitize and preserve their own collections in the capillary system of the organic whole.

A digital library for America might well follow this model, although Europeana has not yet proven that it is workable. When a prototype went live on November 20, 2008, it was flooded with so many attempts at searches that the system crashed. But that failure can be taken as testimony to the demand for such a mega-library. Since then, Europeana has enlarged its capacity. It will resume functioning at full tilt in the near future; and by 2015 it expects to make thirty million items, a third of them books, available free of charge.

Who will pay for it? The European Union will do so, drawing on contributions from its member states. (Europeana's current budget is €4,923,000, but most of the expenses fall on the institutions that create and preserve the digital files.) This financial model may not be suitable for the United States, but we Americans benefit from something that Europe lacks: a rich array of independent foundations dedicated to the public welfare. By combining forces, a few dozen foundations could provide enough money to get the DPLA up and running. It is impossible at this point to provide even ballpark estimates of the overall cost, but it should come to less than the €750 million that President Sarkozy pledged for the digitization of France's "cultural patrimony."

Moreover, in building up its basic collections, it could draw on the public-domain books that are currently stored in the digital archives of not-for-profit organizations like Hathi Trust and the Internet Archive—or (why not?) in the servers of Google itself, Google willing.

Once its basic structure has been erected, the Digital Public Library of America could be enlarged incrementally. And after it has proven its capacity to provide services—for education at all levels, for the information needs of businesses, for research in every conceivable field—it might attract public funds. Long-term sustainability would remain a problem to be solved.

Other problems must be confronted in the near future. As the Google case demonstrated, nearly everything published since 1923, when copyright restrictions begin to apply, is now out of bounds for digitization and distribution. The DPLA must respect copyright. In order to succeed where Google failed, it will have to include several million orphan books; and it will not be able to do that unless Congress clears the way by appropriate legislation. Congress nearly passed bills concerning orphan books in 2006 and 2008. It failed in part because of the uncertainty surrounding Google Book Search. A not-for-profit digital library truly devoted to the public welfare could be of such benefit to their constituents that members of Congress might pass a new bill carefully designed to protect the DPLA from litigation should rightsholders of orphan books be located and bring suit for damages.

Even better, Congress could create a mechanism to compensate authors for the downloading of books that are out of print but covered by copyright. In addition, voluntary collective agreements among authors of in-print books, similar to those in Norway and the Netherlands, could make much contemporary literature accessible through the DPLA. The copyright problems connected with works produced outside the United States might be resolved by agreements between the DPLA and Europeana as well as by similar alliances with aggregators on other continents. Items that are born in diverse formats such as e-books pose still more problems. But the noncommercial character of the DPLA and its commitment to the public good would make all such difficulties look less formidable than they seemed to be when they were confronted by a company intent on maximizing profit at the expense of the public and of its competitors.

In short, the collapse of the settlement has a great deal to teach us. It should help us emulate the positive aspects of Google Book Search and avoid the drawbacks that made Google's enterprise flawed from the beginning. The best way to do so and to provide the American people with what they need in order to thrive in the new information age is to create a Digital Public Library of America.

Note

1. See, for example, "Can We Create a National Digital Library?," *The New York Review*, October 28, 2010. © 1963–2011 NYREV, Inc. All rights reserved.

Critical Thinking

1. What was the first free lending library in the United States? What famous figure in American history helped found it? This figure founded many other civic associations (see the introduction to Unit 4). Name a few of them.

2. Why do you suppose that intellectual property is treated differently than other types of property?

3. Why do you suppose that copyright protection has been extended from 14 years (subject to renewal for an additional 14) to the life of the author plus seventy years?

4. Darnton assumes you already know something about Google's plan to digitize books. Use the Internet to find out about it in more detail.

5. What are orphan books? What role did they play in Judge Chin's ruling?

6. Use the Internet to learn more about Darnton's proposed Digital Public Library.

Archiving Writers' Work in the Age of E-Mail

STEVE KOLOWICH

L eslie Morris is used to handling John Updike's personal effects. For decades, Mr. Updike had been sending a steady stream of manuscripts and papers to Harvard University's Houghton Library, where Ms. Morris serves as a curator.

But in late February, several weeks after the iconic writer died, some boxes arrived with unexpected contents: approximately 50 three-and-a-half and five-and-a-quarter-inch floppy disks—artifacts from late in the author's career when he, like many of his peers, began using a word processor.

The floppies have presented a bit of a problem. While relatively modern to Mr. Updike—who rose to prominence back when publishers were still using Linotype machines—the disks are outmoded and damage-prone by today's standards. Ms. Morris, who curates modern books and manuscripts, has carefully stored them alongside his papers in a temperature-controlled room in the library "until we have a procedure here at Harvard on how to handle these materials."

Harvard isn't the only university puzzling over new media from old—and not-so-old—masters. Emory University recently received four laptops, an external hard drive, and a Palm Treo personal digital assistant from Salman Rushdie. The University of Texas at Austin recently acquired a series of Zip disks and a laptop containing Norman Mailer's files.

"Once we learned how to preserve paper, we were good," says Naomi L. Nelson, interim director of the manuscript, archives, and rare-book library at Emory University's Robert W. Woodruff Library. "That really hasn't changed a lot. With computers it's a whole different ballgame."

Still, three things are becoming clear. First, these trappings of the digital age will transform the way libraries preserve and exhibit literary collections. Second, universities are going to have to spend money on new equipment and training for their archivists. And finally, scholars will be able to learn more about writers than they ever have before.

In with the Old

Personal computers and external storage devices have been around for more than a quarter-century, but only now, as the famous literary figures of the 20th century begin to pass away, are these technologies showing up on archivists' doorsteps.

According to Ms. Morris, the Updike papers will be the first in the Houghton catalog to have a "significant magnetic-media component," and she realizes that old floppy disks are just the tip of the iceberg. The great American novelists of the digital era—the ones who own BlackBerrys, use Gmail, Facebook, and Twitter, and compose only on computer screens—will soon begin shipping their hard drives off to university libraries.

What happens then is something much on the minds of Matthew G. Kirschenbaum (The Chronicle, August 17, 2007) and Douglas L. Reside. Both Mr. Kirschenbaum, associate director of the Maryland Institute for Technology in the Humanities at the University of Maryland, and Mr. Reside, an assistant director at the institute, possess the collection of skills that may eventually be required of all 21st-century curators. In addition to holding doctorates in English, they are computer experts.

The institute, located in an austere warren of offices in the basement of the university's McKeldin Library, houses a mix of sleek new machines and clunky old ones. An easy office-chair roll away from his newest computer sits Mr. Kirschenbaum's oldest one: a small, gray box known as the Apple II. Mr. Reside's office contains similar artifacts, including a Commodore 64 gaming console.

Amid the institute's state-of-the-art machines, these ridiculous-looking antiques are stark reminders of how rapidly computer technology has evolved, producing one of the major challenges of preservation in the digital age: compatibility.

The problem with the dizzying pace of computer evolution is that new machines are often incapable of learning old tricks—even if the tricks are not really that old. For instance, most new computers don't come with floppy-disk drives. And while Harvard will surely procure machines that can safely read Mr. Updike's disk-based papers, what if those papers were trapped inside an even older storage device—say, something resembling a Commodore 64 game cartridge? Future archivists must have the skills to retrieve them.

Brave New World

Archivists must also know how to transfer their data to new machines, since old machines can survive for only so long before their circuits give out.

That, Ms. Nelson says, calls for people with intimate knowledge of how the new stuff works, plus the resourcefulness to retrofit modernity's round holes to accommodate antiquity's square pegs. "We're still going to need people who are experts in the history of the book, people who study handwriting, organize paper collections, handle obsolete video formats, traditional photography. . . . We're going to do everything we've been doing, and then we're going to be doing this."

Ms. Nelson understands this better than most: While Mr. Updike's floppy disks at Harvard probably contain simple text documents, the digital devices Mr. Rushdie donated to Emory contain entire ecosystems of data.

Writers today do a lot more on computers than they used to, and modern devices hold a lot more information about their users than old ones did. The laptop (and now the mobile device) has become the locus of social life as correspondence has migrated from letters and phone calls to e-mail and text chatting. Recreational reading and research have also increasingly moved to the Web.

Since a laptop logs basically everything its user does, preserving these data environments will allow the scholars of the future unprecedented insight into the minds of literary geniuses. "It's basically like giving someone the keys to your house," says Mr. Kirschenbaum.

The influence of authors' environments on their writing has always interested scholars. Marcel Proust, for example, is known to have been heavily influenced by the paintings he surrounded himself with when he penned the novel *Remembrance of Things Past,* between 1909 and 1922. Imagine if Proust had been writing 100 years later, on a laptop: What else we might be able to learn about his creative process?

The implications for scholarship are tremendous, Mr. Kirschenbaum says. Take a great digital-era author: "You could potentially look at a browser history, see that he visited a particular website on a particular day and time," he says. "And then if you were to go into the draft of one of his manuscripts, you could see that draft was edited at a particular day and hour, and you could establish a connection between something he was looking at on the Web with something that he then wrote."

In some cases, computer forensics can even hint at an author's influences beyond the screen. Mr. Reside recently mined data from old equipment belonging to Jonathan Larson, the late composer and playwright who earned a Pulitzer Prize posthumously for the musical *Rent.* In an early draft, Larson had a character suggest that the moonlight coming through the window is really "fluorescent light from the Gap." In the final draft, the lyric was "Spike Lee shooting down the street."

"From the time stamp on the digital files," Mr. Reside says, "I learned that the lyric was changed in the spring of 1992 . . . when, I believe, Spike Lee was shooting *Malcolm X* in New York City."

A Deluge of Data

That is really just scratching the surface. Imagine how mapping the content of an author's Facebook profile, MySpace page, Flickr account, or Twitter feed might help scholars dissect that author's life and letters. The social-media generation has developed a habit of casually volunteering biographical information. When the great authors of that generation emerge, scholars may be pleased to find plenty of fodder for study already on the public record.

But that is where things get tricky. Information that lives inside a writer's personal hardware—like the data on Mr. Updike's floppy disks or Mr. Rushdie's hard drives—may not have physical dimensions, but it is at least attached to a single device that is owned by somebody. "It's physically here," says Mr. Kirschenbaum, gesturing toward a shelf of Apple Classic computers, donated to the Maryland institute by the poet Deena Larsen. "I can wrap my arms around it."

Not so with e-mail and social-media content. These are not programs run on individual computers; they are Web-based services, hosted remotely by companies like Facebook and Google. The content exists in an ethereal mass of data known in information-technology circles as "the cloud." There, Mr. Kirschenbaum says, "you get into this wilderness of competing terms of service."

With more and more information being stored on the Web, it is no longer clear who owns what.

For example, in February, Facebook rewrote its terms of service to stake a claim on all content that users put on their profiles. After a backlash, the company hastily backed off and reiterated that users own their own profile content. But the case is a reminder of the fluidity and ambiguity of ownership laws in the dawning era of shared media.

"Consumers don't really know their rights here, and many are so wowed with the convenience that they aren't asking themselves the tough questions yet," says Susan E. Thomas, digital archivist at the University of Oxford's Bodleian Library. "Right now we can collect boxes from the attic, but if the family request a cloud service to transfer the archive of their loved one to the Bodleian Library, will that happen? We haven't tried it yet, so I can't tell you."

"That's sort of the brick wall that every archivist knows they're hurtling toward at 100 miles per hour," says Mr. Kirschenbaum.

No Manual

Many other questions also remain unanswered. For example, how much information is too much? A 20th-century author's personal papers might be of manageable quantity—say, what she was able to store in her attic. Digital storage, on the other hand, is cheap, easy, and virtually unlimited. Mining, sorting, and archiving every bit of data stored in author's computers could become a chore of paralyzing tedium and diminishing value.

At present, researchers are wary of discarding anything. "The work of an author over their entire lifetime is such a fraction of the space you have on a server hard disk, so there's no reason to throw any of that away," says Mr. Kirschenbaum. However, he added, unless scholars are able to find what they want in that sea of data, it is not worth archiving in the first place.

The good news is that as computers are logging more data, reference technology is growing more sophisticated. And Ms. Nelson suggests that the new tools for interacting with born-digital artifacts—including a wiki functionality that could allow researchers to annotate materials and share their insights with others—may not be too far away.

New tools and new training, however, mean new money. Richard Ovenden, associate director of Oxford's Bodleian Library, says the speed at which universities adopt digital curation may depend on their willingness to divert funds from more traditional areas. And that could be at a slower pace than the speed of technological invention itself.

Critical Thinking

1. Kolowich early on points out a problem associated with digitizing library holdings: Digital formats and the computers on which they are stored change rapidly. Within a very short time, neither the hardware on which library holdings are stored nor the software nor the expertise to link the two might exist. How are libraries coping with this eventuality?

2. Has Google publicly addressed the problem of how its soon to be massive collection of digitized books will be ported to new generations of computing equipment?

3. Microfiche/microfilm has been used by libraries since the 1930s to archive newspapers. Find out how microfiche/microfilm is being used (or not used) in your library.

4. A while back there was an effort to digitize library holdings of newspapers because they were printed, it was argued, on acidic paper that would deteriorate over time. How is that project progressing?

Degrees, Distance, and Dollars

The Internet is making higher education accessible to a whole new class of students—but not necessarily at a lower cost.

MARINA KRAKOVSKY

Podcasting, high-speed Internet, email, message boards—the technology for distance learning has made it less and less necessary for students to go to college the old-fashioned way. Yet, the demand for higher education continues to rise at double-digit rates, boosting the number of students taking one or more online courses in the U.S. in the fall of 2008 to 2.4 million, up from 1.6 million in 2002, according to the most recent survey by the Sloan Consortium, an organization supporting online education.

These numbers do not include the free non-credit courses available through iTunes U, which offers 250,000 free lectures from more than 600 schools, including Yale and Massachusetts Institute of Technology. Yet while elite schools are reaching the masses as a philanthropic gesture, they tend to avoid granting more degrees. "Your Stanfords and Columbias and NYUs and Boston Colleges of the world—they have terrific incentives not to grow," says Guilbert C. Hentschke, a professor at the University of Southern California's (USC's) Rossier School of Education. That's because exclusive schools are, by definition, highly selective—and admitting more students would dilute their brands.

A similar dynamic works in other traditional universities, as well. A school's *U.S. News & World Report* annual ranking depends in part on teacher salaries and per-student spending, so going online and reducing costs can tarnish a school's image. If public universities graduate many students who have taken online courses, it's only because the schools are by far the largest sector in American higher education, Hentschke says. State funding has kept most of them from going online in a substantial way, though severe budget cuts in recent months are prompting the University of California, Berkeley and Rutgers University, among others, to consider online instruction to help fill budget gaps.

Even so, the biggest growth in online schooling has been among for-profit universities, which includes obscure institutions and more familiar names like Kaplan, DeVry University, and the biggest gorilla of all, the University of Phoenix, which currently has 455,600 students, more than half of whom take at least some courses online. As public community colleges turn away tens of thousands of students each year, they create a huge opportunity for for-profits offering associate degrees and higher. The online schools lure students with Internet ads touting instant enrollment and 24/7 access. And whereas traditional universities use tuition from large lecture classes to cover losses from costlier or under-subscribed programs, for-profits can aim precisely where the

money is, focusing on degrees in computer science (especially IT), business, health care, education, and other marketable fields.

Most of the students who flock to online programs are nontraditional; their time and locale is constrained by jobs, military service, and dependent children. "Online education is not only more convenient, but for some students it's the only option they've got," says Hentschke.

Education in computer science is a case in point. The National Science Foundation wants to increase the number of advanced placement CS teachers to 10,000 by 2015, which is five times today's number. Current undergraduates alone aren't likely to meet that demand, but by taking online classes after work, other candidates, such as math teachers, can branch out into teaching CS, suggests Mark Guzdial, a professor at George Institute of Technology and expert in computer science education. Similarly, if female managers in tech firms hit the glass ceiling in part by not finding time to learn the latest tools, as an Anita Borg Institute study suggests, then being able to take classes from home should help close the gender gap in upper management. "These two audiences are poorly served by face-to-face CS courses, but may be well served by distance learning," Guzdial says.

Online education in computer science varies in quality, but the range of offerings is impressive, covering everything from introductory programming and Microsoft certification to graduate-level courses in database theory, network security, and human-computer interaction.

Convenience at a Price

You might expect online courses to also be cheaper, but that is rarely the case. Although online students save time, living expenses, and transportation costs, they typically pay at least as much in tuition as they would for a traditional education. The University of Phoenix, for example, charges the same for both formats, and according to the College Board the average sticker price at a for-profit university is about $14,000 for the 2009–2010 academic year.

Why the high price even online? Some education experts contend that good instruction is always labor-intensive. "I could set up an online course and have a thousand students and teach it myself, but what's the quality going to be?" says Donald Heller, who directs the Center for the Study of Higher Education at Pennsylvania State University. It is true that technology enables a small team to design a course and a lower-paid army of instructors to deliver it, grade papers, and interact with students, but that is not very different from what traditional colleges have been doing for decades, Heller argues. Diane Harley, a University of California, Berkeley anthropologist who directs the university's Higher Education in the Digital Age research project, agrees. "It's not cheap to produce high-quality online courses from soup to nuts," she says, quoting the oft-cited $1 million per state-of-the-art course such as those produced by Carnegie Mellon University's Open Learning Initiative.

Nonetheless, because schools can add students without erecting new buildings, a school's costs for each additional student can be quite small—low enough that a company called Straighterline profitably sells basics on algebra and English composition for just $99 per month, plus $39 per course. Although it doesn't grant degrees, Straighterline grades coursework and issues transcripts that students can turn into credits at the colleges where they are enrolled.

But this low-priced model remains the exception in online education, where for a host of reasons schools have not passed their savings on to students. In fact, sometimes an online degree costs more than its brick-and-mortar equivalent—a price premium not just for convenience, but for hassle-free admissions, suggests Vicky Phillips, founder and chief analyst of GetEducated.com, a watchdog group for online learning. "People research schools with online MBA programs and find out that Indiana University has a price that's one-third of the University of Phoenix's price, and then they find out they have to take the GRE and GMAT and 12 prerequisite courses [for Indiana University]. Welcome to the age of 'I'm not going to do it.'"

The ease of enrolling with little more than a credit card may bring to mind diploma mills and doubts about credibility with employers, but that is less a concern for many of the students who seek their education online. "If I grew up in southern rural Indiana, if I say, 'I have an MBA,' I'm going to blow people away. They don't care where that degree came from," says Phillips. And in a market where objective measures of educational quality are hard to come by, consumers look to price as a signal of quality.

High prices, oddly enough, also keep students enrolled. "If it's too cheap, the school risks losing its accreditation," says Eric Bettinger, associate professor of economics and education at Stanford University's Graduate School of Business. That's because low prices make it more tempting for students to drop out, and high drop-out rates are a red flag to regional accrediting bodies. Some experts believe that Pell Grants, military subsidies, and other federal student aid, all of which for-profit schools urge students to pursue, have also inflated the price of online schooling.

The Future of Higher Ed

Despite their rapid growth, the for-profits are not giving traditional universities a run for their money just yet. Most students still prefer face-to-face contact and a well-recognized credential. Unlike print newspapers, whose survival the Internet has helped endanger, traditional colleges offer much more than information. The schools that are not secure have more impetus to go online,

says GetEducated.com's Phillips, is "this vast wasteland of private mediocre schools." She cites schools like Michigan's Baker College, which has historically catered to the auto industry. With this local customer base eroding, Baker needed to extend its geographic reach to stay in business. But, as Phillips puts it, "the problem with the Internet is the whole world is your marketplace—and it's also your competition."

Specialization can make it easier to compete. By offering classes online, USC's School of Gerontology, for example, can attract a large number of students even to a niche program for managers of nursing homes. Similarly, Penn State Online offers a master's degree in homeland security. Indeed, whereas only about 33% of providers of bachelor's degree programs surveyed by the Sloan Consortium said that online education is critical to their school's long-term strategy, nearly two-thirds of master's, doctoral, and specialized programs said so. All that shows the Long Tail is at work in higher education, and, says Hentschke, that tail will only get longer. "The model of the 18- to 22-year-old going to a residential campus like USC and watching football games and that kind of stuff will be around for along time," he says, "but the demand for other models is coming from lots of other areas and demographics."

References

Allen, E. and Seaman, J. *Learning on Demand: Online Education in the United States, 2009.* Babson College and The Sloan Consortium, 2009.

Bramble, W.J. and Panda, S.K. *Economics of Distance and Online Learning: Theory, Practice, and Research.* Routledge, New York, NY, 2008.

Carey, K. *College for $99 a month.* Washington Monthly, September/October 2009.

Kumar, A.N. The effect of using problem-solving software tutors on the self-confidence of female students. Proceedings of the Thirty-Ninth Special Interest Group on Computer Science Education, March 12–15, 2008, Portland, OR.

Tierney, W.G. and Hentschke, G.C. *New Players, Different Game: Understanding the Rise of For-Profit Colleges and Universities.* Johns Hopkins University Press, Baltimore, MD, 2007.

Critical Thinking

1. Does your university/department offer online courses? Do these appear on transcripts as having been taken online?

2. Suppose you were a manager. Would a résumé listing an online degree carry the same weight in your eyes as one with a conventional degree? Why or why not?

3. What do the authors mean by hassle-free admissions?

4. Have you taken an online course? How does it compare to an on-site course?

5. Is there a relationship between an online course and an online relationship?

Small Change

Why the Revolution Will Not Be Tweeted

MALCOLM GLADWELL

Social media can't provide what social change has always required.

At four-thirty in the afternoon on Monday, February 1, 1960, four college students sat down at the lunch counter at the Woolworth's in downtown Greensboro, North Carolina. They were freshmen at North Carolina A. & T., a black college a mile or so away.

"I'd like a cup of coffee, please," one of the four, Ezell Blair, said to the waitress.

"We don't serve Negroes here," she replied.

The Woolworth's lunch counter was a long L-shaped bar that could seat sixty-six people, with a standup snack bar at one end. The seats were for whites. The snack bar was for blacks. Another employee, a black woman who worked at the steam table, approached the students and tried to warn them away. "You're acting stupid, ignorant!" she said. They didn't move. Around five-thirty, the front doors to the store were locked. The four still didn't move. Finally, they left by a side door. Outside, a small crowd had gathered, including a photographer from the Greensboro *Record*. "I'll be back tomorrow with A. & T. College," one of the students said.

By next morning, the protest had grown to twenty-seven men and four women, most from the same dormitory as the original four. The men were dressed in suits and ties. The students had brought their schoolwork, and studied as they sat at the counter. On Wednesday, students from Greensboro's "Negro" secondary school, Dudley High, joined in, and the number of protesters swelled to eighty. By Thursday, the protesters numbered three hundred, including three white women, from the Greensboro campus of the University of North Carolina. By Saturday, the sit-in had reached six hundred. People spilled out onto the street. White teen-agers waved Confederate flags. Someone threw a firecracker. At noon, the A. & T. football team arrived. "Here comes the wrecking crew," one of the white students shouted.

By the following Monday, sit-ins had spread to Winston-Salem, twenty-five miles away, and Durham, fifty miles away. The day after that, students at Fayetteville State Teachers College and at Johnson C. Smith College, in Charlotte, joined in, followed on Wednesday by students at St. Augustine's College and Shaw University, in Raleigh. On Thursday and Friday, the protest crossed state lines, surfacing in Hampton and Portsmouth, Virginia, in Rock Hill, South Carolina, and in Chattanooga, Tennessee. By the end of the month, there were sit-ins throughout the South, as far west as Texas. "I asked every student I met what the first day of the sitdowns had been like on his campus," the political theorist Michael Walzer wrote in *Dissent*. "The answer was always the same: 'It was like a fever. Everyone wanted to go.'" Some seventy thousand students eventually took part. Thousands were arrested and untold thousands more radicalized. These events in the early sixties became a civil-rights war that engulfed the South for the rest of the decade—and it happened without e-mail, texting, Facebook, or Twitter.

The world, we are told, is in the midst of a revolution. The new tools of social media have reinvented social activism. With Facebook and Twitter and the like, the traditional relationship between political authority and popular will has been upended, making it easier for the powerless to collaborate, coördinate, and give voice to their concerns. When ten thousand protesters took to the streets in Moldova in the spring of 2009 to protest against their country's Communist government, the action was dubbed the Twitter Revolution, because of the means by which the demonstrators had been brought together. A few months after that, when student protests rocked Tehran, the State Department took the unusual step of asking Twitter to suspend scheduled maintenance of its Web site, because the Administration didn't want such a critical organizing tool out of service at the height of the demonstrations. "Without Twitter the people of Iran would not have felt empowered and confident to stand up for freedom and democracy," Mark Pfeifle, a former national-security adviser, later wrote, calling for Twitter to be nominated for the Nobel Peace Prize. Where activists were once defined by their causes, they are now defined by their tools. Facebook warriors go online to push for change. "You are the best hope for us all," James K. Glassman, a former senior State Department official, told a crowd of cyber activists at a recent conference sponsored by Facebook, A. T. & T., Howcast, MTV, and Google. Sites like Facebook, Glassman said, "give the U.S. a significant competitive advantage over terrorists. Some time ago, I said that Al Qaeda was 'eating our lunch on the Internet.' That is no longer the case. Al Qaeda is stuck in Web 1.0. The Internet is now about interactivity and conversation."

These are strong, and puzzling, claims. Why does it matter who is eating whose lunch on the Internet? Are people who log on to their Facebook page really the best hope for us all? As for Moldova's so-called Twitter Revolution, Evgeny Morozov, a scholar at Stanford who has been the most persistent of digital evangelism's critics, points out that Twitter had scant internal significance in Moldova, a country where very few Twitter accounts exist. Nor does it seem to have been a revolution, not least because the protests—as Anne Applebaum suggested in the *Washington Post*—may well have been a bit of stagecraft cooked up by the government. (In a country paranoid about Romanian revanchism, the protesters flew a Romanian flag over the Parliament building.) In the Iranian case, meanwhile, the people tweeting about the demonstrations were almost all in the West. "It is time to get Twitter's role in the events in Iran right," Golnaz Esfandiari wrote, this past summer, in *Foreign Policy*. "Simply put: There was no Twitter

Revolution inside Iran." The cadre of prominent bloggers, like Andrew Sullivan, who championed the role of social media in Iran, Esfandiari continued, misunderstood the situation. "Western journalists who couldn't reach—or didn't bother reaching?—people on the ground in Iran simply scrolled through the English-language tweets post with tag #iranelection," she wrote. "Through it all, no one seemed to wonder why people trying to coordinate protests in Iran would be writing in any language other than Farsi."

Some of this grandiosity is to be expected. Innovators tend to be solipsists. They often want to cram every stray fact and experience into their new model. As the historian Robert Darnton has written, "The marvels of communication technology in the present have produced a false consciousness about the past—even a sense that communication has no history, or had nothing of importance to consider before the days of television and the Internet." But there is something else at work here, in the outsized enthusiasm for social media. Fifty years after one of the most extraordinary episodes of social upheaval in American history, we seem to have forgotten what activism is.

Greensboro in the early nineteen-sixties was the kind of place where racial insubordination was routinely met with violence. The four students who first sat down at the lunch counter were terrified. "I suppose if anyone had come up behind me and yelled 'Boo,' I think I would have fallen off my seat," one of them said later. On the first day, the store manager notified the police chief, who immediately sent two officers to the store. On the third day, a gang of white toughs showed up at the lunch counter and stood ostentatiously behind the protesters, ominously muttering epithets such as "burr-head nigger." A local Ku Klux Klan leader made an appearance. On Saturday, as tensions grew, someone called in a bomb threat, and the entire store had to be evacuated.

The dangers were even clearer in the Mississippi Freedom Summer Project of 1964, another of the sentinel campaigns of the civil-rights movement. The Student Nonviolent Coordinating Committee recruited hundreds of Northern, largely white unpaid volunteers to run Freedom Schools, register black voters, and raise civil-rights awareness in the Deep South. "No one should go *anywhere* alone, but certainly not in an automobile and certainly not at night," they were instructed. Within days of arriving in Mississippi, three volunteers—Michael Schwerner, James Chaney, and Andrew Goodman—were kidnapped and killed, and, during the rest of the summer, thirty-seven black churches were set on fire and dozens of safe houses were bombed; volunteers were beaten, shot at, arrested, and trailed by pickup trucks full of armed men. A quarter of those in the program dropped out. Activism that challenges the status quo—that attacks deeply rooted problems—is not for the faint of heart.

What makes people capable of this kind of activism? The Stanford sociologist Doug McAdam compared the Freedom Summer dropouts with the participants who stayed, and discovered that the key difference wasn't, as might be expected, ideological fervor. "*All* of the applicants—participants and withdrawals alike—emerge as highly committed, articulate supporters of the goals and values of the summer program," he concluded. What mattered more was an applicant's degree of personal connection to the civil-rights movement. All the volunteers were required to provide a list of personal contacts—the people they wanted kept apprised of their activities—and participants were far more likely than dropouts to have close friends who were also going to Mississippi. High-risk activism, McAdam concluded, is a "strong-tie" phenomenon.

This pattern shows up again and again. One study of the Red Brigades, the Italian terrorist group of the nineteen-seventies, found that seventy per cent of recruits had at least one good friend already in the organization. The same is true of the men who joined the mujahideen in Afghanistan. Even revolutionary actions that look spontaneous, like the demonstrations in East Germany that led to the fall of the Berlin Wall, are, at core, strong-tie phenomena. The opposition movement in East Germany consisted of several hundred groups, each with roughly a dozen members. Each group was in limited contact with the others: at the time, only thirteen per cent of East Germans even had a phone. All they knew was that on Monday nights, outside St. Nicholas Church in downtown Leipzig, people gathered to voice their anger at the state. And the primary determinant of who showed up was "critical friends"—the more friends you had who were critical of the regime the more likely you were to join the protest.

So one crucial fact about the four freshmen at the Greensboro lunch counter—David Richmond, Franklin McCain, Ezell Blair, and Joseph McNeil—was their relationship with one another. McNeil was a roommate of Blair's in A. & T.'s Scott Hall dormitory. Richmond roomed with McCain one floor up, and Blair, Richmond, and McCain had all gone to Dudley High School. The four would smuggle beer into the dorm and talk late into the night in Blair and McNeil's room. They would all have remembered the murder of Emmett Till in 1955, the Montgomery bus boycott that same year, and the showdown in Little Rock in 1957. It was McNeil who brought up the idea of a sit-in at Woolworth's. They'd discussed it for nearly a month. Then McNeil came into the dorm room and asked the others if they were ready. There was a pause, and McCain said, in a way that works only with people who talk late into the night with one another, "Are you guys chicken or not?" Ezell Blair worked up the courage the next day to ask for a cup of coffee because he was flanked by his roommate and two good friends from high school.

The kind of activism associated with social media isn't like this at all. The platforms of social media are built around weak ties. Twitter is a way of following (or being followed by) people you may never have met. Facebook is a tool for efficiently managing your acquaintances, for keeping up with the people you would not otherwise be able to stay in touch with. That's why you can have a thousand "friends" on Facebook, as you never could in real life.

This is in many ways a wonderful thing. There is strength in weak ties, as the sociologist Mark Granovetter has observed. Our acquaintances—not our friends—are our greatest source of new ideas and information. The Internet lets us exploit the power of these kinds of distant connections with marvellous efficiency. It's terrific at the diffusion of innovation, interdisciplinary collaboration, seamlessly matching up buyers and sellers, and the logistical functions of the dating world. But weak ties seldom lead to high-risk activism.

In a new book called "The Dragonfly Effect: Quick, Effective, and Powerful Ways to Use Social Media to Drive Social Change," the business consultant Andy Smith and the Stanford Business School professor Jennifer Aaker tell the story of Sameer Bhatia, a young Silicon Valley entrepreneur who came down with acute myelogenous leukemia. It's a perfect illustration of social media's strengths. Bhatia needed a bone-marrow transplant, but he could not find a match among his relatives and friends. The odds were best with a donor of his ethnicity, and there were few South Asians in the national bone-marrow database. So Bhatia's business partner sent out an e-mail explaining Bhatia's plight to more than four hundred of their acquaintances, who forwarded the e-mail to their personal contacts; Facebook pages and YouTube videos were devoted to the Help Sameer campaign. Eventually, nearly twenty-five thousand new people were registered in the bone-marrow database, and Bhatia found a match.

But how did the campaign get so many people to sign up? By not asking too much of them. That's the only way you can get someone you don't really know to do something on your behalf. You can get thousands of people to sign up for a donor registry, because doing so is pretty easy. You have to send in a cheek swab and—in the highly unlikely event that your bone marrow is a good match for someone in need—spend a few hours at the hospital. Donating bone marrow isn't a trivial matter. But it doesn't involve financial or personal risk; it doesn't mean spending a summer being chased by armed men in pickup trucks. It doesn't require that you confront socially entrenched norms and practices. In fact, it's the kind of commitment that will bring only social acknowledgment and praise.

The evangelists of social media don't understand this distinction; they seem to believe that a Facebook friend is the same as a real friend and that signing up for a donor registry in Silicon Valley today is activism in the same sense as sitting at a segregated lunch counter in Greensboro in 1960. "Social networks are particularly effective at increasing motivation," Aaker and Smith write. But that's not true. Social networks are effective at increasing *participation*—by lessening the level of motivation that participation requires. The Facebook page of the Save Darfur Coalition has 1,282,339 members, who have donated an average of nine cents apiece. The next biggest Darfur charity on Facebook has 22,073 members, who have donated an average of thirty-five cents. Help Save Darfur has 2,797 members, who have given, on average, fifteen cents. A spokesperson for the Save Darfur Coalition told *Newsweek,* "We wouldn't necessarily gauge someone's value to the advocacy movement based on what they've given. This is a powerful mechanism to engage this critical population. They inform their community, attend events, volunteer. It's not something you can measure by looking at a ledger." In other words, Facebook activism succeeds not by motivating people to make a real sacrifice but by motivating them to do the things that people do when they are not motivated enough to make a real sacrifice. We are a long way from the lunch counters of Greensboro.

The students who joined the sit-ins across the South during the winter of 1960 described the movement as a "fever." But the civil-rights movement was more like a military campaign than like a contagion. In the late nineteen-fifties, there had been sixteen sit-ins in various cities throughout the South, fifteen of which were formally organized by civil-rights organizations like the N.A.A.C.P. and CORE. Possible locations for activism were scouted. Plans were drawn up. Movement activists held training sessions and retreats for would-be protesters. The Greensboro Four were a product of this groundwork: all were members of the N.A.A.C.P. Youth Council. They had close ties with the head of the local N.A.A.C.P. chapter. They had been briefed on the earlier wave of sit-ins in Durham, and had been part of a series of movement meetings in activist churches. When the sit-in movement spread from Greensboro throughout the South, it did not spread indiscriminately. It spread to those cities which had preëxisting "movement centers"—a core of dedicated and trained activists ready to turn the "fever" into action.

The civil-rights movement was high-risk activism. It was also, crucially, strategic activism: a challenge to the establishment mounted with precision and discipline. The N.A.A.C.P. was a centralized organization, run from New York according to highly formalized operating procedures. At the Southern Christian Leadership Conference, Martin Luther King, Jr., was the unquestioned authority. At the center of the movement was the black church, which had, as Aldon D. Morris points out in his superb 1984 study, "The Origins of the Civil Rights Movement," a carefully demarcated division of labor, with various standing committees and disciplined groups. "Each group was task-oriented and coordinated its activities through authority structures," Morris writes. "Individuals were held accountable for their assigned duties, and important conflicts were resolved by the minister, who usually exercised ultimate authority over the congregation."

This is the second crucial distinction between traditional activism and its online variant: social media are not about this kind of

hierarchical organization. Facebook and the like are tools for building *networks,* which are the opposite, in structure and character, of hierarchies. Unlike hierarchies, with their rules and procedures, networks aren't controlled by a single central authority. Decisions are made through consensus, and the ties that bind people to the group are loose.

This structure makes networks enormously resilient and adaptable in low-risk situations. Wikipedia is a perfect example. It doesn't have an editor, sitting in New York, who directs and corrects each entry. The effort of putting together each entry is self-organized. If every entry in Wikipedia were to be erased tomorrow, the content would swiftly be restored, because that's what happens when a network of thousands spontaneously devote their time to a task.

There are many things, though, that networks don't do well. Car companies sensibly use a network to organize their hundreds of suppliers, but not to design their cars. No one believes that the articulation of a coherent design philosophy is best handled by a sprawling, leaderless organizational system. Because networks don't have a centralized leadership structure and clear lines of authority, they have real difficulty reaching consensus and setting goals. They can't think strategically; they are chronically prone to conflict and error. How do you make difficult choices about tactics or strategy or philosophical direction when everyone has an equal say?

The Palestine Liberation Organization originated as a network, and the international-relations scholars Mette Eilstrup-Sangiovanni and Calvert Jones argue in a recent essay in *International Security* that this is why it ran into such trouble as it grew: "Structural features typical of networks—the absence of central authority, the unchecked autonomy of rival groups, and the inability to arbitrate quarrels through formal mechanisms—made the P.L.O. excessively vulnerable to outside manipulation and internal strife."

In Germany in the nineteen-seventies, they go on, "the far more unified and successful left-wing terrorists tended to organize hierarchically, with professional management and clear divisions of labor. They were concentrated geographically in universities, where they could establish central leadership, trust, and camaraderie through regular, face-to-face meetings." They seldom betrayed their comrades in arms during police interrogations. Their counterparts on the right were organized as decentralized networks, and had no such discipline. These groups were regularly infiltrated, and members, once arrested, easily gave up their comrades. Similarly, Al Qaeda was most dangerous when it was a unified hierarchy. Now that it has dissipated into a network, it has proved far less effective.

The drawbacks of networks scarcely matter if the network isn't interested in systemic change—if it just wants to frighten or humiliate or make a splash—or if it doesn't need to think strategically. But if you're taking on a powerful and organized establishment you have to be a hierarchy. The Montgomery bus boycott required the participation of tens of thousands of people who depended on public transit to get to and from work each day. It lasted a *year.* In order to persuade those people to stay true to the cause, the boycott's organizers tasked each local black church with maintaining morale, and put together a free alternative private carpool service, with forty-eight dispatchers and forty-two pickup stations. Even the White Citizens Council, King later said, conceded that the carpool system moved with "military precision." By the time King came to Birmingham, for the climactic showdown with Police Commissioner Eugene (Bull) Connor, he had a budget of a million dollars, and a hundred full-time staff members on the ground, divided into operational units. The operation itself was divided into steadily escalating phases, mapped out in advance. Support was maintained through consecutive mass meetings rotating from church to church around the city.

Boycotts and sit-ins and nonviolent confrontations—which were the weapons of choice for the civil-rights movement—are high-risk strategies. They leave little room for conflict and error. The moment even one protester deviates from the script and responds to provocation, the moral legitimacy of the entire protest is compromised. Enthusiasts for social media would no doubt have us believe that King's task in Birmingham would have been made infinitely easier had he been able to communicate with his followers through Facebook, and contented himself with tweets from a Birmingham jail. But networks are messy: think of the ceaseless pattern of correction and revision, amendment and debate, that characterizes Wikipedia. If Martin Luther King, Jr., had tried to do a wiki-boycott in Montgomery, he would have been steamrollered by the white power structure. And of what use would a digital communication tool be in a town where ninety-eight per cent of the black community could be reached every Sunday morning at church? The things that King needed in Birmingham—discipline and strategy—were things that online social media cannot provide.

The bible of the social-media movement is Clay Shirky's "Here Comes Everybody." Shirky, who teaches at New York University, sets out to demonstrate the organizing power of the Internet, and he begins with the story of Evan, who worked on Wall Street, and his friend Ivanna, after she left her smart phone, an expensive Sidekick, on the back seat of a New York City taxicab. The telephone company transferred the data on Ivanna's lost phone to a new phone, whereupon she and Evan discovered that the Sidekick was now in the hands of a teen-ager from Queens, who was using it to take photographs of herself and her friends.

When Evan e-mailed the teen-ager, Sasha, asking for the phone back, she replied that his "white ass" didn't deserve to have it back. Miffed, he set up a Web page with her picture and a description of what had happened. He forwarded the link to his friends, and they forwarded it to their friends. Someone found the MySpace page of Sasha's boyfriend, and a link to it found its way onto the site. Someone found her address online and took a video of her home while driving by; Evan posted the video on the site. The story was picked up by the news filter Digg. Evan was now up to ten e-mails a minute. He created a bulletin board for his readers to share their stories, but it crashed under the weight of responses. Evan and Ivanna went to the police, but the police filed the report under "lost," rather than "stolen," which essentially closed the case. "By this point millions of readers were watching," Shirky writes, "and dozens of mainstream news outlets had covered the story." Bowing to the pressure, the N.Y.P.D. reclassified the item as "stolen." Sasha was arrested, and Evan got his friend's Sidekick back.

Shirky's argument is that this is the kind of thing that could never have happened in the pre-Internet age—and he's right. Evan could never have tracked down Sasha. The story of the Sidekick would never have been publicized. An army of people could never have been assembled to wage this fight. The police wouldn't have bowed to the pressure of a lone person who had misplaced something as trivial as a cell phone. The story, to Shirky, illustrates "the ease and speed with which a group can be mobilized for the right kind of cause" in the Internet age.

Shirky considers this model of activism an upgrade. But it is simply a form of organizing which favors the weak-tie connections that give us access to information over the strong-tie connections that help us persevere in the face of danger. It shifts our energies from organizations that promote strategic and disciplined activity and toward those which promote resilience and adaptability. It makes it easier for activists to express themselves, and harder for that expression to have any impact. The instruments of social media are well suited to making the existing social order more efficient. They are not a natural enemy of the status quo. If you are of the opinion that all the world needs is a little buffing around the edges, this should not trouble you. But if you think that there are still lunch counters out there that need integrating it ought to give you pause.

Shirky ends the story of the lost Sidekick by asking, portentously, "What happens next?"—no doubt imagining future waves of digital protesters. But he has already answered the question. What happens next is more of the same. A networked, weak-tie world is good at things like helping Wall Streeters get phones back from teen-age girls. *Viva la revolución.*

Critical Thinking

1. This article was quite controversial when it appeared in October 2010. Use the Internet to research the responses. Are you convinced by Gladwell? By his critics?

2. Gladwell says that genuine activism is a strong-tie phenomenon. What does he mean by that?

3. Gladwell makes much of the fact that the "Facebook page of the Save Darfur Coalition has 1,282,339 members, who have donated an average of nine cents apiece." The amount of the donation appears to be, in Gladwell's eyes, a proxy for the strength of the tie. Does this persuade you?

4. Gladwell says that "the instruments of social media are well suited to making the existing social order more efficient." What story did he tell to illustrate this tendency? Are you persuaded?

Don't Fear the Reaper
Four Misconceptions about How We Think about Drones

CHARLI CARPENTER AND LINA SHAIKHOUNI

Killer robots. Video-game warfare. Unlawful weapons. Terminators. Drone-attack commentary has become synonymous with reports of civilian carnage, claims of international-law violations, and worries about whether high-tech robotic wars have become too easy and fun to be effectively prevented. But the debate over drones is misleading the public about the nature of the weaponry and the law. It is also distracting attention from some more important and bigger issues: whether truly autonomous weapons should be permitted in combat, how to track the human cost of different weapons platforms and promote humanitarian standards in war, and whether targeted killings—by drones *or* SEAL teams—are lawful means to combat global terrorism. Based on our analysis of recent op-eds, we unpack four sets of misconceptions below and offer some sensible ways for the anti-drone lobby to reframe the debate.

Misconception No. 1: Drones Are "Killer Robots."

This is actually two assumptions; neither is precisely wrong, but both are misleading. First, drones themselves are not necessarily "killers": They are used for many nonlethal purposes as well. Drones (unmanned aerial vehicles) can carry anything ranging from cameras to sensors to weapons and have been deployed for nonlethal purposes such as intelligence gathering and surveillance since the 1950s. Yet the nonlethal applications of drones are often lost in a discussion that treats the technology per se as deadly; 90 percent of the op-eds we analyzed focus solely on drones as killing machines.

Of course, it's true that drones *can* be used to kill. Some drones over Libya are now armed, and armed drones have been launching strikes in Afghanistan, Pakistan, and Yemen for years. Second, even weaponized drones are not "killer robots," despite the frequent reference in the op-eds we studied to "robotic weapons" or "robotic warfare." Their flight and surveillance systems are able to extract information from their environment and use it to move safely in a purposive manner, but the weapons themselves are controlled by a human operator and are not autonomous. With a human-in-the-loop navigating the aircraft and controlling the weapon, the "killer" aspect of these specific drones may be remote-controlled, but it's not robotic.

This important distinction is easily lost on a concerned public, but the distinction matters. Indeed, the debate over "killer robot drones" that actually *aren't* autonomous is preventing public attention from being directed to a more ground-breaking development in military technology: preparations to delegate targeting decisions to truly autonomous weapons platforms, many of which are not drones at all. As Brookings Institution scholar Peter W. Singer has argued, a shift toward fully autonomous weapons systems would represent a sea change in the very nature of war. Groups like the International Committee for Robot Arms Control have called for a multilateral discussion to stem or at least regulate these developments. Those worried about drones might usefully refocus their attention to on the debate over whether to keep humans in the loop for unmanned aerial vehicles and other weapons platforms globally. The big issue here is not drones per se. It is the extent to which life-and-death targeting decisions should ever be outsourced to machines.

Misconception No. 2: Drones Make War Easy and Game-Like, and Therefore Likelier.

Remote-controlled violence even with a human in the loop also has people concerned: Nearly 40 percent of the op-eds we studied say that remote-control killing makes war too much like a video game. Many argue this increases the likelihood of armed conflict.

It's a variation on an old argument: Other revolutions in military technology—the longbow, gunpowder, the airplane—have also progressively removed the weapons-bearer from hand-to-hand combat with his foe. Many of these advances, too, were initially criticized for degrading the professional art of war or taking it away from military elites. For example, European aristocrats originally considered the longbow and firearms unchivalrous for a combination of these reasons.

It's true that all killing requires emotional distancing, and militaries throughout time have worked hard to devise ways to ease the psychological impact on soldiers of killing for the state in the national interest. Yet it's not so clear whether the so-called Nintendo effect of drones increases social distance or makes killing easier. Some anecdotal evidence suggests the opposite: Drone pilots say they suffer mental stress precisely because they have detailed, real-time images of their targets, and because they go home to their families afterward rather than debriefing with their units in the field. Studies haven't yet confirmed which view is accurate or whether it's somehow both.

Even if some variant of the Nintendo effect turns out to be real, there is little evidence that distancing soldiers from the battlefield or the act of killing makes war itself more likely rather than less. If that were true, the world would be awash in conflict. As former Lt. Col. Dave Grossman has documented, at no time in history has the combination of technology and military training strategies made killing so easy—a trend that began after World War I. Yet as political scientist Joshua Goldstein demonstrates in a forthcoming book, the incidence of international war—wars between two or more states—has been declining for 70 years.

The political debate over drones should move away from the fear that military advancements mean war is inevitable and instead focus on whether certain weapons and platforms are more or less useful for preventing conflict at a greater or lesser cost to innocent civilian lives. Activists should keep pressure on elected officials, military personnel, and other public institutions to make armed conflict, where it occurs, as bloodless as possible. For example, some human rights groups say the Nintendo effect itself could be harnessed to serve humanitarian outcomes—by embedding war law programming into game designs.

So the wider issue here, too, is not drones. It is about ensuring that a humanitarian code of conduct in war is protected and strengthened.

Misconception No. 3: Drone Strikes Kill Too Many Civilians.

It's hard to argue with this value judgment—in some ways, even one dead civilian is indeed "too many." But it's hard to single out drones when we know so little about whether they kill more or fewer civilians than manned aerial bombing or ground troops would in the same engagements—which also, in some cases, save lives. So a better question than "how many" is: relative to what, and who's counting, how?

Civilians do die in drone attacks, as they do in other types of combat. But accurate reports on drone-strike casualties—and casualties from other types of attack—are very hard to find because no official body is tasked with keeping track. This should change: All collateral damage, not just that caused by drones, needs to be counted and atoned for, and minimized by the governments that inflict it.

To demonstrate this wider problem, consider efforts to tally drone deaths. These statistics vary wildly among different sources depending on how sources define who is a militant and who is a civilian. Pakistan Body Count, which keeps a dataset based on news reports, defines all drone deaths as civilians unless the report clearly specifies which terrorist organization the dead belonged to. According to its founder, Pakistani computer scientist Zeeshan-ul-hassan Usmani, the resulting numbers suggest civilians account for 88 percent of all drone-strike deaths in Pakistan since 2004.

But the New America Foundation's similar dataset, complied by analysts Peter Bergen and Katherine Tiedemann, shows drastically different results. They too rely on news reports, but they estimate the civilian fatality rate to be only 20 percent on average since 2004. Moreover, they show this percentage is shrinking over time. Unlike Pakistan Body Count, Bergen and Tiedemann code any individuals whose status is unknown as "militants" rather than civilians. A report from the Jamestown Foundation comes up with an even lower number by excluding all men and teenage boys from the "civilian" category—a problematic maneuver from a war law perspective. It's not hard to see why the totals end up being different.

An even bigger problem with all these estimates, however, is that they do not measure actual deaths but rather "reported deaths," relying on news reports. Not all journalists, however, are trained to accurately distinguish civilians deaths from combatants. Reports often conflate militants with "suspected militants" and pool them in the same category, an assumption that discounts civilian casualties. Numbers in media reports are also sometimes vague, leaving it to the discretion of the number crunchers how to interpret them. (Pakistan Body Count translates the term "many civilians" into eight and "several civilians" into four.) Moreover, many of these reports draw on statements by the governments that are doing (or facilitating) the bombing—governments that have an incentive to minimize civilian casualty counts.

Ultimately, the problem here is bigger than drones. It is the absence of a global regime for systematically estimating how many civilians suffer deaths and injuries due to incidental harm from military operations in general. Knowing whether drones constitute the best tool for conducting certain operations requires more than counting drone-strike casualties. The question is not how much collateral damage drones cause, but whether that damage is greater or less than that from aerial attacks by manned aircraft or from ground troops.

Such data is necessary to make the case that drones either are or aren't a suitably discriminate weapon. The world needs a standardized reporting system for tracking civilian and combatant deaths globally in order to really understand the effects of different weapons technologies on civilians. Only then can we have an informed debate about how to minimize war's impact on civilians—while enabling governments to use force when necessary and legitimate. Until then, we're really just guessing.

Misconception No. 4: Drones Violate the International Law of Armed Conflict.

No, they don't—at least, no more so than any other weapons platform when it is used improperly or in the wrong context.

The Hague and Geneva conventions actually place very few restrictions on specific weapons. Nothing in the laws of war, for example, requires that weapons make killing difficult or that they level the playing field. Value judgments aside, the treaties allow for a significant amount of injury and harm both to combatants and civilians. They ask only that harm to combatants be as humane as possible and that harm to noncombatants be minimized.

Weapons have been banned outright when by design they fail on one of these criteria. Chemical weapons and certain types of land mines and cluster munitions are considered to be inherently indiscriminate because they can't be controlled once deployed. Blinding lasers were banned not because they are indiscriminate (quite the opposite) but because international society judged that permanently blinding a soldier or airman constituted superfluous suffering beyond that required by military necessity.

Weaponized drones are not themselves weapons, but rather are platforms for launching air-to-ground kinetic weapons that kill through blasts and explosions. They differ from other types of bombing platforms only in that they are remotely controlled. Although some have argued that explosive weapons used in civilian population areas do not meet the proportionality test—meaning the benefits of their use don't outweigh the humanitarian damage they cause—bombing is currently an accepted practice in international society. It is hard to argue that remotely controlled drone-fired missiles are any more unnecessarily injurious than bombs launched from the air by human pilots.

Military operations inside Pakistan *do* pose international legal problems, but it's not because of the drones. It's because the United States is technically not at war with Pakistan and because U.S. drone operations in Pakistan are being conducted by the CIA rather than the armed forces. The former violates the U.N. Charter; the latter arguably violates the rules on lawful combat in the Geneva Conventions. These dynamics create legal problems for U.S. military operations in Pakistan whether they are carried out by drones or by SEAL teams on the ground, as in the Abbottabad raid that killed Osama bin Laden. A drone, in short, can be one means by which international law is violated, but it itself is not the source of the violation.

The legal debate over drones needs to refocus on what drones are being used *for,* not on the nature or effects of the weapons themselves. The real issue is not drones, but the summary execution of suspected criminals without evidence or trial, in complete secrecy, at perhaps an unacceptable cost to innocent lives. Whether this is happening with or without the consent of the Pakistani or Yemeni government is irrelevant. Whether it is being conducted by the CIA or by the U.S. military is irrelevant. Whether it is occurring with remotely piloted drones, manned aircraft, special operations forces, or death squads is irrelevant. What matters is whether extrajudicial execution is or is not the best way to protect citizens against terrorist attacks.

Those who oppose the way drones are used should shift focus to one of the big normative problems touched by the drone issue: the military robotics revolution, collateral-damage control, and the return of extrajudicial execution. Focusing on the drones themselves misses this bigger picture.

Critical Thinking

1. What is the Reaper?

2. The authors say that drones have been "launching strikes in Afghanistan, Pakistan, and Yemen for years." Afghanistan aside, is the United States at war with these countries?

3. Many commentators have criticized the drone program, saying that by minimizing American casualties, it makes war too easy. Are you persuaded by the author's counter-arguments?

4. The authors argue that "the real issue is not drones, but the summary execution of suspected criminals without evidence or trial, in complete secrecy." Do you agree? Now recall a recent summary execution, much in the news. Do you still agree?

CHARLI CARPENTER is associate professor of international relations at the University of Massachusetts, Amherst, and blogs about human security at the *Duck of Minerva*. **LINA SHAIKHOUNI** is completing a degree in political science at the University of Massachusetts, Amherst, with an emphasis on human rights and humanitarian law.

Update: This article has been changed to reflect factual issues with the characterization of the New America Foundation dataset.

Reprinted in entirety by McGraw-Hill with permission from *Foreign Policy,* June 7, 2011. www.foreignpolicy.com. © 2011 Washingtonpost.Newsweek Interactive, LLC.

Autonomous Robots in the Fog of War

Networks of autonomous robots will someday transform warfare, but significant hurdles remain.

Lora G. Weiss

Two small planes fly low over a village, methodically scanning the streets below. Within minutes, they spot their target near the edge of town. With no way to navigate through the streets, they radio for help. Soon after, a metallic blue SUV begins moving cautiously but purposefully along the dirt roads leading to town, seeking out the target's GPS coordinates. Meanwhile, the planes continue to circle overhead, gathering updated information about the target and its surroundings. In less than half an hour after the planes take to the sky, the SUV has zeroed in on its quarry. Mission accomplished.

Last fall, my research team fielded these vehicles at Fort Benning, Ga., during the *U.S. Army's Robotics Rodeo*. That's right, the two quarter-scale Piper Cub aircraft and the Porsche Cayenne *operated without any humans* at the controls. Instead, each robot had an onboard computer running collaborative software that transformed the three machines into an autonomous, interoperable system.

The demonstration may sound simple—the target was just a tarp staked to the ground—but had this been the streets of Kabul or Baghdad, where any pile of debris can conceal a deadly improvised explosive device, such autonomous tracking robots in the future could help keep soldiers out of harm's way. Indeed, military leaders have increasingly embraced the use of unmanned aerial vehicles (UAVs) and other robotic systems over the past decade, to handle the "three D's": the dull, dirty, and dangerous tasks of war. Back in 2000, the U.S. Department of Defense (DOD) had fewer than 50 UAVs in its inventory; by early 2010, it had *more than 7000*. In 2009, the *U.S. Air Force started training* more pilots to operate unmanned systems than to fly fighters and bombers. And according to market research firm ABI Research, *65 countries now use military robots* or are in the process of acquiring them.

The ranks of battlefield robots will only grow: The U.S. Congress has mandated that by the year 2015, *one-third of ground combat vehicles* will be unmanned, and the DOD is now developing a multitude of unmanned systems that it intends to rapidly field. Meanwhile, thousands of robotics researchers worldwide are making impressive gains in networking robots and boosting the sophistication and autonomy of these systems. Despite the advances in both their performance and safety, these robots are still far from perfect, and they routinely operate in situations for which they may not have been designed and in which their responses cannot always be anticipated. Some of the DOD's most advanced UAVs carry dozens of sensors, including high-resolution night-vision cameras, 3-D imagers, and acoustic arrays. Yet most cannot distinguish a sleeping dog from a bush, even at high noon. Humans are still needed to operate the vehicles, interpret the data, and coordinate tasks among multiple systems. If we are ever to see fully autonomous robots enter the battlefield—those capable of planning and carrying out missions and learning from their experiences—several key technological advances are needed, including improved sensing, more agile testing, and seamless interoperability. Even then, a basic question will remain: How can we equip these robots to make critical decisions on their own?

A reporter on the phone asks me what will happen when robots become so smart that they can clone themselves. He seems to assume it's a given: Robots will someday be agile enough to create exact copies of their mechanical bodies and of the software code comprising their "brains." All he wants to know from me is when—not if—this great day will arrive. I suggest that he not hold his breath.

As a researcher at the *Georgia Tech Research Institute* and a board member of the world's largest association for unmanned systems— the *Association for Unmanned Vehicle Systems International*—I've been working with robots for more than two decades, starting with underwater vehicles, then moving to air and ground vehicles, and most recently addressing collaborations among robots like those we demonstrated at the Robotics Rodeo. I can attest that while robots are definitely getting smarter, it is no easy task to make them so smart that they need no adult supervision. And call me a skeptic, but I doubt they'll be cloning themselves anytime soon.

That said, I'm amazed at the pace of progress in the field. With thousands of researchers now engaged in advancing the intelligence and autonomy of unmanned systems, new breakthroughs are announced seemingly every week. Both the variety and the number of unmanned systems now deployed are breathtaking. UAVs run the gamut from the 1-metric-ton *MQ-1 Predator drone* made by General Atomics to AeroVironment's tiny 430-gram *Wasp micro air vehicle.* There are unmanned ground vehicles that roll on treads like tanks, *walk like dogs,* and *slither like snakes.* Unmanned maritime vehicles include submarine-like vessels that can cruise underwater for kilometers and boatlike craft that patrol for pirates, smugglers, and other criminal types.

But none of these systems are fully autonomous. The *RQ-4 Global Hawk UAV,* made by Northrop Grumman, is guided by satellite waypoint navigation, yet it still requires a human pilot sitting in a remote ground station, plus others to operate the drone's sensors and analyze the data being sent back. *iRobot's PackBot* tactical robot is teleoperated by means of a video-game-style controller, complete with joystick. Even the driverless vehicles that participated in the *Defense Advanced Research Projects Agency's Grand Challenge* competitions

Predator

DEVELOPER: *General Atomics*

DESCRIPTION: Unmanned aerial vehicle (UAV) for surveillance and, when equipped with Hellfire missiles, for combat. Can be remotely piloted or programmed to follow GPS waypoints.

STATUS: First deployed in 1995. Since 2001, primarily used for combat. Currently, 360 operated by U.S. military in Afghanistan, Iraq, Pakistan, and elsewhere. Also used by Italian Air Force and the United Kingdom's Royal Air Force.

Talon

DEVELOPER: *Foster-Miller/Qinetiq Group*

DESCRIPTION: 52-kilogram remotely operated unmanned ground vehicle that can be equipped for various missions, including infrared and night-vision cameras for reconnaissance, manipulator arm for improvised explosive device (IED) disposal, and rifle or grenade launcher for combat.

STATUS: Deployed by U.S. military in Bosnia, Iraq, Afghanistan, and elsewhere.

Bluefin Hauv

DEVELOPER: *Bluefin Robotics Corp./Battelle Memorial Institute*

DESCRIPTION: 79-kg unmanned underwater vehicle for ship hull inspection using high-resolution sonar. When equipped with a manipulator arm and camera, it can also do IED detection and disposal. Conducts surveys autonomously or can be remotely operated via fiber-optic tether.

STATUS: U.S. Navy awarded Bluefin US $30 million production contract in March 2011.

Mapping Swarmbots

DEVELOPERS: Georgia Tech, University of Pennsylvania, and Jet Propulsion Laboratory

DESCRIPTION: Collaborative robots that can autonomously map an entire building for first-responder and military applications. Each palm-sized robot is equipped with a video camera for identifying doorways and windows and a laser scanner for measuring walls.

STATUS: Developed under U.S. Army Research Lab's five-year, $38 million *Micro Autonomous Systems and Technology program.* Mapping experiment conducted in 2010; next iteration to include small UAVs.

T-Hawk

DEVELOPER: *Honeywell International*

DESCRIPTION: Vertical takeoff and landing 8-kg micro air vehicle equipped with color and infrared video cameras for intelligence, surveillance, and reconnaissance. Can hover and observe for up to 50 minutes at altitudes of up to 3000 meters.

STATUS: Deployed in Iraq starting in 2007 for roadside bomb detection. *Surveyed damage* at Fukushima nuclear power plant following March 2011 earthquake and tsunami in northeastern Japan.

X-47B

DEVELOPER: *Northrop Grumman Corp.*

DESCRIPTION: U.S. Navy's stealth unmanned combat aerial vehicle designed for takeoff and landing on an aircraft carrier. Has a range of 3380 kilometers and can carry up to 2000 kg of ordnance in two weapons bays. Originated as a project of the Defense Advanced Research Projects Agency.

STATUS: First test flight February 2011. Scheduled deployment by 2018.

---

in 2004, 2005, and 2007 weren't entirely autonomous, as the courses they had to negotiate were tightly controlled.

So why haven't we seen a fully autonomous robot that can sense for itself, decide for itself, and seamlessly interact with people and other machines? Unmanned systems still fall short in three key areas: sensing, testing, and interoperability. Although the most advanced robots these days may gather data from an expansive array of cameras, microphones, and other sensors, they lack the ability to process all that information in real time and then intelligently act on the results. Likewise, testing poses a problem, because there is no accepted way to subject an autonomous system to every conceivable situation it might encounter in the real world. And interoperability becomes an issue when robots of different types must interact; even more difficult is getting manned and unmanned systems to interact.

To appreciate the enormous challenge of robotic sensing, consider this factoid, *reported last year in The Economist:* "During 2009, American drone aircraft . . . sent back 24 years' worth of video footage. New

models . . . will provide ten times as many data streams . . . and those in 2011 will produce 30 times as many." It's statistics such as those that once prompted colleagues of mine to print up lanyards that read "It's the Sensor, Stupid."

But a robot is more than just a platform of sensors. Let's say an unmanned jeep is traveling down a city street. Its cameras may detect a parked car along the curb, an open manhole in the middle of the road, and a knot of school kids crossing at the intersection. But unless the jeep can correctly classify the car as a car, the manhole as a manhole, and the children as children, it won't have sufficient information to avoid those obstacles.

So the sensing problem in robotics extends well beyond just designing sophisticated new sensors. An autonomous robot needs to be able to automatically process the data from those sensors, extract relevant information from those data, and then make decisions in real time based on that information and on information it has gathered in the past. The goal is to achieve what researchers call situational understanding.

And with no humans in the loop to help interpret the data, reason about the data, and decide how to respond, situational understanding gets even trickier. Using current technology, no robot has all the onboard sensors needed to precisely decipher its environment. What's more, decisions have to be made based on uncertainties and incomplete or conflicting information. If a robo-sentry armed with a semiautomatic rifle detects someone running from a store, how can it know whether that person has just robbed the store or is simply sprinting to catch a bus? Does it fire its weapon based on what it thinks is happening?

Humans, too, may struggle to read such a situation, but perhaps unsurprisingly, society holds robots to a higher standard and has a lower tolerance for their errors. This bias may create a reluctance to take the leap in designing robots for full autonomy and so may prevent the technology from moving ahead as quickly as it could. It should not take five people to fly one UAV; one soldier should be able to fly five UAVs.

On the other hand, because military robots typically operate in geopolitically sensitive environments, some added caution is certainly warranted. What happens, for example, if a faulty sensor feeds a UAV erroneous data, causing it to cross a border without authorization? What if it mistakenly decides that a "friendly" is a target and then fires on it? If a fully autonomous, unmanned system were to make such a grave mistake, it could compromise the safety of other manned and unmanned systems and exacerbate the political situation.

The Predator UAV, developed in the 1990s, went from concept to deployment in less than 30 months, which is extremely fast by military procurement standards.

Little wonder, then, that the UAV exhibited quite a few kinks upon entering the field. Among other things, it often failed when flying in bad weather, it was troublesome to operate and maintain, and its infrared and daylight cameras had great difficulty discerning targets. But because commanders needed the drone quickly, they were willing to accept these imperfections, with the expectation that future upgrades would iron out the kinks. They didn't have time to wait until the drone had been thoroughly field-tested.

But how do you test a fully autonomous system? With robots that are remotely operated or that navigate via GPS waypoints, the vehicle's actions are known in advance. Should it deviate from its instructions, a human operator can issue an emergency shutdown command.

However, if the vehicle is making its own decisions, its behavior can't be predicted. Nor will it always be clear whether the machine is behaving appropriately and safely. Countless factors can affect the outcome of a given test: the robot's cognitive information processing, external stimuli, variations in the operational environment, hardware and software failures, false stimuli, and any new and unexpected situation a robot might encounter. New testing methods are therefore needed that provide insight and introspection into why a robot makes the decisions it makes.

Gaining such insight into a machine is akin to performing a functional MRI on a human brain. By watching which areas of the brain experience greater blood flow and neuronal activity in certain situations, neuroscientists gain a better understanding of how the brain operates. For a robot, the equivalent would be to conduct software simulations to tap the "brain" of the machine. Subjecting the robot to certain conditions, we could then watch what kinds of data its sensors collect, how it processes and analyzes those data, and how it uses the data to arrive at a decision.

Another illuminating form of testing that is often skipped in the rush to deploy today's military robots involves simply playing with the machines on an experimental "playground." The playground has well-defined boundaries and safety constraints that allow humans as well as other robots to interact with the test robot and observe its behavior. Here, it's less important to know the details of the sensor data and the

Robots in Combat

Books have been written about the feasibility and ethics of weaponizing robots, and it's not my intent to explore that topic in any great detail here. The fact is, weaponized robots—missile-launching unmanned combat air vehicles, rifle-toting unmanned combat ground vehicles, and mine-deploying unmanned combat underwater vehicles—are already a reality.

At present the decision of whether these robots attack is still left to humans. But as robots gain more autonomy, will we or won't we allow them to decide to fire weapons on their own? The U.S. Defense Department continues to mull the issue. In 2007, for instance, it released a report called *Unmanned Systems Safety Guide for DOD Acquisition* [PDF], which includes a section on designing weaponized unmanned systems. It lays out a number of ethical, legal, and technical areas of concern that any designer of armed autonomous robots should be prepared to address. These include the inadvertent firing of weapons, erroneous target discrimination, and the possibility of the enemy taking control of the unmanned system.

John Canning of the Naval Surface Warfare Center Dahlgren Division, in Virginia, has pointed out that deploying weaponized robots while maintaining a human operator to do the actual firing is costly. He's put forth several concepts of operation that might allow autonomous armed robots to coexist on the battlefield with other manned and unmanned systems. One of Canning's key concepts is to "let machines target other machines." That is, design armed unmanned systems so that they can automatically identify, target, and neutralize or destroy the weapons used by adversaries, but not the people using the weapons.

In those instances when it becomes necessary to target humans, Canning proposes that an armed unmanned system not be allowed to act autonomously but rather be remotely controlled by humans. The machine, he suggests, should be designed with "dial-a-level" autonomy so that it can switch among operational modes according to its environment and other circumstances. It would also be equipped with both nonlethal and lethal weapons, the former for convincing the enemy to abandon its arms and the latter for actually destroying those weapons.

Ronald C. Arkin, director of the Mobile Robot Laboratory at Georgia Tech, has been looking at ways to imbue robots with a sense of "ethics" [PDF] and even an artificial "conscience" so that they adhere to international rules of warfare. That should make it possible, he believes, for autonomous robots to conduct themselves on the battlefield at least as well as humans—and probably better.

—Lora G. Weiss

exact sequence of decisions that the machine is making; what emerges on the playground is whether or not the robot's behavior is acceptably safe and appropriate.

Moving to smarter and more autonomous systems will place an even greater burden on human evaluators and their ability to parse the outcomes of all this testing. But they'll never be able to assess all possible outcomes, because this would involve an infinite number of possibilities. Clearly, we need a new way of testing autonomous systems that is statistically meaningful and also inspires confidence in the results. And of course, for us to feel confident that we understand the machine's behavior and trust its decision making, such tests will need to be completed before the autonomous robot is deployed.

A swarm of small robots scatters across the floor of an abandoned warehouse. Each tread-wheeled bot, looking like a tiny tank with a mastlike antenna sticking out of its top, *investigates the floor space* around it using a video camera to identify windows and doors and a laser scanner to measure distances. Employing a technique called SLAM (for "*simultaneous localization and mapping*"), it creates a map of its surroundings, keeping track of its own position within the map. When it meets up with another robot, the two exchange maps and then head off to explore uncharted territory, eventually creating a detailed map of the entire floor.

These ingenious mapping robots, designed by researchers through the U.S. Army–funded *Micro Autonomous Systems and Technology* program, represent the cutting edge of robot autonomy. In future iterations, their designers plan to equip the machines with wall-penetrating radar and infrared sensors, as well as a flexible "whisker" to sense proximity to obstacles. Clever as they are, though, these robots lack a key capability that all future robots will need: They cannot easily interact with other kinds of robots.

Now consider the *U.S. Navy's Littoral Combat Ship.* Rather than having a fixed architecture, it will have swappable "mission modules" that include vertical takeoff unmanned aerial vehicles, unmanned underwater vehicles, and unmanned surface vehicles. All these robotic systems will have to operate in concert with each other as well as with manned systems, to support intelligence, surveillance, and reconnaissance missions, oceanographic surveys, mine warfare, port security, and so on.

Achieving this interoperability will be no small feat. While significant progress has been made on automating a single robot as well as a team of identical robots, we are not yet at the point where an unmanned system built for the Army by one contractor can seamlessly interact with another robotic system built for the Navy by another contractor. Lack of interoperability isn't exclusively a robotics problem, of course. For decades, developers of military systems of all kinds have tried and often failed to standardize their designs to allow machines of different pedigrees to exchange data. But as different branches of the military continue to add to the ranks of their battlefield robots, the enormous challenge of interoperability among these disparate systems only grows.

A particular difficulty is that most automation and control approaches, especially those used for collaborating, assume that all the unmanned systems have the same level of autonomy and the same software architecture. In practice, that is almost never the case, unless the robots have been designed from scratch to work together. Clearly, new approaches are needed so that you can introduce an unknown, autonomous system without having to reconfigure the entire suite of robots.

Interoperability between manned and unmanned systems is even more challenging. The ultimate goal is to have autonomous systems collaborate with humans as equal partners on a team, instead of simply following commands issued by their operators. For that to happen, though, the robots will need to understand human language and intent, and they will need to learn to communicate in a way that is natural for humans.

Interoperability also requires standards, procedures, and architectures that enable effective integration. Today, for instance, unmanned ground and maritime systems use a messaging standard called the *Joint Architecture for Unmanned Systems* (JAUS). The messaging standard for unmanned air systems, meanwhile, is *STANAG-4586,* a NATO-mandated format. Within their respective domains, both of these serve their purpose.

But when a UAV needs to communicate with an unmanned ground vehicle, should it use JAUS or STANAG-4586 or something else entirely? The most promising effort in this arena is the *JAUS Tool Set,* an open, standards-based unmanned vehicle messaging suite that is in beta testing. Using the tool set seems to improve interactions among unmanned vehicles. In the future, the tool set should allow the two message formats to be merged. Ultimately, that should accelerate the deployment of compatible and interoperable unmanned systems.

As robotic systems become more autonomous, they will also need the ability to consider the advice, guidance, and opinions of human users. That is, humans won't be dictating behavior or issuing hard directives, but they should still be able to influence the robot's planning and decision making. Integrating such information, including its vagaries, nuances, and uncertainties, will be a challenge for any autonomous system as its intelligence increases. But attaining these capabilities is within our reach. Of that, I am not skeptical.

Critical Thinking

1. The author states somewhat matter-of-factly that she has been "working with robots for more than two decades." Most people with highly technical skill sets ask themselves this question at some point in their careers: "Should I work on weaponry?" How would you answer that question?

2. The author appears surprised that a reporter asks her how long it will be before robots clone themselves. Were you surprised at her answer?

3. What are some of the problems researchers face in developing a fully autonomous robot?

4. Reread the sidebar, "Robots in Combat." It tells us that the director of the Mobile Robot Laboratory at Georgia Tech "has been looking at ways to imbue robots with a sense of 'ethics' and even an artificial 'conscience.'" Why are "ethics" and "conscience" in scare quotes? Use the Internet to see if you can learn how this work is progressing.

5. The military has been at the center of computing research since the beginning. To give two examples, ENIAC, the first modern computer, was developed to compute ballistics tables and ARPANET, the early Internet, was developed as a fail-safe mechanism for military communications in the event of attack. Both were put to work in the civilian sector. Use the Internet to discover other military projects that turned out to have had civilian applications.

LORA G. WEISS is a lab chief scientist at the Georgia Tech Research Institute. Her PhD work on signal processing for underwater systems first got her interested in robotics. "Signals don't propagate well underwater, so you can't rely on a human operator for control," she says. "I quickly realized that the vehicles would have to start making decisions on their own."

UNIT 6

Risk and Avoiding Risk

Unit Selections

Learning Outcomes

After reading this Unit, you will be able to:

- Understand the contours of cyber warfare and cyber espionage.

- Have a thorough understanding of the historical and legal issues surrounding privacy in the digital age.

- Understand how you pay to visit the most popular websites through the sale of your preferences to advertisers.

- Understand that offshore oil extraction depends upon highly complex, sometimes inadequately tested software.

- Have engaged in a discussion of the issues surrounding the Internet and risk youthful behavior.

Student Website

www.mhhe.com/cls

Internet References

AntiOnline: Hacking and Hackers
www.antionline.com/index.php

Copyright & Trademark Information for the IEEE Computer Society
www.computer.org/copyright.htm

Electronic Privacy Information Center (EPIC)
www.epic.org

Internet Privacy Coalition
www.epic.org/crypto

Center for Democracy and Technology
www.cdt.org

Survive Spyware
www.reviews.cnet.com/4520-3688_7-6456087-1.html

Cyber Warfare
www.en.wikipedia.org/wiki/Cyberwarfare

If literature and film are guides, we in the United States and Western Europe have tangled feelings about technology. On the one hand, we embrace each technical marvel that enters the market place. On the other, a world in which machines have gained the upper hand is a cultural staple. Not long ago, Michael Crichton's novel, *Prey,* frightened us with killer robots that evolved by natural selection to inhabit bodies, snatch souls, and take over the world. A few years later, teenagers around the country were watching the handsome couple from *The Matrix,* Neo and Trinity, take on technology run amuck. That time, our creations farmed humankind and harvested their capacity to produce energy. More recently, *Children of Men* creates a world, torn by war, in which there has not been a human birth in twenty years. Any science fiction fan could extend this list almost endlessly.

As it happens, we have good reason to worry about technology, especially computer technology. They include privacy intrusions, the deliberate (and legal) harvesting of our shopping habits for sale to advertisers, software that cannot be made error free, deliberate sabotage, and, now, cyber warfare. We even have grounds to fear that much of our cultural heritage, now digitized, will be inaccessible when the software used to encode it becomes obsolete. These are issues that concern practicing computer scientists and engineers. *The Communications of the ACM,* the leading journal in the field, has run a column for many years called Inside Risks, dedicated to exploring the unintended consequences of computing. Another ACM journal, *Software Engineering Notes,* devotes a large part of each issue to chronicling software failures.

In fact, technology, and not just computing technology, has been biting back for some time. Edward Tenner published a book chronicling what he calls "revenge effects" fifteen years ago. Revenge effects occur, he writes, "because new structures, devices, and organisms react with real people in real situations in ways we could not foresee."[1] Thus when stronger football helmets were developed in the 1960s and 1970s, players began charging with their heads forward and spines straight, resulting in more broken necks and damaged spinal columns. Similarly soldiers in Iraq have suffered more frequent brain injuries than those who served in Vietnam, largely the result of body armor and rapid evacuation of the wounded. We equip our soldiers with body armor to withstand small weapons fire and insurgents respond with head-trauma inducing rocket-propelled grenades and IEDs.[2] The moral of Tenner's story is to look beyond technological fixes for our predicaments to the social and economic systems in which they are embedded. "Technology giveth and technology taketh away."

Those who remember Y2K, remember countless news stories about the interconnectedness of computers and our increasing dependence upon them. The global communication network is vastly larger now. Since 1995, the number of Internet users around the world has grown from none to nearly a third of the world's population. Interconnected computer systems are not just more pervasive than they were a few years ago; their dispersion and our dependence on them make them more vulnerable. Greg Bruno's primer on cyber warfare ("The Evolution of Cyber Warfare"), and a piece from *The Economist* ("War in the

© Yvan Dube/Getty Images

Fifth Domain") underscore the risks. The techniques of cyber war include denial of service attacks in which there is a coordinated effort to flood servers with requests for data, invasion of communications networks, and malicious programs implanted into computers to disrupt or steal information. According to a retired lieutenant colonel, "one US response, D5, an all-encompassing term that embraces the ability to deceive, deny, disrupt, degrade, and destroy an enemy's computer information systems," comes with risks of its own.[3]

To imagine that cyber warfare is analogous to conventional warfare is to miss some obvious differences, once they have been pointed out, of course. The first is that old standby of the nuclear age, mutual assured destruction, probably will not work in the digital age. Why? As Robert Knake points out in "Untangling Attribution," cyber warfare is asymmetrical: "Many countries that possess sophisticated offensive capabilities do not have extensive societal reliance on the Internet or networked systems." Another difference is what is called in cyber warfare circles, "the problem of attribution." Just as it's tough to find out who is sending you spam, a country under digital attack will not necessarily know who the perpetrators are. The problem of attribution is not insurmountable in technical terms, but the unfortunate side effect would be to turn "the Internet into the ultimate tool of surveillance." But cyber warfare does not have to be an all-out attack to be destructive. Many will remember the Stuxnet virus, thought to target Iran's nuclear weapons program. One report notes that Iran replaced about 1,000 centrifuges in late 2009 or early 2010, perhaps as a result of the attack. As it happens, our "electrical power grid is easier to break into than any nuclear enrichment facility." Read "Hacking the Lights Out" for a disturbing story of just how vulnerable power networks might be.

As the Patriot Act enacted during the Bush years has shown, a normal response of government during times of threatened public safety is to threaten civil liberties. In theory, a free press, a concerned citizenry, and the normal checks and balances built into our system should prevent the worst abuses. If only the federal government were all we had to worry about. In a world of networked computers, e-commerce, and social networking, we blithely hand over valuable data to providers of services we usually think of as free. To take a simple example, imagine that you're a Gmail subscriber. You may well think you have deleted private messages. But they are stored on a server, who knows where for who knows how long, with access by who knows whom. We Americans (but not Europeans and Canadians whose governments were farsighted enough to pass privacy legislation in the 1980s and 1990s) are in a privacy fix. Read "The Web's New Gold Mine" to learn how all that free stuff on the Internet got to be free. Turns out that the fifty most visited websites install on average sixty-four "pieces of tracking technology" onto our computers. Who is the worst offender? Dictionary.com with 234 files. The best-behaved is Wikipedia, which installs no tracking technology at all.

To change pace a little, have you ever read those pages that you must agree to before a software publisher allows you to install its product? Essentially, they exempt the manufacturer from any liability resulting from its use. Imagine such a thing with your car or your dishwasher. Imagine signing an agreement that says the manufacturer is not liable for either, no matter what happens. This is problematic for many reasons. An important one is that much commercial software is simply too complex to be fully tested or truly understood. The BP oil spill of spring and summer 2010 is a case in point. Turns out that the complexity of the alarm system on a typical rig—one inventory produced a 90-page list of 2,700 alarms—could cause one or more alarms to be overlooked. The authors acknowledge that this is speculative. Yet knowing what we know about the tendency of technology to bite back, that worry is not misplaced. We end this unit with a piece on a subject that has been part of the national conversation about the Internet since the beginning, sexual predation, harassment, and youth exposure to adult content ("The Conundrum of Visibility"). The authors contend that despite real dangers associated with unrestricted access to the Internet, technology has made an old problem more visible.

What is a reasonable person to make of all of this? We can communicate with almost anyone almost anywhere on the planet at almost no cost. The wealth of the world is available on Amazon or eBay for those with credit cards. Google, Wikipedia, and an ocean of other sites provide information in an abundance and at a speed that would have seemed like science fiction a generation ago. Yet thieves get hold of digitally-stored personal information. Our digital records are disintegrating even as we digitize more and more of them. Political debate reaches new lows as unattributed allegations swarm through the Internet. The government compiles massive databases about terrorism and catches the innocent in its nets. Disruption of the global communications network could be catastrophic, as financial markets and global supply chains collapse. One strives for the equanimity of Neil Postman: "Technology giveth and technology taketh away."

Notes

1. Edward Tenner, *Why Things Bite Back,* Vintage, 1996, p. 4.
2. Emily Singer, *Technology Review,* Brain Trauma in Iraq, 2008.
3. William Astore, Geeks and Hackers, Uncle Sam's Cyber Force Wants You!, *The Nation,* June 5, 2008.

The Evolution of Cyber Warfare

GREG BRUNO

Introduction

In the spring of 2007, when Estonian authorities moved a monument to the Red Army from the center of its capital city, Tallinn, to the outskirts of town, a diplomatic row erupted with neighboring Russia. Estonian nationalists regard the army as occupiers and oppressors, a sentiment that dates to the long period of Soviet rule following the Second World War, when the Soviet Union absorbed all three Baltic states. Ethnic Russians, who make up about a quarter of Estonia's 1.3 million people, were nonetheless incensed by the statue's treatment and took to the streets in protest. Estonia later blamed Moscow for orchestrating the unrest; order was restored only after U.S. and European diplomatic interventions. But the story of the "Bronze Statue" did not end there. Days after the riots the computerized infrastructure of Estonia's high-tech government began to fray, victimized by what experts in cybersecurity termed a coordinated "denial of service" attack. A flood of bogus requests for information from computers around the world conspired to cripple (*Wired*) the websites of Estonian banks, media outlets, and ministries for days. Estonia denounced the attacks as an unprovoked act of aggression from a regional foe (though experts still disagree on who perpetrated it—Moscow has denied any knowledge). Experts in cybersecurity went one step further: They called it the future of warfare.

Cyber Warfare: The New Frontier

The attack on Estonia's "paperless government" (BBC) was one of the most publicized hacks in recent computing history. But it wasn't the first case of cyber espionage, nor the most egregious. It's the "tip of the iceberg of the quantity and quality of attacks that are going on," says O. Sami Saydjari, president of the Cyber Defense Agency, a security consultant, and a former Pentagon computer security expert. Israel, India, Pakistan, and the United States have all been accused of launching similar attacks on adversaries.

> **"Chinese [cyber warfare] capabilities have evolved from defending networks from attack to offensive operations against adversary networks."**
>
> —Richard P. Lawless,
> U.S. Deputy Under Secretary for Defense

China, however, may be the most active. Washington has accused the Chinese of hacking into government computer networks at the U.S. Departments of State, Commerce, and Defense—in some instances making off with data. But accusations of Chinese cyber-meddling reached a crescendo in June 2007, when, according to the *Financial Times,* hackers broke into a Pentagon network that serves the Office of the Secretary of Defense, briefly shutting it down. Chinese electronic espionage has also been suspected against British companies (Rolls Royce is one example), as well as government agencies in France, Germany, South Korea, and Taiwan. "Chinese capabilities in this area have evolved from defending networks from attack to offensive operations against adversary networks," Deputy Undersecretary for Defense Richard P. Lawless told (PDF) a House committee in June 2007. China, like Russia, denies the accusations. Both countries argue any attacks originating from IP addresses inside their countries have been directed by rogue citizens, not their governments. Western targets, however, continue to accuse the Chinese of ratcheting up their cyber attack capabilities.

> **"Our ability to penetrate into enemy computer networks, our ability to exploit communication networks, to manipulate digital information, is real."**
>
> —William M. Arkin, Defense Analyst

U.S. Cyber Warfare on the Offensive

The United States, of course, is no innocent bystander. William M. Arkin, a defense analyst who writes the Early Warning blog for the *Washington Post,* says "our ability to penetrate into enemy computer networks, our ability to exploit communication networks, to manipulate digital information, is real," but little is known about the precise nature of Washington's offensive capabilities. Some details, however, have leaked. For instance, in March 2004 the Pentagon announced the formation of an Information Operations team—the Network Attack Support Staff—to streamline the military's cyber attack capabilities (PDF).

The aim, senior military officials said at the time, was to create an "interface between the combatant commanders and the intelligence community."

Arkin, who has reported on cybersecurity issues for over two decades, says the U.S. military also has technologies capable of penetrating and jamming enemy networks, including the classified "Suter" system of airborne technology. According to *Aviation Week,* Suter has been integrated into unmanned aircraft and "allows users to invade communications networks, see what enemy sensors see, and even take over as systems administrator so sensors can be manipulated into positions so that approaching aircraft can't be seen." Some speculate the Israeli military used the capability during its air raid on a Syrian construction site in September 2007. The United States made use of nascent capabilities in the 1999 Kosovo War (MSNBC.com), and built on those lessons in Iraq *(Wired).*

Cyber-Warfare Tactics

Other cyber tactics are less sophisticated. The attack that temporarily brought down Estonian networks began with a flood of bogus messages targeting government servers, called a "denial of service" attack. The approach harnesses "botnets"—massive networks of interconnected computers—to bombard targeted networks with information requests while masking the location of the primary attacker. James Lewis, a security expert with the Center for Strategic and International Studies (CSIS), says hackers in the Estonia example likely took control of tens of thousands of computers around the world without the knowledge of their owners and directed them at the government's servers. The result, he says, was a relatively minor attack that was nearly impossible to trace (PDF).

Another technique is the use of "malware," "spyware," and other malicious programs imbedded into computer systems to steal information without user knowledge. The software is designed to hide undetected and siphon information from its host—everything from secrets stored on personal computers to Pentagon military mainframes. A December 2007 analysis of U.S. Air Force cyber vulnerabilities (PDF) notes much of the Pentagon's operating systems are off-the-shelf components manufactured overseas, due to cheaper costs. But pinching pennies has potentially opened U.S. military networks to intrusion. "Foreign countries could place hidden components inside the computers, making the computers vulnerable for attack and/or spying," the analysis concludes.

Less common but far more worrisome are cyber attacks aimed at critical infrastructure—like nuclear-power-plant control systems, banks, or subways. In March 2007 the Department of Energy's Idaho Lab conducted an experiment to determine whether a power plant could be compromised by hacking alone. The result—a smoking, self-combusting diesel generator incapacitated by nothing more than keystrokes—sent shivers (CNN) through the private sector. The worries were apparently well-founded. In January 2008 a CIA analyst told U.S. utilities that hackers had succeeded in infiltrating electric companies in undisclosed locations outside the United States and, in at least one instance, shut off power to multiple cities. The hackers then demanded money (AP). "The [U.S.] government is scrambling to

try and protect its own systems, to try and check the Chinese from reading government email," says economist Scott Borg, director of the U.S. Cyber Consequences Unit, a nonprofit research institute that studies cyber threats. "But the focus probably needs to be critical infrastructure. That's what we need to defend."

Patching the Holes

On paper the U.S. government appears to agree. For over a decade government-sanctioned studies have delved into the subject; the Pentagon published a report on "Information Warfare-Defense" (PDF) in 1996, when public use of the Internet was still in its infancy. Saydjari says all of these studies reached the same conclusion: "The threat and vulnerabilities to our national infrastructure is serious, it's getting worse, and it's getting worse at an increasingly fast rate." But only recently has the concern been a constant focus of attention for the security and intelligence communities. Part of the attention deficit lies with the difficulty in defining the cyber threat. A 2006 Air Force task force termed cyberspace "a warfighting domain bounded by the electromagnetic spectrum," but air force officials acknowledge "a full understanding of the domain is years away."

> **"Our information infrastructure . . . increasingly is being targeted for exploitation and potentially for disruption or destruction by a growing array of state and non-state adversaries."**
>
> —Michael McConnell, Director of National Intelligence

What is understood is how potentially devastating the loss of cyberspace dominance could be to U.S. interests. In his annual threat assessment to Congress delivered in February 2008, Director of National Intelligence Michael McConnell discussed "cyber threats" before talking about the war in Afghanistan. "Our information infrastructure . . . increasingly is being targeted for exploitation and potentially for disruption or destruction by a growing array of state and non-state adversaries," McConnell said. "We assess that nations, including Russia and China, have the technical capabilities to target and disrupt" the United States' information infrastructure.

The Pentagon, too, has acknowledged the threat to its infrastructure. The Defense Department is considering banning nonofficial traffic (*Federal Computer Week*) from its servers, and the U.S. Air Force is creating a Cyber Command to defend Pentagon networks. "When we talk about the speed range and flexibility of air power, the thing that enables this for us is the fact of our cyber-dominance," Air Force Gen. Robert Elder told United Press International.

The recent flurry of high-level pronouncements also comes amid a renewed funding commitment from Washington. In November 2007 the Bush administration called on the National Security Agency to coordinate with the Department of Homeland Security to protect government and civilian communication networks from hackers. The $144 million plan, unveiled quietly in White House budget documents (PDF), aims to enhance "civilian agency cybersecurity and strengthen defenses to combat terrorism." In January 2008 President George W. Bush signed two presidential directives calling for the creation of a comprehensive national cybersecurity initiative. According to an article by the *Wall Street Journal,* the White House's 2009 budget request takes the program exponentially further, with an estimated $6 billion request to build a secretive system to protect U.S. communications networks. Details of the proposed program remain classified, angering some civil libertarians who fear monitoring of civilian networks could infringe on privacy rights. Rep. Bennie G. Thompson (D-MS), chairman of the House Homeland Security Committee, has called for the program to be put on hold (PDF) until Congress can adequately review it.

Measuring the Threat

Cyber experts don't dispute that electronic espionage is a vexing problem, or that the United States is a prime target. But they do disagree on how pervasive such attacks are, who is behind them, and how disruptive they may prove to be. According to a tally by the Heritage Foundation, a conservative Washington think tank, the hackers may already be winning: In 2007 the Department of Homeland Security logged an estimated 37,000 attempted breaches of private and government computer systems, and over 80,000 attacks on Pentagon systems. Some hacks "reduced the U.S. military's operational capabilities," the report says (PDF).

Economist Borg says the biggest threat from cyber attacks may be economic. He estimates a shutdown of electric power to any sizable region for more than ten days would stop over 70 percent of all economic activity in that region. "If you can do that with a pure cyber attack on only one critical infrastructure, why would you bother with any traditional military attack?" CSIS' Lewis takes a less alarmist view. "The U.S. is a very big set of targets, and some of our important networks are very secure. So you could inflict damage on the U.S. but it wouldn't be crippling or decisive," he says. "I've seen people who say a cyber attack could turn the United States into a third-world nation in a matter of minutes. That's silly. We have to be realistic about this."

Critical Thinking

1. What is a denial of service attack?

2. Who is Robert Tappan Morris? His family history is interesting. Why?

3. Use the Internet to investigate an explosion on a Soviet gas pipeline in 1982. It could have been one of the earliest known instances of malware.

4. Who is Kevin Mitnick? Where does he work now? What does this say about the way we view white-collar crime in the United States?

5. Who is Bruce Schneier? Use the Internet to find out what his views on cyber warfare are. Whom do you believe, Schneier or Bruno?

From *Backgrounder*, February 27, 2008. Copyright © 2008 by Foreign Affairs. Reprinted by permission.

War in the Fifth Domain

Are the mouse and keyboard the new weapons of conflict?

At the height of the cold war, in June 1982, an American early-warning satellite detected a large blast in Siberia. A missile being fired? A nuclear test? It was, it seems, an explosion on a Soviet gas pipeline. The cause was a malfunction in the computer-control system that Soviet spies had stolen from a firm in Canada. They did not know that the CIA had tampered with the software so that it would "go haywire, after a decent interval, to reset pump speeds and valve settings to produce pressures far beyond those acceptable to pipeline joints and welds," according to the memoirs of Thomas Reed, a former air force secretary. The result, he said, "was the most monumental non-nuclear explosion and fire ever seen from space".

This was one of the earliest demonstrations of the power of a "logic bomb". Three decades later, with more and more vital computer systems linked up to the internet, could enemies use logic bombs to, say, turn off the electricity from the other side of the world? Could terrorists or hackers cause financial chaos by tampering with Wall Street's computerised trading systems? And given that computer chips and software are produced globally, could a foreign power infect high-tech military equipment with computer bugs? "It scares me to death," says one senior military source. "the destructive potential is so great".

After land, sea, air and space, warfare has entered the fifth domain: cyberspace. President Barack Obama has declared America's digital infrastructure to be a "strategic national asset" and appointed Howard Schmidt, the former head of security at Microsoft, as his cyber-security tsar. In May the Pentagon set up its new Cyber Command (Cyber-com) headed by General Keith Alexander, director of the National Security Agency (NSA). His mandate is to conduct "full-spectrum" operations—to defend American military networks and attack other countries' systems. Precisely how, and by what rules, is secret.

Britain, too, has set up a cyber-security policy outfit, and an "operations centre" based in GCHQ, the British equivalent of the NSA. China talks of "winning informationised wars by the mid-21st century". Many other countries are organising for cyberwar, among them Russia, Israel and North Korea. Iran boasts of having the world's second-largest cyber-army.

What will cyberwar look like? in a new book Richard Clarke, a former White House staffer in charge of counter-terrorism and cyber-security, envisages a catastrophic breakdown within 15 minutes. Computer bugs bring down military e-mail systems; oil refineries and pipelines explode; air-traffic-control systems collapse; freight and metro trains derail; financial data are scrambled; the electrical grid goes down in the eastern United States; orbiting satellites spin out of control. Society soon breaks down as food becomes scarce and money runs out. Worst of all, the identity of the attacker may remain a mystery.

In the view of Mike McConnell, a former spy chief, the effects of full-blown cyberwar are much like nuclear attack. Cyberwar has already started, he says, "and we are losing it." Not so, retorts Mr Schmidt. There is no cyberwar. Bruce Schneier, an IT industry security guru, accuses securocrats like Mr Clarke of scaremongering. Cyberspace will certainly be part of any future war, he says, but an apocalyptic attack on America is both difficult to achieve technically ("movie-script stuff") and implausible except in the context of a real war, in which case the perpetrator is likely to be obvious.

For the top brass, computer technology is both a blessing and a curse. Bombs are guided by GPS satellites; drones are piloted remotely from across the world; fighter planes and warships are now huge data-processing centres; even the ordinary foot-soldier is being wired up. Yet growing connectivity over an insecure internet multiplies the avenues for e-attack; and growing dependence on computers increases the harm they can cause.

By breaking up data and sending it over multiple routes, the internet can survive the loss of large parts of the network. Yet some of the global digital infrastructure is more fragile. More than nine-tenths of internet traffic travels through undersea fibre-optic cables, and these are dangerously bunched up in a few choke-points, for instance around New York, the Red Sea or the Luzon Strait in the Philippines. Internet traffic is directed by just 13 clusters of potentially vulnerable domain-name servers. Other dangers are coming: weakly governed swathes of Africa are being connected up to fibre-optic cables, potentially creating new havens for cyber-criminals. And the spread of mobile internet will bring new means of attack.

The internet was designed for convenience and reliability, not security. Yet in wiring together the globe, it has merged the garden and the wilderness. No passport is required in cyberspace. And although police are constrained by national borders, criminals roam freely. Enemy states are no longer on the other side of the ocean, but just behind the firewall. The ill-intentioned can mask their identity and location, impersonate others and con their way into the buildings that hold the digitised wealth of the electronic age: money, personal data and intellectual property.

Mr Obama has quoted a figure of $1 trillion lost last year to cybercrime—a bigger underworld than the drugs trade, though such figures are disputed. Banks and other companies do not like to admit how much data they lose. In 2008 alone Verizon, a telecoms company, recorded the loss of 285m personal-data records, including credit-card and bank-account details, in investigations conducted for clients.

About nine-tenths of the 140 billion e-mails sent daily are spam; of these about 16% contain moneymaking scams, including "phishing" attacks that seek to dupe recipients into giving out passwords or bank details, according to Symantec, a security-software vendor. The amount of information now available online about individuals makes it ever easier to attack a computer by crafting a personalised e-mail that is more likely to be trusted and opened. This is known as "spear-phishing".

The ostentatious hackers and virus-writers who once wrecked computers for fun are all but gone, replaced by criminal gangs seeking to harvest data. "Hacking used to be about making noise. Now it's about staying silent," says Greg Day of McAfee, a vendor of IT security products. Hackers have become wholesale providers of malware—viruses, worms and Trojans that infect computers—for others to use. Websites are now the favoured means of spreading malware, partly because the unwary are directed to them through spam or links posted on social-networking sites. And poorly designed websites often provide a window into valuable databases.

Malware is typically used to steal passwords and other data, or to open a "back door" to a computer so that it can be taken over by outsiders. Such "zombie" machines can be linked up to thousands, if not millions, of others around the world to create a "botnet". Estimates for the number of infected machines range up to 100m (see map for global distribution of infections). Botnets are used to send spam, spread malware or launch distributed denial-of-service (DDoS) attacks, which seek to bring down a targeted computer by overloading it with countless bogus requests.

The Spy Who Spammed Me

Criminals usually look for easy prey. But states can combine the criminal hacker's tricks, such as spear-phishing, with the intelligence apparatus to reconnoitre a target, the computing power

to break codes and passwords, and the patience to probe a system until it finds a weakness—usually a fallible human being. Steven Chabinsky, a senior FBI official responsible for cybersecurity, recently said that "given enough time, motivation and funding, a determined adversary will always—always—be able to penetrate a targeted system."

Traditional human spies risk arrest or execution by trying to smuggle out copies of documents. But those in the cyberworld face no such risks. "A spy might once have been able to take out a few books' worth of material," says one senior American military source. "Now they take the whole library. And if you restock the shelves, they will steal it again."

China, in particular, is accused of wholesale espionage, attacking the computers of major Western defence contractors and reputedly taking classified details of the F-35 fighter, the mainstay of future American air power. At the end of 2009 it appears to have targeted Google and more than a score of other IT companies. Experts at a cyber-test-range built in Maryland by Lockheed Martin, a defence contractor (which denies losing the F-35 data), say "advanced persistent threats" are hard to fend off amid the countless minor probing of its networks. Sometimes attackers try to slip information out slowly, hidden in ordinary internet traffic. At other times they have tried to break in by leaving infected memory-sticks in the car park, hoping somebody would plug them into the network. Even unclassified e-mails can contain a wealth of useful information about projects under development.

"Cyber-espionage is the biggest intelligence disaster since the loss of the nuclear secrets [in the late 1940s]," says Jim Lewis of the Centre for Strategic and International Studies, a think-tank in Washington, DC. Spying probably presents the most immediate danger to the West: the loss of high-tech know-how that could erode its economic lead or, if it ever came to a shooting war, blunt its military edge.

Western spooks think China deploys the most assiduous, and most shameless, cyberspies, but Russian ones are probably more skilled and subtle. Top of the league, say the spooks, are still America's NSA and Britain's GCHQ, which may explain why Western countries have until recently been reluctant to complain too loudly about computer snooping.

The next step after penetrating networks to steal data is to disrupt or manipulate them. If military targeting information could be attacked, for example, ballistic missiles would be useless. Those who play war games speak of being able to "change the red and blue dots": make friendly (blue) forces appear to be the enemy (red), and vice versa.

General Alexander says the Pentagon and NSA started cooperating on cyberwarfare in late 2008 after "a serious intrusion into our classified networks". Mr Lewis says this refers to the penetration of Central Command, which oversees the wars in Iraq and Afghanistan, through an infected thumb-drive. It took a week to winkle out the intruder. Nobody knows what, if any, damage was caused. But the thought of an enemy lurking in battle-fighting systems alarms the top brass.

That said, an attacker might prefer to go after unclassified military logistics supply systems, or even the civilian infrastructure. A loss of confidence in financial data and electronic transfers could cause economic upheaval. An even bigger worry is an attack on the power grid. Power companies tend not to keep many spares of expensive generator parts, which can take months to replace. Emergency diesel generators cannot make up for the loss of the grid, and cannot operate indefinitely. Without electricity and other critical services, communications systems and cash-dispensers cease to work. A loss of power lasting just a few days, reckon some, starts to cause a cascade of economic damage.

Experts disagree about the vulnerability of systems that run industrial plants, known as supervisory control and data acquisition (SCADA). But more and more of these are being connected to the internet, raising the risk of remote attack. "Smart" grids", which relay information about energy use to the utilities, are promoted as ways of reducing energy waste. But they also increase security worries about both crime (eg., allowing bills to be falsified) and exposing SCADA networks to attack.

General Alexander has spoken of "hints that some penetrations are targeting systems for remote sabotage". But precisely what is happening is unclear: are outsiders probing SCADA systems only for reconnaissance, or to open "back doors" for future use? One senior American military source said that if any country were found to be planting logic bombs on the grid, it would provoke the equivalent of the Cuban missile crisis.

Estonia, Georgia and WWI

Important thinking about the tactical and legal concepts of cyber-warfare is taking place in a former Soviet barracks in Estonia, now home to NATO's "centre of excellence" for cyber-defence. It was established in response to what has become known as "Web War I", a concerted denial-of-service attack on Estonian government, media and bank web servers that was precipitated by the decision to move a Soviet-era war memorial in central Tallinn in 2007. This was more a cyber-riot than a war, but it forced Estonia more or less to cut itself off from the internet.

Similar attacks during Russia's war with Georgia the next year looked more ominous, because they seemed to be coordinated with the advance of Russian military columns. Government and media websites went down and telephone lines were jammed, crippling Georgia's ability to present its case abroad. President Mikheil Saakashvili's website had to be moved to an American server better able to fight off the attack. Estonian experts were dispatched to Georgia to help out.

Many assume that both these attacks were instigated by the Kremlin. But investigations traced them only to Russian "hack-tivists" and criminal botnets; many of the attacking computers were in Western countries. There are wider issues: did the cyber-attack on Estonia, a member of NATO, count as an armed attack, and should the alliance have defended it? And did Estonia's assistance to Georgia, which is not in NATO, risk drawing Estonia into the war, and NATO along with it?

Such questions permeate discussions of NATO's new "strategic concept", to be adopted later this year. A panel of experts headed by Madeleine Albright, a former American secretary of state, reported in May that cyber-attacks are among the three most likely threats to the alliance. The next significant attack, it said, "may well come down a fibre-optic cable" and may be serious enough to merit a response under the mutual-defence provisions of Article 5.

During his confirmation hearing, senators sent General Alexander several questions. Would he have "significant" offensive cyber-weapons? Might these encourage others to follow suit? How sure would he need to be about the identity of an attacker to "fire back"? Answers to these were restricted to a classified supplement. In public the general said that the president would be the judge of what constituted cyberwar; if America responded with force in cyberspace it would be in keeping with the rules of war and the "principles of military necessity, discrimination, and proportionality".

General Alexander's seven-month confirmation process is a sign of the qualms senators felt at the merging of military and espionage functions, the militarisation of cyberspace and the fear that it may undermine Americans' right to privacy. Cyber-command will protect only the military ".mil" domain. The government domain, ".gov", and the corporate infrastructure, ".com" will be the responsibility respectively of the Department of Homeland Security and private companies, with support from Cybercom.

One senior military official says General Alexander's priority will be to improve the defences of military networks. Another bigwig casts some doubt on cyber-offence. "It's hard to do it at a specific time," he says. "If a cyber-attack is used as a military weapon, you want a predictable time and effect. If you are using it for espionage it does not matter; you can wait." He implies that cyber-weapons would be used mainly as an adjunct to conventional operations in a narrow theatre.

The Chinese may be thinking the same way. A report on China's cyber-warfare doctrine, written for the congressionally mandated US-China Economic and Security Review Commission, envisages China using cyber-weapons not to defeat America, but to disrupt and slow down its forces long enough for China to seize Taiwan without having to fight a shooting war.

Apocalypse or Asymmetry?

Deterrence in cyber-warfare is more uncertain than, say, in nuclear strategy: there is no mutually assured destruction, the dividing line between criminality and war is blurred and identifying attacking computers, let alone the fingers on the keyboards, is difficult. Retaliation need not be confined to cyberspace; the one system that is certainly not linked to the public internet is America's nuclear firing chain. Still, the more likely use of cyber-weapons is probably not to bring about electronic apocalypse, but as tools of limited warfare.

Cyber-weapons are most effective in the hands of big states. But because they are cheap, they may be most useful to the comparatively weak. They may well suit terrorists. Fortunately, perhaps, the likes of al-Qaeda have mostly used the internet for propaganda and communication. It may be that jihadists lack the ability to, say, induce a refinery to blow itself up. Or it may be that they prefer the gory theatre of suicide-bombings to the anonymity of computer sabotage—for now.

Critical Thinking

1. What was one of the earliest demonstrations what the article calls a "logic bomb"?

2. Richard Clarke is an important figure in this article. He was also quite a controversial figure in the Bush administration. Why?

3. Where are some "choke points" where Internet traffic is "dangerously bunched up"?

4. How is cyber-warfare asymmetric? What is meant by asymmetric warfare?

Untangling Attribution: Moving to Accountability in Cyberspace

ROBERT K. KNAKE

Chairman Wu, Ranking Member Smith, and distinguished members of the House Subcommittee on Technology and Innovation, thank you for the opportunity to discuss the role of attack attribution in preventing cyber attacks and how attribution technologies can affect the anonymity and the privacy of Internet users. In your letter of invitation, you asked me to address the following series of questions:

1. As has been stated by many experts, deterrence is a productive way to prevent physical attacks. How can attack attribution play a role in deterring cyber attacks?
2. What are the proper roles of both the government and private industry in developing and improving attack attribution capabilities? What R&D is needed to address capability gaps in attack attribution and who should be responsible for completing that R&D?
3. What are the distinguishing factors between anonymity and privacy? How should we account for both in the development and use of attribution technologies?
4. Is there a need for standards in the development and implementation of attack attribution technologies? Is there a specific need for privacy standards and if so, what should be the government's role in the development of these standards?

Attributions Role in Deterring Cyber Attacks

Let me begin by stating my view that the utility of deterrence in cyber security may be limited and that the problem of attribution has been over-stated for the high end threats that represent a challenge to our national security. In its classic usage, deterrence is the idea of using fear of reprisal in order to dissuade an adversary from launching an attack. For deterrence to work, it is critically important that we know who has carried out the attack and thus attribution is a central component of deterrence strategy. I believe it may be too broad to view deterrence as a productive way to prevent all kinetic attacks. Deterrence was the central concept in preventing a nuclear exchange between the United States and the Soviet Union during the Cold War. It

is not, however, a central part of U.S. strategy to prevent terrorist attacks and its importance in preventing conventional military attacks is more limited than in the nuclear case. During the Cold War, deterrence of the use of nuclear weapons was created through the establishment of "Mutually Assured Destruction" or MAD, in which both the United States and the Soviets understood that any use of nuclear weapons would be responded to in kind. The threat of total annihilation kept both sides at bay. Radar and other warning systems provided the mechanism for attributing any nuclear attack and possession of a second strike capability that could provide a nuclear response even after a successful Soviet launch kept the threat of retaliation credible. Equally important, however, was symmetry.

The Soviets as rational actors did not want to see the loss of their cities, industry, and regime in a retaliatory nuclear strike. As long as we had the ability to hold these assets under threat, a Soviet strike against us would not be to their advantage. Such parity does not exist in cyberspace. Attribution may be a secondary problem to the lack of symmetry. Many countries that possess sophisticated offensive capabilities do not have extensive societal reliance on the Internet or networked systems. If attribution could be achieved, deterrence might not follow because a state conducting an attack in cyberspace, may have little to lose through retaliation. The logical solution to this problem is to threaten retaliation through diplomatic or kinetic means outside of cyberspace, responses that could range from the imposition of sanctions to airstrikes. Thus far, despite the onslaught of attacks in cyberspace, no country has chosen to escalate their response outside of cyberspace. Moreover, it may be difficult to achieve proportionality in response to a cyber attack through other means. Deterrence may simply not be a useful concept to address our current state of cyber insecurity.

If deterrence is to be a central part of our cyber security strategy, I believe it is essential that we can answer three questions: First, what degree of certainty in attribution is necessary to take action? Second, what would that action look like? Third, how will we make potential adversaries understand the answers to these questions prior to an incident so that they will be deterred? To begin, I think it is important to breakdown the attribution problem in cyberspace. There are three broad categories of attack that have their own distinct attribution problem. The first attribution problem, the one on which most attention is focused is the attribution problem for attacks carried over the Internet. These attacks are difficult to deter because of the underlying architecture of the Internet, the lack of security on many hosts, and because the individuals or teams carrying out these attacks can do so remotely, from the safe confines of a non-cooperative country. The second attribution problem is for cyber attacks that are not carried over the Internet. Potentially, many of the most dangerous forms of cyber attacks will be carried out against systems that are not connected to the Internet through other delivery mechanisms including attacks using microwave or other radio transmissions, thumb drives, and other portable media like CDs and DVDs. For these attacks against well-defended military and

industrial systems, the attribution problem is similar to the attribution problem for kinetic attacks and can be addressed through real world forensics, investigation, and intelligence. Finally, there is the problem of attribution for the introduction of malicious code in the supply chain for hardware and software. The threat to the supply chain may be the area of most concern today, yet the attribution problem for the insertion of malicious content into software and hardware is no different from a traditional investigative challenge to identify the opportunity and the motive for inserting malicious content (see Figure 1 for a visual representation of these challenges).

With the exception of flooding attacks, all other forms of Internet-based cyber attack require two way communication between the attacking computer and the victim computer.

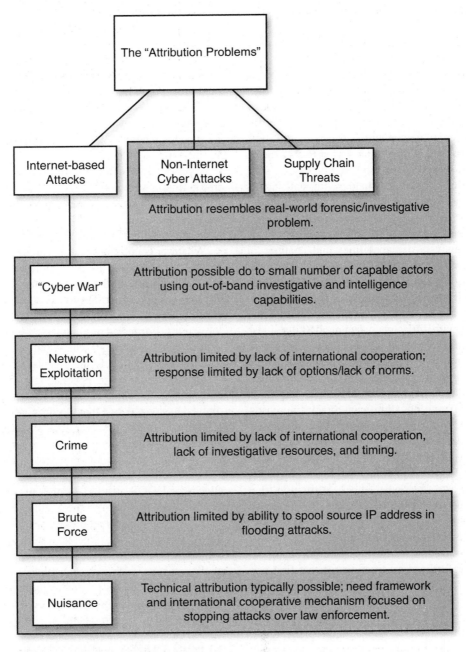

Figure 1   The Attribution Problems

127

Sophisticated adversaries will take steps to obfuscate their true location and identity through the use of proxy systems, whether they are compromised computers or anonymization services or both. Despite these precautions, trace back techniques and digital forensics can provide the technical means to allow the attackers to be discovered. The barriers to the use of these techniques are more legal than technical, due to international boundaries and non-cooperative countries. If we breakdown the various threats carried over the Internet, the scope of the attribution problem can be brought into focus and different solutions for managing each threat begin to emerge.

Attacks can be divided into the following categories ordered by the threat they pose: cyber warfare, cyber espionage, brute force attacks, crime, and nuisance. For each of these, both the attribution problem and the issue of response are different. For the highest level threat, that of cyber warfare, the attribution problem is largely overstated. As with other Internet based attacks, technical attribution may be difficult and the forensics work will take time, but at present there are a limited number of actors that are capable of carrying out such attacks. Moreover, the resources, planning, and timeline for such attacks would provide many opportunities to identify and disrupt such attacks. Estimates vary, but on the low end, many experts believe that only four countries possess the capability to carry out a catastrophic attack in cyberspace, the so-called Cyber Pearl Harbor, Cyber 9/11, or Cyber Katrina. On the high end, up to 100 state actors and private groups closely affiliated with state actors may have the capability. No matter which estimate is accurate, this is a fairly small list of suspects that can be narrowed down through technical means, as well as out of band methods that include intelligence, analysis of capabilities and analysis of intent. If not already a priority, U.S. intelligence agencies should be focused on identifying actors with high-level capabilities and understanding their intentions. While it has become a truism that hacking tools can be downloaded off the Internet and used by an individual with little or no technical skills, these tools do not pose the kind of threat that could cause widespread destruction. If the operators of critical systems cannot defend against such attacks, they are not taking the threat seriously. As the relevant technologies continue to evolve, it is important that the difficulty in carrying out significant attacks increases. Our critical industries, military and government agencies must continue to raise their defense levels in order to keep the ability to cause destruction in the hands of a limited number of state actors.

In the event of a catastrophic cyber attack, attribution to at least some level will almost always be possible. The question becomes to what level of certainty must attribution be demonstrated in order for the President to take action? At the lowest level, attribution that traces an attack back one hop can provide the foundation for further investigations. If that first hop is in a non-cooperative country that is unwilling to assist in the investigation, that may be enough evidence to hold that country accountable. As with the 9/11 attacks when the Taliban refused to turn over Osama Bin Laden, it may be appropriate under such circumstances to hold a non-cooperative country accountable, a concept I will return to later in this testimony.

On the issue of espionage, the capability necessary for network exploitation is generally lower than that required for destructive attacks, particularly in the realm of economic espionage where private sector companies are targeted. What we lack is not so much an ability to attribute attacks, but international norms that keep espionage limited. Espionage is generally recognized to be permissible under certain circumstances and many scholars will argue that it has a stabilizing effect on the international system by reducing paranoia. As has been recently demonstrated by the discovery of a Russian spy ring in the United States, engaging in espionage is not necessarily considered a hostile act and can be resolved without further escalation. The challenge with cyber espionage is that we lack norms that limit the extent to which states engage in it. This problem is exacerbated by the fact that cyber espionage is not constrained by the costs, consequences and limitations of traditional espionage.

By way of example, consider the case of Robert Hanssen, a former FBI agent who spied for the Soviets and then the Russian Federation for over two decades. Over that period, Hanssen smuggled several hundred pages of classified material to the Russians, who paid him several hundred thousand dollars and maintained a network of handlers in order run this operation. Hanssen paid a heavy price for his betrayal. Having been sentenced to life in prison, he spends 23 hours a day in solitary confinement at a Supermax Facility and is addressed by the guards only in the third person ("the prisoner will exit the cell"). The American spies he betrayed inside Russia were not so lucky. Most were executed. During the Cold War, spying had consequences. Now, according to public media reports, foreign intelligence agencies have exfiltrated several terabytes of information from U.S. government systems.

Whatever country or countries are behind this espionage campaign, the people who are carrying it out are working safely from within the borders of their own country at little risk of being discovered or imprisoned. The low cost and low risk of cyber espionage is the problem, not the difficulty in attributing the source of the activity. If ironclad proof emerged of who was behind an incident of cyber espionage, what would the U.S. response be, particularly given the likely intelligence advantages that the United States gains from cyber espionage? It may be time that we recognize cyber espionage to be a different phenomenon from traditional espionage, one that requires a different set of norms and responses. I doubt, however, that we lack sufficient certainty of who is behind these campaigns that we are limited in our response simply because we do not know who is carrying them out.

Brute force attacks, so called distributed denial of service attacks or DDOS attacks, do present a specific technical attribution challenge. During these attacks, compromised systems formed into a botnet flood targets with large numbers of packets that do not require the targeted system to respond. The malware behind these attacks will provide false information on the source of the packets, so that the machines sending the packets cannot be identified. This particular problem is due to the trusting nature of the internet protocol which does not provide any security mechanism to keep this information from being falsified. To deter DDOS attacks, it may be necessary to strengthen the Internet Protocol so that attacks can be traced to the computers that are part of the attacking botnet, and from their to the command

and control servers and potentially to the botnet master himself. It may be equally productive to simply locate compromised computers participating in the attack and shut these down.

For crime, the goal of attribution is to aid in investigation and result in criminal prosecution. Attribution is therefore necessary in the first instance to direct where an investigation should be targeted and for this first step, attribution needs to rise to the level sufficient for "probable cause" to initiate the investigation. This first level of attribution may only need to lead to a system, not to an individual and an IP address is often times all that is sufficient. In turn, the investigation will need to establish attribution to an individual or group of individuals for the purpose of prosecution. For prosecution to be successful, attribution will need to rise to the level of guilt beyond a reasonable doubt. In between, there is the potential to pursue criminals through civil litigation, in which case the standard for attribution would be lower, and guilt would be assigned based upon a preponderance of the evidence. The problem is that currently, many countries lack both the legal framework and resources to pursue cybercrimes committed by their citizens or that use systems within their territory that target victims in another country. Even crimes committed by individuals in the United States against individuals in the United States will make use of intermediary systems in other countries, particularly those that are not likely or able to cooperate with an investigation. What is needed to deal with the problem of crime is not better attribution but stronger legal mechanisms for working across international borders, the ability to shutdown attacks as they are taking place, and more investigative resources. Ultimately, there must be penalties for states that do not cooperate in investigations and do not take steps to secure their portion of cyberspace.

For nuisance attacks, attribution is rarely a problem. The problem is that few if any investigative resources are assigned to cyber criminal activity that does not have a high monetary value associated with it. This is a situation in which the impact of the crimes committed is fairly low but the resources necessary to address them are high given the volume of the problem. As an example, look at the problem of SPAM. The 2003 CAN-SPAM Act requires spammers to provide accurate header information and to provide an opt-out method for recipients so they can choose not to receive future methods. Yet nearly a decade later, SPAM is flourishing as 9 out of 10 emails are SPAM. For most of these messages, the organization that sent the message is identifiable because they are selling a product. What we lack is an enforcement method that fits this problem, one that is focused on stopping the nuisance behavior rather than prosecuting those who are behind it. Similarly, nuisance level network attacks, the type that can be initiated through downloads off the Internet, are rarely investigated and prosecuted yet they distract system administrators and computer response teams from higher level threats. Investigating and prosecuting more of this behavior could deter many of the people who engage in it.

For most of these threats, the challenges are not so much related to attribution as they are to resources and international cooperation. Focusing on deterrence may simply be the wrong way to think about how to handle these problems. The threats are materializing every day, making the abstract theorizing that laid the foundation for deterrence in a nuclear confrontation unnecessary. They are also, in every respect, a lower level concern that in no way threatens the existence of the United States. Instead we should focus in two areas. We need to reduce the scale of the problem by stopping threats as they unfold and by reducing the vulnerabilities that the threat actors make use of in their attacks. An investigative and enforcement approach to all problems is simply not tenable. Instead of trying to trace every incident back to a human user, we need to develop a legal framework for stopping attacking systems. We must move beyond treating intermediary systems as victims, and start viewing them as accomplices. In the United States, such a framework could require ISPs to monitor their network for compromised systems that have become parts of botnets and quarantine those systems until the problem is resolved. Similarly, we need mechanisms that allow companies or individuals that are under attack and have traced the attack to a system or systems to request for those systems to be shutdown. This process needs to take place quickly and mechanisms must be developed to authenticate such requests across international borders. Such a framework, if developed in the United States, could be promoted as a global model.

For higher end threats, there are lessons we can learn from the last decade of dealing with terrorist threats. The key is to move beyond the search for perfect attribution and instead hold states that do not cooperate accountable. Currently, the situation can be summed up like this. When an attack is traced to another country that is not cooperative, the investigation dead ends. If that country is Russia, Russian authorities will typically say that the incident was carried out either by patriotic hackers or cyber criminal groups that the Russian government cannot control. If that country is China, Chinese officials will point out that China is often the victim of cybercrime and that do to the poor security on many Chinese systems, they are often compromised in an effort to cast blame on China. In both cases, national sovereignty will be raised to explain why cooperation cannot be more forthcoming.

To move beyond this stalemate, the United States should make public a position that treats failure to cooperate in investigating a cyber attack as culpability for the attack. Countries should know that they can choose to have the incident treated as a law enforcement matter by cooperating in the investigation or choose not to cooperate and have the incident treated as a hostile attack for which their country will be held accountable. Over the last decade the concept of state sovereignty has evolved so that sovereignty not only comes with rights in the international system but also responsibilities. The evolution of this concept is due to events in one of the least wired parts of the world: the Hindu Kush.

In 1999, Michael Sheehan, the U.S. Ambassador at Large for Counterterrorism delivered a demarche over the phone to the Taliban's foreign secretary. The message was clear: as long as the Taliban continued to harbor and support al Qaeda and its leaders, the United States would hold the Taliban responsible for any al Qaeda attacks against the United States or other countries. To drive home the point, Sheehan used an analogy. He told the Taliban's representative: "If you have an arsonist in your basement; and every night he goes out and burns down a neighbor's house, and you know this is going on, then you can't claim you aren't responsible." The United States made good on Ambassador Sheehan's word after 9/11, and as the international community attempts to address failed states that cannot control their borders or police their internal territory, this new concept of sovereign responsibility is taking hold.

Applying this new concept of sovereignty to cyberspace has its merits. As with al Qaeda in Afghanistan, failure of a state to prevent its territory from being used to stage an international cyber attack should not, in and of itself, constitute a violation of state responsibility. Indeed, a world in which states monitor and constrain citizen activities to prevent crimes before they take place would be a very frightening world. What is crucial, however, is how states respond when confronted with the use of systems within their territory for cyber attack. If the Taliban had responded to requests to turn over bin Laden, the invasion of Afghanistan might never have occurred. Based on this new paradigm of sovereignty, states should be expected to pass laws making international cybercrime illegal and enforce them. They should have mechanisms in place to respond to international requests for assistance and they should have some ability to oversee the hygiene of their national networks. Better attribution through post-incident forensic techniques will be a crucial part of this new paradigm, but the development of ironclad attribution, will not necessarily lead to better security in cyberspace.

The Role of Government and Private Industry in Improving Attack Attribution

In order to improve attack attribution, there are many things that can be done with current technology. The most crucial is for both government and private industry to do a better job detecting significant threats, mitigating them quickly, and capturing evidence that can be used by law enforcement for investigative purposes. Forensic techniques are getting better, but there are genuine civil liberties concerns with them getting too good.

The vision of perfect attribution can best be summed up as the idea of giving packets license plates. Under such a system, compromised systems or other proxies could not be used to hide the identity of attackers because each packet would be labeled with a unique identifier, possibly an IPv6 address that has been assigned to an individual after having that individual's identity authenticated in some verifiable way. Access to the network would require authentication, and each packet produced by the user would be traceable back to that user. The privacy implications of such a system would be obvious, turning the Internet into the ultimate tool of state surveillance. The security benefits for pursuing criminals and state actors, however, would be minimal. Without cooperation from all foreign states, criminal activity will simply gravitate to states that do not authenticate identity before issuing identification numbers or choose not to participate in the system at all. Many states benefit tremendously from cybercrime, both directly through the cash it brings into economies, and indirectly through the bolstering of technology development through the theft of intellectual capital. Moreover,

for less capable states, cybercrime provides the necessary cover of darkness for espionage to take place. By cracking down on cybercriminal groups, the activities of state actors would stand out starkly. Ultimately, such a system would restrict the freedom and privacy of most users, while doing little to curb criminal elements or state actors who would find ways around the system.

As a baseline, of what we should expect from digital forensics, it may be instructive to look at the role forensics plays in the real world. Many people have become familiar with modern forensics techniques through the popular series CSI and its spinoffs, television shows about real-world crime scene investigators. Each episode begins with a body. The crime scene investigators come in and walk the scene collecting forensic evidence and then take it back to the lab and process it for clues. This activity takes us to the first commercial break in an hour-long drama. The forensics have yielded clues about who the victim was, how he or she was killed, and possible attributes of the killer. Then the detective work begins. The detectives try and establish a motive. They delve into the past of the victim. They ask themselves who would have wanted the victim dead? They ask a lot of questions of a lot of people. On television, this process is packed into an hour. In the real world it can take days to weeks, months and years.

Cyberspace isn't so different from the real world. We have digital forensic tools and trace-back techniques that in the latest incident with Google, allowed the company to conclude that the attacks emanated from China. We can't know more than that without some good old-fashioned investigative work but we can ascertain motive based on what systems were infiltrated and what data was stolen. We can narrow down the list of possible suspects by geography. We can further narrow down the set by capability. Only so many people in the world have the ability to put together the kind of code used in the hack. We also know whoever built the exploits wasn't working alone. That's enough leads to get an investigation going in the real world, and it is also enough in cyberspace.

While the Google case illustrates the attribution "problem", it also illustrates the need for Internet Freedom, something the Chinese government is trying to erode. Our law enforcement community might want ironclad attribution on the Internet to combat cyber crime, but the Chinese government and other authoritarian states want it to combat speech. We may want to know who carried out the hacking of Google but we also want to protect the identity of anonymous posters in online forums about Chinese human rights.

Creating the perfect surveillance state online is within our technical means. In real-world equivalents, we could label each packet with its digital DNA, tying it to a single real-world person, and recordings of everything that goes on so we can play back the tape. But cyberspace isn't so different from the real world, especially since more and more of what we used to do by walking we now do online. If we don't want to live in a surveillance society out here, we also do not want to live in one in cyberspace. The tools for digital forensics are getting better. We don't want them to get too good. What the Google incident really demonstrates, isn't a technical problem; it's a legal and diplomatic one. We lack norms for acceptable behavior by states in conducting espionage online and we lack agreements between states to partner in pursuing cross-border cyber criminal activity. Better surveillance wouldn't solve that problem.

In two narrow areas, government and private sector technology companies should collaborate to improve two of the basic protocols that govern internet transactions. First, government and industry must work together to develop a secure version of the basic internet protocol that authenticates the "from" information contained in packet headers. In distributed denial of service or DDOS attacks that do not require the return of information, the ability to supply false sender information makes it difficult to trace and block such attacks. Similarly, the underlying protocols for sending email allow an individual to spoof the identity of a sender so that someone with malicious intent can send email appearing to be from a bank, a friend, or a work colleague. This weakness is typically exploited in social engineering attacks in order to get the recipient to click on a link that will download malware or send back sensitive information. These problems are well known and well documented. After more than two decades, I believe it is safe to conclude that the informal, consensus-based processes used by the Internet Engineering Task Force to develop and adopt new protocols will not solve these problems. The federal government must step in, lay out the challenge, and lead the development and adoption of protocols that solve these problems. An "X-prize" strategy might prove useful in this context.

Privacy and Anonymity in Resolving Attack Attribution

In the early days of the Internet, anonymity was how privacy was obtained when online. As a general trend, anonymity on the web is eroding for most users due to the interactive nature of current web content but new ways of protecting privacy have not developed, at least not for the average user. In terms of protecting privacy, anonymity is only useful in a "web 1.0" context. In the web 1.0 era, users were passive recipients of information posted to the web. Anonymity on the web is still useful for accessing information that you do not want others to know you have accessed, whether it be pornographic material or information on democracy if you live under an authoritarian regime. Increasingly, however, access to information is not what the Internet is being used for. Managing health records and finances and communicating online cannot be done anonymously. What is needed is privacy, something that does not currently exist on the web that must be created through both technical and legal mechanisms.

Most of the so-called "free" web is funded through advertising, and advertising is increasingly targeted to individuals based on information collected about them from their IP address and from various types of cookies placed on their computers when they access sites. By the time my homepage at the nytimes.com has loaded, a total of 12 cookies have been loaded onto my computer, including "flash cookies" that cannot be deleted through standard browser settings. While some of these cookies are used to authenticate my username and password on the site, the vast majority are for advertising, meant to track my use of the internet in order to target advertising at me. Companies sell geo-location services that use IP information to determine

where you live so that advertising can be targeted at you for local services. By default, my browser, my computer, and the websites I visit are set to allow all this to happen without me knowing it. Advanced users may have the skill set and the motivation to set their browser settings and take other steps to avoid privacy loss but most users do not.

At present, only the technically sophisticated, be they law-abiding citizens concerned with their civil liberties or criminal actors, can obtain anonymity, while the average Internet user experiences a total loss of privacy. As the technology develops to improve attribution, we need to ensure that our laws develop to protect their use, both by government and by the private sector. These points to the need for government intervention to require companies that collect information online and track users to be explicit about what they are doing. Surrendering your privacy online in exchange for "free" access to information should not be something that happens behind the scenes, but an explicit decision that users make. The equivalent of the Surgeon General's warning, something short, explicit, prominent and standard should be displayed on sites that use privacy compromising methods to generate advertising revenue.

In order to protect private communication online, we need to implement both technical solutions and stronger legal protections for the content of communication. While law enforcement and intelligence agencies are restricted from accessing private information without due process, private sector entities and criminals have far fewer barriers. The average home users email messages are not secured end-to-end through encryption, and the laws that protect the intercept of these messages are far weaker than those that protect regular mail.

Taken together, these steps would replace the loss of anonymity that was the foundation of privacy on the early web, with privacy for all activities carried out over the Internet, including transactions and two-way communication.

Standards Development for Attack Attribution and Privacy

As stated previously, I believe it is necessary for the US government to work with the Internet engineering community to address known problems in the current suite of protocols. In my view, these problems are both limited and correctable but both funding for development and incentives for adoption post-development are necessary. The goal should not be to create ironclad attribution that would turn the Internet into the ultimate tool of the surveillance state. Rather, the end state should be protocols that prevent the spoofing of IP addresses and email.

On privacy standards, I believe that it is government's role to protect the privacy of individual users. Government must stop assuming that consumers have all the information they need to make informed decisions about privacy. The goal of government intervention in this area should be to make the decision to surrender privacy in exchange for access to information and services a transparent decision. Websites should be required to notify users if access requires the installation of cookies that will track users for the purpose of targeting advertising. Many if not most users may make the decision to surrender their privacy for access to so-called "free content". Others may choose a pay option. Still others may seek out content that neither costs privacy or dollars.

These two issues overlap for Internet Service Providers. The activity of ISPs is largely unregulated in the United States. For ISPs, attribution on their networks is not a problem: they can see malicious activity and trace it back to a customer. When evidence of the next jump on a host has been deleted, ISPs are often able to trace the next hop of packets. Standards are necessary for what ISPs should and should not be required to track, for how long they should store such information, and how this information can be shared with law enforcement or private parties.

Finally, we need standards for the operation of anonymity services. Services like Hotspot Shield, Tor, and others provide a valuable service to many Internet users, particularly those living under authoritarian regimes where accessing certain websites may not be possible or may be tracked in order to identify dissidents. Yet these same systems can be used for criminal purposes. Standards are necessary for regulating these services and they must be promoted internationally. These services provide anonymity, which, as previously discussed, is only useful for accessing information sources and anonymous posting activity. These services should therefore restrict their users to web-based activity. They should also make it easy for companies and government agencies to block the outbound IP addresses to prevent users that have gained anonymity from attempting to access secure systems. If you are trying to access your own bank account online, there is no legitimate reason to use an anonymization service. Finally, these services should retain auditable logs for law enforcement purposes. Users should understand that this information will be kept private, and only released if the service has been used for criminal purposes. Ultimately, as with states, anonymization services should be held accountable for their users' behavior if they do not cooperate with law enforcement.

Conclusion

As I have expressed throughout this testimony, it is my view that the problem of attribution has been largely overstated. Ironclad or perfect attribution would not address the problems of cyber warfare, espionage, crime or other threats in cyberspace. Such a capability would, however, be injurious to freedom of expression and access to information for many people around the world. Stronger mechanisms for international law enforcement cooperation are necessary, as is the ability to stop attacks in progress, and improvements to the general hygiene of the Internet ecosystem. More than anything else, we need to develop better and stronger options for responding to threats in cyberspace and introduce consequences for states that do not cooperate in stopping attacks or in investigating them. Finally, we need to move beyond anonymity as the guarantor of privacy on the Internet and instead work to create privacy through both technical means and legal requirements. Thank you for the opportunity to testify on these important issues. I would be happy to answer any questions at this time.

Critical Thinking

1. What is the attribution problem?

2. Knake says that 9 of 10 e-mails are spam. Use the Internet to see if you can find other estimates.

3. The article draws an analogy between the Taliban harboring al Qaeda in Afghanistan and intermediary computer systems that forward malware to an intended target. By this reasoning, Internet service provides (ISPs) would be required "to monitor their network for compromised systems." In effect, we should "move beyond treating intermediary systems as victims, and start viewing them as accomplices." Do you agree, both with the analogy and with the liability it would impose upon ISPs?

4. Use the Internet to investigate Tor and Hotspot Shield. What do they do? How might they be used by cyber terrorists? How might they be used by free speech advocates living under repressive regimes?

ROBERT K. KNAKE is an International Affairs Fellow in Residence at the Council on Foreign Relations Studying Cyber War. He is currently working on a Council Special Report on Internet Governance and Security. Prior to his fellowship, he was a Principal at Good Harbor Consulting, a security strategy consulting firm with offices in Washington, DC; Boston, MA; and Abu Dhabi, UAE, where he served domestic and foreign clients on cyber security and homeland security projects. Rob joined Good Harbor after earning his MA from Harvard University's Kennedy School of Government. He has written extensively on cyber security, counterterrorism and homeland security issues. He is coauthor (with Richard Clarke) of Cyber War: The Next Threat to National Security and What to Do about It (HarperCollins, April 2010).

Testimony before the House Subcommittee on Technology and Innovation, Committee on Science and Technology, July 15, 2010, U.S. House of Representatives.

Hacking the Lights Out

Computer viruses have taken out hardened industrial control systems. The electrical power grid may be next.

Every facet of the modern electrical grid is controlled by computers. It is our greatest example of physical infrastructure interlinked with electronics.

The Stuxnet virus that infected Iran's nuclear program showed just how vulnerable machines could be to a well-crafted electronic virus. The grid shares many of the vulnerabilities that Stuxnet exposed; being larger, its vulnerabilities are, if anything, more numerous. Although a sophisticated attack could bring down a large chunk of the U.S. electrical grid, security is being ramped up.

DAVID M. NICOL

Last year word broke of a computer virus that had managed to slip into Iran's highly secure nuclear enrichment facilities. Most viruses multiply without prejudice, but the Stuxnet virus had a specific target in its sights—one that is not connected to the Internet. Stuxnet was planted on a USB stick that was handed to an unsuspecting technician, who plugged it into a computer at a secure facility. Once inside, the virus spread silently for months, searching for a computer that was connected to a prosaic piece of machinery: a programmable logic controller, a special-purpose collection of microelectronics that commonly controls the cogs of industry—valves, gears, motors and switches. When Stuxnet identified its prey, it slipped in, unnoticed, and seized control.

The targeted controllers were attached to the centrifuges at the heart of Iran's nuclear ambitions. Thousands of these centrifuges are needed to process uranium ore into the highly enriched uranium needed to create a nuclear weapon. Under normal operating conditions, the centrifuges spin so fast that their outer edges travel just below the speed of sound. Stuxnet bumped this speed up to nearly 1,000 miles per hour, past the point where the rotor would likely fly apart, according to a December report by the Institute for Science and International Security. At the same time, Stuxnet sent false signals to control systems indicating that everything was normal. Although the total extent of the damage to Iran's nuclear program remains unclear, the report notes that Iran had to replace about 1,000 centrifuges at its Natanz enrichment facility in late 2009 or early 2010.

Stuxnet demonstrates the extent to which common industrial machines are vulnerable to the threat of electronic attack.

The virus targeted and destroyed supposedly secure equipment while evading detection for months. It provides a dispiriting blueprint for how a rogue state or terrorist group might use similar technology against critical civilian infrastructure anywhere in the world.

Unfortunately, the electrical power grid is easier to break into than any nuclear enrichment facility. We may think of the grid as one gigantic circuit, but in truth the grid is made from thousands of components hundreds of miles apart acting in unerring coordination. The supply of power flowing into the grid must rise and fall in lockstep with demand. Generators must dole their energy out in precise coordination with the 60-cycle-per-second beat that the rest of the grid dances to. And while the failure of any single component will have limited repercussions to this vast circuit, a coordinated cyberattack on multiple points in the grid could damage equipment so extensively that our nation's ability to generate and deliver power would be severely compromised for weeks—perhaps even months.

Considering the size and complexity of the grid, a coordinated attack would probably require significant time and effort to mount. Stuxnet was perhaps the most advanced computer virus ever seen, leading to speculation that it was the work of either the Israeli or U.S. intelligence agencies—or both. But Stuxnet's code is now available on the Internet, raising the chance that a rogue group could customize it for an attack on a new target. A less technologically sophisticated group such as al Qaeda probably does not have the expertise to inflict significant damage to the grid at the moment, but black hat hackers for hire in China or the former Soviet Union might. It is beyond time we secured the country's power supply.

The Break-In

A year ago I took part in a test exercise that centered on a fictitious cyberattack on the grid. Participants included representatives from utility companies, U.S. government agencies and the military. (Military bases rely on power from the commercial grid, a fact that has not escaped the Pentagon's notice.) In the test scenario, malicious agents hacked into a number of transmission substations, knocking out the specialized and expensive devices that ensure voltage stays constant as electricity flows across long high-power transmission lines. By the end of the exercise half a dozen devices had been destroyed, depriving power to an entire Western state for several weeks.

Computers control the grid's mechanical devices at every level, from massive generators fed by fossil fuels or uranium all the way down to the transmission lines on your street. Most of these computers use common operating systems such as Windows and Linux, which makes them as vulnerable to malware as your desktop PC is. Attack code such as Stuxnet is successful for three main reasons: these operating systems implicitly trust running software to be legitimate; they often have flaws that admit penetration by a rogue program; and industrial settings often do not allow for the use of readily available defenses.

Even knowing all this, the average control system engineer would have once dismissed out of hand the possibility of remotely launched malware getting close to critical controllers, arguing that the system is not directly connected to the Internet. Then Stuxnet showed that control networks with no permanent connection to anything else are still vulnerable. Malware can piggyback on a USB stick that technicians plug into the control system, for example. When it comes to critical electronic circuits, even the smallest back door can let an enterprising burglar in.

Consider the case of a transmission substation, a waypoint on electricity's journey from power plant to your home. Substations take in high-voltage electricity coming from one or more power plants, reduce the voltage and split the power into multiple output lines for local distribution. A circuit breaker guards each of these lines, standing ready to cut power in case of a fault. When one output line's breaker trips, all of the power it would have carried flows to the remaining lines. It is not hard to see that if all the lines are carrying power close to their capacity, then a cyberattack that trips out half of the output lines and keeps the remaining ones in the circuit may overload them.

These circuit breakers have historically been controlled by devices connected to telephone modems so that technicians can dial in. It is not difficult to find those numbers; hackers invented programs 30 years ago to dial up all phone numbers within an exchange and make note of the ones to which modems respond. Modems in substations often have a unique message in their dial-up response that reveals their function. Coupled with weak means of authentication (such as well-known passwords or no passwords at all), an attacker can use these modems to break into a substation's network. From there it may be possible to change device configurations so that a danger condition that would otherwise open a circuit breaker to protect equipment gets ignored.

New systems are not necessarily more secure than modems. Increasingly, new devices deployed in substations may communicate with one another via low-powered radio, which does not stop at the boundaries of the substation. An attacker can reach the network simply by hiding in nearby bushes with his computer. Encrypted Wi-Fi networks are more secure, but a sophisticated attacker can still crack their encryption using readily available software tools. From here he can execute a man-in-the-middle attack that causes all communication between two legitimate devices to pass through his computer or fool other devices into accepting his computer as legitimate. He can craft malicious control messages that hijack the circuit breakers—tripping a carefully chosen few to overload the other lines perhaps or making sure they do not trip in an emergency.

Digital Attacks, Physical Harm As industrial machinery goes online, the potential for wreaking havoc grows. Intrusions over the past decade show that the grid is not the only vulnerability—anything with a microchip can be a target.

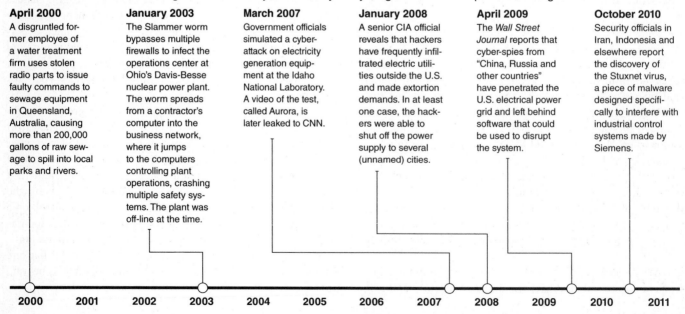

April 2000
A disgruntled former employee of a water treatment firm uses stolen radio parts to issue faulty commands to sewage equipment in Queensland, Australia, causing more than 200,000 gallons of raw sewage to spill into local parks and rivers.

January 2003
The Slammer worm bypasses multiple firewalls to infect the operations center at Ohio's Davis-Besse nuclear power plant. The worm spreads from a contractor's computer into the business network, where it jumps to the computers controlling plant operations, crashing multiple safety systems. The plant was off-line at the time.

March 2007
Government officials simulated a cyber-attack on electricity generation equipment at the Idaho National Laboratory. A video of the test, called Aurora, is later leaked to CNN.

January 2008
A senior CIA official reveals that hackers have frequently infiltrated electric utilities outside the U.S. and made extortion demands. In at least one case, the hackers were able to shut off the power supply to several (unnamed) cities.

April 2009
The *Wall Street Journal* reports that cyber-spies from "China, Russia and other countries" have penetrated the U.S. electrical power grid and left behind software that could be used to disrupt the system.

October 2010
Security officials in Iran, Indonesia and elsewhere report the discovery of the Stuxnet virus, a piece of malware designed specifically to interfere with industrial control systems made by Siemens.

2000 2001 2002 2003 2004 2005 2006 2007 2008 2009 2010 2011

Once an intruder or malware sneaks in through the back door, its first step is usually to spread as widely as possible. Stuxnet again illustrates some of the well-known strategies. It proliferated by using an operating system mechanism called autoexec. Windows computers read and execute the file named AUTOEXEC.BAT every time a new user logs in. Typically the program locates printer drivers, runs a virus scan or performs other basic functions. Yet Windows assumes that any program with the right name is trusted code. Hackers thus find ways to alter the AUTOEXEC.BAT file so that it runs the attackers' code.

Attackers can also use clever methods that exploit the economics of the power industry. Because of deregulation, competing utilities share responsibility for grid operation. Power is generated, transmitted and distributed under contracts obtained in online auctions. These markets operate at multiple timescales—one market might trade energy for immediate delivery and another for tomorrow's needs. A utility's business unit must have a constant flow of real-time information from its operations unit to make smart trades. (And vice versa: operations need to know how much power they need to produce to fulfill the business unit's orders.) Here the vulnerability lies. An enterprising hacker might break into the business network, ferret out user names and passwords, and use these stolen identities to access the operations network.

Other attacks might spread by exploiting the small programs called scripts that come embedded in files. These scripts are ubiquitous—PDF files routinely contain scripts that aid in file display, for example—but they are also a potential danger. One computer security company recently estimated that more than 60 percent of all targeted attacks use scripts buried in PDF files. Simply reading a corrupted file may admit an attacker onto your computer.

Consider the hypothetical case where a would-be grid attacker first penetrates the Website of a software vendor and replaces an online manual with a malicious one that appears exactly like the first. The cyberattacker then sends an engineer at the power plant a forged e-mail that tricks the engineer into fetching and opening the booby-trapped manual. Just by going online to download an updated software manual, the unwitting engineer opens his power plant's gates to the Trojan horse. Once inside, the attack begins.

Search and Destroy

An intruder on a control network can issue commands with potentially devastating results. In 2007 the Department of Homeland Security staged a cyberattack code-named Aurora at the Idaho National laboratory. During the exercise, a researcher posing as a malicious hacker burrowed his way into a network connected to a medium-size power generator. Like all generators, it creates alternating current operating at almost exactly 60 cycles per second. In every cycle, the flow of electrons starts out moving in one direction, reverses course, and then returns to its original state. The generator has to be moving electrons in exactly the same direction at exactly the same time as the rest of the grid.

During the Aurora attack, our hacker issued a rapid succession of on/off commands to the circuit breakers of a test generator at the laboratory. This pushed it out of sync with the power grid's own oscillations. The grid pulled one way, the generator another. In effect, the generator's mechanical inertia fought the grid's electrical inertia. The generator lost. Declassified video shows the hulking steel machine shuddering as though a train hit the building. Seconds later steam and smoke fill the room.

Industrial systems can also fail when they are pushed beyond their limits—when centrifuges spin too fast, they disintegrate. Similarly, an attacker could make an electric generator produce a surge of power that exceeds the limit of what the transmission lines can carry. Excess power would then have to escape as heat. Enough excess over a long enough period causes the line to sag and eventually to melt. If the sagging line comes into contact with anything— a tree, a billboard, a house—it could create a massive short circuit.

Protection relays typically prevent these shorts, but a cyberattack could interfere with the working of the relays, which means damage would be done. Furthermore, a cyberattack could also alter the information going to the control station, keeping operators from knowing that anything is amiss. We have all seen the movies where crooks send a false video feed to a guard.

Control stations are also vulnerable to attack. These are command and control rooms with huge displays, like the war room in *Dr. Strangelove*. Control station operators use the displays to monitor data gathered from the substations, then issue commands to change substation control settings. Often these stations are responsible for monitoring hundreds of substations spread over a good part of a state.

Data communications between the control station and substations use specialized protocols that themselves may have vulnerabilities. If an intruder succeeds in launching a man-in-the-middle attack, that individual can insert a message into an exchange (or corrupt an existing message) that causes one or both of the computers at either end to fail. An attacker can also try just injecting a properly formatted message that is out of context— a digital non sequitur that crashes the machine.

Attackers could also simply attempt to delay messages traveling between control stations and the substations. Ordinarily the lag time between a substation's measurement of electricity flow and the control station's use of the data to adjust flows is small—otherwise it would be like driving a car and seeing only where you were 10 seconds ago. (This kind of lack of situational awareness was a contributor to the Northeast Blackout of 2003.)

Many of these attacks do not require fancy software such as Stuxnet but merely the standard hacker's tool kit. For instance, hackers frequently take command over networks of thousands or even millions of ordinary PCs (a botnet), which they then instruct to do their bidding. The simplest type of botnet attack is to flood an ordinary Website with bogus messages, blocking or slowing the ordinary flow of information. These "denial of service" attacks could also be used to slow traffic moving between the control station and substations.

Botnets could also take root in the substation computers themselves. At one point in 2009 the Conficker botnet had

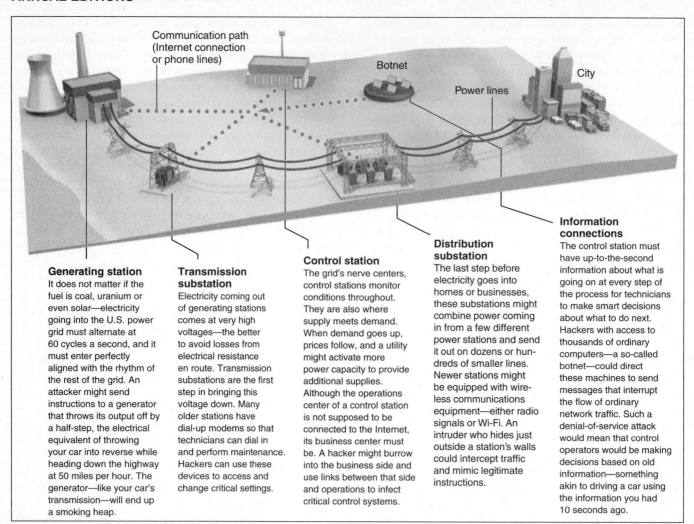

Communication path (Internet connection or phone lines)

Botnet

City

Power lines

Generating station
It does not matter if the fuel is coal, uranium or even solar—electricity going into the U.S. power grid must alternate at 60 cycles a second, and it must enter perfectly aligned with the rhythm of the rest of the grid. An attacker might send instructions to a generator that throws its output off by a half-step, the electrical equivalent of throwing your car into reverse while heading down the highway at 50 miles per hour. The generator—like your car's transmission—will end up a smoking heap.

Transmission substation
Electricity coming out of generating stations comes at very high voltages—the better to avoid losses from electrical resistance en route. Transmission substations are the first step in bringing this voltage down. Many older stations have dial-up modems so that technicians can dial in and perform maintenance. Hackers can use these devices to access and change critical settings.

Control station
The grid's nerve centers, control stations monitor conditions throughout. They are also where supply meets demand. When demand goes up, prices follow, and a utility might activate more power capacity to provide additional supplies. Although the operations center of a control station is not supposed to be connected to the Internet, its business center must be. A hacker might burrow into the business side and use links between that side and operations to infect critical control systems.

Distribution substation
The last step before electricity goes into homes or businesses, these substations might combine power coming in from a few different power stations and send it out on dozens or hundreds of smaller lines. Newer stations might be equipped with wireless communications equipment—either radio signals or Wi-Fi. An intruder who hides just outside a station's walls could intercept traffic and mimic legitimate instructions.

Information connections
The control station must have up-to-the-second information about what is going on at every step of the process for technicians to make smart decisions about what to do next. Hackers with access to thousands of ordinary computers—a so-called botnet—could direct these machines to send messages that interrupt the flow of ordinary network traffic. Such a denial-of-service attack would mean that control operators would be making decisions based on old information—something akin to driving a car using the information you had 10 seconds ago.

Holes in the Grid. The modern electrical grid involves an intricate balance between the amount of energy needed by society and the amount generated at power plants. Dozens of components orchestrate the flow of electrons over distances of hundreds of miles, aligning the alternating currents and making sure no single component gets stretched beyond its limits. Any one of these parts might suffer from the attention of malicious actors. Here are some of the most troublesome choke points and the ways they might be compromised.

insinuated itself into 10 million computers; the individuals, as yet unknown, who control it could have ordered it to erase the hard drives of every computer in the network, on command. A botnet such as Conficker could establish itself within substations and then have its controller direct them simultaneously to do anything at any time. According to a 2004 study by researchers at Pennsylvania State University and the National Renewable Energy Laboratory in Golden, Colo., an attack that incapacitated a carefully chosen minority of all transmission substations—about 2 percent, or 200 in total—would bring down 60 percent of the grid. Losing 8 percent would trigger a nationwide blackout.

What to Do

When microsoft learns of a potential security liability in its Windows software, it typically releases a software patch. Individual users and IT departments the world over download the patch, update their software and protect themselves from the threat. Unfortunately, things are not that simple on the grid.

Whereas the power grid uses the same type of off-the-shelf hardware and software as the rest of the world, IT managers at power stations cannot simply patch the faulty software when bugs crop up. Grid control systems cannot come down for three hours every week for maintenance; they have to run continuously. Grid operators also have a deep-rooted institutional conservatism. Control networks have been in place for a long time, and operators are familiar and comfortable with how they work. They tend to avoid anything that threatens availability or might interfere with ordinary operations.

In the face of a clear and present danger, the North American Electric Reliability Corporation (NERC), an umbrella body of grid operators, has devised a set of standards designed to protect critical infrastructure. Utilities are now required to identify their critical assets and demonstrate to NERC-appointed auditors that they can protect them from unauthorized access.

Yet security audits, like financial audits, cannot possibly be exhaustive. When an audit does go into technical details, it does so only selectively. Compliance is in the eye of the auditor.

The most common protection strategy is to employ an electronic security perimeter, a kind of cybersecurity Maginot line. The first line of defense is a firewall, a device through which all electronic messages pass. Each message has a header indicating where it came from, where it is going, and what protocol is used to interpret the message. Based on this information, the firewall allows some messages through and stops others. An auditor's job is partly to make sure the firewalls in a utility are configured properly so that they do not let any unwanted traffic in or out. Typically the auditors would identify a few critical assets, get a hold of the firewall configuration files, and attempt to sort through by hand the ways in which a hacker might be able to break through the firewall.

Firewalls, though, are so complex that it is difficult for an auditor to parse all the myriad possibilities. Automated software tools might help. Our team at the University of Illinois at Urbana-Champaign has developed the Network Access Policy Tool, which is just now being used by utilities and assessment teams. The software needs only a utility's firewall configuration files—it does not even have to connect to the network. Already it has found a number of unknown or long-forgotten pathways that attackers might have exploited.

The DOE has come out with a roadmap that lays out a strategy for enhancing grid security by 2015. (A revision due this year extends this deadline to 2020.) One focus: creating a system that recognizes an intrusion attempt and reacts to it automatically. That would block a Stuxnet-like virus as soon as it jumped from the USB stick. But how can an operating system know which programs are to be trusted?

One solution is to use a one-way hash function, a cryptographic technique. A hash function takes a fantastically huge number—for example, all the millions of 1s and 0s of a computer program, expressed as a number—and converts it to a much smaller number, which acts as a signature. Because programs are so large, it is highly unlikely that two different ones would result in the same signature value. Imagine that every program that wants to run on a system must first go through the hash function. Its signature then gets checked against a master list; if it does not check out, the attack stops there.

The DOE also recommends other security measures, such as physical security checks at operator workstations (think radio chips in identification badges). It also highlights the need to exert tighter control over communication between devices inside the network. The 2007 Aurora demonstration involved a rogue device tricking a generator's network into believing it was sending authoritative commands. These commands eventually led to the destruction of the generator.

These worthwhile steps will require time and money and effort. If we are going to achieve the DOE roadmap to a more secure grid in the next decade, we are going to have to pick up the pace. Let us hope we have even that much time.

References

Roadmap to Secure Control Systems in the Energy Sector.
Jack Eisenhauer et al. Energetics Incorporated, January 2006. www.oe.energy.gov/csroadmap.htm

Security of Critical Control Systems Sparks Concern. David Geer in *IEEE Computer,* Vol. 39, No. 1, pages 20–23; January 2006.

Trustworthy Cyber Infrastructure for the Power Grid.
Multiuniversity research project funded by the U.S. Department of Energy. www.tcipg.org

What Is the Electric Grid, and What Are Some Challenges It Faces? U.S. Department of Energy. www.eia.doe.gov/energy_ in_brief/power_grid.cfm

Scientific American Online
For an extended look at the history of electronic attacks on physical structures, visit ScientificAmerican.com/jul2011/lights-out

Critical Thinking

1. Use the Internet to research the Stuxnet virus. Who is thought to have been responsible for it?

2. The author mentions a type of cyber-attack known as at Trojan horse. Use the Internet to read about the Trojan horse attack. While you're at it, where was the first Trojan horse described?

3. The author uses the phrase "clear and present danger." Use the Internet to learn who first used it and in what context. Is the phrase being misused in the article?

4. Reread the description of the one-way hash function toward the end of the article. Now read about one-way hash functions in Wikipedia. You will come across Merkle-Damgard hashing. Its co-inventor is Ralph Merkle, whom you'll learn more about in "Die Another Day," reprinted in Unit 8. Take a few minutes to read that essay now. What do you think about technical fixes for technical vulnerabilities now?

5. Think about technology biting back. Is there a simpler solution to protecting the grid than those proposed? Again, use the Internet to do some research.

DAVID M. NICOL is director of the Information Trust Institute and a professor in the department of electrical and computer engineering at the University of Illinois at Urbana-Champaign. He has worked as a consultant for the U.S. Department of Homeland Security and Department of Energy.

The Web's New Gold Mine: Your Secrets

A Journal investigation finds that one of the fastest-growing businesses on the Internet is the business of spying on consumers. First in a series.

JULIA ANGWIN

Hidden inside Ashley Hayes-Beaty's computer, a tiny file helps gather personal details about her, all to be put up for sale for a tenth of a penny.

The file consists of a single code—4c812db292272995e-5416a323e79bd37—that secretly identifies her as a 26-year-old female in Nashville, Tenn.

The code knows that her favorite movies include "The Princess Bride," "50 First Dates" and "10 Things I Hate About You." It knows she enjoys the "Sex and the City" series. It knows she browses entertainment news and likes to take quizzes.

"Well, I like to think I have some mystery left to me, but apparently not!" Ms. Hayes-Beaty said when told what that snippet of code reveals about her. "The profile is eerily correct."

Ms. Hayes-Beaty is being monitored by Lotame Solutions Inc., a New York company that uses sophisticated software called a "beacon" to capture what people are typing on a website—their comments on movies, say, or their interest in parenting and pregnancy. Lotame packages that data into profiles about individuals, without determining a person's name, and sells the profiles to companies seeking customers. Ms. Hayes-Beaty's tastes can be sold wholesale (a batch of movie lovers is $1 per thousand) or customized (26-year-old Southern fans of "50 First Dates").

"We can segment it all the way down to one person," says Eric Porres, Lotame's chief marketing officer.

One of the fastest-growing businesses on the Internet, a Wall Street Journal investigation has found, is the business of spying on Internet users.

The Journal conducted a comprehensive study that assesses and analyzes the broad array of cookies and other surveillance technology that companies are deploying on Internet users. It reveals that the tracking of consumers has grown both far more pervasive and far more intrusive than is realized by all but a handful of people in the vanguard of the industry.

- The study found that the nation's 50 top websites on average installed 64 pieces of tracking technology onto the computers of visitors, usually with no warning. A dozen sites each installed more than a hundred. The nonprofit Wikipedia installed none.

- Tracking technology is getting smarter and more intrusive. Monitoring used to be limited mainly to "cookie" files that record websites people visit. But the Journal found new tools that scan in real time what people are doing on a Web page, then instantly assess location, income, shopping interests and even medical conditions. Some tools surreptitiously re-spawn themselves even after users try to delete them.

- These profiles of individuals, constantly refreshed, are bought and sold on stock-market-like exchanges that have sprung up in the past 18 months.

The new technologies are transforming the Internet economy. Advertisers once primarily bought ads on specific Web pages—a car ad on a car site. Now, advertisers are paying a premium to follow people around the Internet, wherever they go, with highly specific marketing messages.

In between the Internet user and the advertiser, the Journal identified more than 100 middlemen—tracking companies, data brokers and advertising networks—competing to meet the growing demand for data on individual behavior and interests.

The data on Ms. Hayes-Beaty's film-watching habits, for instance, is being offered to advertisers on BlueKai Inc., one of the new data exchanges.

"It is a sea change in the way the industry works," says Omar Tawakol, CEO of BlueKai. "Advertisers want to buy access to people, not Web pages."

The Journal examined the 50 most popular U.S. websites, which account for about 40% of the Web pages viewed by Americans. (The Journal also tested its own site, WSJ.com.) It then analyzed the tracking files and programs these sites downloaded onto a test computer.

As a group, the top 50 sites placed 3,180 tracking files in total on the Journal's test computer. Nearly a third of these were innocuous, deployed to remember the password to a favorite site or tally most-popular articles.

But over two-thirds—2,224—were installed by 131 companies, many of which are in the business of tracking Web users to create rich databases of consumer profiles that can be sold.

The top venue for such technology, the Journal found, was IAC/InterActive Corp.'s Dictionary.com. A visit to the online dictionary site resulted in 234 files or programs being downloaded onto the Journal's test computer, 223 of which were from companies that track Web users.

The information that companies gather is anonymous, in the sense that Internet users are identified by a number assigned to their computer, not by a specific person's name. Lotame, for instance, says it doesn't know the name of users such as Ms. Hayes-Beaty—only their behavior and attributes, identified by code number. People who don't want to be tracked can remove themselves from Lotame's system.

And the industry says the data are used harmlessly. David Moore, chairman of 24/7 RealMedia Inc., an ad network owned by WPP PLC, says tracking gives Internet users better advertising.

"When an ad is targeted properly, it ceases to be an ad, it becomes important information," he says.

Tracking isn't new. But the technology is growing so powerful and ubiquitous that even some of America's biggest sites say they were unaware, until informed by the Journal, that they were installing intrusive files on visitors' computers.

The Journal found that Microsoft Corp.'s popular Web portal, MSN.com, planted a tracking file packed with data: It had a prediction of a surfer's age, ZIP Code and gender, plus a code containing estimates of income, marital status, presence of children and home ownership, according to the tracking company that created the file, Targus Information Corp.

Both Targus and Microsoft said they didn't know how the file got onto MSN.com, and added that the tool didn't contain "personally identifiable" information.

Tracking is done by tiny files and programs known as "cookies," "Flash cookies" and "beacons." They are placed on a computer when a user visits a website. U.S. courts have ruled that it is legal to deploy the simplest type, cookies, just as someone using a telephone might allow a friend to listen in on a conversation. Courts haven't ruled on the more complex trackers.

The most intrusive monitoring comes from what are known in the business as "third party" tracking files. They work like this: The first time a site is visited, it installs a tracking file, which assigns the computer a unique ID number. Later, when the user visits another site affiliated with the same tracking company, it can take note of where that user was before, and where he is now. This way, over time the company can build a robust profile.

One such ecosystem is Yahoo Inc.'s ad network, which collects fees by placing targeted advertisements on websites. Yahoo's network knows many things about recent high-school graduate Cate Reid. One is that she is a 13- to 18-year-old female interested in weight loss. Ms. Reid was able to determine this when a reporter showed her a little-known feature on Yahoo's website, the Ad Interest Manager, that displays some of the information Yahoo had collected about her.

Yahoo's take on Ms. Reid, who was 17 years old at the time, hit the mark: She was, in fact, worried that she may be 15 pounds too heavy for her 5-foot, 6-inch frame. She says she often does online research about weight loss.

"Every time I go on the Internet," she says, she sees weight-loss ads. "I'm self-conscious about my weight," says Ms. Reid, whose father asked that her hometown not be given. "I try not to think about it. . . . Then [the ads] make me start thinking about it."

Yahoo spokeswoman Amber Allman says Yahoo doesn't knowingly target weight-loss ads at people under 18, though it does target adults.

"It's likely this user received an untargeted ad," Ms. Allman says. It's also possible Ms. Reid saw ads targeted at her by other tracking companies.

Information about people's moment-to-moment thoughts and actions, as revealed by their online activity, can change hands quickly. Within seconds of visiting eBay.com or Expedia.com, information detailing a Web surfer's activity there is likely to be auctioned on the data exchange run by BlueKai, the Seattle startup.

Each day, BlueKai sells 50 million pieces of information like this about specific individuals' browsing habits, for as little as a tenth of a cent apiece. The auctions can happen instantly, as a website is visited.

Spokespeople for eBay Inc. and Expedia Inc. both say the profiles BlueKai sells are anonymous and the people aren't identified as visitors of their sites. BlueKai says its own website gives consumers an easy way to see what it monitors about them.

Tracking files get onto websites, and downloaded to a computer, in several ways. Often, companies simply pay sites to distribute their tracking files.

But tracking companies sometimes hide their files within free software offered to websites, or hide them within other tracking files or ads. When this happens, websites aren't always aware that they're installing the files on visitors' computers.

Often staffed by "quants," or math gurus with expertise in quantitative analysis, some tracking companies use probability algorithms to try to pair what they know about a person's online behavior with data from offline sources about household income, geography and education, among other things.

The goal is to make sophisticated assumptions in real time—plans for a summer vacation, the likelihood of repaying a loan—and sell those conclusions.

Some financial companies are starting to use this formula to show entirely different pages to visitors, based on assumptions about their income and education levels.

Life-insurance site AccuquoteLife.com, a unit of Byron Udell & Associates Inc., last month tested a system showing visitors it determined to be suburban, college-educated baby-boomers a default policy of $2 million to $3 million, says Accuquote executive Sean Cheyney. A rural, working-class senior citizen might see a default policy for $250,000, he says.

"We're driving people down different lanes of the highway," Mr. Cheyney says.

Consumer tracking is the foundation of an online advertising economy that racked up $23 billion in ad spending last year. Tracking activity is exploding. Researchers at AT&T Labs and Worcester Polytechnic Institute last fall found tracking technology on 80% of 1,000 popular sites, up from 40% of those sites in 2005.

The Journal found tracking files that collect sensitive health and financial data. On Encyclopaedia Britannica Inc.'s dictionary website Merriam-Webster.com, one tracking file from Healthline Networks Inc., an ad network, scans the page a user is viewing and targets ads related to what it sees there. So, for example, a person looking up depression-related words could see Healthline ads for depression treatments on that page—and on subsequent pages viewed on other sites.

Healthline says it doesn't let advertisers track users around the Internet who have viewed sensitive topics such as HIV/AIDS, sexually transmitted diseases, eating disorders and impotence. The company does let advertisers track people with bipolar disorder, overactive bladder and anxiety, according to its marketing materials.

Targeted ads can get personal. Last year, Julia Preston, a 32-year-old education-software designer in Austin, Texas, researched uterine disorders online. Soon after, she started noticing fertility ads on sites she visited. She now knows she doesn't have a disorder, but still gets the ads.

It's "unnerving," she says.

Tracking became possible in 1994 when the tiny text files called cookies were introduced in an early browser, Netscape Navigator. Their purpose was user convenience: remembering contents of Web shopping carts.

Back then, online advertising barely existed. The first banner ad appeared the same year. When online ads got rolling during the dot-com boom of the late 1990s, advertisers were buying ads based on proximity to content—shoe ads on fashion sites.

The dot-com bust triggered a power shift in online advertising, away from websites and toward advertisers. Advertisers began paying for ads only if someone clicked on them. Sites and ad networks began using cookies aggressively in hopes of showing ads to people most likely to click on them, thus getting paid.

Targeted ads command a premium. Last year, the average cost of a targeted ad was $4.12 per thousand viewers, compared with $1.98 per thousand viewers for an untargeted ad, according to an ad-industry-sponsored study in March.

The Journal examined three kinds of tracking technology—basic cookies as well as more powerful "Flash cookies" and bits of software code called "beacons."

More than half of the sites examined by the Journal installed 23 or more "third party" cookies. Dictionary.com installed the most, placing 159 third-party cookies.

Cookies are typically used by tracking companies to build lists of pages visited from a specific computer. A newer type of technology, beacons, can watch even more activity.

Beacons, also known as "Web bugs" and "pixels," are small pieces of software that run on a Web page. They can track what a user is doing on the page, including what is being typed or where the mouse is moving.

The majority of sites examined by the Journal placed at least seven beacons from outside companies. Dictionary.com had the most, 41, including several from companies that track health conditions and one that says it can target consumers by dozens of factors, including zip code and race.

Dictionary.com President Shravan Goli attributed the presence of so many tracking tools to the fact that the site was working with a large number of ad networks, each of which places its own cookies and beacons. After the Journal contacted the company, it cut the number of networks it uses and beefed up its privacy policy to more fully disclose its practices.

The widespread use of Adobe Systems Inc.'s Flash software to play videos online offers another opportunity to track people. Flash cookies originally were meant to remember users' preferences, such as volume settings for online videos.

But Flash cookies can also be used by data collectors to re-install regular cookies that a user has deleted. This can circumvent a user's attempt to avoid being tracked online. Adobe condemns the practice.

Most sites examined by the Journal installed no Flash cookies. Comcast.net installed 55.

That finding surprised the company, which said it was unaware of them. Comcast Corp. subsequently determined that it had used a piece of free software from a company called Clearspring Technologies Inc. to display a slideshow of celebrity photos on Comcast.net. The Flash cookies were installed on Comcast's site by that slideshow, according to Comcast.

Clearspring, based in McLean, Va., says the 55 Flash cookies were a mistake. The company says it no longer uses Flash cookies for tracking.

CEO Hooman Radfar says Clearspring provides software and services to websites at no charge. In exchange, Clearspring collects data on consumers. It plans eventually to sell the data it collects to advertisers, he says, so that site users can be shown "ads that don't suck." Comcast's data won't be used, Clearspring says.

Wittingly or not, people pay a price in reduced privacy for the information and services they receive online. Dictionary.com, the site with the most tracking files, is a case study.

The site's annual revenue, about $9 million in 2009 according to an SEC filing, means the site is too small to support an extensive ad-sales team. So it needs to rely on the national ad-placing networks, whose business model is built on tracking.

> **"Think about how these technologies and the associated analytics can be used in other industries and social settings (e.g. education) for real beneficial impacts. This is nothing new for the web, now that it has matured, it can be a positive game-changer."**
>
> —Mitchell Weisberg

Dictionary.com executives say the trade-off is fair for their users, who get free access to its dictionary and thesaurus service.

"Whether it's one or 10 cookies, it doesn't have any impact on the customer experience, and we disclose we do it," says Dictionary.com spokesman Nicholas Graham. "So what's the beef?"

The problem, say some industry veterans, is that so much consumer data is now up for sale, and there are no legal limits on how that data can be used.

Until recently, targeting consumers by health or financial status was considered off-limits by many large Internet ad companies. Now, some aim to take targeting to a new level by tapping online social networks.

Media6Degrees Inc., whose technology was found on three sites by the Journal, is pitching banks to use its data to size up consumers based on their social connections. The idea is that the creditworthy tend to hang out with the creditworthy, and deadbeats with deadbeats.

"There are applications of this technology that can be very powerful," says Tom Phillips, CEO of Media6Degrees. "Who knows how far we'd take it?"

Critical Thinking

1. What is a cookie (in the context of a web browser)?

2. What is a beacon?

3. Many websites, like broadcast TV, appear to be free. The bills are paid through advertising. Would you prefer to pay directly to use websites or to continue to allow their owners to collect and sell information about you?

Emily Steel, Jennifer Valentino-DeVries and Tom McGinty contributed to this report.

The BP Oil Spill: Could Software Be a Culprit?

DON SHAFER AND PHILLIP A. LAPLANTE

Computing Now Exclusive: Interview with Don Shafer

Author Don Shafer, chief safety and technology officer with the Athens Group, an independent software-consulting firm that provides risk-mitigation services to the offshore oil-drilling industry, details how software failures on oil rigs include mishandled software alarms, untested software, frozen computer screens, and lack of data recorders for oil rigs. Yet, the most important failure might be the lack of standards across the oil drilling industry.

> No one yet knows what caused the Deepwater Horizon oil rig explosion that killed 11 workers and poured millions of gallons of oil into the Gulf of Mexico. But considering the fact that offshore oil rigs comprise dozens of complex subsystems that use or are controlled by software, is it possible a software failure could have contributed to this disaster?

In April 2010, an explosion occurred on the Deepwater Horizon oil rig operated by BP Petroleum and its subcontractor, Transocean. The explosion killed 11 workers, destroyed and sank the rig, and caused millions of gallons of oil to pour into the Gulf of Mexico, about 40 miles off of the Louisiana coast.

As we write this, it appears that the gushing well, about a mile under the sea, has finally been brought under control after more than three months of frenetic attempts. The total damage to the environment, economy, and future of deepwater fossil-fuel drilling in the US has yet to be determined.

While the American government and press are scrambling to assign blame for this catastrophe, no one knows what caused the explosion that led to this disaster. The cause might never be known. However, we wonder . . . could a software failure have contributed to this disaster?

Speculation of a Software Connection

We don't have access to all the data from this incident. However, Transocean's interim report, submitted to Representative

Henry Waxman's committee in the US House of Representatives on 8 June 2010, stated the following under an "Action items/work needed" section: "Full control-system software review. Software code requested from manufacturer for investigation."[1] Apparently, in studying the disaster, there's speculation of a software connection.

Additionally, an article appearing in the 19 July 2010 issue of the *Houston Chronicle* stated that "display screens at the primary workstation used to operate drill controls on the Deepwater Horizon, called the A-chair, had locked up more than once before the deadly accident."[2] According to Stephen Bertone, Transocean's chief engineer on the Deepwater Horizon, "Basically, the screens would freeze [and] all the data . . . would lock up." Bertone noted, however, that hard drives had been replaced, and he wasn't aware of any problems with the equipment the day of the accident.[2]

We'll learn more about software's role in this disaster as additional evidence surfaces. However, since one of us (Don Shafer) has extensive experience in software testing for oil rig technology and in post-incident analysis of fatal software-related equipment failures, let's speculate further about how a software problem could have caused the Deepwater Horizon incident.

Software Control on Oil Rigs

Offshore oil rigs comprise dozens of complex subsystems that use embedded software or are operated under software control. For numerous reasons, each system is a potential point of failure.

For example, three rigs with the same design built over four years can end up with different equipment and software versions that might not integrate as expected. This could also lead to serious configuration-management problems.

Another problem is that much of the software residing in or controlling components is routinely delivered well after the equipment is onboard the rig. Engineers test the interfaces at the last minute—if they even test the software at all. Equipment interfaces thus present the weakest link in offshore oil rig systems in terms of reliability and safety, because the industry lacks interface standards and sufficient testing methods.[3]

Table 1 Industry recommendations for "manageable" alarm rates[5–7] versus rates reported in the Abnormal Situation Management Consortium study[4]

Organization	Standard	Normal Alarm Rate	Peak Alarm Rate
The Engineering Equipment and Materials Users' Association	EEMUA 191	1 alarm per 5 minutes	Less than 10 alarms per 10 minutes
International Society of Automation	ISA 18.2	Approximately 2 alarms per 10 minutes	10 alarms per 10 minutes for less than approximately 2.5 hours per month*
Nowegian Petroleum Directorate	NPD YA 711	1 alarm per 5 minutes	Less than 1 alarm per minute
Abnormal Situation Management Consortium	Study results	Average rate: 2.3 alarms every 10 minutes	95% of unique consoles experience 31-50 alarms every 10 minutes

*Adapted from ISA 18.2: 16.5.2. Calculation is based on an eight-hour workday.

Mishandled Software Alarms

There are several possible scenarios in which a software failure could have manifested as a serious rig failure. For example, any one of the many software systems controlling the equipment . . . could have started failing weeks or months before the Deepwater Horizon incident, causing accumulative problems. However, here we focus on one possible scenario—a mishandled alarm.

In an oil rig system, the many devices coupled with insufficient testing and alarm management lead to numerous software alarms popping up on the driller's work station (see Table 1). In some cases, up to 50 alarms can occur every 10 minutes,[4] which is much higher than industry standards recommend.[5–7]

Typical alarm issues include calibration errors, flooding, buried alarms, improper prioritization, nuisance alarms, and alarms that are missing altogether. Athens Group recently performed a Failure Modes, Effects, and Criticality Analysis (FMECA) report and found that vital alarms might not be acted upon in time for two main reasons:

- the alarms aren't categorized by priority, or
- thousands or even tens of thousands of alarms are being displayed every day.

The typical number of potential alarms on a drilling rig is astounding. In one project, for example, researchers created an inventory of all alarms created by drill floor equipment. The final list was over 90 pages long and contained more than 2,700 alarms.[8]

There is, unfortunately, a great deal of precedent for software failures having a serious impact on rig equipment.[9] Many of these failures led to loss of life, injury to rig hands, or expensive damage to equipment. Some of the failures led to environmental issues. To illustrate the relationship of missed alarms to certain failures in rigs, consider the following real cases.

Case 1: Buried Alarm

While *tripping out*—that is, pulling the drill pipe out of the well—a driller on an offshore rig arrived at the lower portion of the drill pipe. When you pull a drill pipe out of a well, a volume of mud equal to that which the pipe displaced must be pumped back in as a replacement. To ensure that this process was functioning correctly, the driller performed a flow check before continuing the process. No irregularities were found, so the driller continued.

When an alarm sounded to indicate that the trip tank (a receptacle used to ascertain the exact amount of mud displaced by the drill pipe) had overflowed, the assistant driller acknowledged the alarm, not realizing that it had indicated a full trip tank. The trip tank then overflowed, causing approximately 60 barrels of synthetic-based mud to be discharged overboard. An assessment of alarm priority and annunciation could have helped prevent this alarm from being overlooked.

Case 2: Missed Alarm

In this incident, a mud pump failed on a particular rig. The driller assumed that a bad sensor caused the problem, so he replaced the sensor and the mud pump. However, a subsequent failure of the replacement mud pump then occurred in the same manner as the first. An alarm had indicated the problem's real cause, but it was buried so deep on the alarm screen that the driller never saw it.

Because no one had ever tested the possible alarms, no one knew that the driller was mishandling this alarm. As a result, unnecessary hardware was purchased. Additionally, the mud pump replacement resulted in the loss of productive time. A review of the alarms supported by the system—of their prioritization and their mapping into the human-machine interface on the driller's chair—could have prevented this.

Case 3: Alarm Calibration Error

During production on a Floating Production, Storage, and Offloading unit, the compressor flow transmitter offset began to increase. The change wasn't automatically detected, so operations personnel didn't notice it, and the offset continued to increase.

Sometime later, compressor vibrations changed signature, indicating bearing changes. The vibration remained below alarm level and thus went undetected. Later, the seal gas cavity temperature increased significantly during an aborted restart, but the temperature increase didn't trigger an alarm, so no corrective action was taken.

As a result, a fire occurred in the gas compression process module, halting production on a US$720 million venture. In this scenario, an alarm audit could have helped prevent this problem by identifying possible failures in alarm communication paths and ensuring that alarms trigger under the appropriate circumstances.

There is a strong possibility that the Deep Water Horizon driller or tool pusher in charge of the drill floor never saw one or more alarm signals issued in relation to the problems that eventually led to the explosion. Unfortunately, we can't reconstruct the software events leading to the BP spill disaster because there's no "black box" on the rigs. Some rigs carry a "flight recorder," but it only records some of the messages on the drilling control network. The subsea, power, and vessel-management system networks are totally ignored.

The 2010 Toyota Prius braking problem was very quickly blamed on a software failure, without proof. In fact, to date, no software defect has been found, and Toyota is now suggesting that driver error was most likely to blame.[10] Yet no one is claiming that a software problem caused the BP oil disaster. Unfortunately, the oil industry is in the same state as the U.S. manufacturing industry in the 1970s—that is, standards have yet to be fully adopted, and there are no universal risk-mitigation strategies or tight safety controls.

We might never know whether a software problem caused the 2010 Gulf oil spill, but there's clearly the need for better interface standards and software testing for oil rig technology. Perhaps in the future, software could help prevent a catastrophic spill from occurring.

References

1. "Deepwater Horizon Incident—Internal Investigation," draft report, Transocean, 8 June 2010, p. 15; http://energycommerce.house.gov/documents/20100614/Transocean.DWH.Internal.Investigation.Update.Interim.Report.June.8.2010.pdf.
2. B. Clanton, "Drilling Rig Had Equipment Issues, Witnesses Say—Irregular Procedures also Noted at Hearing," *Houston Chronicle,* 19 July 2010; www.chron.com/disp/story.mpl/business/7115524.html.
3. "Can You Afford the Risk? The Case for Collaboration on Risk Mitigation for High-Specification Offshore Assets," white paper, Athens Group, Feb. 2010.
4. *Achieving Effective Alarm System Performance: Results of ASM Consortium Benchmarking against the EEMUA Guide for Alarm Systems,* Abnormal Situation Management Consortium, Feb. 2005; www.applyhcs.com/publications/interface_design/EffectiveAlarmSystemPerformance_CCPS05.pdf.
5. *EEMUA 191: Alarm Systems: A Guide to Design, Management and Procurement,* Eng. Equipment and Materials Users' Assoc., 1999.
6. *ISA 18.2: Management of Alarm Systems for the Process Industries,* Int'l Soc. Automation, 2009.
7. *NPD YA-711: Principles for Alarm System Design,* Norwegian Petroleum Directorate, 2001.
8. Athens Group, "How to Stop the Flood of Superfluous Alarms and Achieve Alarm Management Compliance," to appear in *Proc. Int'l Assoc. Drilling Contractors World Drilling Conf.,* 2010.
9. D. Shafer, "Would You Like Software with That? Where Do We Stand with Oil and Gas (O&G) Exploration and Production (E&P) Software?" white paper, Athens Group, 2005; http://athensgroup.com/nptqhse-resources/articles-and-whitepapers.html.
10. J. Garthwaite, "It Wasn't the Software: Toyota Finds Driver Error (Not Code) to Blame," Earth2tech.com, 14 July 2010; http://earth2tech.com/2010/07/14/toyota-finds-driver-error-not-software-to-blame-in-some-runaway-cars

Critical Thinking

1. Which of the software plagues (the vegematic promise, the big technical leap, etc.) chronicled in Article 27, "The Software Wars," are the authors referring to when speculating about software problems leading to the BP oil spill problem.
2. The authors refer to both the number and complexity of alarms and the apparently inadequate testing of software. "In some cases," they say, "up to 50 alarms can occur every ten minutes." Use the Internet to read Aesop's fable, "The Boy Who Cried Wolf." What happened to the boy in the story? Is there a lesson for software engineering?

DON SHAFER is Chief Safety and Technology Officer of the Athens Group. His research interests include software safety and configuration management. Shafer has an MBA from the University of Denver and is a Certified Software Development Professional (CSDP). Contact him at dshafer@athensgroup.com. **PHILLIP A. LAPLANTE** is professor of software engineering at Pennsylvania State University. His research interests include software project management, software testing, requirements engineering, and cyber security. Laplante has a PhD from the Stevens Institute of Technology and is a licensed professional engineer in Pennsylvania and a CSDP. He's a fellow of IEEE and a member of the IEEE Computer Society's Board of Governors. Contact him at plaplante@psu.edu.

The Conundrum of Visibility: Youth Safety and the Internet

Danah Boyd and Alice Marwick

The complexities of the Internet continue to be a source of consternation for parents, educators, and policy makers. Some embrace the Internet, evangelizing about its tremendous potential. Others fear it, preaching en masse about its dangers. These cycles of polarizing doctrine make it difficult to understand that the Internet is quickly becoming just another aspect of everyday life, mirroring dynamics that shape every environment that people inhabit. Are there risks and dangers online? Certainly—just as there are offline. There is little doubt that technology inflects age-old issues in new ways, and these shifts must be understood. But when we focus exclusively on technology, we lose track of the bigger picture. For many youth, technology is part of their everyday lives, and must be examined in that context. The key to addressing online safety is to take a few steps back and make sense of the lives of youth, the risks and dangers they face, and the personal, social, and cultural logic behind their practices.

Four issues dominate contemporary conversations about online safety: 1) sexual solicitation; 2) harassment; 3) exposure to inappropriate content; and 4) youth-generated problematic content. Data on these issues have been well-documented, especially in the U.S. (Shrock and Boyd 2008), but let's look briefly at each of these concerns before turning to think about the most significant opportunity provided by the Internet: visibility.

Sexual Solicitation

The image of the online predator is pervasive. He is portrayed as an older, unattractive man who falsifies his identity to deceive, groom, kidnap, and rape children. A handful of devastating but rare cases that fit this stereotype are put forward as proof that the Internet is dangerous. Statistics about sexual solicitation are misinterpreted to convey the idea that these men are lurking everywhere online. The image is perpetrated by TV shows where fake profiles of children are used to "catch a predator." The danger of this manufactured image is that it is misleading and obscures the very real risks youth face with regard to sexual solicitation.

Consider the findings of the Crimes Against Children Research Center, who found that one in seven minors in a national U.S. sample are sexually solicited online (Wolak et al. 2006). Peers and young adults—not older adults—account for 90% of solicitations in which approximate age is known (Wolak et al. 2006). Many acts of online solicitation are harassing or teasing communications that are not designed to seduce youth into offline sexual encounters; 69% of solicitations involve no attempt at offline contact and youth typically ignore or deflect the experience without distress (Wolak et al. 2006). A study of U.S. criminal cases in which adult sex offenders were arrested after meeting young victims online found that victims were adolescents—not children; few (5%) were deceived by offenders claiming to be teens or lying about their sexual intentions; and 73% of youth who met an offender in person did so more than once (Wolak et al. 2008b). Interviews with police indicate that most victims are underage adolescents who knowingly meet adults for sexual encounters. These offenses tended to fit a model of statutory rape involving a post-pubescent minor having non-forcible sexual relations with an adult, most frequently adults in their twenties (Wolak et al. 2008a).

Let us not dismiss these crimes, for they are crimes. Statutory rape is illegal in many countries because our society believes that minors cannot truly consent to sexual relations with adults. But this problem is not unique to the Internet. Most youth are not at-risk online, and those who are tend to also have problems offline (Mitchell et al. 2007). In other words, the Internet provides a new forum for a type of problematic interaction that predates the technology. But the Internet is also a tremendous tool to see at-risk youth engaging in risky behaviors. Instead of deploring the Internet as the cause of age-old problems, we should use it to understand why youth do these things, and how we can reach out to prevent them from happening.

Harassment

Bullying, gossip-mongering, and harassment have been a cruel presence in the lives of children for a very long time. While the numbers vary wildly, as do the definitions for bullying or harassment, there is little doubt that the Internet has provided new ways for youths to torment each other. Ignoring highly celebrated and exceptional examples, the vast majority of online harassment targeted at children and teens stems from other youth.

While the Internet is certainly used for harassment, the term "cyberbullying" implies that what takes place online radically departs from offline behavior. Anonymity is often cited as a core difference. Yet, while online perpetrators may appear to be anonymous, this does not mean that victims do not know the perpetrators or cannot figure out who is harassing them. Hinduja and Patchin (2009) found that 82% of victims in their U.S. sample knew their perpetrator (and that 41% of all perpetrators were friends or former friends). Others claim that online harassment is more harmful. There is little doubt that online harassment can be more persistent and is thus visible to more people, including peers and adults. One could reasonably argue that the potential reputational damage of visible harassment is greater than physical and emotional blows shelled out in the locker room. But visibility is a double-edged sword. Increasing the transparency of harassment means that more people can observe the harm and intervene. More importantly, it is easier for adults—parents, teachers, counselors—to see what takes place online than what goes on in private. This is an amazing opportunity to address a long-standing problem, but adults must stop blaming the technology and focus on the youth hurting and being hurt.

Exposure to Inappropriate Content

As a society, we believe that some content that is acceptable for adults is inappropriate for minors. The increased flow of information facilitated by the Internet means that content of all types is easier to access now than ever, including inappropriate content. We worry that youth might gain access to forbidden content or be inadvertently exposed to it during otherwise innocuous activities.

Pornographic content is usually front and center in this discussion. Encounters with pornography are not universal and rates of exposure are heavily debated. Wolak et al. (2006) found that 42% of youth in a U.S. sample reported unwanted or wanted exposure or both; of these, 66% reported only unwanted exposure, and only 9% of those indicated being "very or extremely upset." Furthermore, rates of unwanted exposure were higher among youth who were older, suffered from depression, and reported being harassed or solicited online or victimized offline (Wolak et al. 2007). This suggests that unwanted exposure might be linked to specific activities, particularly at-risk online behavior.

While use of the Internet is assumed to increase the likelihood of unwanted exposure to pornography, this may not be true among all demographics. Younger children report encountering pornographic content offline more frequently than online (Ybarra and Mitchell 2005) and a study of seventh and eighth graders in the U.S. found that of those who are exposed to nudity (intentionally or not), more are exposed through TV (63%) and movies (46%) than on the Internet (35%) (Pardun et al. 2005). This raises questions about whether the boundaries that we assume offline actually exist.

Youth-Generated Problematic Content

One of the Internet's core benefits it is that it enables consumers of culture to become producers and distributors. But not all user-generated content is considered healthy, particularly when youth produce content that society deems immoral, illegal, or detrimental. Eating disorders and self-harm have a long history, but the Internet provides a way for youth to document their "lifestyles" and find like-minded others. Teens once used Polaroids to capture their burgeoning sexuality; today, youth leverage mobile phones to capture and disseminate naked photographs, both for fun and harm. Gangs, violence, and hate are not new, but they are now documented and disseminated through fight videos and shock content. The content that results from these activities is undoubtedly disturbing, as is the ease with which it can be disseminated but shouldn't we be more concerned with the underlying issues than the content itself?

Most troubling is the determination by some lawyers to prosecute minors who produce and disseminate naked photos of themselves and their peers as child pornographers. The legal apparatus around child pornography is meant to uncover, prosecute, and severely punish those who produce and consume content that records—or appears to record—the sexual assault of a child by an adult. When minors are prosecuted, child pornography laws are devalued and minors are victimized in entirely new ways.

Youth-generated problematic content is indeed disturbing. And technology does make it easier to distribute. But the underlying problems are the same. Once again, just because technology makes an issue more noticeable does not mean that we should focus on eliminating its visibility. Instead, we should use visibility to get to the root of the problem.

The Conundrum of Visibility

Many of our fears and concerns regarding online safety stem from the ways in which the Internet uncovers many things that were previously hidden. Simply put, we see more risky behaviors not because risky acts have increased, but because the technology makes them more conspicuous. Most of the risks youth take and face online parallel those they take and face offline. But many of us do not see at-risk youth seeking the attention of older men offline. Many of us are unaware of all of the hateful gossip and bullying that takes place in our schools. Many of us are oblivious to the availability of inappropriate content to those seeking it. And, finally, many of us do not realize how many youth are struggling with mental health issues, making risky decisions, or living in worlds of hate and violence. It's easier not to notice.

The Internet demands that we notice. It illuminates that which we least want to see. It shows many of our youth struggling and hurting and crying out for help. Of course, the Internet does not do this by itself. It does it because we're looking. But we're not seeing. We're giving agency to the Internet so that we can blame it for what it reveals, rather than forcing ourselves to contend with what we see. At the end of the day, the Internet is not the issue. The issue is us. We cannot provide perfect protection for our children. We don't have the social or organizational infrastructure to help all youth who are in need. We don't know how to stop bullying. We don't have a magic bullet to end mental illness or insecurity or anger. And we, the adults of the world, are scared. We want something to blame. So we blame what we don't understand, that which is forcing us to see. We blame the Internet because we are unwilling to blame ourselves for not knowing how to solve the problems of this world.

Perhaps it's time that we look beyond the Internet and begin addressing the fundamental problems of our society. Thanks to the Internet, they are staring us right in the face. It's high time we do something about it.

Bibliography

Hinduja, Sameer and Justin Patchin. 2009. *Bullying Beyond the Schoolyard: Preventing and Responding to Cyberbullying.* Thousand Oaks, CA: Sage.

Mitchell, Kimberly J., Janis Wolak, and David Finkelhor. 2007. "Trends in Youth Reports of Sexual Solicitations, Harassment, and Unwanted Exposure to Pornography on the Internet." *Journal of Adolescent Health* 40(2): 116–126.

Pardun, Carol J., Kelly Ladin L'Engle, and Jane D. Brown. 2005. "Linking Exposure to Outcomes: Early Adolescents' Consumption of Sexual Content in Six Media." *Mass Communication & Society* 8(2): 75–91.

Schrock, Andrew and Danah Boyd. 2008. "Online Threats to Youth: Solicitation, Harassment, and Problematic Content." Report of the Internet Safety Technical Task Force, 62–142. (http://cyber.law.harvard.edu/pubrelease/isttf/).

Wolak, Janis, David Finkelhor, and Kimberly Mitchell. 2008a. "Is Talking Online to Unknown People Always Risky? Distinguishing Online Interaction Styles in a National Sample of Youth Internet Users." *CyberPsychology & Behavior* 11(3): 340–343.

Wolak, Janis, David Finkelhor, Kimberly Mitchell, and Michele Ybarra. 2008b. "Online 'Predators' and Their Victims: Myths, Realities, and Implications for Prevention and Treatment." *American Psychologist* 63(2): 111–128.

Wolak, Janis, Kimberly J. Mitchell, and David Finkelhor. 2007. "Unwanted and Wanted Exposure to Online Pornography in a National Sample of Youth Internet Users." *Pediatrics* 119(2): 247–257.

Wolak, Janis, Kimberly Mitchell, and David Finkelhor. 2006. "Online Victimization of Youth: Five Years Later." National Center for Missing and Exploited Children, #07-06-025. (www.unh.edu/ccrc/pdf/CV138.pdf).

Ybarra, Michele and Kimberly J. Mitchell. 2005. "Exposure to Internet Pornography among Children and Adolescents: A National Survey." *CyberPsychology & Behavior* 8(5): 473–486.

Critical Thinking

1. The authors argue that the image of the adult predator is greatly overstated and, that, in fact, most of the solicitation of minors online is done by other minors and young adults. Further, most victims seem to be adolescents, not young children. Are you comforted?

2. Do you think minors should be prosecuted as child pornographers for disseminating "naked photos of themselves and their peers"? Use the Internet to see if you can find out how common such prosecutions are.

3. The authors argue, toward the end of the article, "the Internet is not the issue. The issue is us." Have you been persuaded?

4. Are the authors arguing that the Internet is only a tool and it is how we use it that counts?

5. Continuing the previous questions, are the authors arguing that the Internet is transformative in that it brings to light the more problematic side of our culture that reproduces itself online?

DANAH BOYD and **ALICE MARWICK** (2009). "The Conundrum of Visibility." *Journal of Children & Media, 3*(4): 410–414.

UNIT 7

International Perspectives and Issues

Unit Selections

Learning Outcomes

After reading this Unit, you will be able to:

- Have a deeper understand of the role of Twitter in Iran's recent elections.

- Have contended with an especially counterintuitive argument: the contributions of the Internet to political change are not as obvious as is usually portrayed.

- Have read about some unlikely governmental censors.

- Have learned that even Google can misstep when dealing with China.

- Have learned that other countries take privacy more seriously than does our own.

- Have seen an example of true Internet addiction in one of the world's most wired nations.

Student Website

www.mhhe.com/cls

Internet Reference

Oxford Internet Institute
   www.oii.ox.ac.uk

For the past decade or so, we have been hearing a great deal about a global economy, the exchange of goods, services, and labor across national boundaries. Yet human beings have been trading across long distances for centuries. Roman artifacts in India and sea shells in the Mississippi Valley are two of many, many examples. The beginnings of capitalism in the fifteenth century accelerated an existing process. When most commentators speak of globalization, though, they refer increasingly to the interdependent trade we have witnessed since the collapse of the former Soviet Union, and the global availability of the Internet and satellite communications. Without the new information technologies, the global marketplace would not be possible. We can withdraw money from our bank accounts using ATMs in Central Turkey, make cell phones calls from nearly anywhere on the planet, and check our e-mail from a terminal located in an Internet café in Florence or Katmandu. They also make it possible for businesses to transfer funds around the world and, if you happen to be a software developer, to employ talented—and inexpensive—software engineers in growing tech centers like Bangalore, India.

Not all governments that censor the new media are what we generally think of as repressive regimes. In August 2011, transit officials in San Francisco shut down underground cell phone service to thwart protestors angry over police behavior. As the "The List" points out, Australia, France, India, Argentina, and South Korea have all set up Internet firewalls, to combat child pornography, to eliminate file sharing, to tamp down political radicalism. Each government, including transit officials in San Francisco itself, can cite perfectly good reasons for its actions. One important lesson is that all media, no matter how apparently decentralized, rely upon an infrastructure that is vulnerable to central disruption.

Sometimes the clash between censorious governments and the free-wheeling Internet are played out on the front pages, especially if the clash is between two titans like China and Google. Google, whose well-known motto is "don't be evil," earned the scorn of free speech advocates in 2006 when it permitted the Chinese government to censor search results from Google.cn. In 2010 Google reversed itself, announcing that it would leave China in the wake of cyber attacks on its source code and the Gmail accounts of its users. You can read about the diplomatic dance between Google and China, almost as if Google were just another sovereign power, in "Google and Saving Face in China."

It was only a matter of time before Facebook was drawn into the fray. In "Does Facebook Have a Foreign Policy?," Tim Wu argues that Facebook will soon face "a new intensity of international and domestic scrutiny." In the United States there is growing concern over the company's privacy policies. But since European privacy standards are considerably more stringent than our own, the first legal challenges to Facebook will probably come from that quarter.

Like so much in computing, online games were first developed in the United States. And like so much that the United States has pioneered—think cars—the highest expression is elsewhere, South Korea, as it happens, in the world of online games. Internet

© Comstock Images/Jupiterimages

addiction has been a staple of reports from South Korea for a number of years, now. But these reports reached a new low in the story of a couple of South Koreans whose infant died of malnutrition while they were "exploring mythical lands and slaying monsters." A memorable character in Lawrence Sterne's eighteenth century novel, *A Sentimental Journey,* tells us that "there is nothing unmixed in this world." That goes double for transformative (and disruptive) technologies like computing.

The global interconnectedness that Marshall McLuhan observed forty years ago has only increased in complexity with developments in computer technology.[1] Now instead of merely receiving one-way satellite feeds, as in McLuhan's day, we can talk back through e-mail, websites, blogs, and Facebook pages. It is not surprising that all of this communication is having unanticipated effects across the planet. Who, for instance, during the Tiananmen Square uprising of 1989, could have predicted that a newly market-centered China would become the world's second largest economy? Or who would have predicted international enthusiasm for a technology that resembles an American high school yearbook circa 1965? Or its acceptance among those for whom high school is a distant memory? No one, in fact, which is why the study of computing is so fascinating (and why so few visionaries continue to get so rich).

Note

1. Marshal McLuhan, *Understanding Media,* MIT Press, 1994.

The List: Look Who's Censoring the Internet Now

Countries like Iran and China are notorious for their Internet censorship regimes. But a growing number of democracies are setting up their own great fire walls.

JOSHUA KEATING

Australia
What's targeted?
Officially, child pornography and terrorism, but recent reports suggest the scope might be expanded.

What's behind the wall?
In January 2008, the Australian Parliament began considering a law to require all Internet service providers (ISPs) to filter the content they provide to users in order to block a blacklist of objectionable sites prepared by the Australian Communications and Media Authority. Although the law is still in the planning stages, ISPs are required to have their filtering systems ready for testing by June 2009.

The government claimed that the blacklist would combat child pornography and terrorism-related sites, but in March 2009, the list of 2,935 sites was leaked by anticensorship website Wikileaks and revealed a much broader scope of content, including online poker, Satanism, and euthanasia. Some seemingly uncontroversial private businesses, such as a Queensland dentist's office, were also included for unknown reasons. The release of the list has dampened public support for the law, and one of Australia's largest ISPs recently announced it would not participate in the filtering tests.

France
What's targeted?
File-sharing.

What's behind the wall?
The French Parliament is debating and seems likely to pass the world's toughest antipiracy law to date. Other countries have begun cracking down on file-sharers with fines, but the French law would require ISPs to deny Internet access to those who have been repeatedly caught illegally downloading material. A new administrative body would be created and granted judicial power to enforce the law. The controversial measure is strongly supported by music and film industry leaders, as well as President Nicolas Sarkozy (whose wife Carla Bruni recently released an album incidentally), and opposed by privacy groups and cable companies.

One of the law's most controversial aspects is that it would penalize anyone whose Internet connection was used for downloading illegal material, even if the person wasn't aware of it or the network was used without permission. All people in France, in effect, would be legally required to secure their wireless networks.

India
What's targeted?
Political radicalism, terrorist tools.

What's behind the wall?
India's Internet filtering is still sporadic, but the seemingly arbitrary nature of its enforcement has censorship watchdogs nervous. In 2003, the Indian Computer Emergency Response Team (CERT-In) was created to enforce the country's filtering regime. CERT-In is the sole authority empowered to block websites, and there is no review or appeals process once it blacklists a site. Many blocked sites have been found to contain obscene material, but CERT-In has also shut down Hindu nationalists and other radical groups on social networking sites such as Orkut. In 2003, thousands of Indian Internet users were blocked from accessing Yahoo! Groups because CERT-In objected to a message board for a minor North Indian separatist group consisting of 25 people.

When it was revealed that the terrorists responsible for the November 2008 Mumbai attacks used Google Earth to plan their assault, a prosecutor petitioned the Bombay High Court to block the popular site. The motion was ultimately thrown out, but security concerns are also dogging a rival satellite-mapping site being developed by the Indian government itself. The government agency building the program suggests that some sensitive sites might be blurred out in the final version.

Argentina
What's targeted?
Celebrity dirt.

What's behind the wall?
Argentine soccer legend Diego Maradona is best known for his controversial 1986 "hand of God" goal, but he also has a hand in one of the world's most brazen acts of Web censorship. Maradona and about 70 other celebrities filed a class action suit in mid-2007 against Google and Yahoo!, claiming that their names were being associated with pornography or libelous sites against their will. A judge ruled in favor of the plaintiffs, essentially holding the search engines responsible for the content of other sites, a standard that a Google Argentina spokesperson told *Time* was like "suing the newsstand for what appears in the newspapers it sells."

The search engines are appealing the ruling, but for now, if you search for Maradona or any of his co-plaintiffs on the Argentine version of Google or Yahoo!, you'll get a message saying the search engine is "obliged to temporarily suspend all or some of the results related to this search," followed by an abridged list of links to major news sites. It's one thing for Maradona to try to cover up gossip about his past partying, but the plaintiffs also included several judges whose decisions have provoked online discussion, a fact many see as a major conflict of interest for the justices deciding the case. Unfortunately for Maradona, though, getting the dirt on him is as easy as loading up another country's version of the search engines.

South Korea
What's targeted?
North Korean propaganda.

What's behind the wall?
South Korea is one of the world's most wired countries, with about 90 percent of households hooked up to the Web, but the Korean Internet is also one of the world's most heavily policed. ISPs are reportedly required to block as many as 120,000 sites from an official government blacklist. Some sites on the list are for pornography and gambling—South Korea requires ISPs to self-police content that could be deemed harmful to youth—but much of it is content sympathetic to North Korea or advocating Korean reunification.

The medium may be new, but the justification is decades old. Thanks to the 1948 anticommunist National Security Law, South Koreans can be imprisoned for up to seven years for vaguely defined "antistate" activities. In recent years such activities have extended to the Internet, with communist activists being arrested for downloading material on Marxism. The National Security Law is controversial, and the South Korean government recently stated that it will relax restrictions on access to pro-North Korea sites, many of which are hosted in Japan. However, recent testing by the OpenNet Initiative has revealed that filtering is still pervasive.

Critical Thinking

1. Are you surprised to learn that France and Australia block websites? What do you know about governmental censorship in the United States?

2. Suppose you were named czar of the Internet and could censor anything. What would you censor? Why? If you wouldn't censor anything at all, why?

JOSHUA KEATING is deputy Web editor at FP.

Google and Saving Face in China

Adam Segal

After several weeks of negotiations with the Chinese government, Google announced on March 22 that it was redirecting users of google.cn—its China-based search engine—to google.com.hk where results are not filtered or censored. Google will keep some R&D and advertising on the mainland.

For Google, it is a clever maneuver in very difficult circumstances. The company does not back down from its January 12 announcement that it could no longer censor results on google.cn after discovering that its source code had been hacked and the Gmail accounts of human rights activists targeted. Yet by moving to Hong Kong, the search giant can claim that it is not abandoning Chinese users—an important issue not only to those who argue that Google's presence in China was a force for good that increased the flow of information, but also, perhaps more importantly, to advertisers who want to reach Chinese consumers.

Now the other shoe has dropped. The day before the announcement, Beijing mounted an aggressive public relations campaign against the company, calling its actions "totally wrong" and claiming that it had "violated its written promise (ChannelNewsAsia)". The New York Times reports that Beijing is already filtering and sometimes blocking access to search results on Google in Hong Kong. China Mobile and China Unicom have either announced or are expected to announce the cancellation of business deals for mobile search and Google's Android phone.

These early moves are likely to feed into the feeling in the foreign business community that China has become an increasingly hostile market. A recent survey by the American Chamber of Commerce in China shows companies that feel unwelcome jumping to 38 percent, up from 26 percent in 2009 and 23 percent in 2008 (WSJ). These feelings are also likely to spill over into U.S.-China relations since many in China believe that Google has closely coordinated with, if not been directed by, the State Department in its calls for Internet freedom. Public criticism by Chinese officials is not going to be well received in the United States as both sides grow increasingly snappish about the bilateral economic relationship and the valuation of China's currency, the yuan, in particular.

These initial countermoves by Beijing may be enough for it to declare victory. To its more nationalistic netizens, the government can claim it did not back down in the face of foreign pressure (and still continue to filter sensitive material). Some access to Google will remain and so the government can show that it is sensitive to scientists and others worried (Nature) about the impact Google's departure will have on the country's innovative capability.

If this is indeed where Beijing stops, it will be a welcome sign that the Chinese leadership both cares about the increasingly negative view of China in U.S. domestic politics and can do something about it by moderating its own foreign policy pronouncements. China's increasingly assertive (Economist) international stance over the last six months suggests, however, that foreign businesses and U.S. policymakers can expect things to get worse before they get better.

Critical Thinking

1. This article was published March 23, 2010. In the fast-changing world of computing and international relations much could have changed since then. What is the current status of the relationship between China and Google?

2. Should Google have made the original deal with China allowing it to censor search results?

3. Use the Internet to see if you can find an example of exactly what (not what kind, but what specifically) Google search results China has censored.

ADAM SEGAL, is an Ira A. Lipman Senior Fellow for Counterterrorism and National Security Studies.

Does Facebook Have a Foreign Policy?

Right now, it all looks rosy for Mark Zuckerburg. But Facebook's global rise has limits—and real dangers—as it taps markets in unfriendly countries.

TIM WU

If it hadn't already been Facebook's moment, it certainly is now. It has become obvious, even to skeptics, that the firm is not just an interesting fad (remember GeoCities?), but an integral part of the world's social architecture.

In the near future, we can expect a new intensity of international and domestic scrutiny of what has become one of the most powerful tools on the planet for planning events and mapping connections between people. How Facebook reacts to such scrutiny will give us a sense of the soul of this company, more so than any recent movie ever could.

In the United States, most of the attention has been on Facebook's privacy policies, which once again have come under criticism for lapses due to third-party applications sharing personal data. At root, what makes Facebook interesting is a mutual agreement to tell others who you are, what you like, and what you are doing. In the United States, the pressure on Facebook, relatively mild so far, comes mostly from journalists and advocacy groups like the Electronic Privacy Information Center.

But the time is coming when Facebook will begin to face ever more intense international pressure from foreign governments unpleased, for one reason or another, with how the site operates.

It is a truism that any Internet firm, or in fact any information firm, once established, begins to gain the attention of governments, which are naturally suspicious of anything that rivals their power over information. In the late 1990s and early 2000s, sites like Yahoo and eBay were the first Internet darlings to face serious international pressure. In 2000, a French Jewish group sued Yahoo for allowing Nazi paraphernalia to be sold on its auction site. (Yahoo initially insisted the Internet could not be regulated, but ended up paying up.) In 2004, an eBay executive was briefly imprisoned in India because pornographic DVDs were available for purchase through the site. This year, three Google executives were convicted and found guilty of criminal defamation in their absence, by an Italian court that held the men responsible for an unseemly YouTube video that showed students bullying a disabled child. Google, which owns YouTube, took the video down, but not quickly enough for the Italian judge.

The Italian decision is an outlier, and frankly outrageous, but it should give a sense that European nations tend to take breaches of privacy and matters of defamation more seriously than the United States. The European Union Data Privacy Directive, signed in 1995, obliged every member of the European Union to enact laws that govern data controllers—that is, anyone who collects personal data (that obviously includes a lot of Internet companies.) The directive then imposes duties of "notice, fidelity, and proportionality," along with additional rules for "special information," i.e., sensitive topics, like health, ethnicity, or religious orientation. On paper, European privacy rules are the strictest in the industrialized world; the European Union likes to refer to privacy as a fundamental right. Consequently, much as California effectively sets U.S. emissions standards, European regulators often set the world's privacy standards.

For Facebook, this strongly suggests that a European privacy challenge could have a powerful impact on how the firm operates. As it stands, Facebook remains a relatively new phenomenon in Europe, but its usage is growing: There are now about 123 million European users, according to statistics collected in February. This year, European privacy regulators, led by the Germans and Swiss, have begun investigations of Facebook's photo tagging and the use of privacy data by applications. Depending on the outcome, Facebook might need to change how the site works in Europe. Assuming the firm capitulates, the question will be whether Facebook changes its global product—or creates European pages with different privacy settings than its American counterparts. Either way, European privacy regulators have the power to insist on pretty fundamental changes in what we think of as Facebook.

This year, Facebook faced some of its first challenges from outside the Western World when someone posted a page advertising an "Everybody Draw Mohammed Day," available to users in Pakistan and Bangladesh, among other places. Both countries blocked Facebook by court order on the grounds of blasphemy, until it apologized and agreed to delete the page, which it did, promising to never let such a thing happen again, according to Pakistani officials. As this case suggests, the real tests, or at least the real ethical tests, will come when Facebook begins to face the demands of the world's authoritarian regimes. As it stands, Facebook is banned in China, Iran, Syria, Vietnam, and other countries (though savvy users can access Facebook using proxy servers).

On this, Yahoo provides an object lesson. Once considered a champion of an open Internet, Yahoo in 2002 signed something called the "Public Pledge on Self-Discipline for the Chinese Internet Industry." It was an agreement to monitor and report on its users for the Chinese party-state, whether on email, in chatrooms, or elsewhere. Things came to a head when Yahoo turned over emails from a Chinese journalist named Shi Tao, containing a memo related to the Tiananmen Square protests. He was imprisoned for 10 years. Yahoo eventually retreated from the Chinese market; its business ventures there were mostly a failure.

Facebook's other predecessor in China is, of course, Google. The company decided to enter the Chinese market in 2007, with trepidation. Google was certainly more careful than Yahoo. It declined, for example, to operate email services in China, for fear of another Shi Tao incident. But Google did agree to censor its Chinese search engine, google.cn. And like Yahoo, it went

on to lose so much market share (to a Chinese firm, Baidu) that it, too, made a well publicized retreat from the Chinese market, complaining about censorship and cyber-attacks.

So what will Facebook do when faced with such predicaments in trying to enter, or stay in, tricky overseas markets? How Facebook reacts to the scrutiny that's coming will be a new test of its philosophy as a company. It's not just an important question for Facebook, but for all of us. It's one thing giving Facebook access to your private information. It's something else entirely if governments then obtain access, too.

Critical Thinking

1. Use the Internet to learn more about the European Union Data Privacy Directive.

2. How does the Data Privacy Directive differ from privacy statues in the United States?

3. Use the Internet to read about the conviction of three Google executives in an Italian court. The writer calls the decision "frankly outrageous." What reasons were given for the conviction? Do you agree or disagree? Why?

A Fantasy World Is Creating Problems in South Korea

CHOE SANG-HUN

Suwon, South Korea—Neither had a job. They were shy and had never dated anyone until they met each other on an online chat site in 2008. They knew so little about childbearing that the 25-year-old wife did not know when her baby was due until her water broke.

But in the fantasy world of Internet gaming, they were masters of all they encountered, swashbuckling adventurers exploring mythical lands and slaying monsters. Every evening Kim Jae-beom, 41, and his wife, Kim Yun-jeong, left their one-room apartment for an all-night Internet cafe where they role-played, often until dawn. Each one raised a virtual daughter, who followed them everywhere, and was fed, dressed and cuddled—all with a few mouse clicks.

On the morning of Sept. 24, they returned home after a 12-hour game session to find their actual daughter, a 3-month-old named Sa-rang, or "Love," dead—shriveled with malnutrition.

In South Korea, one of the world's most wired societies, addiction to online games has long been treated as a teenage affliction, alarming to parents and teachers. But the Kims' case has drawn attention to the growing problem here of Internet game addiction among adults.

Sa-rang, born prematurely and sickly, was fed milk two or three times a day—before and after her parents' overnight gaming and sometimes when the father woke up from the couple's daytime slumber, prosecutors said. The baby died "eyes open and her ribs showing," said their lawyer, Kim Dong-young.

"I am sorry for being such a bad mother to my baby," Ms. Kim said, sobbing, during the couple's trial earlier this month. After six months on the run, they were arrested in March and charged with negligent homicide. Prosecutors are asking for a five-year prison sentence. A verdict in the case is expected on Friday.

In recent years, thanks partly to government counseling programs, the estimated number of teenagers with symptoms of Internet addiction has steadily declined, to 938,000 in 2009, the Ministry of Public Administration and Safety said in April.

But the number of addicts in their 20s and 30s has been increasing, to 975,000 last year. Many of these adult addicts are former teenagers who grew up with online games and now resort to them when they are unemployed or otherwise feel alienated from society, said Dr. Ha Jee-hyun, a psychiatrist at Konkuk University Hospital.

This development and a recent string of cases like that of the Kims have prompted the government to announce plans to open rehabilitation centers for adult addicts and expand counseling for students and the unemployed, groups considered the most vulnerable to compulsive gaming.

"Unlike teenagers, these grown-ups don't have parents who can drag them to counselors," said Dr. Ha. He treats an average of four adults a month for game addiction, he said. Two years ago, it was one a month.

At about 700 won, or 55 cents, an hour, online games provide "the cheapest diversion available for the jobless and a liberating exit for children suffocated by the country's over-competitive educational system," said Kim Boo-ja, herself an avid online gamer and a professor at Sogang University's Game Education Center, which trains software developers for online games.

South Korea's virtual-reality game industry took off during the Asian financial crisis in the late 1990s and expanded in the recent recession, both times of higher unemployment.

More than 90 percent of South Korean homes are fitted with high-speed Internet. Nearly every street corner has a PC Bang, or "PC Room." In these dim, 24-hour-a-day gaming parlors, "the line blurs between reality and the virtual world," said Jung Young-chul, a psychiatrist at Yonsei University.

Critical Thinking

1. Use the Internet to find out about professional gaming in South Korea.

2. The article says that South Korea is "one of the world's most wired societies." Investigate the average download speeds available to South Koreans and their costs. Compare this to what's available in the United States.

3. Use the Internet to investigate the response of the South Korean government to the case of infant neglect by gaming described in the article.

4. What is meant, say to a mental health professional, by Internet addiction? Use the Internet to investigate the scope of the problem in the United States.

UNIT 8

The Frontier of Computing

Unit Selections

Learning Outcomes

After reading this Unit, you will be able to:

- Have learned what the developers of relational companions have in store for us and what it means.

- Have a deeper understanding of cloud computing.

- Know why Google is now in the business of constructing an operating system.

- Understand how one man, deeply connected to the publishing industry, thinks the transition to digital books "is now underway and irreversible."

- Have engaged in a discussion about machines that exhibit human-like behaviors.

- Have learned more about Watson, the IBM heavyweight that recently defeated two *Jeopardy!* champions.

- Have considered the possibility of immortality from a geek's perspective.

Student Website

www.mhhe.com/cls

Internet References

Introduction to Artificial Intelligence (AI)
www.formal.stanford.edu/jmc/aiintro/aiintro.html
Kasparov vs. Deep Blue: The Rematch
www.research.ibm.com/deepblue/home/html/b.html
PHP-Nuke Powered Site: International Society for Artificial Life
www.alife.org

According to the U.S. Census Bureau statistics not long ago, the output of the meat and poultry industry was worth more than the output of the computer and software industries. Though this is not exactly a fair comparison—computers are used to build still other products—it does get at something significant about computers: they figure more importantly in our imaginations than they do in the economy. Why is this? Part of the answer has to do with who forms opinions in developed nations. The computer is an indispensable tool for people who staff the magazine, newspaper, publishing, and education sectors. If meat packers were the opinion makers, we might get a different sense of what is important. Recall "Five Things We Need to Know about Technological Change." Postman says that "Embedded in every technology there is a powerful idea. . . . To a person with a computer, everything looks like data."

We can concede Postman's point but still insist that there is something special about computing. Before computers became a household appliance, it was common for programmers and users alike to attribute human-like properties to them. Joseph Weizenbaum, developer of Eliza in the 1970s, a program that simulated a Rogerian psychotherapist, became a severe critic of certain kinds of computing research, in part because he noticed that staff in his lab had begun to arrive early to ask its advice. In 1956, a group of mathematicians interested in computing gathered at Dartmouth College and coined the term "Artificial Intelligence." AI, whose goal is to build into machines something that we can recognize as intelligent behavior, has become perhaps the best-known and most criticized area of computer science. Since intelligent behavior, like the ability to read and form arguments, is often thought to be the defining characteristic of humankind (we call ourselves "homo sapiens," after all), machines that might exhibit intelligent behavior have occupied the dreams and nightmares of western culture for hundreds of years.

All of our ambiguous feelings about technology are congealed in robots. The term itself is surprisingly venerable, having been invented by the Czech playwright Karel Copek in 1921. Robots can be loveable like R2D2 from *Star Wars* or Robbie from *The Forbidden Planet* of a generation earlier. They can be forbidding but loyal, like Gort from *The Day the Earth Stood Still.* They can even be outfitted with logical safety mechanisms that render them harmless to humans. This last, an invention of Isaac Asimov in *I, Robot,* is a good thing, too, since so many of our robotic imaginings look like *The Terminator.* As of this writing (August 2011), a particular kind of fearsome robot, semi-autonomous warriors, is much in the news (see Unit 5). Sherry Turkle of MIT has been studying the relationship between humans and their computing machines for twenty years. In her article for this unit, subtitled, "On the Threshold of Robotic Companions," she asks, as always, the really big questions. Attitudes toward computing have changed since she began her research in the 1980s. Telling the story of one her graduate students who would happily trade her boyfriend for a robot as long as it exhibited "caring behavior," she observes among her subjects a "certain fatigue with the difficulties of dealing with people." Do you suspect overstatement here? Then consider one of Professor Turkle's subjects, a seventy-four-year-old Japanese participant who said of her furry robot, "When

© ERproductions Ltd/Blend Images LLC

I looked into his large, brown eyes, I feel in love after years of being quite lonely. . . . I swore to protect and care for the little animal."

We have more than robots to excite our imaginations. Consider Google. Fifteen years ago, the study of database systems was an important but unheralded part of computer science. For all its importance, how an insurance company organizes its data could seem a little dull. But that was before Google began to tame the chaos of the Internet through sophisticated storage and retrieval techniques and, above all, through clusters of computers it calls "the cloud." Brian Hayes, an excellent reporter on developments in computing, provides an accessible introduction to cloud computing. Turns out that the Google cloud is, in a sense, a return to the centralized computing of forty years ago. This will have major implications for companies like Microsoft who package software to be run on local computers.

The cloud is not all that Microsoft has to fear from Google. Think about what happens when you turn your computer on. A massive collection of programs called the operating system—Windows, Apple, or Linux variants on most machines—is transferred from the hard disk to volatile memory and a multitude of setup routines are performed, like activating interfaces to hardware, restarting your virus protection software, and configuring your windowing layout, one small piece of which is an icon that gives you access to your browser. This takes about forty-five seconds, much more on some machines, depending on their age and network connections. Turns out that most people spend most of the time on applications that are funneled through the browser, activities like Google searches, Facebook, Web-based e-mail, and so on. Somebody had to ask the question: "Who needs 500-gigabyte hard drives and 6-megabyte L2 cache when lots of input ports and a fast wireless connection will do?" "Chrome the Conqueror" recounts how the Google Chrome OS team answered it.

One of the truly remarkable pieces in this volume is Jason Epstein's reflections on the future of publishing. Once married to Barbara Epstein, hired by Bennett Cerf, colleague of Elizabeth Hardwick and Robert Lowell, co-founder of *The New York Review of Books,* a man more tied to world of books would be hard to find. We already know the import of movable type on human consciousness (see the Preface). Epstein calls digitization "a technological shift orders of magnitude greater than the momentous evolution from monkish scriptoria to movable type launched in Gutenberg's German city of Mainz six centuries ago." "Publishing: The Revolutionary Future" is the wisdom of an insider. Listen carefully.

Yet another technology that is moving from the laboratories to the mainstream is computer speech recognition. Read "Computers Learn to Listen, and Some Talk Back," for a quick tour of what could well lay ahead. Oddly, the authors never mention surveillance in their description of the wonders of intelligent computing. The National Security Agency recently built a 470,000-square-foot data warehouse in San Antonio. The amount of data stored there is beyond the capacity of humans to process. Though, of course, the workings of the NSA are classified, it is easy to imagine the agency employing voice recognition software to scan phone calls looking for words that indicate a threat to national security.[1]

Praised by some as a leap forward in language processing and machine intelligence, Watson, a 2880 core machine from IBM, suitably programmed, roundly defeated two *Jeopardy!* champions. Some readers will recall IBM's Deep Blue that beat chess world champion Garry Kasparov in a hard-fought match back in 1997. Though critics remain skeptical about both accomplishments, much to the dismay of AI researchers, watching Watson at work in fall 2010 was impressive. Read "Weighing Watson's Impact" to see for yourself. The final piece in this unit, appropriately, is a meditation on death, or rather on non-death for a few lucky stiffs frozen in Scottsdale, Arizona. Computer scientists figure prominently among supporters of Alcor, a cryonics company that charges $150,000 to freeze a body in the hope that some future scientist/engineer/entrepreneur will develop what it takes to cure what killed it.

Robots, cloud computing, language processing, and immortality, the articles in this unit have a common theme: the technologies described are neither fully-formed nor have their impact on society been large—Goggle excepted. Computing history is filled with bad predictions. Perhaps the most spectacularly wrong prediction is widely attributed to Thomas Watson, head of IBM, who in 1943 is supposed to have said, "I think there is a world market for maybe five computers." But there have been many, many others. Will robots get no further than furbies? Is the "Wisdom of Clouds" just a reprise of centralized data processing? Will Chrome OS spell the end of the need for increasingly powerful and complex computers on one's desk? Will Alcor resurrect its clients? Who knows? But who wants to be the next Tom Watson?

Note

1. James Bamford, *The Shadow Factory: The Ultra-Secret NSA from 9/11 to the Eavesdropping on America,* Random House, 2008.

In Good Company?
On the Threshold of Robotic Companions

Most contributors to this volume believe that only technical matters stand between where we are now and a time when robots will be our Companions and teachers. In this view, robots need to expand their domains of understanding, and if those domains should be emotional, well, that will be a technical matter as well. So while this volume expresses designers' enthusiasm about robots as technical objects, it challenges us to see robots as something more, as evocative objects. What are we thinking about when we are thinking about robots? We are thinking about aliveness and authenticity, love and spirituality. We are thinking about what it means to build a psychology. We are thinking about what makes people special. Or perhaps that they are not so special after all.

SHERRY TURKLE

If one thinks of a classic "upstairs/downstairs" scenario, it is no longer clear where the robots will be lodging. For some years, robot vacuum cleaners have staked their claim as household helpers, but more recently, roboticists would expand the domain of the robotic from doing chores to offering companionship and care. But to make this step, one needs a new kind of robot, one equipped to be good company. These are sociable robots, robots programmed to have mental states that shift as they interact with people. To take those already on the scene, consider, for example, the robotic doll My Real Baby. Bounce the doll and it gets happy; bounce it too much and it might get ornery. Or Pleo, a small dinosaur robot advertised for its psychological '*autonomy*'; or Paro, a baby seal robot designed as a therapeutic Companion. Like the others, Paro has "states of mind," even if primitive ones. Interacting with Paro requires understanding its states, a demand for vigilance that, in the end, contributes to its appeal. Such digital creatures are the shock troops of a cultural moment when figuring out how a robot is "feeling" in order to get along with it, begins to seem a natural thing.

When robots make eye contact, recognize faces, mirror human gestures, they push our Darwinian buttons, exhibiting the kinds of behavior people associate with sentience, intentions, and emotions. Once people see robots as creatures, people feel a desire to nurture them. With this feeling comes the fantasy of reciprocation: as we begin to care for robots, we want them to care about us. In our nascent robotics culture, nurturance turns out to be a "killer app". Eleven-year-old Fara reacts to a play session with Cog, a humanoid robot at MIT that can meet her eyes, follow her position, and imitate her movements, by saying that she could never get tired of the robot because "it's not like a toy because you can't teach a toy; it's like something that's part of you, you know, something you love, kind of like another person, like a baby."

What seems natural to the contributors to this volume—that robots are part of our relational futures—is now a widely shared idea, and not just among experts. Indeed, it is so widely shared that it is easy to forget that, until recently, it was hardly shared at all. In the 1980s, one common response to the computer presence could be summed up as a "romantic reaction."[1] It accepted that people might well be a kind of computer (a major concession to models of mind as program) but stressed the soul and the spirit in the human machine: simulated thinking might be thinking but simulated feeling is never feeling, simulated love is never love. Computers were fine, more than fine, if they were doing instrumental jobs, or jobs that could be neatly compartmentalized in the '*thinking*' category. But computational objects—robots included—should not be allowed into the realm of human relationships.[2] So, when in 1984 I called the computer a "second self" and demonstrated people's strong personal connection to them, many objected by insisting on the truism: "the computer is just a tool."

Over the next decade, opinions shifted.[3] Computers became everyday objects and it became commonplace to see one's laptop as an extension of self. "What is on your PowerBook?" was a good advertising slogan in the mid-1990s because it acknowledged the degree to which a computer desktop reflected personal as well as intellectual commitments. People still saw computers as tools but recognized that they were tools with a difference. They had special vocations: not-yet-minds, but on the boundaries of mind, they were close to being minds whose opinions counted.[4]

These days, in studying reactions to sociable robots, robots that do such things as look you in the eye, remember your name, and track your motion, I find numbers of people who consider such objects as potential friends, confidants, and (as they imagine technical improvements) even lovers. I listen for what stands behind this new attitude and I hear three things. There is openness to seeing computational objects as "other minds"; there is willingness to consider what a computer and human mind have in common; and, in a different register, there is evidence of a certain fatigue with the difficulties of dealing with people. A female graduate student comes up to me after a lecture and tells me she would gladly trade in her boyfriend for a sophisticated humanoid robot as long as the robot could produce what she calls "caring behavior." She tells me that "I need the feeling of civility in the house and I don't want to be alone." She says: "If the robot could provide a civil environment, I would be happy to help produce the illusion that there is somebody really with me." What she is looking for, she says, is a no-risk relationship that will stave off loneliness; a responsive robot, even if it were just exhibiting scripted behavior, seems better to her than a demanding boyfriend.

The distance travelled over the past twenty years has been impressive. Bruce, a thirteen-year old I interviewed in 1983, thinks of computers and robots as "perfect" and therefore different from flawed and frail people. Robots do everything right; people do the best they know how. But for Bruce, it is human imperfection that makes for the ties that bind. Specifically, his own limitations make him feel close to his father ("I have a lot in common with my father . . . we both have chaos"). Perfect robots could not understand this very important relationship. Twenty years later, Howard, fourteen, compares his father to the idea of a robot counsellor and the human does not fare as well. Howard thinks that the robot would be better able to grasp the intricacies in the day of a high school student. He comments on what the robot would bring to the table: "Its database would be larger than Dad's. Dad has knowledge of basic things, but not enough of high school. Robots can be made to understand things like "feelings."

With the belief that robots can understand them, people are, of course, more likely to warm to their company. In the presence of sociable robots people feel attachment and loss; they want to reminisce and feel loved. In a year-long study of human-robot bonding, one seventy-four-year-old Japanese participant said of her Wandukun, a furry robot creature designed to resemble a koala bear: "When I looked into his large, brown eyes, I feel in love after years of being quite lonely . . . I swore to protect and care for the little animal."[5] In my study of robots in Massachusetts nursing homes, seventy-four-year-old Jonathan responds to his My Real Baby robot doll by wishing it were a bit smarter because he would prefer to talk to a robot about his problems than to a person. "The robot wouldn't criticize me." Andy, also seventy-four, says that the My Real Baby, which responds to caretaking by exhibiting different states of mind, bears a resemblance to his ex-wife Rose, "something in the eyes." He likes chatting with the robot about events of the day. "When I wake up in the morning and see her face [the robot] over there, it makes me feel so nice, like somebody is watching over me."

I recently had an exchange with colleagues who wrote about the 'I-Thou' dyad of people and robots and I could only see Martin Buber spinning in his grave.[6] The *I* was the person in the relationship, but how could the robot be the *Thou?* In the past, I might have focused on how my colleagues' projected feelings on a robot that definitionally could not have them. But I had taken that position when I interpreted attitudes toward robots as a kind of Rorschach for better understanding people's hopes and frustrations. Now, there was a new earnestness, a new literal-mindedness to the consideration of a robot Companion. My colleagues saw the robot in the wings and were eager to welcome it onstage.

It seemed no time at all that a book came out, *Love and Sex with Robots* and a reporter from *Scientific American* was interviewing me about the psychology of robot marriage.[7] I found the conversation memorable. I was asked if my opposition to people marrying robots didn't put me in the same camp as those who oppose the marriage of lesbians or gay men. I tried to explain that just because I didn't think people could marry machines didn't mean that that any mix of people with people was fair play. The reporter accused me of species chauvinism. Wasn't this the kind of talk that homophobes once used, not considering gays as "*real*" people? Our culture had clearly come to a new place.

To me, robots represent the new uncanny in our culture of simulation. Here I refer to the uncanny in Freud's sense—something known of old and long familiar, yet now made strangely unfamiliar.[8] They are not like the dolls of the past that offered possibilities for pure projection. The new relational robots are built with psychologies and needs of their own. As uncanny objects, objects on the boundaries of categories, robotic creatures provoke us to ask questions about traditional categories, questions such as, *What kinds of relationships are appropriate to have with machines?* And more generally, *What is a relationship?* The question is not whether children will grow up to love their robots more than other toys, or indeed, their parents, but what will loving come to mean?

The psychoanalyst Heinz Kohut describes how some people may temporarily strengthen their fragile sense of self by turning another person into a "self-object."[9] In the role of self-object, the other is experienced as part of the self, thus in perfect tune with the fragile individual's inner state. Disappointments inevitably follow. The relationships people form on social networking sites (whether in MySpace or Facebook chat or in virtual worlds) are excellent contenders for the role of self-object. There, we come to know people through a curious half-light, where people can be imagined to be what the fragile self needs them to be.[10]

Similarly, robots that look into your eyes, trace your movements, perhaps say your name, clearly present themselves as candidates for the role of self-object. If they can give the appearance of aliveness and yet not disappoint, they may even have a "comparative advantage" over people for this job, and thus open new possibilities for narcissistic experience with machines. Why do I say, "comparative advantage"? When people turn other people into self-objects, one might say they are making an effort to turn a person into a kind of "spare part" rather than taking him or her as an autonomous, individual personality. The artificial Companion or robot is, of course, already a spare part.

The seductions of the robotic provide a window onto how much people are tempted to sidestep encounters with friends and family. Over-stressed, over-worked, people claim exhaustion and overload. Loneliness is failed solitude. Are cyber-connections paving the way to considering robotic Companions as sufficient unto the day? These days, people readily admit that they would rather leave a voice mail or send an email than talk face-to-face. And from there, they say: "I'd rather talk to the robot. Friends can be exhausting. The robot will always be there for me. And whenever I'm done, I can walk away." Or as one woman said about AIBO, Sony's household entertainment robot, "It is better than a real dog . . . It won't do dangerous things, and it won't betray you . . . Also, it won't die suddenly and make you feel very sad." The romantic reaction to the computer presence stressed that simulation had no place in matters of love. These days, people are likely to speculate on the possibility that humans, like robots, get by on simulation. One thirty-year-old puts it this way: "How do I know that my lover is not just simulating everything he says he feels?" A fifty-nine-year-old man said: "My first wife faked her orgasms for twenty-five years . . . so what would make a robot inauthentic? She set the bar pretty low." Or recall the graduate student who was willing to "help produce the illusion that there is somebody really with me" if a robot would just provide some background.

In the 1980s, people insisted that the bedrock of human uniqueness was what computers could not do or be, placing special value on the importance of the human life cycle in defining what was essential about being a person. One man, considering the possibility of confiding in a computer psychotherapist put it this way: "How can I talk about sibling rivalry to something that never had a mother?" It put a premium on the idea that only people can give each other understanding and empathy. It was invested in the idea that there is something essential about the human spirit, and that this essential quality resides in human inner states. Now this essentialist assumption is challenged. Today one does not linger over inner states. The new focus is on behavior. What matters is how the robots perform and how we perform for each other—the essence, after all, of life in virtual communities where we create an avatar and put it on a self-built stage. With the focus on behavior rather than inner states, a creature that behaves appropriately is an appropriate creature.

In the 1980s, debates in Artificial Intelligence centred on the question of whether machines could "really" be intelligent. These debates were about the objects themselves, what they could and could not do. Our new debates about relational and sociable machines—debates that will have an increasingly high profile in mainstream culture—are not only about the machines' capabilities but about our vulnerabilities, both to machines that push our Darwinian buttons and to the promise of relationship, any relationship, in a world where humans so often seem to disappoint. For many who are lonely yet fearful of intimacy, a robotic Companion offers the illusion of Companionship without the demands of sustained, intimate friendship. One can be a loner yet never alone. It is a small step from this position to

the question, one implicit in so many of the contributions in this volume: *What are the purposes of living things?*

From the perspective of today's young people, the answers may not be obvious. Recall fourteen-year-old Howard who thinks that robots might be better than people when it comes to understanding the intricacies of high school and eleven-year-old Fara who looks forward to nurturing a baby-like robot. As for me, the question has been raised very close to home. I took my daughter, then fourteen, to visit the Darwin exhibit at the American Museum of Natural History. The exhibit documented Darwin's life and thought, and with a somewhat defensive tone (in light of current challenges to evolution by proponents of intelligent design), presented the theory of evolution as the central truth that underpins contemporary biology. The Darwin exhibit wanted to convince and it wanted to please. At its entrance was a turtle from the Galapagos Islands, a seminal object in the development of evolutionary theory. The turtle rested in its cage, utterly still. "They could have used a robot," commented my daughter. She considered it a shame to bring the turtle all this way and put it in a cage for a performance that draws so little on the turtle's "aliveness." I was startled by her comments, both solicitous of the imprisoned turtle because it is alive and unconcerned about its authenticity. The museum had been advertising these turtles as wonders, curiosities, and marvels—among the plastic models of life at the museum, here is the life that Darwin saw.

I began to talk with others at the exhibit, parents and children. It was Thanksgiving weekend. The line was long, the crowd frozen in place. My question, "Do you care that the turtle is alive?" was welcome diversion. A ten-year-old girl would prefer a robot turtle because aliveness comes with aesthetic inconvenience: "its water looks dirty. Gross." More usually, votes for the robots echoed my daughter's sentiment that in this setting, aliveness doesn't seem worth the trouble. A twelve-year-old girl opined: "For what the turtles do, you didn't have to have the live ones." Her father looked at her, uncomprehending: "But the point is that they are real, that's the whole point."

The Darwin exhibit gave authenticity major play: on display were the actual magnifying glass that Darwin used, the actual notebooks in which he recorded his observations, indeed, the very notebook in which he wrote the famous sentences that first described his theory of evolution. But, in the children's reactions to the inert but alive Galapagos turtle, the idea of the original was in crisis. I recall my daughter's reaction when she was seven to a boat ride in the postcard blue Mediterranean. Already an expert in the world of simulated fish tanks, she saw a creature in the water, pointed to it excitedly and said: "Look mommy, a jellyfish! It looks so realistic!" When I told this story to a friend who was a research scientist at the Walt Disney Company, he was not surprised. When Animal Kingdom opened in Orlando, populated by "real", that is, biological animals, its first visitors complained that these animals were not as "realistic" as the animatronic creatures in Disneyworld, just across the road. The robotic crocodiles slapped their tails, rolled their eyes, in sum, displayed "essence of crocodile" behavior. The biological crocodiles, like the Galapagos turtle, pretty much kept to themselves. What is the gold standard here?

I have long believed that in our culture of simulation, the notion of authenticity is for us what sex was to the Victorians—threat and obsession, taboo and fascination. I have lived with this idea for many years, yet at the museum, I found the children's position strangely unsettling. For them, in this context, aliveness seemed to have no intrinsic value. Rather, it was useful only if needed for a specific purpose. "If you put in a robot instead of the live turtle, do you think people should be told that the turtle is not alive?" I ask. "Not really", said several of the children. Data on "aliveness" can be shared on a "need to know" basis, for a purpose. This volume with its enthusiastic embrace of machines as kin both provokes and challenges: What indeed are the purposes of living things?

Notes

1. Turkle, *The Second Self.*
2. Ibid.
3. Turkle, *Life on the Screen.* There I discuss the case of computer psychotherapy to illustrate a turning away from the romantic reaction as a response to programs as appropriate dialogue partners in the realm of the personal.
4. Ibid.
5. Suvendi Kakushi, "Robot Lovin," Asia Week Magazine Online, November 9, 2001. www.asiaweek.com/asiaweek/magazine/life/0.8782.182326.00html. Accessed on 5/9/05.
6. *Interaction Studies,* ibid.
7. David Levy, *Love and Sex With Robots: The Evolution of Human-Robot Relationships* (New York: HarperCollins, 2007).
8. Sigmund Freud, "The Uncanny," In *The Standard Edition of the Complete Works of Sigmund Freud,* edited by James Strachey, et al. London: The Hogarth Press and The Institute of Psychoanalysis, 1953–74.
9. P. H. Ornstein, Ed., *The Search for the self: Selected writings of Heinz Kohut: 1950–1978,* (Vol. 2). New York: International Universities Press, Inc., 1978.
10. On this, see Sherry Turkle, "Whither Psychoanalysis in Computer Culture," *Psychoanalytic Psychology,* Vol. 21, 2004.

Critical Thinking

1. Turkle says that in the 1980s claims that computers would one day simulate behaviors we think of as quintessentially human produced the "romantic reaction" in people. What is the romantic reaction? Do have the romantic reaction in the face of similar claims.

2. Turkle claims a newly found openness to "seeing computational objects as 'other minds.'" Are you open to such a point of view? Why or why not?

3. Turkle says that there similarities between the relationships formed through Facebook and those that might be formed with furry robots. What is her argument? Are you persuaded?

4. Do you believe that "there is something essential about the human spirit and that this something resides in human inner states"? Or are you with those who focus on behavior (if it walks like a duck, etc.)?

5. 2003 marked the 30th anniversary of the publication of an essay entitled "Animals, Men and Morals" by Peter Singer in *The New York Review of Books.* This essay is often credited with beginning the animal rights movement. Singer argues that because animals have feelings, they can suffer. Because they can suffer, they have interests. Because they have interests, it is unethical to conduct experiments on them. Suppose scientists succeed in developing machines that feel pain and fear. What obligations will we have toward them? If this is difficult to imagine, watch the movie *Blade Runner* with Harrison Ford. What do you think now?

From/Based on "In Good Company: On the Threshold of Robotic Companions." In Yorik Wilks (Editor), *Close Engagements with Artificial Companions,* 2010, pp. 2–10. With kind permission by John Benjamin Publishing Company, Amsterdam/Philadelphia. www.benjamins.com. Reprinted by permission.

Cloud Computing

As software migrates from local PCs to distant Internet servers, users and developers alike go along for the ride.

Brian Hayes

The Greek myths tell of creatures plucked from the surface of the Earth and enshrined as constellations in the night sky. Something similar is happening today in the world of computing. Data and programs are being swept up from desktop PCs and corporate server rooms and installed in "the compute cloud."

Whether it's called *cloud computing* or *on-demand computing, software as a service,* or *the Internet as platform,* the common element is a shift in the geography of computation. When you create a spreadsheet with the Google Docs service, major components of the software reside on unseen computers, whereabouts unknown, possibly scattered across continents.

The shift from locally installed programs to cloud computing is just getting under way in earnest. Shrink-wrap software still dominates the market and is not about to disappear, but the focus of innovation indeed seems to be ascending into the clouds. Some substantial fraction of computing activity is migrating away from the desktop and the corporate server room. The change will affect all levels of the computational ecosystem, from casual user to software developer, IT manager, even hardware manufacturer.

In a sense, what we're seeing now is the second coming of cloud computing. Almost 50 years ago a similar transformation came with the creation of service bureaus and time-sharing systems that provided access to computing machinery for users who lacked a mainframe in a glass-walled room down the hall. A typical time-sharing service had a hub-and-spoke configuration. Individual users at terminals communicated over telephone lines with a central site where all the computing was done.

When personal computers arrived in the 1980s, part of their appeal was the promise of "liberating" programs and data from the central computing center. (Ted Nelson, the prophet of hypertext, published a book titled *Computer Lib/Dream Machines* in 1974.) Individuals were free to control their own computing environment, choosing software to suit their needs and customizing systems to their tastes.

But PCs in isolation had an obvious weakness: In many cases the sneaker-net was the primary means of collaboration and sharing. The client-server model introduced in the 1980s offered a central repository for shared data while personal computers and workstations replaced terminals, allowing individuals to run programs locally.

In the current trend, the locus of computation is shifting again, with functions migrating outward to distant data centers reached through the Internet. The new regime is not quite a return to the hub-and-spoke topology of time-sharing systems, if only because there is no hub. A client computer on the Internet can communicate with many servers at the same time, some of which may also be exchanging information among themselves. However, even if we are not returning to the architecture of time-sharing systems, the sudden stylishness of the cloud paradigm marks the reversal of a long-standing trend. Where end users and corporate IT managers once squabbled over possession of computing resources, both sides are now willing to surrender a large measure of control to third-party service providers. What brought about this change in attitude?

For the individual, total control comes at a price. Software must be installed and configured, then updated with each new release. The computational infrastructure of operating systems and low-level utilities must be maintained. Every update to the operating system sets off a cascade of subsequent revisions to other programs. Outsourcing computation to an Internet service eliminates nearly all these concerns. Cloud computing also offers end users advantages in terms of mobility and collaboration.

For software vendors who have shifted their operations into the cloud, the incentives are similar to those motivating end users. Software sold or licensed as a product to be installed on the user's hardware must be able to cope with a baffling variety of operating environments. In contrast, software offered as an Internet-based service can be developed, tested, and run on a computing platform of the vendor's choosing. Updates and bug fixes are deployed in minutes. (But the challenges of diversity don't entirely disappear; the server-side software must be able to interact with a variety of clients.)

Although the new model of Internet computing has neither hub nor spokes, it still has a core and a fringe. The aim is to concentrate computation and storage in the core, where high-performance machines are linked by high-bandwidth connections, and all of these resources are carefully managed. At the fringe are the end users making the requests that initiate computations and who receive the results.

Although the future of cloud computing is less than clear, a few examples of present practice suggest likely directions:

Wordstar for the Web. The kinds of productivity applications that first attracted people to personal computers 30 years ago are now appearing as software services. The Google Docs programs are an example, including a word processor, a spreadsheet, and a tool for creating PowerPoint-like presentations. Another undertaking of this kind is Buzzword, a Web-based word processor acquired by Adobe Systems in 2007. Another recent Adobe product is Photoshop Express, which has turned the well-known image-manipulation program into an online service.

Enterprise computing in the cloud. Software for major business applications (such as customer support, sales, and marketing) has generally been run on corporate servers, but several companies now provide it as an on-demand service. The first was Salesforce.com, founded in 1999, offering a suite of online programs for customer relationship management and other business-oriented tasks; the company's slogan is "No software!"

Cloudy infrastructure. It's all very well to outsource the chore of building and maintaining a data center, but someone must still supply that infrastructure. Amazon.com has moved into this niche of the Internet ecosystem. Amazon Web Services offers data storage priced by the gigabyte-month and computing capacity by the CPU-hour. Both kinds of resources expand and contract according to need. IBM has announced plans for the "Blue Cloud" infrastructure. And Google is testing the App Engine, which provides hosting on Google server farms and a software environment centered on the Python programming language and the Bigtable distributed storage system.

For most applications, the entire user interface resides inside a single window in a Web browser.

The cloud OS. For most cloud-computing applications, the entire user interface resides inside a single window in a Web browser. Several initiatives aim to provide a richer user experience for Internet applications. One approach is to exploit the cloud-computing paradigm to provide all the facilities of an operating system inside a browser. The eyeOS system, for example, reproduces the familiar desktop metaphor—with icons for files, folders, and applications—all living in a browser window. Another solution would bypass the Web browser, substituting a more-capable software system that runs as a separate application on the client computer and communicates directly with servers in the cloud. This is

the idea behind AIR (formerly Apollo) being tested by Adobe Systems. Open-Laszlo, an open-source project, works in much the same way.

For those deploying software out in the cloud, scalability is a major issue—the need to marshal resources in such a way that a program continues running smoothly even as the number of users grows. It's not just that servers must respond to hundreds or thousands of requests per second; the system must also coordinate information coming from multiple sources, not all of which are under the control of the same organization. The pattern of communication is many-to-many, with each server talking to multiple clients and each client invoking programs on multiple servers.

The other end of the cloud-computing transaction—the browser-based user interface—presents challenges of another kind. The familiar window-and-menu layer of modern operating systems has been fine-tuned over decades to meet user needs and expectations. Duplicating this functionality inside a Web browser is a considerable feat. Moreover, it has to be done in a comparatively impoverished development environment. A programmer creating a desktop application for Windows or one of the Unix variants can choose from a broad array of programming languages, code libraries, and application frameworks; major parts of the user interface can be assembled from pre-built components. The equivalent scaffolding for the Web computing platform is much more primitive.

A major challenge of moving applications to the cloud is the need to master multiple languages and operating environments. In many cloud applications a back-end process relies on a relational database, so part of the code is written in SQL or other query language. On the client side, program logic is likely to be implemented in JavaScript embedded within HTML documents. Standing between the database and the client is a server application that might be written in a scripting language (such as PHP, Java, and Python). Information exchanged between the various layers is likely to be encoded in some variation of XML.

Even though the new model of remote computing seems to reverse the 1980s "liberation" movement that gave individual users custody over programs and data, the shift does not necessarily restore control to managers in the corporate IT department.

To the extent that cloud computing succeeds, it represents an obvious competitive challenge to vendors of shrink-wrap software. Ironically, the open-source movement could also have a tough time adapting to the new computing model. It's one thing to create and distribute an open-source word processor competing with Microsoft Word; not so obvious is how a consortium of volunteers would create a Web service to compete with Google Docs.

Finally, cloud computing raises questions about privacy, security, and reliability—a major subject of discussion at a workshop held last January at the Center for Information Technology Policy at Princeton University. Allowing a third-party service to take custody of personal documents raises awkward questions about control and ownership: If you move to a competing service provider, can you take your data with you? Could you lose access to your documents if you fail to pay your bill? Do you have the power to expunge documents that are no longer wanted?

The issues of privacy and confidentiality are equally perplexing. In one frequently cited scenario, a government agency presents a subpoena or search warrant to the third party that has possession of your data. If you had retained physical custody, you might still have been compelled to surrender the information, but at least you would have been able to decide for yourself whether or not to contest the order. The third-party service is presumably less likely to go to court on your behalf. In some circumstances you might not even be informed that your documents have been released. It seems likely that much of the world's digital information will be living in the clouds long before such questions are resolved.

Critical Thinking

1. What is meant by "cloud computing"?

2. Hayes says that "what we're seeing now is the second coming of cloud computing." What does he mean by that?

3. How does cloud computing raise issues of privacy and security?

4. What companies are likely to gain by advances in cloud computing?

5. What companies are likely to lose by advances made in cloud computing?

BRIAN HAYES writes about science and technology from Durham, NC.

Chrome the Conqueror

Google's new online operating system could be the Windows killer.

SALLY ADEE

Is Google God? There's a test for that: omnipresent, omniscient, and omnipotent. Omnipresence? Check. There's Gmail, Google Maps, Google Calendar, Google Earth, Google Mars, Google Apps (the word-processing, spreadsheeting service). They're all everywhere, all the time.

Omniscience? The eponymous search engine is perhaps as close to a complete index of the sum total of human knowledge as has ever existed. (There's even the PowerMeter application, which can tell when you've been naughty or nice with your electricity usage.)

Omnipotence? That's a tough one. Google could annoy you in myriad ways if it wanted to. It could frustrate your flailing attempts to find out where the hyoglossus muscle is. Gmail could gobble up your feverish love letters; Maps could send you down an endless series of side streets long ago blocked by freeways and housing developments. Off you go to the howling wastelands of Yahoo Search and MapQuest.

But, really, why should Google bother with you when, with its superpowers, it can take on much bigger game? Like, say, Microsoft?

Last year saw the introduction of Google's Chrome browser, a variant of which can live inside Microsoft Internet Explorer. Ouch! Then came another smack with the unveiling of Google Wave, a sort of supercharged e-mail and messaging application that merges those functions and seamlessly adds other niceties—social networking, automatic translation, and other services. And later this year will come the most punishing blow of all: an entirely Web-based operating system, Google Chrome OS, which will live in ultraportable netbooks.

Although you'll never hear it from Google, the Chrome suite looks an awful lot like a dagger aimed straight at Microsoft's heart.

Who needs 500-gigabyte hard drives and a 6-megabyte L2 cache when lots of input ports and a fast wireless connection will do? That's the rhetorical question that has lately prompted the meteoric rise of the netbook, a bare-bones laptop that gets most of its muscle from online services.

Google, in Mountain View, Calif., is the first software company to truly capitalize on the promise of these machines: to allow casual users to live entirely in the cloud, without realizing they're there.

Chrome OS has no built-in applications—no iCal, no Outlook, no TextEdit, no Word. You just turn on your netbook and you're on the Web, in what we now call the cloud, where all your stuff lives: all your photos on Flickr, a long trail of your daily foibles and frustrations on Twitter, your purchasing history on PayPal, your prolix unpublished novel on LiveJournal, your music collection on Rhapsody, and the stuff that might be a little embarrassing if your coworkers came across it on Facebook. In fact, cloud computing is what makes Google's strategy possible. "There's only a browser," says Linus Upson, a director of engineering at Google, who is in charge of Chrome OS. "And all it does is get you onto the Web really, really fast."

Cloud computing has become an everyday transaction. Those computer users who don't need to store sensitive documents locally can put everything up in the cloud without missing a beat. Nearly any application you desire—for e-mail, social networking, maps, shopping, even music—no longer needs to be stored on your computer. A significant number of people no longer use their computers for much that isn't Web-based. So why not make it as easy as possible to open your laptop, press the on button, and be where you want to be?

As an increasing number of applications become virtual—Microsoft is even taking Office 2010 into the cloud—you can use them without using a lick of your own computer's resources. Experts call the new paradigm "appliance computing," likening your netbook to your television: Your TV doesn't care whether it's fed an HD or a standard signal as long as the hardware can make sense of it. At last year's Supercomputing conference, Nvidia showed off precisely that idea: A featherweight netbook with only rudimentary graphics capabilities displayed completely photo-realistic three-dimensional rendered images courtesy of a server 500 miles away. Your Web apps—Gmail, Google Calendar, Google Docs, YouTube—are just small-scale versions of that concept.

But first, some untangling of terms, because Google insists on sowing confusion by naming the OS after the browser. The new technology is called Chrome OS, an operating system that is mostly a Web browser, but it's not Chrome, which actually is a browser. Confused? You're not alone. Google punted on the naming conventions, but the company insists that it all makes sense. And it does. But it requires a little bit of explaining.

> **"No more managing, tracking, and backup—my data and applications will be available instantly from any Internet-connected terminal. Thank you, Google."**
>
> Nick Tredennick

Chrome OS is Google's stab at reinventing the operating system. To understand why, you need a little background in what makes an operating system in a regular computer and why it's in need of an upgrade.

Chrome OS is based on Chrome, a free, open-source Web browser Google introduced in 2008 to compete with Apple's Safari and Mozilla Firefox. Google is working with equipment manufacturers to create special hardware around the Chrome operating system, based on Linux, which will run on x86 and ARM chips. Chrome OS–compatible netbooks are expected to appear by the fourth quarter of 2010, just in time for the holiday shopping season.

So if the whole operating system runs inside a browser, why can't any computer use it right now? Well, at press time, there were still some pesky technical challenges that Google engineers had to solve, which is why they released the first open-source version of the code in November. Among the issues: How much storage do you build into a machine that isn't intended for off-line use? How do you come up with a smarter way to let users print to any printer without worrying about drivers? Can people with no intention of ever having a Google account happily get by using a Chrome netbook?

The same basic pain points that users hate about bad browsers—sluggishness, complexity, malware, and the constant crashing—have also been the most common complaints about operating systems. That's how the Chrome operating system grew out of the Chrome browser, says Upson.

The rationale for the Chrome browser was that the vast majority of users don't need duplicate commands or such dubious features as the Home button—that house-shaped icon that takes you back to the first page that loads each time the browser is opened anew. Really, how many computer users even know what that button means? Research has shown that button to be worse than useless—inexperienced users often end up having their home pages set for them by

enterprising Web sites, their browsers doomed to perpetually redirect them to GetRichByGamblingInNigeria.com. So Google built a basic, no-frills browser chassis and let third-party developers build optional extensions for the people who need to pimp their browsers with bells and whistles.

Naturally, critics complain that the Chrome browser is too plain, while conceding that it runs much faster than other browsers and takes up less memory. That's a particular plus for Windows users, whose other applications grind to a halt when an application like Firefox or Internet Explorer 6 hogs memory.

Like the browser, Chrome OS will rely on HTML 5, the latest incarnation of the predominant language used to structure Web pages. HTML 5 will make Chrome OS more powerful, mainly by improving access to rich media. Right now, in order to look at video in older browsers, you need a plug-in—a piece of software that augments your browser's basic capabilities. Think Quicktime, which lets you watch YouTube videos of skateboarding cats, or Adobe Reader, which lets you look at a PDF document right in your browser window. But HTML 5 displays rich media without the assistance of plug-ins. Chrome not only won't need them—it might not even support them.

So what does Google get out of all this? After all, apart from the netbooks (which by some estimates will sell for between US $400 and $700), Google is giving the entire Chrome suite away for free. Recall that Google makes its money from the ads that people see during the course of their everyday Web surfing. So if these people surf more, Google profits more. "We noticed that when people can use the Internet faster and more easily, they are able to use the Internet more," says Chrome OS engineer Upson. "And that means Google makes more money."

To that end, Google's main bragging right is "power button to Web" speed, or how fast you can get from having a shut-down computer to reading your e-mail. Google Chrome, the company promises, will do it in 7 seconds. Contrast that with even the best computers, which can take 45 seconds to boot up. Where does that big difference come from? A computer that runs many applications has a lot of chores to do when you hit the on button. Among these are loading the firmware (a kind of software that deals with the most basic operations, which allow a device to function—for example, by making it aware that its various components exist so it can start delegating tasks to them), initializing various drives and ports, and looking for any external devices. Some of these don't exist anymore, but the legacy firmware will spend time checking for them anyway. Raise your hand if you remember Zip drives.

That eats into the boot-up time before the operating system has even loaded. But even after it does load, you're still not out of the woods. The next obstacles are the auto-start applications that have been configured to fire themselves up the moment the system starts: virus protection, office reminders, updaters, self-monitors, and so on. These applications grow on your hard drive like ivy. If you don't prune them mercilessly, within a few years they'll have clogged up your system's memory and your once blazingly fast computer will creak like an old rocking chair.

Google trashed most of these processes. By getting rid of all software except the browser, engineers were able to prune a tremendous amount of legacy software. Virus protection? Part of the browser. Calendar reminders? In the cloud; subtract a couple of seconds. Google's partners will replace the hard disk drives in the new Chrome netbooks with solid-state drives (the kind that are on your mobile phone). That means no moving mechanical parts—subtract a few more seconds. An operating system that's also a browser means you'll never have to double-click an application icon again—subtract another second. And so on.

Not surprisingly, Microsoft isn't too happy about all this. The software giant can't complain about an unseen OS, which leaves it to talk up Windows 7. A Microsoft spokeswoman told *IEEE Spectrum* in a canned statement that people have purchased Windows 7 twice as often as they purchased any of Microsoft's previous operating systems.

Microsoft's confidence may stem from a misconception that Chrome will be bound to the netbook. However, given the open-source nature of the code, Chrome's migration into other hardware is just a matter of time. In late November, Google cofounder Sergey Brin intimated that Google Chrome OS will not stay in the netbook ghetto for long. Eventually, he said, the operating system will also be available on notebooks and desktops. "There are no technical limits," he said.

Fast, secure, free—is that where the Web is headed? If it is, it wouldn't be the first time. Consider the story of Microsoft's "free" Hotmail. In 1999, Hotmail offered users 2 MB of free storage, but for most users spam quickly devoured that allotment if they weren't vigorous about maintaining their pittance of free space. Disingenuously, Microsoft (or MSN) made available a paid upgrade if you couldn't live on that pittance: Various plans charged users between $19.95 and $59.95 a year to upgrade to between 10 and 100 MB. In 2004, Google blew a hole in that business plan with Web mail that gave away shocking amounts of storage: 1000 MB, a number that kept growing at such a rate that users couldn't keep up with supply (it now stands at 7384 MB). Lo and behold, in 2004 Microsoft announced that it was upping its free storage offering to 250 megabytes at no charge. Now it's all free—even Yahoo offers theoretically unlimited free storage.

And yet, even a plan as seemingly bulletproof as "let me give you this great thing for free" has its skeptics. "I think we still have a long way to go before cloud computing becomes something that we can all use on a day-to-day basis," says Mike Halsey, an IT support engineer and teacher based in Sheffield, England, and the author of the *Windows 7 Power Users Guide.* "What about playing music or video on the move, or editing photos on one service when they're stored on another?" Halsey asks.

Halsey's particular beef is that the cloud is not yet reliable enough to support Google's Web-only vision. "It's certainly not ready for the mainstream as things stand," Halsey concludes. Let's say you're in the clouds (you're stuck on an airplane without Wi-Fi), and yet, ironically, cut off from your access to The Cloud. The thought of a $400 brick sitting in your lap for the entire 6 hours you spend on a flight between New York and Frankfurt might give you pause. A Google spokesperson told *IEEE Spectrum* that Google has no plans to mitigate the issue by installing off-line applications—a word processor, say, or an e-mail client—as insurance against the times when no Internet connection is available.

So the cloud is still the kink, but the cloud will improve. And so will Google, right along with it. It's worth pointing out that many companies store sensitive documents in the cloud right now, and some of them use the enterprise version of Google Apps. Here's the predictable scenario: The programs will evolve with use, as more developers testdrive Chrome's capabilities and more geeks customize it with every extension you can possibly imagine. In the end, Google's user base will expand the extensions to areas that not even Google can imagine. People will spend even more time surfing, and out of the corners of their eyes they will see ads from Google, making a rich company even richer. And that means the benevolent deity will continue to make fast and fun toys.

> "I will admit that Google is a deity, but even they have bad-hair days. They can't have my data in their cloud. I don't trust them."
>
> Robert W. Lucky

But before you sign your entire life over to Google, you might consider a minor sticking point. "Google has been able to treat users really well because it's been so profitable," says Siva Vaidhyanathan, a cultural historian and media scholar, who is an associate professor of media studies and law at the University of Virginia. He is working on a book called *The Googleization of Everything.* Google's benevolence, Vaidhyanathan says, isn't something we should get too used to. "Henry Ford thought he was saving the world, too," he says. "It's really important to be suspicious about any egalitarian claim by any corporation. Corporations are, and should be, in the business of business. Any claims of making the world better should not be important to those of us who use the services and products. In fact, we are Google's products, because Google actually sells us."

Critical Thinking

1. What is the difference between Google Chrome and Google Chrome OS?

2. Watch the You Tube video on Chrome OS:www.youtube.com/watch?v=0QRO3gKj3qw. Is it true that you spend 90% of your time on the computer using a browser?

3. Suppose that you have a computer running Chrome OS. Is there anyplace where you go that does not have Internet service available? Is there anything you do on your computer in these places? What would you do there with a Chrome OS equipped machine?

4. Reread "The Web's Goldmine" in Unit 6. What do you think Google might do with the data you've stored in its cloud?

5. Use the Internet to read about the social contributions of three giants from another era: Thomas Edison (and the electric chair), George Pullman (and his utopia), Henry Ford (and the *Verdienstkreutz Deutscher Adler*). On a brighter note, read about Andrew Carnegie (and his libraries). Do you agree with the author's informant that "it's really important to be suspicious about any egalitarian claim by any corporation"?

Publishing: The Revolutionary Future

JASON EPSTEIN

The transition within the book publishing industry from physical inventory stored in a warehouse and trucked to retailers to digital files stored in cyberspace and delivered almost anywhere on earth as quickly and cheaply as e-mail is now underway and irreversible. This historic shift will radically transform worldwide book publishing, the cultures it affects and on which it depends. Meanwhile, for quite different reasons, the genteel book business that I joined more than a half-century ago is already on edge, suffering from a gambler's unbreakable addiction to risky, seasonal best sellers, many of which don't recoup their costs, and the simultaneous deterioration of backlist, the vital annuity on which book publishers had in better days relied for year-to-year stability through bad times and good. The crisis of confidence reflects these intersecting shocks, an overspecialized marketplace dominated by high-risk ephemera and a technological shift orders of magnitude greater than the momentous evolution from monkish scriptoria to movable type launched in Gutenberg's German city of Mainz six centuries ago.

Though Gutenberg's invention made possible our modern world with all its wonders and woes, no one, much less Gutenberg himself, could have foreseen that his press would have this effect. And no one today can foresee except in broad and sketchy outline the far greater impact that digitization will have on our own future. With the earth trembling beneath them, it is no wonder that publishers with one foot in the crumbling past and the other seeking solid ground in an uncertain future hesitate to seize the opportunity that digitization offers them to restore, expand, and promote their backlists to a decentralized, worldwide marketplace. New technologies, however, do not await permission. They are, to use Schumpeter's overused term, disruptive, as nonnegotiable as earthquakes.

Gutenberg's technology was the sine qua non for the rebirth of the West, as if literacy, scientific method, and constitutional government had been implicit all along, awaiting only Gutenberg to throw the switch. Within fifty years presses were operating from one end of Europe to the other, halting only at the borders of Islam, which shunned the press. Perhaps from the same fear of disruptive literacy that alarmed Islam, China ignored a phonetic transcription of its ideographs, attributed to a Korean emperor, that might have permitted the use of movable type.

The resistance today by publishers to the onrushing digital future does not arise from fear of disruptive literacy, but from the understandable fear of their own obsolescence and the complexity of the digital transformation that awaits them, one in which much of their traditional infrastructure and perhaps they too will be redundant. Karl Marx wrote of the revolutions of 1848 in his *Communist Manifesto* that all that is solid melts into air. His vision of a workers' paradise was of course wrong by 180 degrees, the triumph of wish over experience. What melted soon solidified as industrial capitalism, a paradise for some at the expense of the many. But Marx's potent image fits the publishing industry today as its capital-intensive infrastructure—presses, warehouses stacked with fully returnable physical inventory, its retail market constrained by costly real estate—faces dissolution within a vast cloud in which all the world's books will eventually reside as digital files to be downloaded instantly title by title wherever on earth connectivity exists, and printed and bound on demand at point of sale one copy at a time by the Espresso Book Machine[1] as library-quality paperbacks, or transmitted to electronic reading devices including Kindles, Sony Readers, and their multiuse successors, among them most recently Apple's iPad. The unprecedented ability of this technology to offer a vast new multilingual marketplace a practically limitless choice of titles will displace the Gutenberg system with or without the cooperation of its current executives.

Digitization makes possible a world in which anyone can claim to be a publisher and anyone can call him- or herself an author. In this world the traditional filters will have melted into air and only the ultimate filter—the human inability to read what is unreadable—will remain to winnow what is worth keeping in a virtual marketplace where Keats's nightingale shares electronic space with Aunt Mary's haikus. That the contents of the world's libraries will eventually be accessed practically anywhere at the click of a mouse is not an unmixed blessing. Another click might obliterate these same contents and bring civilization to an end: an overwhelming argument, if one is needed, for physical books in the digital age.

Amid the literary chaos of the digital future, readers will be guided by the imprints of reputable publishers, distinguishable within a worldwide, multilingual directory, a function that Google seems poised to dominate—one hopes with the cooperation of great national and university libraries and their skilled bibliographers, under revised world copyright standards in keeping with the reach of the World Wide Web. Titles will also be posted on authors' and publishers' own Web sites and on reliable Web sites of special interest where biographies of Napoleon or manuals of dog training will be evaluated by competent critics and downloaded directly from author or publisher to end user while software distributes the purchase price appropriately, bypassing traditional formulas. With inventory expense, shipping, and returns eliminated, readers will pay less, authors will earn more, and book publishers, rid of their otiose infrastructure, will survive and may prosper.

This future is a predictable inference from digitization in its current stage of development in the United States, its details widely discussed in the blogosphere by partisans of various outcomes, including the utopian fantasy that in the digital future content will be free of charge and authors will not have to eat.

Digitization will encourage an unprecedented diversity of new specialized content in many languages. The more adaptable of today's general publishers will survive the redundancy of their traditional infrastructure but digitization has already begun to spawn specialized publishers occupying a variety of niches staffed by small groups of like-minded editors, perhaps not in the same office or even the same country, much as software firms themselves are decentralized with staff in California collaborating online with colleagues in Bangalore and Barcelona.

The difficult, solitary work of literary creation, however, demands rare individual talent and in fiction is almost never collaborative. Social networking may expose readers to this or that book but violates the solitude required to create artificial worlds with real people in them. Until it is ready to be shown to a trusted friend or editor, a writer's work in progress is intensely private. Dickens and Melville wrote in solitude on paper with pens; except for their use of typewriters and computers so have the hundreds of authors I have worked with over many years.

In preliterate cultures, the great sagas and epics were necessarily communal creations committed to tribal memory and chanted under priestly supervision over generations. With the invention of the alphabet, authors no longer depended on communal memory but stored their work on stone, papyrus, or paper. In modern times, communal projects are limited mainly to complex reference works, of which Wikipedia is an example. Though social networking will not produce another Dickens or Melville, the Web is already a powerful resource for writers, providing conveniently online a great variety of updated reference materials, dictionaries, journals, and so on instantly and everywhere, available by subscription or, like Google search and Wikipedia, free. Most time-sensitive reference materials need never again be printed and bound.

Informed critical writing of high quality on general subjects will be as rare and as necessary as ever and will survive as it always has in print and online for discriminating readers. Works of genius will emerge from parts of the world where books have barely penetrated before, as such works after Gutenberg emerged unbidden from the dark and silent corners of Europe. Gutenberg's press, however, did not give Europe, with its tight cultural boundaries, a common tongue. Digitization may produce a somewhat different outcome by giving worldwide exposure to essential scientific and literary texts in major languages: Rome redux, while translators will still find plenty of work.

The cost of entry for future publishers will be minimal, requiring only the upkeep of the editorial group and its immediate support services but without the expense of traditional distribution facilities and multilayered management. Small publishers already rely as needed upon such external services as business management, legal, accounting, design, copyediting, publicity, and so on, while the Internet will supply viral publicity opportunities of which YouTube and Facebook are forerunners. Funding for authors' advances may be provided by external investors hoping for a profit, as is done for films and plays. The devolution from complex, centralized management to semi-autonomous editorial units is already evident within the conglomerates (for example, Nan A. Talese at Random House and Jonathan Karp at Hachette), a tendency that will strengthen as the parent companies fade. As conglomerates resist the exorbitant demands of best-selling authors whose books predictably dominate best-seller lists, these authors, with the help of agents and business managers, will become their own publishers, retaining all net proceeds from digital as well as traditional sales. With the Espresso Book Machine, enterprising retail booksellers may become publishers themselves, like their eighteenth-century forebears.

Traditional territorial rights will become superfluous and a worldwide, uniform copyright convention will be essential. Protecting content from unauthorized file sharers will remain a vexing problem that raises serious questions about the viability of authorship, for without protection authors will starve and civilization will decline, a prospect recognized by the United States Constitution, which calls for copyright to sustain writers not primarily as a matter of equity but for the greater good of public enlightenment.

Some musicians make up for lost royalties by giving concerts, selling T-shirts, or accompanying commercials. For authors there is no equivalent solution. Refinements of today's digital rights management software, designed to block file sharing, will be an ongoing contest with file sharers who evade payment for themselves and their friends, often in the perverse belief that "content wants to be free"—much as antiviral software is engaged in a continuing contest with hackers. Unauthorized file sharing will be a problem but not in my opinion a serious one, perhaps at the level that libraries and individual readers have always shared books with others.

These and other solutions will emerge opportunistically in response to need, as such solutions usually have. It is futile at this early stage, however, to anticipate the new publishing landscape in detail or to specify the rate of evolution, which will be sporadic and complex, or the future role of traditional publishers as digitization advances along a ragged and diverse front, while publishers, writers, and readers adapt accordingly. Timing will be apparent only in retrospect.

So far I have attempted to foresee the digital future in instrumental terms. There is also a moral dimension, for we are a troublesome species with a long history of self-destruction. The industry that Gutenberg launched eventually made possible wide distribution of Montaigne, Shakespeare, and Cervantes, to say nothing of *Babar the Elephant* and *The Cat in the Hat*. But his technology also gave us *The Protocols of the Elders of Zion, Mein Kampf,* and the nonsense that turned Pol Pot in Paris from a mere fool into a mass murderer. Digitization will amplify our better nature but also its diabolic opposite. Censorship is not the answer to these evils.

Digital content is fragile. The secure retention, therefore, of physical books safe from electronic meddlers, predators, and the hazards of electronic storage is essential. Amazon's recent arbitrary deletion of Orwell's *1984* at its publisher's request from Kindle users who had downloaded it suggests the ease with which files can be deleted without warning or permission, an inescapable hazard of electronic distribution.[2] In Denmark music downloaded by subscription self-destructs when the subscription expires. So does my annual subscription to the online *Oxford English Dictionary* unless I renew it. Much other reference material that is usually time-sensitive and for that reason need never be printed and bound is already sold by renewable subscription. If I were a publisher today I would consider a renewable rental model for all e-book downloads—the "lending library" technique of the Depression era—that more accurately reflects the conditional relationship, enforced by digital rights management software, between content provider and end user.

I would like to add a few words about the evolution of my own interest in digitization. From the beginning of my career I have been obsessed with the preservation and distribution of backlist—the previously published books, still in print, that are the indispensable component of a publisher's stability and in the aggregate the repository of civilizations. In this sense, it is fair to say that book publishing is more than a business. Without the contents of our libraries—our collective backlist, our cultural memory—our civilization would collapse.

By the mid-Eighties I had become aware of the serious erosion of publishers' backlists as shoals of slow-moving but still viable titles were dropped every month. There were two reasons for this: a change in the tax law that no longer permitted existing unsold inventory to be written off as an expense; but more important, the disappearance as Americans left the cities for the suburbs of hundreds of well-stocked, independent, city-based bookstores, and their replacement by chain outlets in suburban malls that were paying the same rent as the shoe store next door for the same minimal space and requiring the same rapid turnover.

This demographic shift turned the book business upside down as retailers, unable to stock deep backlist, now demanded high turnover, often of ephemeral titles. Best-selling authors whose loyalty to their publishers had previously been the norm were now chips in a high-stakes casino: a boon for authors and agents with their nonrecoverable overguarantees and a nightmare for publishers who bear all the risk and are lucky if they break even. Meanwhile, backlist continued to decline. The smaller houses, unable to take these risks, merged with the

larger ones, and the larger ones eventually fell into the arms of today's conglomerates.

To offset the decline of backlist I launched in the mid-Eighties the Reader's Catalog, an independent bookstore in catalog form from which readers could order 40,000 backlist titles by telephone. The Internet existed but had not yet been commercialized. The Reader's Catalog was an instant success, confirming my belief in a strong worldwide market for backlist titles. But I had underestimated the cost of handling individual orders and concluded, with my backers, that if we continued our losses would become intolerable. The Internet was now available commercially. Amazon bravely took advantage of it and in the beginning suffered the losses that I feared. But by this time I had begun to hear of digitization and its buzzword, disintermediation, which meant that publishers could now look forward to marketing a practically limitless backlist without physical inventory, shipping expense, or unsold copies returned for credit. Customers would pay in advance for their purchases. This meant that even Amazon's automated shipping facilities would eventually be bypassed by electronic inventory. This was twenty-five years ago. Today digitization is replacing physical publishing much as I had imagined it would.

Relatively inexpensive multipurpose devices fitted with reading applications will widen the market for e-books and may encourage new literary forms, such as Japan's cell-phone novels. Newborn revolutions often encourage utopian fantasies until the exigencies of human nature reassert themselves. Though bloggers anticipate a diversity of communal projects and new kinds of expression, literary form has been remarkably conservative throughout its long history while the act of reading abhors distraction, such as the Web-based enhancements—musical accompaniment, animation, critical commentary, and other metadata—that some prophets of the digital age foresee as profitable sidelines for content providers.

The most radical of these fantasies posits that the contents of the digital cloud will merge or be merged—will "mash up"—to form a single, communal, autonomous intelligence, an all-encompassing, single book or collective brain that reproduces electronically on a universal scale the synergies that occur spontaneously within individual minds. To scorn a bold new hypothesis—the roundness of the earth, its rotation around the sun—is always a risk but here the risk is minimal. The nihilism—the casual contempt for texts—implicit in this ugly fantasy is nevertheless disturbing as evidence of cultural impoverishment,[3] more offensive than but not unrelated to the assumption of e-book maximalists that authors who spend months and years at their desks will not demand physical copies as evidence of their labors and hope for posterity.

The huge, worldwide market for digital content, however, is not a fantasy. It will be very large, very diverse, and very surprising: its cultural impact cannot be imagined. E-books will be a significant factor in this uncertain future, but actual books printed and bound will continue to be the irreplaceable repository of our collective wisdom.

I must declare my bias. My rooms are piled from floor to ceiling with books so that I have to think twice about where to put another one. If by some unimaginable accident all these books were to melt into air leaving my shelves bare with only a memorial list of digital files left behind I would want to melt as well for books are my life. I mention this so that you will know the prejudice with which I celebrate the inevitability of digitization as an unimaginably powerful, but infinitely fragile, enhancement of the worldwide literacy on which we all—readers and nonreaders—depend.

Notes

1. A project that I helped found.
2. See also Amazon's more recent attempt to block sales of books by a major publisher because of a pricing dispute.
3. For a critical account of this view, see Jaron Lanier, *You Are Not a Gadget: A Manifesto* (Knopf, 2010), pp. 26, 46.

Critical Thinking

1. What is a publisher's backlist? Why have these books been dropped?
2. What is Epstein's argument for the demise of the independent bookstore?
3. What would be the role of book publishers in digitized world?
4. Does Epstein address where digital books will be stored and who will be their conservator?

Computers Learn to Listen, and Some Talk Back

STEVE LOHR AND JOHN MARKOFF

"Hi, thanks for coming," the medical assistant says, greeting a mother with her 5-year-old son. "Are you here for your child or yourself?" The boy, the mother replies. He has diarrhea.

"Oh no, sorry to hear that," she says, looking down at the boy.

The assistant asks the mother about other symptoms, including fever ("slight") and abdominal pain ("He hasn't been complaining").

She turns again to the boy. "Has your tummy been hurting?" Yes, he replies.

After a few more questions, the assistant declares herself "not that concerned at this point." She schedules an appointment with a doctor in a couple of days. The mother leads her son from the room, holding his hand. But he keeps looking back at the assistant, fascinated, as if reluctant to leave.

Maybe that is because the assistant is the disembodied likeness of a woman's face on a computer screen— a no-frills avatar. Her words of sympathy are jerky, flat and mechanical. But she has the right stuff—the ability to understand speech, recognize pediatric conditions and reason according to simple rules—to make an initial diagnosis of a childhood ailment and its seriousness. And to win the trust of a little boy.

"Our young children and grandchildren will think it is completely natural to talk to machines that look at them and understand them," said Eric Horvitz, a computer scientist at Microsoft's research laboratory who led the medical avatar project, one of several intended to show how people and computers may communicate before long.

For decades, computer scientists have been pursuing artificial intelligence—the use of computers to simulate human thinking. But in recent years, rapid progress has been made in machines that can listen, speak, see, reason and learn, in their way. The prospect, according to

scientists and economists, is not only that artificial intelligence will transform the way humans and machines communicate and collaborate, but will also eliminate millions of jobs, create many others and change the nature of work and daily routines.

The artificial intelligence technology that has moved furthest into the mainstream is computer understanding of what humans are saying. People increasingly talk to their cellphones to find things, instead of typing. Both Google's and Microsoft's search services now respond to voice commands. More drivers are asking their cars to do things like find directions or play music.

The number of American doctors using speech software to record and transcribe accounts of patient visits and treatments has more than tripled in the past three years to 150,000. The progress is striking. A few years ago, supraspinatus (a rotator cuff muscle) got translated as "fish banana." Today, the software transcribes all kinds of medical terminology letter perfect, doctors say. It has more trouble with other words and grammar, requiring wording changes in about one of every four sentences, doctors say.

"It's unbelievably better than it was five years ago," said Dr. Michael A. Lee, a pediatrician in Norwood, Mass., who now routinely uses transcription software. "But it struggles with 'she' and 'he,' for some reason. When I say 'she,' it writes 'he.' The technology is sexist. It likes to write 'he.'"

Meanwhile, translation software being tested by the Defense Advanced Research Projects Agency is fast enough to keep up with some simple conversations. With some troops in Iraq, English is translated to Arabic and Arabic to English. But there is still a long way to go. When a soldier asked a civilian, "What are you transporting in your truck?" the Arabic reply was that the truck was "carrying tomatoes." But the English translation became "pregnant tomatoes." The speech software understood "carrying," but not the context.

Yet if far from perfect, speech recognition software is good enough to be useful in more ways all the time. Take call centers. Today, voice software enables many calls to be automated entirely. And more advanced systems can understand even a perplexed, rambling customer with a misbehaving product well enough to route the caller to someone trained in that product, saving time and frustration for the customer. They can detect anger in a caller's voice and respond accordingly—usually by routing the call to a manager.

So the outlook is uncertain for many of the estimated four million workers in American call centers or the nation's 100,000 medical transcriptionists, whose jobs were already threatened by outsourcing abroad. "Basic work that can be automated is in the bull's-eye of both technology and globalization, and the rise of artificial intelligence just magnifies that reality," said Erik Brynjolfsson, an economist at the Sloan School of Management at the Massachusetts Institute of Technology.

Still, Mr. Brynjolfsson says artificial intelligence will also spur innovation and create opportunities, both for individuals and entrepreneurial companies, just as the Internet has led to new businesses like Google and new forms of communication like blogs and social networking. Smart machines, experts predict, will someday tutor students, assist surgeons and safely drive cars.

The Digital Assistant

"Hi, are you looking for Eric?" asks the receptionist outside the office of Eric Horvitz at Microsoft.

This assistant is an avatar, a time manager for office workers. Behind the female face on the screen is an arsenal of computing technology including speech understanding, image recognition and machine learning. The digital assistant taps databases that include the boss's calendar of meetings and appointments going back years, and his work patterns. Its software monitors his phone calls by length, person spoken to, time of day and day of the week. It also tracks his location and computer use by applications used—e-mail, writing documents, browsing the Web—for how long and time of day.

When a colleague asks when Mr. Horvitz's meeting or phone call may be over, the avatar reviews that data looking for patterns—for example, how long have calls to this person typically lasted, at similar times of day and days of the week, when Mr. Horvitz was also browsing the Web while talking? "He should be free in five or six minutes," the avatar decides.

The avatar has a database of all the boss's colleagues at work and relationships, from research team members to senior management, and it can schedule meetings. Mr. Horvitz has given the avatar rules for the kinds of meetings that are more and less interruptible. A session with a research peer, requiring deep concentration, may be scored as less interruptible than a meeting with a senior executive. "It's O.K. to interrupt him," the assistant tells a visitor. "Just go in."

As part of the project, the researchers plan to program the avatar to engage in "work-related chitchat" with colleagues who are waiting.

The conversation could be about the boss's day: "Eric's been in back-to-back meetings this afternoon. But he's looking forward to seeing you." Or work done with the boss: "Yes, you were in the big quarterly review with Eric last month." Or even a local team: "How about that Mariners game last night?"

Mr. Horvitz shares a human administrative assistant with other senior scientists. The avatar's face is modeled after her. At Microsoft, workers typically handle their own calendars. So the main benefit of the personal assistant, Mr. Horvitz says, is to manage his time better and coordinate his work with colleagues. "I think of it as an extension of me," he said. "The result is a broader, more effective Eric."

Computers with artificial intelligence can be thought of as the machine equivalent of idiot savants. They can be extremely good at skills that challenge the smartest humans, playing chess like a grandmaster or answering "Jeopardy!" questions like a champion. Yet those skills are in narrow domains of knowledge. What is far harder for a computer is common-sense skills like understanding the context of language and social situations when talking—taking turns in conversation, for example.

The scheduling assistant can plumb vast data vaults in a fraction of a second to find a pattern, but a few unfamiliar words leave it baffled. Jokes, irony and sarcasm do not compute.

That brittleness can lead to mistakes. In the case of the office assistant, it might be a meeting missed or a scheduling mix-up. But the medical assistant could make more serious mistakes, like an incorrect diagnosis or a seriously ill child sent home.

The Microsoft projects are only research initiatives, but they suggest where things are headed. And as speech recognition and other artificial intelligence technologies take on more tasks, there are concerns about the social impact of the technology and too little attention paid to its limitations.

Smart machines, some warn, could be used as tools to isolate corporations, government and the affluent from the rest of society. Instead of people listening to restive customers and citizens, they say, it will be machines.

"Robot voices could be the perfect wall to protect institutions that don't want to deal with complaints," said Jaron Lanier, a computer scientist and author of You Are Not a Gadget (Knopf, 2010).

Smarter Devices

"I'm looking for a reservation for two people tomorrow night at 8 at a romantic restaurant within walking distance."

That spoken request seems simple enough, but for a computer to respond intelligently requires a ballet of more than a dozen technologies.

A host of companies—AT&T, Microsoft, Google and startups—are investing in services that hint at the concept of machines that can act on spoken commands. They go well beyond voice-enabled Internet search.

Perhaps the furthest along is Siri, a Silicon Valley company offering a "virtual personal assistant," a collection of software programs that can listen to a request, find information and take action.

In this case, Siri, presented as an iPhone application, sends the spoken request for a romantic restaurant as an audio file to computers operated by Nuance Communications, the largest speech-recognition company, which convert it to text. The text is then returned to Siri's computers, which make educated guesses about the meaning.

"It's a bit like the task faced by a waiter for whom English is a second language in a noisy restaurant," said Tom Gruber, an artificial intelligence researcher and co-founder of Siri. "It isn't perfect, but in context the waiter can usually figure out what you want."

The Siri system taps more data to decide if it is seeking a romantic restaurant or romantic comedy. It knows the location of the phone and has rules for the meaning of phrases like "within walking distance." It scans online restaurant review services like Yelp and Gayot for "romantic."

Siri takes the winnowed list of restaurants, contacts the online reservation service Open Table and gets matches for those with tables available at 8 the next day. Those restaurants are then displayed on the user's phone, and the reservation can be completed by tapping a button on the screen. The elaborate digital dance can be completed in a few seconds—when it works.

Apple is so impressed that it bought Siri in April in a private transaction estimated at more than $200 million.

Nelson Walters, an MTV television producer in New York, is a Siri fan. It saves him time and impresses his girlfriend. "I will no longer get lost in searching Yelp for restaurant recommendations," he said. But occasionally, Mr. Walters said, Siri stumbles. Recently, he asked Siri for the location of a sushi restaurant he knew. Siri replied with directions to an Asian escort service. "I swear that's not what I was looking for," he said.

Mr. Gruber said Siri had heard an unfamiliar Japanese word, but did not know the context and guessed wrong.

In cars, too, speech recognition systems have vastly improved. In just three years, the Ford Motor Company, using Nuance software, has increased the number of speech commands its vehicles recognize from 100 words to 10,000 words and phrases.

Systems like Ford's Sync are becoming popular options in new cars. They are also seen by some safety specialists as a defense, if imperfect, against the distracting array of small screens for GPS devices, smartphones and the like.

Later this summer, a new model of the Ford Edge will recognize complete addresses, including city and state spoken in a single phrase, and respond by offering turn-by-turn directions.

To the Customer's Rescue

"Please select one of the following products from our menu," the electronics giant Panasonic used to tell callers seeking help with products from power tools to plasma televisions.

It was not working. Callers took an average of 2 1/2 minutes merely to wade through the menu, and 40 percent hung up in frustration. "We were drowning in calls," recalled Donald Szczepaniak, vice president of customer service. Panasonic reached out to AT&T Labs in 2005 for help.

The AT&T researchers worked with thousands of hours of recorded calls to the Panasonic center, in Chesapeake, Va., to build statistical models of words and phrases that callers used to describe products and problems, and to create a database that is constantly updated. "It's a baby, and the more data you give it, the smarter it becomes," said Mazin Gilbert, a speech technology expert at AT&T Labs.

The goal of the system is to identify key words— among a person's spoken phrases and sentences—so an automated assistant can intelligently reply.

"How may I help you?" asked the automated female voice in one recording.

"I was watching 'American Idol' with my dog on Channel 5," a distraught woman on the line said recently, "and suddenly my TV was stuck in Spanish."

"What kind of TV?" the automated assistant asked, suggesting choices that include plasma, LCD and others.

"LCD," replied the woman, and her call was sent to an agent trained in solving problems with LCD models.

Simple problems—like product registration or where to take a product for repairs—can be resolved in the automated system alone. That technology has improved, but callers have also become more comfortable speaking to the system. A surprising number sign off by saying, "Thank you."

Some callers, especially younger ones, also make things easier for the computer by uttering a key phrase like "plasma help," Mr. Szczepaniak said. "I call it the Google-ization of the customer," he said.

Over all, half of the calls to Panasonic are handled in the automated system, up from 10 percent five years ago, estimated Lorraine Robbins, a manager.

But the other half of calls are more complex problems—like connecting a digital television to a cable box. In those cases, the speech recognition system quickly routes a call to an agent trained on the product, so far more problems are resolved with a single call. Today, Panasonic resolves one million more customer problems a year with 1.6 million fewer total calls than five years ago. The cost of resolving a customer issue has declined by 50 percent.

The speech technology's automated problem sorting has enabled Panasonic to globalize its customer service, with inquiries about older and simpler products routed to its call centers in the Philippines and Jamaica. The Virginia center now focuses on high-end Panasonic products like plasma TVs and home theater equipment. And while the center's head count at 200 is the same as five years ago, the workers are more skilled these days. Those who have stayed have often been retrained.

Antoine Andujar, a call center agent for more than five years, attended electronics courses taught at the call center by instructors from a local community college. He used to handle many products, but now specializes in issues with plasma and LCD televisions.

Mr. Andujar completed his electronics certification program last year, and continues to study. "You have to move up in skills," he said. "At this point, you have to be certified in electronics to get in the door here as a Panasonic employee."

The Efficient Listener

"This call may be recorded for quality assurance purposes."

But at a growing number of consumer call centers, technical support desks and company hot lines, the listener is a computer. One that can recognize not only words but also emotions—and listen for trends in customer complaints.

In the telephone industry, for example, companies use speech recognition software to provide an early warning about changes in a competitor's calling plans. By detecting the frequent use of names like AT&T and other carriers,

the software can alert the company to a rival that lowered prices, for example, far faster than would hundreds of customer service agents. The companies then have their customer agents make counteroffers to callers thinking of canceling service.

Similar software, used by Aetina, began to notice the phrase "cash for clunkers" in hundreds of calls to its call center one weekend last year. It turned out that tens of thousands of car shoppers responding to the government incentive were calling for insurance quotes. Aetna created insurance offers for those particular callers and added workers to handle the volume.

And as Apple's new smartphone surged in popularity several years ago, GoDaddy, an Internet services company, learned from its call-monitoring software that callers did not know how to use GoDaddy on their iPhones. The company rushed to retrain its agents to respond to the calls and pushed out an application allowing its users to control its service directly from the iPhone.

Certain emotions are now routinely detected at many call centers, by recognizing specific words or phrases, or by detecting other attributes in conversations. Voicesense, an Israeli developer of speech analysis software, has algorithms that measure a dozen indicators, including breathing, conversation pace and tone, to warn agents and supervisors that callers have become upset or volatile.

The real issue with artificial intelligence, as with any technology, is how it will be used. Automation is a remarkable tool of efficiency and convenience. Using an A.T.M. to make cash deposits and withdrawals beats standing in line to wait for a teller. If an automated voice system in a call center can answer a question, the machine is a better solution than lingering on hold for a customer service agent.

Indeed, the increasing usefulness of artificial intelligence—answering questions, completing simple tasks and assisting professionals—means the technology will spread, despite the risks. It will be up to people to guide how it is used.

"It's not human intelligence, but it's getting to be very good machine intelligence," said Andries van Dam, a professor of computer science at Brown University. "There are going to be all sorts of errors and problems, and you need human checks and balances, but having artificial intelligence is way better than not having it."

Critical Thinking

1. Much of what is described in this article falls under the heading, "computational linguistics." Go to the Association for Computational Linguistics' website (www.aclweb.org) to see what computational linguists are up to in their native habitat.

2. Use the Internet to see if you can find out which government agencies support research in speech recognition.

3. Besides marveling at what's coming down the road, do the researchers who produce these artifacts bear any responsibility for how they will be used—mostly to replace humans who are doing the same jobs quite well?

4. Current research in speech recognition and translation depends on the clever compilation of mountains of statistical data. Use the Internet to see if you can get a more detailed understanding of the underlying principles. Possible search keys include Hidden Markov Models, Statistical Language Processing, the Viterbi algorithm, Machine Translation, Speech Recognition.

Weighing Watson's Impact

Does IBM's Watson represent a distinct breakthrough in machine learning and natural language processing or is the 2,880-core wunderkind merely a solid feat of engineering?

IBM's Watson soundly defeated the two most successful contestants in the history of the game show "Jeopardy!," Ken Jennings and Brad Rutter, in a three-day competition in February.

KIRK L. KROEKER

In the history of speculative fiction, from the golden age of science fiction to the present, there are many examples of artificial intelligences engaging their interlocutors in dialogue that exhibits self-awareness, personality, and even empathy. Several fields in computer science, including machine learning and natural language processing, have been steadily approaching the point at which real-world systems will be able to approximate this kind of interaction. IBM's Watson computer, the latest example in a long series of efforts in this area, made a television appearance earlier this year in a widely promoted human-versus-machine "Jeopardy!" game show contest. To many observers, Watson's appearance on "Jeopardy!" marked a milestone on the path toward achieving the kind of sophisticated, knowledge-based interaction that has traditionally been relegated to the realm of fiction.

The "Jeopardy!" event, in which Watson competed against Ken Jennings and Brad Rutter, the two most successful contestants in the game show's history, created a wave of coverage across mainstream and social media. During the three-day contest in February, hints of what might be called Watson's quirky personality shone through, with the machine wagering oddly precise amounts, guessing at answers after wildly misinterpreting clues, but ultimately prevailing against its formidable human opponents.

Leading up to the million-dollar challenge, Watson played more than 50 practice matches against former "Jeopardy!" contestants, and was required to pass the same tests that humans must take to qualify for the show and compete against Jennings, who broke the "Jeopardy!" record for the most consecutive games played, resulting in winnings of more than $2.5 million, and Rutter, whose total winnings amounted to $3.25 million, the most money ever won by a single "Jeopardy!" player. At the end

of the three-day event, Watson finished with $77,147, beating Jennings, who had $24,000, and Rutter, who had $21,600. The million-dollar prize money awarded to Watson went to charity.

Named after IBM founder Thomas J. Watson, the Watson system was built by a team of IBM scientists whose goal was to create a standalone platform that could rival a human's ability to answer questions posed in natural language. During the "Jeopardy!" challenge, Watson was not connected to the Internet or any external data sources. Instead, Watson operated as an independent system contained in several large floor units housing 90 IBM Power 750 servers with a total of 2,880 processing cores and 15 terabytes of memory. Watson's technology, developed by IBM and several contributing universities, was guided by principles described in the Open Advancement of Question-Answering (OAQA) framework, which is still operating today and facilitating ongoing input from outside institutions.

Judging by the sizeable coverage of the event, Watson piqued the interest of technology enthusiasts and the general public alike, earning "Jeopardy!" the highest viewer numbers it had achieved in several years and leading to analysts and other industry observers speculating about whether Watson represents a fundamental new idea in computer science or merely a solid feat of engineering. Richard Doherty, the research director at Envisioneering Group, a technology consulting firm based in Seaford, NY, was quoted in an Associated Press story as saying that Watson is "the most significant breakthrough of this century."

Doherty was not alone in making such claims, although the researchers on the IBM team responsible for designing Watson have been far more modest in their assessment of the technology they created. "Watson is a novel approach and a powerful architecture," says David Ferrucci, director of the IBM DeepQA research team that created Watson. Ferrucci does characterize

Watson as a breakthrough in artificial intelligence, but he is careful to qualify this assertion by saying that the breakthrough is in the development of artificial-intelligence systems.

"The breakthrough is how we pulled everything together, how we integrated natural language processing, information retrieval, knowledge representation, machine learning, and a general reasoning paradigm," says Ferrucci. "I think this represents a breakthrough. We would have failed had we not invested in a rigorous scientific method and systems engineering. Both were needed to succeed."

Contextual Evidence

The DeepQA team was inspired by several overarching design principles, with the core idea being that no single algorithm or formula would accurately understand or answer all questions, says Ferrucci. Rather, the idea was to build Watson's intelligence from a broad collection of algorithms that would probabilistically and imperfectly interpret language and score evidence from different perspectives. Watson's candidate answers, those answers in which Watson has the most confidence, are produced from hundreds of parallel hypotheses collected and scored from contextual evidence.

Ferrucci says this approach required innovation at the systems level so individual algorithms could be developed independently, then evaluated for their contribution to the system's overall performance. The approach allowed for loosely coupled interaction between algorithm components, which Ferrucci says ultimately reduced the need for team-wide agreement. "If every algorithm developer had to agree with every other or reach some sort of consensus, progress would have been slowed," he says. "The key was to let different members of the team develop diverse algorithms independently, but regularly perform rigorous integration testing to evaluate relative impact in the context of the whole system."

Ferrucci and the DeepQA team are expected to release more details later this year in a series of papers that will outline how they dealt with specific aspects of the Watson design. For now, only bits and pieces of the complete picture are being disclosed. Ferrucci says that, looking ahead, his team's research agenda is to focus on how Watson can understand, learn, and interact more effectively. "Natural language understanding remains a tremendously difficult challenge, and while Watson demonstrated a powerful approach, we have only scratched the surface," he says. "The challenge continues to be about how you build systems to accurately connect language to some representation, so the system can automatically learn from text and then reason to discover evidence and answers."

Lillian Lee, a professor in the computer science department at Cornell University, says the reactions about Watson's victory echo the reactions following Deep Blue's 1997 victory over chess champion Garry Kasparov, but with several important differences. Lee, whose research focus is natural language processing, points out that some observers were dismissive about Deep Blue's victory, suggesting that the system's capability was due largely to brute-force reasoning rather than machine learning. The same criticism, she says, cannot be leveled at Watson because

the overall system needed to determine how to assess and integrate diverse responses.

"Watson incorporates machine learning in several crucial stages of its processing pipeline," Lee says. "For example, reinforcement learning was used to enable Watson to engage in strategic game play, and the key problem of determining how confident to be in an answer was approached using machine-learning techniques, too."

Lee says that while there has been substantial research on the particular problems the "Jeopardy!" challenge involved for Watson, that prior work should not diminish the team's accomplishment in advancing the state of the art to Watson's championship performance. "The contest really showcased real-time, broad-domain question-answering, and provided as comparison points two extremely formidable contestants," she says. "Watson represents an absolutely extraordinary achievement."

Lee suggests that with language processing technologies now maturing, with the most recent example of such maturation being Watson, the field appears to have passed through an important early stage. It now faces an unprecedented opportunity in helping sift through the massive amounts of user-generated content online, such as opinion-oriented information in product reviews or political analysis, according to Lee.

While natural-language processing is already used, with varying degrees of success, in search engines and other applications, it might be some time before Watson's unique question-answering capabilities will help sift through online reviews and other user-generated content. Even so, that day might not be too far off, as IBM has already begun work with Nuance Communications to commercialize the technology for medical applications. The idea is for Watson to assist physicians and nurses in finding information buried in medical tomes, prior cases, and the latest science journals. The first commercial offerings from the collaboration are expected to be available within two years.

Beyond medicine, likely application areas for Watson's technology would be in law, education, or the financial industry. Of course, as with any technology, glitches and inconsistencies will have to be worked out for each new domain. Glitches notwithstanding, technology analysts say that Watsonlike technologies will have a significant impact on computing in particular and human life in general. Ferrucci, for his part, says these new technologies likely will mean a demand for higher-density hardware and for tools to help developers understand and debug machine-learning systems more effectively. Ferrucci also says it's likely that user expectations will be raised, leading to systems that do a better job at interacting in natural language and sifting through unstructured content.

To this end, explains Ferrucci, the DeepQA team is moving away from attempting to squeeze ever-diminishing performance improvements out of Watson in terms of parsers and local components. Instead, they are focusing on how to use context and information to evaluate competing interpretations more effectively. "What we learned is that, for this approach to extend beyond one domain, you need to implement a positive feedback loop of extracting basic syntax and local semantics from language, learning from context, and then interacting with users and a broader community to acquire knowledge that is otherwise difficult to extract," he says. "The system must be able to boot-strap and learn from its own failing with the help of this loop."

In an ideal future, says Ferrucci, Watson will operate much like the ship computer on "Star Trek," where the input can be expressed in human terms and the output is accurate and under-standable. Of course, the "Star Trek" ship computer was largely humorless and devoid of personality, responding to queries and commands with a consistently even tone. If the "Jeopardy!" chal-lenge serves as a small glimpse of things to come for Watson—in particular, Watson's precise wagers, which produced laughter in the audience, and Watson's visualization component, which appeared to express the state of a contemplative mind through moving lines and colors—the DeepQA team's focus on active learning might also include a personality loop so Watson can accommodate subtle emotional cues and engage in dialogue with the kind of good humor reminiscent of the most person-able artificial intelligences in fiction.

Further Readings

Baker, S. *Final Jeopardy: Man vs. Machine and the Quest to Know Everything.* Houghton Mifflin Harcourt, New York, NY, 2011.

Ferrucci, D., Brown, E., Chu-Carroll, J., Fan, J., Gondek, D., Kalyanpur, A.A., Lally, A., Murdock, J.W., Nyberg, E., Prager, J., Schlaefer, N., and Welty, C. Building Watson: An overview of the DeepQA project, *AI Magazine 59,* Fall 2010.

Ferrucci, D., et al. Towards the Open Advancement of Question Answering Systems. *IBM Research Report RC24789 (W0904-093),* April 2009.

Simmons, R.F. Natural language question-answering systems, *Communications of the ACM 13,* 1, Jan. 1970.

Strzalkowski, T., and Harabagiu, S. (Eds.) *Advances in Open Domain Question Answering.* Springer-Verlag, Secaucus, NJ, 2006.

Critical Thinking

1. IBM maintains a website about the Watson project: www-03.ibm.com/innovation/us/watson. Watch a few of the videos. IBM thinks that "this technology will impact the way humans communicate with computers." Do you agree?

2. Can you think of a downside to a Watson-like machine handing your health-care and finance questions? What about a Watson descendent teaching your classes?

3. What imperative is driving the computer industry to produce question-answering software? Who/what performs these tasks right now?

4. David Ferucci, the manager of the Watson project, is proud but modest about its accomplishments. Do they fall under the heading of science or engineering or both?

5. Watson defeated its opponents much more easily than Deep Blue did Gary Kasparov fifteen years ago. Use the Internet to see if anyone has commented on the two matches. Is chess harder or Watson smarter?

Based in Los Angeles, **KIRK L. KROEKER** is a freelance editor and writer specializing in science and technology.

Geek Life
Die Another Day

Thousands of bodies are already cryonically frozen, waiting for faster computers and medical advances that will undo their cause of death.

SUSAN KARLIN

What is death? Over the centuries, the line dividing life and death has moved from the cessation first of breathing, then of the heartbeat, and finally of brain activity. But cryogenic methods first contemplated in science fiction may push the line even further. The idea is to freeze legally dead people in liquid nitrogen in the hope of regenerating them at some future date.

Today's cryonics scientists believe that this future may be a mere 100 years away. Alcor Life Extension Foundation, in Scottsdale, Ariz., the world's largest cryonics company, charges US$150,000 to freeze and maintain a body and $80,000 for a head, typically paid for with a life insurance policy.

Ralph Merkle, a nanotechnology expert and a director at Alcor, believes the best approach lies in developing nanorobots that can repair the body at the cellular level before thawing. They would fix or replace diseased and deteriorated tissue as well as the tissue fractures and denatured proteins that result from the freezing process itself. The revival process would, ideally, restore the physiology of dead persons to a pristine level, not only undoing the damage of whatever disease or accident killed them but also enabling them to return smarter and healthier than they ever were in life.

"We're talking about a fundamentally more powerful medical technology than we have today that will continue the evolution of the concepts of life and death," says Merkle, who holds bachelor's and master's degrees in computer science from the University of California, Berkeley, and a Ph.D. in electrical engineering from Stanford. "People will be able to suffer more damage and still fully recover."

Before the body is cooled to −196° C (the temperature at which liquid nitrogen becomes a gas), the person's blood is replaced by a cryoprotective solution that doesn't freeze at those temperatures. Technically, the body and cryoprotective solution are not frozen but vitrified—that is, they solidify into a glassy substance that's free of ice crystals and the damage they can cause. The first step in the future regeneration process would remove this vitrified liquid, letting physicians use the circulatory system as a series of tunnels through which they could run nanomedical robots, nanomaterials, and a removable high-speed fiber-optic network connecting to an external supercomputer.

"It takes about 10^{25} bits to store the molecular structure of the brain," says Merkle. "The processing power to repair the brain alone might be 10^{37} switching operations (10^{31} floating-point operations)—the equivalent of 100 million copies of today's fastest supercomputer running flat out for three years. With Moore's Law doubling computer power every year, we'll have that kind of computational power in a single supercomputer in about 26 years," he adds. "Give it another 10 years and the price will drop from $100 million to $100,000. Somewhere around 2050, that much computational power will be readily available to individuals." And it doesn't matter if Moore's Law slows down, Merkle says: "A person at the temperature of liquid nitrogen can literally wait centuries."

That loose deadline was a selling point for Merkle when he first investigated life-extension technologies for himself and his wife. Cryonics offered the only potential solution that wasn't tied to a person's lifetime.

But is it a solution—or a pointless gamble? In *The Skeptics Dictionary: A Collection of Strange Beliefs, Amusing Deceptions, and Dangerous Delusions* (Wiley, 2003), retired philosophy professor Robert Todd Carroll wrote: "A business based on little more than hope for developments that can be imagined by science is quackery. There is little reason to believe that the promises of cryonics will ever be fulfilled."

Stephen Barrett, a retired psychiatrist in Chapel Hill, N.C., who operates the Web site Quackwatch, a health-care consumer-advocacy network, agrees. "The odds are pretty close to zero that people who are pronounced dead would have any remaining brain function or restorability. Brain cells die fairly quickly and would have to be regenerated in sufficient order and numbers to restore functionality. And then you'd have to restore the rest of the body. The obstacles are so enormous, it's a foolish investment. You're better off putting the money toward improving your life today or doing something worthwhile for others."

Critical Thinking

1. Use the Internet to see if you can find the names of some of the people on Alcor's client list; then use the Internet to find out something about them. Does a pattern emerge?

2. Who was Immanuel Kant? He is famous for the categorical imperative: "Act only according to that maxim whereby you can, at the same time, will that it should become a universal law." Does the use of Alcor violate the categorical imperative?

3. What if what Alcor promises were possible? What might be the consequences?

4. Suppose Alcor's promise is possible. Is Alcor any different than a very expensive pharmaceutical or surgical intervention?

5. Ralph Merkle is an important figure in this article. Use the Internet to read about him, especially with respect to public key cryptography. Now read about the clipper-chip and key escrow proposal from the Clinton administration. What development in cryptography resulted in the proposal? What do you think about it?

Test-Your-Knowledge Form

We encourage you to photocopy and use this page as a tool to assess how the articles in *Annual Editions* expand on the information in your textbook. By reflecting on the articles you will gain enhanced text information. You can also access this useful form on a product's book support website at www.mhhe.com/cls

NAME: _____ DATE: _____

_____

TITLE AND NUMBER OF ARTICLE:

_____

BRIEFLY STATE THE MAIN IDEA OF THIS ARTICLE:

_____

LIST THREE IMPORTANT FACTS THAT THE AUTHOR USES TO SUPPORT THE MAIN IDEA:

_____

WHAT INFORMATION OR IDEAS DISCUSSED IN THIS ARTICLE ARE ALSO DISCUSSED IN YOUR TEXTBOOK OR OTHER READINGS THAT YOU HAVE DONE? LIST THE TEXTBOOK CHAPTERS AND PAGE NUMBERS:

_____

LIST ANY EXAMPLES OF BIAS OR FAULTY REASONING THAT YOU FOUND IN THE ARTICLE:

_____

LIST ANY NEW TERMS/CONCEPTS THAT WERE DISCUSSED IN THE ARTICLE, AND WRITE A SHORT DEFINITION: